I0456245

PRODIGAL

a novel by
Scott L. Miller

To every teacher and patient I've ever had, Thank you for teaching me about life.

It's a good thing most people bleed on the inside or this would be
a gory, blood-smeared earth."
Beatrice Sparks, Go Ask Alice

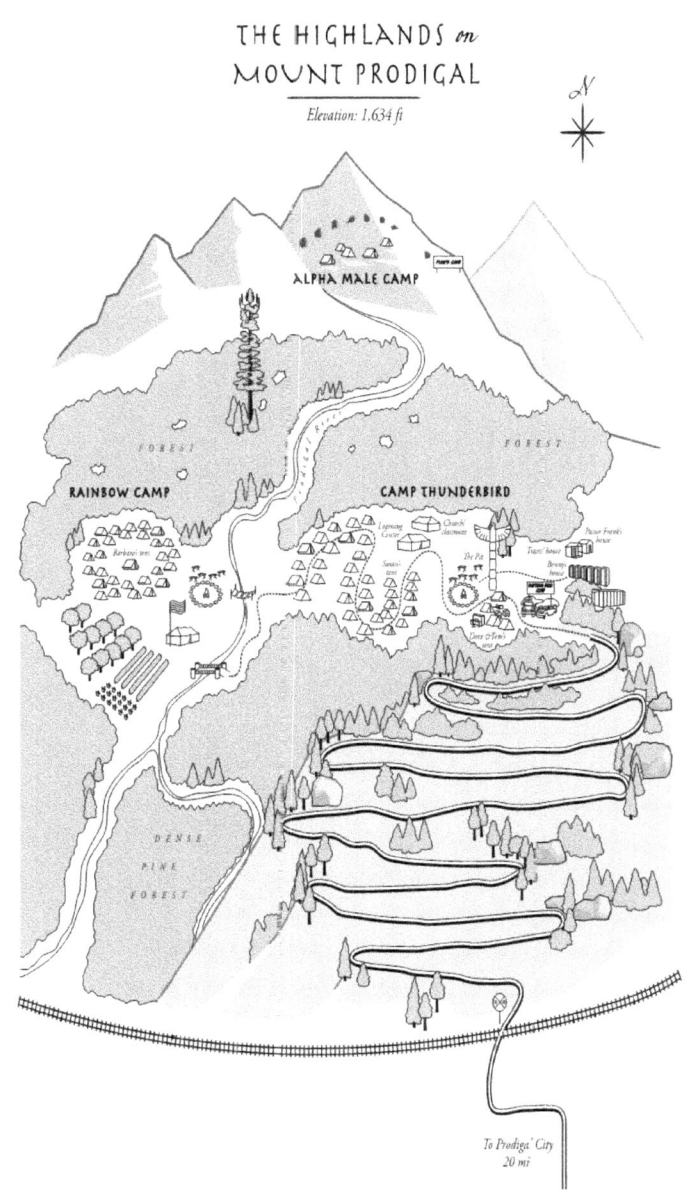

THE HIGHLANDS on MOUNT PRODIGAL

Elevation: 1,634 ft

N

ALPHA MALE CAMP

FOREST

FOREST

RAINBOW CAMP

CAMP THUNDERBIRD

Barbeque tent

Lightning Center

Church Classroom

Pastor Frank's house

Feast house

Sunrise tent

Be Pit

Bronty house

Camp Office

DENSE
PINE
FOREST

To Prodigal City
20 mi

3

PART ONE: A WALK IN THE WOODS

"I went to the woods because I wished to live deliberately,

To front only the essential facts of life,

And see if I could not learn what it had to teach,

And not, when I came to die, discover that I had not lived."

Henry David Thoreau, Walden

HOSTAGES

My husband screams at me. We're locked in the same argument loop tonight.

When I turn away, an object misses my head by inches. I feel it whiz by my hair and shatter against the wall. I cower and freeze. Shards from his coffee cup bounce off my face. Some land in my hair. Terrified, I slide down the wall onto the floor.

I cringe when he closes the distance between us with sudden speed. His face crimson, he makes sweeping gestures with his arms, his hands balled into fists. He's never been violent before tonight, but I brace for his impact.

He looms over me. "I want a divorce. I want you out of this house. Now! This isn't a marriage. I don't even know what *this* is anymore, Susan. We do nothing together."

Heat flushes through me. I'm scared, and my stomach churns. My throat is so dry I can't find my voice. I look up and feel myself shake. The truth? Every word he says rings true.

I repeat my part of the loop right on cue, like a good little hostage. "That's because once you're home from work, you listen to the police scanner all night. Is that even legal?"

He runs his hands through his hair. "Of course. It's only illegal if I make non-emergency transmissions on police channels."

My mouth drops open, and I shake my head. "What kind of person does this? What are you listening for?"

He presses his hands to his temples and begins to pace. "We're getting nowhere. I will not live like this anymore. I want a divorce."

I rise and keep the sofa between us while he paces and fumes.

"You haven't heard a word I've said, have you? You're lost in your own world." He recycles his list of grievances against me.

This go-around, I hear maybe a third of the loop.

His flared nostrils and nose hairs distract me while he rants. I stare into the gaping chasm that is Jim's mouth. For a man who almost always avoids confrontation, I've never seen him act like such a lout.

Something has changed.

At last, I sever the loop and connect the dots. "What's her name?"

He stops in his tracks. He wears an exaggerated look of incredulity. He lowers his voice. "What? How can you say that? There's no one else."

I raise my chin. "Whoever she is must have given you the courage to do this. But the house belongs to both of us, and I'm not leaving. *You're* free to go. So, if you've finished repeating your litany of my failings, I'm tired and going upstairs."

His lips pinch together and disappear. "You're always tired. From the depression, from work, and from twelve-hour days at the school. You should be exhausted from pretending to be a wife. You never talk about the hospital. I begged you for years to get help, but you wouldn't. You moved out of our bedroom when you found Danny's stash. And now you're worse since he left."

I stand there cradling my belly. Sometimes I look at people while they're talking and wonder: is this the same person I used to know? I stare at the man who looks like Jim and wonder if he's in there somewhere. Is he right—is this all my fault? I wish I could remember. I turn to the stairs.

He resumes pacing. "After all these years, you have nothing else to say other than you're tired. Unbelievable! When I return, I want you gone."

He storms through the kitchen and into the garage. The roar of his SUV snaps me back to the present. I release my belly and rush to the front window. He backs down the driveway in a hurry. His headlights vanish down the rain-drenched street. Another Jim move: cut and run.

Since Danny left. Ha! That's one way to put it. I kicked our son out while he sat on his hands and let me be the heavy lifter.

Now he chooses our son's birthday to tell me he wants a divorce. What a shit move.

Jim still believes the world is a fair, moral, and just place. I used to admire that about him before we married. Like me, he works hard. He believes that when everyone does their job, things fall into place like clockwork. Now he thinks I've slipped a cog.

I trudge upstairs to the bathroom and open the medicine cabinet. I stare at the lower shelf. Antidepressants, anti-anxiety pills, estrogen, Ambien, and more. I close the cabinet door, and my reflection appears.

My reflection.

Sometimes I look at myself and wonder the same thing. I'm not the same person I was last year, ten years ago, and certainly not during my pregnancy. Every so often, the cells in our bodies die and regenerate. Yet my past failings taint the new cells. If there is a God, He enjoys being cruel or simply doesn't give a shit.

I examine the faint lines near my eyes and test my skin for tautness. I just turned sixty and had a mini-facelift two summers ago. It hurt like hell but was worth every penny. We argued over it. He said I waste too much money, but it sickens me that women age so much faster than men. I open the medicine cabinet again and scan the products that crowd the upper shelves. I spread a dab of moisturizing cream under my eyes. I take care of my shell, though I don't know why I bother anymore. Standing here now, I take a deep breath and wonder: What does Jim see? What mirror image of me do I project to him?

Sartre once said that hell is other people. Sometimes it feels that way. But what if hell is in us? What if it establishes a foothold so subtle that we're not even aware of it?

Sometimes I view my life as a story, certain a key aspect of it is missing. What does this say about me? I feel like I'm living half a life while the missing link remains hidden behind the mirror.

I change into warmer clothes in the guest room where I sleep. I do not pack suitcases, for I'm not leaving. I have a late appointment with the stranger who responded to my latest flier about Danny. He insisted on meeting me in the city.

I grab my raincoat and expect this meeting to end like the others. With nothing.

Expectations can be a real kick in the head.

A TIP

My name is Susan Crusoe, and I live in a nice home in the suburbs of the town of Prodigal, which is like any prosperous modern American city undergoing a construction renaissance. I've been married for thirty years to my husband. He broke off an engagement with his college sweetheart to marry me. We hold down stable jobs; he is a financial officer for a large automobile dealership, and I teach high school English. Suffice it to say that he is the major breadwinner. Jim manages our money and lords over it with an iron fist. We make hefty payments on two late-model cars. Our 401(k) retirement accounts are zeroed out, and there's a second mortgage on our two-story colonial, which Jim reminds me is my fault; each time our son relapsed, I fought tooth and nail with Jim to pay for the help Danny needed.

I was a homewrecker when I met Jim.

And once again, after I kicked Danny out.

Tonight, I drive to the north side of town through pelting sideways rain that obscures the street signs. This dimly lit last vestige of old Prodigal City is slated for demolition and rehab soon. I become hopelessly lost and try to use Google Maps, but my iPhone is dead, and Jim has my car charger. When I find the address, I realize I've driven past it half a dozen times. I didn't think anything was unusual about it when the man refused to speak about my son over the phone. I agreed to meet him at 11:30, after his shift; I assumed that meant he worked at the hospital several blocks over. I park half a block away under the lone streetlight and trudge back in the rain, which has thankfully slowed to a light shower. I pass storefronts that loom black and steel-caged for the night amid others long since abandoned, the warped plywood graffitied over with faded gang insignia. The signs on this side of the street advertise Chinese takeout, fortune-teller readings, Quick Nails, and Fast Cash. I had no idea this degree of urban blight still existed in Prodigal. I walk faster. A disheveled man squats under a faded marquee, extends his hand, and asks me for spare change. His doleful eyes stare into mine until I look away and quicken my pace to a near jog. If I give people like him money, they just buy booze. No wonder this area has a date with the wrecking ball.

I arrive thirty minutes late and take shelter under a rotted awning. I shiver when the rain intensifies again and drops the size of quarters ping off my coat collar and slither down my back. Up and down the block, the neon light casts a gray shroud over the neighborhood.

What the hell have I gotten myself into? I chastise myself for not charging my phone.

I pull out a cigarette and fumble for my lighter when a figure emerges from the fog. Up close, he looms nearly two feet taller than me. He turns back his hoodie, and his rheumy eyes walk all over me as he assesses me, a beer can in one gargantuan hand. Then he flashes a gap-toothed grin, and his ears protrude like wing nuts.

"There a reward for finding this dude?"

I hadn't considered this. I'd assumed people would respond to a missing person flier out of the goodness of their hearts. I arch my neck to meet his eyes while I show him Danny's picture. He notices my hand tremble.

"If your information leads me to him," I say, "I will give you two hundred dollars *after* I find this man. I have your phone number and promise to call."

He ignores the picture and sips his beer while his eyes lock on mine. He leers and bends forward so close I smell beer and pot on his breath. "How do I know you'll keep your end of the bargain?"

"You have my word."

He laughs and throws the empty can into the street. The noise rattles my bones. "You a long way from home, Suzie Homemaker. You better go home and bake some cookies."

More raindrops fall from the awning and meander down my spine. Lightning flashes above the buildings, as if repairs are being made in a distant, iron-dark part of the world not meant for me. I shift my weight and realize I'm still holding my unlit cigarette.

"You said you have information for me. Do you?"

I freeze when he reaches into a pocket.

I imagine many things—all bad—about to appear from that enormous hand except what does . . . a ratty pack of matches.

I cup his scarred hand with mine and light up. Now I see his acne scars and the teardrop tattoo below his eye. "Thanks."

"Your hands are shaking. You may think you a little Miss Hard Case comin' downtown, but you ain't."

I exhale smoke through my nose. "Well? What can you tell me?"

He ignores the picture again. He's so tall his arms stretch above my head and grab the top of the eaves. "Your husband know you're here, Suzie?"

That's a whole other can of worms. I take a deep breath and lie. "Yes, he does."

The grin morphs into a leer as he leans closer. "You musta been a looker in your day. I got weed, uppers. I say we go to my place and party."

My blood pressure shoots through the roof. "Pass. Just tell me what you know, if anything."

He scans the wet and desolate street, tilting his head toward my blue BMW parked half a block away. His voice lowers an octave. "That your ride under the streetlight?"

I'm in deep shit.

"Why don't you hand over your purse and keys, and we can end this little transaction? Unless you wanna get to know me better. My place is a few blocks away." He snickers like a horse. "Maybe you can bake me some cookies, Suzie."

I look for the homeless beggar I ignored under the marquee earlier, but he's gone. The street's deserted. There's no way I can outrun the giant or call for help, so I steel myself and try a different tactic. I sigh and grind my cigarette under my boot on the cracked sidewalk. "You don't have anything for me. I'm leaving." I take a step forward.

He grabs my arm and smirks as I drop Danny's flier. "Damn, you got some sack after all. Got a smoke?" I offer him one, and he takes the pack. The sickening grin returns with a wink.

"Thanks for wasting my time," I say, pushing past him toward the car, praying he doesn't stop me again. The chill rain plasters my bangs to my forehead when I leave the shelter of the awning.

He shouts after me, "Don't walk away from me. These are my streets, Suzie Homemaker. I make the rules!"

I stop in the middle of the road and turn to see whether he's coming for me.

He remains under the awning. The hoodie cloaks his pale face in shadow, but his right hand holds a .38 against his thigh. "The keys, Suzie Homemaker."

Two police cars speed down the nearest cross street toward the hospital, and he pockets the gun.

A switch flips in me, and I laugh at him. "You're nothing but hot air." I hurl the foulest of insults at him from the empty street and raise my arms, making myself an easy target. "Give me something to go on! Where is my son?" I scream into the night.

The silence seems to last forever as I wait, expecting him to bridge the gap between us with those long strides and put a bullet in my forehead. He looks to the street where we last saw the cop cars. "You are one crazy bitch. Get the fuck outta here, Suzie Homemaker. Ain't nothing here for you but more pain. Last I heard, he was in the Highlands." He points to the flier on the ground with the gun barrel. "Hope he got your balls. He gonna need them to survive up there."

I run to my car as a soaked, emaciated black cat crosses in front of me and scampers down the street. I climb inside and lock the doors. I turn to look for the giant, but he's not there. Hyperventilating, I rev the engine and floor the accelerator. I drive blindly behind my fogged windshield until I run over something on the right and hit the brake. My forehead strikes the steering wheel. I rub my head and run the defroster full blast.

My heart's in my throat, and I'm sweating as I tug at my coat collar and power down the window so the cold, wet air hits me. A familiar nemesis climbs up my spine and sits on my chest. I dry-swallow three Xanax and watch sheets of water slough off the windshield. I feel like I'm drowning. I can't stop shaking. My vision blurs. I shut my eyes and cover my ears, but the flashing lights and beeping noises overwhelm me. I struggle through my grounding exercises: name five things out loud near me that I can touch; call out four things I can hear; name three things I can see. Slow, deep breaths return in time, and the beeps and flashing lights fade. I get out to discover I jumped the curb and stopped four feet short of a parking meter. I laid rubber braking, but the tires seem okay. I look back and realize I blew through three stop signs. It's a wonder I didn't crash into a building, a parked car, or that mailbox at the corner along the way.

It's past one in the morning. The sky pelts down more rain that washes away nothing.

I sit on the straps of my fastened seat belt—new behavior for me. It's my deference to fate: if I'm in a head-on collision, I'll be more likely to be thrown from the car and die.

I drive south from the city back to the suburbs, past the bridge abutments that materialize from the darkness like gray behemoths. These bridges are buttressed by steel barricades or battleship-gray water barrels stacked like bowling pins, but thirty miles south of home, unprotected rural overpasses dot the flat farmlands—my fallback plan should the suicidal impulses win.

I take the exit for our subdivision. Lightning flashes in the distance, closer now. No repairs are being made in this dark part of the world, either.

Jim's SUV is in the garage. The hood is cold. He probably had a few drinks at Marcel's Pub. I bet he's in the master bedroom with the door closed.

A note taped to the guest bedroom door bears his handwriting: *I mean it. LEAVE*. My green suitcases stand by the door like silent sentinels. I smile sadly; assertiveness never was his forte.

I turn the key to the padlock I installed months ago and lock the door behind me. I shed my wet clothes and step into the shower, running water hotter than I can tolerate until mist surrounds me. My skin blotches like a lobster. I towel off, don a robe, and fall onto the bed. Spidery white fingers of mist from the bath reach out to me like ghosts from the past. I close my eyes, and Danny's crooked grin appears. Or at least what I remember of it. Funny how fast you lose sight of someone you used to see every day. After a year, you begin to wonder what they even look like. I smoke in the darkened room, four fingers of Woodford Reserve on the nightstand. The lone light comes from the bath, and I reflect on the brief moment I felt alive today—when I tried to bait a giant into shooting me. Should I feel happy or sad for surviving Danny's birthday this year? I choose to feel nothing.

If Danny is in the Highlands, I need to act soon. Life off the grid the last year means he could pull up stakes, and I'd miss him again.

I slip on my wedding ring and weigh my options.

The potential to never see Danny again versus the inherent dangers of the lawless Highlands.

I wrestle with this for three hours until the alarm sounds at six a.m.

ROAD TRIP

I invited death last night, and this morning I'm faced with a Hobson's choice: stay or go. Home is a place I can't leave and can't stay. Part of me is angry the giant didn't shoot me.

I can remain here in my current unraveled state and welcome death's release in some direct or indirect form. Jim and Danny wouldn't care, but my students, their families, and the school community would be devastated. I've encouraged and challenged my students to find new ways to learn in and outside the classroom. The countless hours of free tutoring outside of school would all be for naught. The parent and community groups I established would end. I'd be a failure and a fraud in their eyes . . .

I write fresh notes in pen on the Great Wall of Danny (Jim will lose his mind when he sees what I've done to this room) and reread my journal entries from last night. I make the bed, clean the bathroom, vacuum the carpet, and dust the nightstand a final time. I place the journals in my backpack with some other items and padlock the guest bedroom door behind me.

I call in sick for the week and leave a note on the kitchen table for Jim, who remains sequestered in the master bedroom. The suitcases he left for me last night remain untouched in the hallway.

I'm about to climb in the car when I remember my Faraday bag. I considered Jim paranoid when he suggested we buy them. Faraday bags block electromagnetic impulses and help prevent hackers from obtaining your personal information. They also prevent you from being tracked via your cell phone. I used mine for a few weeks, then tossed it up on the shelf in the hallway closet. If things go south, I may not want to be found. I re-enter the foyer, stand on my tiptoes to reach the bag, and toss it on the passenger seat.

I came unglued last night, but the thought of entering the Highlands terrifies me more. It's a tent city perched on Mount Prodigal, some twenty miles north of the city and forty miles from home. The news reports the place is rife with crime and drug abuse; that a man died in a fire there last year when the entire forest nearly burned to the ground. The residents live in squalor, and the encampment is a sanctuary for illegal immigrants. The unsanitary conditions must serve as a Petri dish for all sorts of diseases.

Ironically, the thought of *not* checking out the homeless camp now looms as my ultimate fear.

I plug my phone into the charger I recovered from Jim's car last night and type "the Highlands" into the maps app, then head north from the suburbs and through Prodigal until the four-lane concrete road becomes two-lane blacktop. Elms and oaks and stone cottages yield to pines and firs and granite outcroppings. Mine is now the lone car on the road. The last turn is a right, so I rumble over a set of train tracks, and there it is. Mount Prodigal, all of its 1,634 feet in elevation, towers before me.

My pulse quickens, and my breath grows shallow. There's a turnaround ahead. I stop the car in it, facing the mountain, and take a deep breath. What awaits? I recall other Highland horror stories, one about a rape.

But each month brings fewer leads about Danny. Last night's was the lone response from the latest round of fliers I've posted on telephone poles and bus stops throughout Prodigal. The private investigator I hired six months ago snooped around the Highlands and found nothing. I try to convince myself this is a wild-goose chase, but there's no comfort in that. I imagine the road ahead and the one behind. I recall the giant's warning. I'm losing every battle after the war is over.

My thoughts wander to the last Japanese soldier (an intelligence officer, no less) found in 1974 on an island near Luzon in the Philippines. Convinced that rumors of Japan's surrender in 1945 were an American trick, he continued to live in the jungle as a soldier despite pictures and letters airdropped from family members urging him to come out of hiding, that the war was long lost. How did he see himself in the mirror when he was no longer a fighter? What were his final years like?

I drive forward. Before I've gone thirty feet, my phone says I've reached my destination and to park in 250 feet. I ignore it and begin the gradual ascent up the mountain. In the 1850s, miners worked Mount Prodigal for its gold and precious metals, grading tracks for horses and wagons to negotiate the sixteen-hundred-foot climb. The blacktop becomes a gravel road compacted from the night rains. I encounter many dead ends and switchbacks along the unmarked lane. I feel trapped inside a giant maze. The BMW continues to climb as ferns and saplings give way to mature pines. The car automatically shifts gears in response to the incline.

Old forest surrounds me, and hawks glide through the gray mist in slow circles, hunting above colossal white pines. Near the shoulder of the road, massive knotted trees, some with trunks two feet wide, gnarled and oozing sap, dot the sheer drop-off along hairpin turns. The Highlands is situated higher up, nestled somewhere nearby in these green mountains. It is a city, but one not found on any map; there are no street signs, mailboxes, or addresses. A whisper of smoke billows over tall treetops ahead in lazy ashen plumes, the first sign of people, and the gravel road abruptly ends.

I park in a copse of mature pines, stow my wedding ring and billfold in the Faraday bag, and hide it under the front passenger seat. I hoist my backpack and take a deep breath. *I can do this.*

Two hundred yards into the trail, the mounted head of a six-point buck missing an eye stares down at me. Below it, a carved and weathered sign reads,

WELCOME TO THE HIGHLANDS

ABANDON EXPECTATION ALL YE WHO ENTER

Christ on a cracker. I glance back down the path and can still see my car. What am I doing? A sane woman wouldn't place herself in jeopardy twice in twenty-four hours. A sensible and practical person would return home and try to mend the remaining broken pieces of life. But this guilt is crushing me. I'm no good to anybody unless this fog lifts and I make peace with Danny and my crimes.

I tighten the straps of my backpack and crest a gentle rise, my senses on high alert. I cover a long flat stretch of ground, head west, and leave bright sunlight for shade. I feel a presence, but when I turn around, no one is there. I zip my coat all the way up. My breath visible as the forest swallows me, I hear sounds that seem to come from every direction, yet none at the same time. A shiver hitches a ride up my spine. The air is thick with the smell of resin. The woods feel threatening, laced with shafts of sunlight.

I flinch when an animal darts across my path. A frenzied beating of wings precedes the squawking of chickens, who pause to consider me before they resume foraging. I laugh. I swap the prescription sunglasses for my regular pair. Voices filter through the dense foliage to my right. I turn that way and keep going.

I spot movement near the base of a pine and feel eyes follow me when I continue along the main path. A thin blonde girl with straight, limp hair beneath a green wool cap regards me from behind a trunk. Upon closer inspection, she's actually a young woman with large, unblinking eyes so bright and alert she reminds me of a fox. I blink and lose her in the woods. A train whistle blows forlornly in the valley below.

Highlanders slowly materialize ahead of me in the lengthening shadows. My heart a lump in my throat. I swallow to relieve the tension. Will they frisk me when they see a stranger enter their turf? Will they steal my phone, confiscate my car keys? Others follow in pairs, heads down, quietly speaking to each other. No gun-toting, wild-eyed person engaged in a conversation with himself. The first group I come across pays me no mind. My fear lessens. Apparently, I'm free to move about as I please.

Under the shade of massive pine trees, near a sign that reads *Daytona 500 Club*, I pass a row of RV shells and junked cars on blocks, cages with doghouses of various shapes and sizes packed with straw, chicken coops, and a rabbit hutch. A wider path appears, and I follow it through a forest of ferns and larger conifers that shelter the sweet earthy smells of mulch, pine needles, and wintergreen. Smoke rises to my right, beyond a stand of honeysuckle and bramble bushes. The first structure I reach is not a tent, but a Goldbergian hut the size of a tool shed, only shorter, cobbled together with bits of different colored wood, rusted tin, and corrugated aluminum. The door, a flap of blue tarp, is tethered to a stake. It reminds me of the Hoovervilles of the Great Depression. I wasn't aware people still live this way.

I come upon RV trailers on tires with dry rot, more antlers hanging from trees, and tumbledown huts. This woebegone place is the antithesis of Danny.

I keep to the path until the pines thin and a small clearing appears, still bathed in partial shade by a canopy of towering trees. I freeze when I see what casts its shadow over me. Brightly colored, it stands fifteen feet tall and has the head of an eagle and a ten-foot wingspan. Its eyes look down on me, and its hooked yellow beak gapes open. What in the hell?

I approach a group of weathered gray picnic tables near a row of grills fashioned from 55-gallon metal drums cut lengthwise. A trio of people works nearby, talking among themselves. Beyond them, a large campfire crackles to life, encircled by wide flat stones and stumps hewn level for seats. My mouth waters: I haven't eaten all day, and it's already late afternoon.

My stomach growls as a woman walks past me with a smiling black Lab on a leash. The dog stops to turn and regard me. No one notices when I pause at a picnic table and root in my backpack. Two women, an older white one wearing a blue bandana scarf and a young black one in a wool sweater, share a laugh while they shuck corn near the cooking drums. A thick-set black man in worn jeans and a hoodie hefts a cardboard box to the table and begins to scrape the grills. Milk crates of canned food and boxes of paper plates occupy half of the long work table. Behind the tables are several large plastic coolers of various colors. From the darkening woods, a bird screams like a lost soul and flits from tree to tree. The temperature drops. I fend off another rush of anxiety and dry-swallow two Xanax.

I approach the women, who are tossing armfuls of husks into a rusted trash drum, the kind you used to see at ball fields twenty years ago. The women pick corn silk from between their fingers. The man tending the drums notices me first but pays no mind and resumes his prep work.

My foot snaps a twig on the path, and the women raise their heads. The older one smiles but the other stares, wary.

I point back down the path I traveled. "The totem pole almost gave me a heart attack."

"It can have that effect on first-timers," the older woman says, squinting.

I hold up the picture of Danny. "Have you seen this man?"

Wool Sweater looks first and quickly turns away. She exchanges a hardened look with the man in the hoodie while Blue Bandana studies the photo. No one answers until Bandana shakes her head. She's missing several teeth, and the hair that protrudes from the front of her bandana is gray and thinning. She turns to the others, who shake their heads in unison without taking a second look at the photograph.

I turn around and see others when Blue Bandana speaks. "You hungry, child?"

I study her weathered face and think, I'm probably older than you. My stomach growls again, and the corners of my mouth upturn on their own. "I thought I smelled food when I arrived."

"Wind shifts a lot up here. We never know what the hell it blows into camp until it does," Hoodie says, frowning, as he shoots a harsh look at Wool Sweater. "You prob'ly smell the grill from the west camp. I'm gonna fire up Lucille soon. Won't be long." His demeanor shifts from aggravation to detachment when his focus returns to the grills.

Wool Sweater takes my arm and smirks. "Lucille. You know men be silly that way. Always gotta name things like cars and their trouser monkeys," she says, overly loud, which I take as an attempt to lighten the mood. She looks at Hoodie, who fails to make eye contact, and turns back to me. "Look, we got a lot of work to do. We could use some help. Put down your gear and start shucking or scrub potatoes. Your choice."

I place my backpack on the bench and grab an ear of corn. I keep an eye on my pack while Blue Bandana disappears behind the tables.

In a soft voice, wool Sweater sidles closer and asks, "You a cop?"

What an odd question. I smile because I often felt like one when Danny lived at home. "Do I look like a cop?"

She stares, reading my body language. "PI?"

I laugh. "If I am, I'm a lousy one."

She huffs. "I take that as a no. Are you INS? ATF?"

"I'm just looking for the man in the picture. He's my son."

She freezes for an instant, then grabs another ear.

"Have you seen him?"

She shakes her head and scowls. "Every Highlander has lost someone close or had something taken from them. Go back to Prodigal while you still can. Before one of the homeless by choice latches onto you. This ain't your world."

I don't know what she means, so I say, "My son is missing. His name is Danny. I got a tip in Prodigal that he may be here and is in trouble." I embellish the last part in a play for sympathy, as I hope I'm not the one in danger. A loud whoosh startles me. Hoodie tosses a match into a cooking drum, and the flames dance between the coals and lick the curved sides of the pit. He's staring at me; he's been listening to our conversation. "I feel for you," he says, "more than you know, but names and faces here come and go."

Wool Sweater shakes her head and mumbles something about karma.

I'm about to ask what she means when Hoodie levels a finger at her. "We are not homeless by choice. *I* take responsibility for me being here. I don't blame anyone else."

Wool Sweater rolls her eyes and walks away, covering her ears.

Hoodie turns back to the grill and rips open a large box marked MEAT in red block letters. Over his shoulder, he says to me, "Some stay here because they refuse to follow any rules. They avoid responsibility and accountability."

Wool Sweater returns.

"That may be," she says. "A lot of people here are fooling themselves, but *my* eyes are wide open. Don't think otherwise." She casts furtive looks his way, but Hoodie keeps his back to her. She turns to scowl at me, then her eyes shift to something behind me.

Something hits me square in the back. I cringe, then see a red Frisbee at my feet, and I smile. A thin young man with long hair and a beard jogs over and apologizes. I reach to show him Danny's picture until Wool Sweater says harshly, "Best not show that around anymore." She returns to shucking.

Blue Bandana appears with a load of potatoes cradled in her baggy coat. She places them on the table, her cheeks puffing.

"You scrub those potatoes, Dora?" Wool Sweater says.

"Of course, and I pricked them all." Dora winks at me and offers a sly smile and a brief head shake. In her gravelly voice, she says, "What's your name, child?"

I place a shucked ear of corn with the others on a warped cookie tray. "Susan." Then to Wool Sweater: "Why can't I show the picture to people?"

The trio stares at each other until Wool Sweater says, "I'm not saying you can't, but there's a right way and a wrong way to go about it. You should run it by the mayor."

"Who?"

Wool Sweater frowns and points an ear of corn at me. "You're from town. I bet you like your privacy. Well, we do too. We don't like strangers asking a lot of questions, looking for people, causing problems, stirring up shit. Maybe some people don't want to be found. You ever think of that?"

Countless times.

"Go home. You won't survive here. You run into someone who *wants* to live here because they hate society and rules, they gonna take everything from you. You a babe in these woods."

I'm flabbergasted that she has the nerve to talk down to me. I cross my arms. "I have no desire to stay here, but I will speak with the mayor about my son. Where is he?"

An awkward silence descends. Once the coals have turned gray, Hoodie deposits the potatoes rolled in foil, corn cobs in and out of the husk, and finally, the hamburger patties on the grills with assembly-line efficiency. He squirts the husks with a water bottle and wipes his brow while the two women look to him for direction. He does a double-take and looks at me. "You can't," he says.

For an instant, I wonder if he is the mayor. My nose is cold and runny. I pull a tissue from a pocket. "What do you mean?"

He uses the old metal spatula to rearrange the food with the fluid dexterity of a short-order cook. "Just what I said. He's a busy man. Besides, he ain't here but should be later. You can speak with him then, if he'll agree to talk. I can't speak for the man." Flames dance and shoot in jets between the grillwork and are met with more squirts from the water bottle. Hoodie motions with his head to Dora as people begin to mill around, drawn by the smell. The growing crowd ignores me. The shadow of a plane crosses over us and vanishes in the blink of an eye.

"Come with me, child," Dora urges, leading me to a table. "Wilbur and Flossie mean no harm. They're protective, is all. You must be tired from your journey." She hands me one of two plastic pint bottles of orange juice and opens hers. "*Are* you from town?"

I blow my nose as a gust of wind almost knocks me from the bench. It's much colder up here. A young man rides slowly through the clearing on a bike and acknowledges Dora. I stand and dart toward him. "I'm looking for the man in this picture. Have you seen him?" The cyclist gives me a wide berth and abruptly pedals away, a quizzical look on his face.

Dora asks to see the photo again and handles it with care. It was windy the day I took it; Danny sported a week-long beard and seemed to be gazing beyond the camera, a wistful look and wan smile on his face, his dark brown hair curled up behind his ears. Like his dad's.

"A handsome young man." She looks at me and smiles. "I see the resemblance around the eyes. I don't think I've seen him, but my memory isn't what it used to be."

I almost forget an important part. "The picture is two years old. He turned thirty-five yesterday. His hair could be longer, he could have a beard. He could be thinner." He could be . . . many things.

She takes time to study it carefully. "I'm sorry. I don't remember." She leans closer, and a musty smell wafts to me from her worn coat. She folds her gnarled hands in her lap and, in a voice raspy as sandpaper, says, "You've had a difficult journey. They take your heart and break it, don't they?"

A short, thin, elderly man with longish, unkempt white hair idles by and winks at Dora.

I bite my lip and notice the approaching twilight. The temperature drops sharply with the sun now behind the mountain. I hope I can find my way back to the car; my phone's compass should help. "Where does the mayor live?"

Music begins behind me. I do a double take when I see the white-haired man now sitting on a bench playing a slow boogie-woogie tune from memory on a small upright piano under a tarp suspended from pine branches.

I turn to Dora. "How did a piano get all the way up here?"

She smiles and says in that gritty voice, "Where there's a will . . . Most Highlanders bring all their earthly possessions with them. We were no different. Tom's had that old thing for thirty years. At times I swear it's attached to his fingers."

We listen as a crowd forms. Dora nudges my knee. "We haven't seen our children in years. It still makes me heartsick. The best advice I have is don't chew on somethin' that's eating you, child."

I purse my lips and smile briefly. I find her folksy bromides damn near offensive. And stop calling me *child*.

I open my mouth to tell her to mind her own business and point me to the mayor's tent when a bell clangs loudly five or six times. Those milling nearby form an orderly line.

Dora rises. "Welcome to the Highlands, Susan. Food's ready."

When we join the back of the line, I spot a tarnished brass ship's bell nailed to a tree near the grills. Tom segues to a lively bluegrass tune I also recognize but can't name. I didn't have much time or use for music after I married. Popular songs are so damn frivolous, and the lyrics, especially to love songs, are mostly nonsense. But here, the riff injects energy into the residents, and the chatter increases. Some people dance in line or around the totem pole.

Stacks of buns, plates of pickles and tomato and onion slices, a large block of government cheese, napkins, and condiments are there for the taking. Flossie shoos flies from the food. Lights wink on, and portable lanterns repel patches of advancing darkness; the bonfire blazes while more than forty people gather round it to eat and talk. The campfire hisses and pops with a great cascade of dancing sparks, belching motes of dust and ash into the air like an active volcano.

"Let's get some hot food in you. You look so thin and cold." Dora motions me in front of her. We reach the first of the tables, where Wilbur deftly places a grilled burger and steaming ear of corn on my paper plate. I help myself to a bun, pickle, and potato salad from one of the many-gallon containers. I ate like this when I was young, when I was thirty pounds heavier and sluggish all the time. Jim, who's always been lean, began to make comments about my weight. When I hit middle age, I cut my carbs and shed weight by eating kale salads, veggies, fish, and quinoa. Maybe a protein shake for lunch. The sizzling meat smells wonderful. The seats around the bonfire are taken, so we settle at one of the picnic tables while people sing along to the music, and a few call out requests. I wasn't expecting this at all, especially after the run-in with Flossie.

Dora turns to me. "Is Danny your only child?"

I cringe at the prospect of questions about my personal failures. I turn to grab my drink, hoping Dora will assume I didn't hear her. Flossie gingerly takes the spot between us. That's when

I notice her tiny baby bump. Winter approaches, and this woman is homeless and pregnant. I'm an interloper in a world of castoffs and freeloaders who face shattered hopes and failure daily. Flossie grunts and says, "You gonna answer her question?"

We stare at each other in silence while the music plays. I put myself in their shoes and feel my face redden. Am I embarrassed for being here? Yes. Do I regret my failings as a parent? You bet. Am I fearful that it reflects poorly on me? Yes, but Dora isn't to blame, and I need to swallow my pride if I want their help.

"Yes, he is my only child."

I stand and pour a cup of coffee from the pot on our table, mostly to warm my hands. My nose feels frozen, and I place the hot cup to my face. Although my sole attempt at camping years ago failed miserably due to my aversion to bugs and the heat—the thought makes me want to hang myself from the tallest pine—my one positive memory is that food tastes fantastic when grilled and eaten in the woods.

While I wait for the charred corn to cool, I take a bite of burger. I close my eyes as the hot beef melts and slides down my throat like a little piece of heaven. My eyes roll over. It's the only food I've had all day. My insides begin to warm, and I start in on the potato salad. Low clouds scud across the sky, and the stars shine bright in the mountain air.

Dora pushes back her tangled gray bangs and leans closer, waving a plastic fork in my direction. "Forgive my forwardness, but you want him to be the prodigal son, don't you? The one who returns to his mother." Her kind blue-gray eyes scan my face. "What a joyous irony that would be, a prodigal son who returns to Prodigal!"

I stare at my plate and do a slow boil. My anxiety kicks in. I close my eyes while the beeps grow louder and morph into a deafening *scree* of cicadas. I cover my ears. A wave of guilt washes over me. When I open my eyes, the long shadows thrown by the fire and totem pole seem to spring to life and advance toward me. I know it's impossible, but I see it happen. People stare. Flossie cracks a smile. They must think I'm crazy. I toss the rest of my dinner into a trash can.

I sit back down and wait for the beeps to stop. I find myself cradling my belly again and don't want to let go of it. I turn to Dora. "People like you don't know what the word means." I'm surprised by the sarcasm I hear in my lowered voice. People at our table glare at me. Several move away. A murmur builds among the crowd.

Dora looks put in her place—worse, humiliated—which I now realize was my intent. I breathe and count to ten before I speak.

She puts down her fork and wipes her mouth gingerly with a napkin. She speaks in a slow, measured voice. "Maybe I don't know what the word means, but I have a feeling you are about to tell me."

I clear my throat and straighten my posture. "A prodigal spends lavishly and foolishly. He, or she, is characterized by profuse self-indulgence." Danny personified.

"Huh," Dora says, looking me in the eyes. "I thought it was someone who returns after being gone a long time, like it says in the Good Book."

"The Bible is a poor substitute for a dictionary."

Flossie has been eyeballing me the entire time. Her frown returns stronger than ever. "Looky here, Dora, we got ourselves an educated woman . . . with an attitude to match those designer clothes and that expensive watch."

I briefly place a hand over my watch as I stand to leave, but a hand grabs my shoulder.

It's Dora. "I hope he returns to you. I pray that he does." She looks toward Tom at the piano. "Ours disowned us the day we moved here." Those within earshot nod in affirmation.

"They did that to you for being homeless?"

She nods. "We put them through college, but now we embarrass them. They have stressful jobs in town, children of their own at home, and no room for us." She hangs her head. "We haven't seen our grandchildren in three years."

"What I said was cruel. I'm struggling with . . . things. I was wrong to take it out on you. I'm sorry."

She reaches for my hand. "I was out of line for pressing you about the photograph. I should have kept my pie hole shut. That's not what we're about up here." She stands, wipes away a tear, and says in her damaged, guttural voice, "We all have our demons. You will have your audience with the mayor when he returns, but for now, let's enjoy tonight."

A fiddler rosins up his bow, and an accordionist joins Tom in a lively version of "The Beer Barrel Polka" while people dance and sing around the bonfire. The numbers swell to perhaps a hundred. We take seats near the fire on the stones and tree trunks. Bottles snick open, and I hear the whoosh of aluminum cans. Flossie passes me a bottle, and—as surreptitiously as possible—I wipe its mouth with a clean tissue before I drink. My belly warms while I hand the bottle to Dora. She leans forward and whispers, "We don't have cooties up here, Susan." She smiles and passes the bottle without drinking. The unmistakable smell of pot fills the air, and I notice small groups sharing joints. Two men huddle together, cleaning their rifles.

An owl hoots in the dark forest, and luminous silver stars freckle the clear night sky. I ask when the mayor is due, but no one seems to know. The trio /performs quality renditions of "The Devil Went Down to Georgia," "If I Were a Rich Man," and a medley of dance and show tunes while more bottles circle the bonfire. I begin to feel tipsy. It no longer seems as cold as before, and somehow the world is more expansive here than the one down below.

I look at my watch and am shocked at the time. If the mayor doesn't return soon, I'm going to have to drive out of here, and negotiating all those switchbacks in the dark will be a challenge. Someone offers another bottle, but I pass it on. More Highlanders gather as the music and dancing continue, and I hear mention of other encampments on the mountain. Could Danny live in one of them?

I turn to Dora. "I have to pee."

"What do you know, you are human," she says, grinning. "Follow me."

I return her smile. She balances her trash on top of an overflowing drum, and we walk a slippery needle-carpeted path. Every so often, a lamp droops from a branch, swaying in the breeze, to guide the way.

"If the mayor still isn't here, I will come back tomorrow. Do you know his schedule?"

Before Dora answers, we pass a burly man in a red flannel jacket and hat with matching earflaps. He belches as he urinates against a tree, his back to us, and mutters something incomprehensible in drunk-speak. Dora reminds him to follow the rules, then calls back to him.

"Bert, is the mayor back from town?"

"No, he's working late again. I'll use the pissers from now on. Don't tell him, Dora."

That's it, then. I'll use the commode and drive home or find a hotel. I can figure it out on the way down the mountain.

Owls call to each other high above us. I look up and see the horned moon in a now cloudless sky. The path descends and widens into a small clearing bordered by ferns. A herd of deer looks up to consider us; the flash of white tails signals their departure. The smell of rotting trees soon mingles with the unmistakable odor of human waste.

In the soft amber glow of two lanterns, a row of portable commodes emerges. Dora knocks on the nearest door, finds it unoccupied, and motions me forward. Thin, faint ribbons of light slant through the doorframe once the door closes. As I lower my jeans, a man's bass voice floats in the air nearby, chanting, muffled, and incomprehensible. Have I had that much to drink? Maybe it's an illusion, an anomaly of the wind, or my mind playing tricks on me again.

Crickets chirp, and as I squat over the seat, some *thing* jumps on my exposed leg. I swat at it and lose my balance. I land on the commode with a thud and get stuck because the seat is up. Shock waves of cold rattle my bones, and the warm buzz from the liquor vanishes. I struggle to free myself, and the stench hits hard. I fumble for the latch and throw open the door, but it's too late— the flashing lights and beeping noises are back. I cover my ears, but the syringes in the trampled grass send me over the edge. The world goes black.

I dream of Danny's birth and the year that followed.

I remember the terror. The blood on our bed. Jim's frantic 911 call. The ambulance ride. The drips, the drugs. The looks on the faces of the EMTs. Wheeling down the halls on a stretcher, blinking under each fluorescent light, drifting in and out of consciousness.

The OR nurses, identical in their gowns and masks, glance at me and avert their eyes. One shakes her head briefly. How bad is it? Did I do something wrong? Jim's face is ashen; a fist hides his mouth. He watches the doctor intently. Maybe the lady doctor's done something wrong.

Every day for months, I prayed for a healthy baby. That's all I wanted. Boy or girl, it didn't matter. I wanted to see my baby and the look of unabashed joy on my husband's face when it was born. I got neither.

Masked staff hovers over me, but their voices drift to me as if from the bottom of an elevator shaft, and their words do not register. Are they coordinating their stories to cover up the doctor's mistake? They clean me and sew me up. Someone wheels me somewhere and leaves me alone with my drug-induced thoughts.

Jim isn't here.

At some point, a social worker enters my room and offers to talk, but I tell her all I want is to see my baby. She leaves her card on the hospital tray. I fall into a deep sleep. When I wake, there is no card.

When the drugs wear off, a nurse wheels me to the NICU, where my son looks like a tiny lump in an incubator. He's eleven inches long and weighs a pound and a half. A CPAP machine helps him breathe. An NG tube carries nutrition through his nose to his stomach. A pliable splint attached to his tiny arm keeps the central line and tubing in place. I'd give anything to hold him, to trade places with him, but the only contact I'm allowed is through the side openings, which offer limited skin-to-skin contact. I fear this physical separation will cause bonding issues with my baby, but the nurse assures me being close to him now helps.

I sit in a wheelchair in the NICU touching his tiny hand. It is the twenty-fifth week of what I'd been told was a routine pregnancy. I learn that the sudden blood loss was a result of a complete placental abruption, the separation of the placenta from my uterine wall. Abruptions occur in about one percent of pregnancies. Most of the time, they're relatively minor; sometimes, they can complicate a birth. In rare cases, they can kill the baby, the mother, or both. The doctor says it's a miracle Danny's brain received enough oxygen in the ambulance to keep his underdeveloped lungs pumping. She says I'm lucky to be alive.

I lay shaking during the blood transfusion that night, terrified that my son's next breath will be his last. I haven't been allowed to hold him yet. The doctors monitor me for signs of organ failure. I cry, pray, and curse God. I bargain with Him to let my son live. *Take me and let him live, if you must.*

I visit him in the NICU as often as they let me. Sometimes they bring him in a portable incubator to my room. The staff bends over backward for me and Danny. Jim says he followed Danny to the NICU after my emergency C-section; that's why he wasn't there when I woke up from the hysterectomy. He apologizes for not being with me.

The transfusions over the next week help me regain my strength. When my renal panel and other major organs stabilize, they discharge me without my son.

I visit the hospital several times a day. I stay for hours. Jim stops by when he can on his lunch break. I hold our son for the first time a month after his birth.

Each night when visiting hours end, the nurses smile and offer hugs and prayers. They urge me to go home and remind me to take care of myself, but they don't tell me how.

They don't know about the voices I keep hearing, ones that, in time, I will come to suspect may not actually be there. The voices say that I committed a monstrous act for which I will be punished. Are they telling the truth?

The dark whisperings persist after we bring Danny home. One whispers that Jim plans to get rid of me and keep our son for himself. If I tell people this, they won't believe me, so I never let Danny out of my sight. I write everything down in my journal, in case harm befalls me.

Jim thinks I'm overprotective. He's concerned and wants me to see the doctor, but I know better: Jim and the doctor are in it together. The doctor will commit me, and Jim will take Danny.

I know something is haywire inside me, and I fear I've gone mad. Maybe Jim wanted this all along. I start to think the only way out is to kill myself. Or take Danny, change our names, and start a new life somewhere far away. The voices persist for months before they begin to ease up. They stop on their own around Danny's first birthday.

What a hellish year.

As I begin to wake, I remember fainting outside in a cold, unfamiliar place.

I feel toasty warm. Something nearby hisses and pops, and I look up to see a crinkled, silver sky. Where the hell am I?

AN AUDIENCE WITH THE MAYOR

Something sweeps across my face, and I worry the bugs are back. I turn my head to the side and find Dora sitting close, wetting my forehead with a washcloth. She squeezes the rag into a bedpan and turns back to me. "You had quite a nightmare."

My eyes track her hand on its way to the bedpan, and she smiles. "Don't worry. This one's clean."

"Where am I?"

"In our home."

I look upward, confused.

"It's silver tent lining, to retain heat."

I run my fingers across the worn comforter above me and the thin mattress below. I turn my head to see a narrow, warped bookcase crammed with books and sheet music, a folding table with a wooden bowl filled with cereal packets. A small green floral sofa sits next to a portable commode. A black Franklin stove, the source of the pops and hisses, radiates warmth in the corner; its flue extends through the roof. Dancing light fills the room. I swivel my head the other way and see Tom sitting in front of a battered upright piano set on large casters.

"Welcome back to the world," he says, waving at me and flashing an impish smile that shows a few missing upper and lower teeth.

The wet cloth feels good on my clammy forehead. "What happened?"

Dora brushes wayward gray bangs from her face and smiles, revealing a missing front tooth. "You passed out last night by the porta-potties. Looked like you saw a ghost and fell facedown. Even though you don't weigh a hundred pounds soaking wet, I couldn't lift you, so I had Bert bring you here in a wheelbarrow." Her smile fades. "How do you feel?"

I couldn't begin to answer that one truthfully if I wanted to. "I'm fine. I haven't had much of an appetite lately. Maybe my blood sugar is low."

She straightens; concern etches her round face. "You diabetic? We don't have a doctor here, but the bus—"

"I'm fine."

My head spins, and a marching band blares between my ears when I sit up. My tongue feels hairy. I remember feeling threatened at dinner and in the commode—the return of the beeps and lights.

I don't belong here. I don't want to be here, but this is where I need to be. Maybe Flossie's right. I am a babe in these woods.

"You want to try and stand?" Dora says.

She helps me to the sofa while Tom, reading my mind, offers me a cup of hot coffee from the stove ledge.

"Would you like cream or sugar?" he asks.

"Black is fine, thanks," I say.

Tom bows theatrically.

The coffee is strong, just the way I like it, and I peer over the cup while Dora pours water from a steaming kettle into a bowl. "Would you like sugar and cinnamon with your oatmeal, Susan?"

"Both, please. This is very kind of you."

She places the oatmeal, a sugar packet, a paper towel, and a plastic jar of ground cinnamon on a TV tray between the sofa and stove, then adds logs to the fire. When Tom announces he's off to do chores in camp, she calls, "Bring back water for boiling, old man," without looking up.

I take tentative bites of the instant oatmeal and close my eyes. The world spins slower, and my head feels a bit clearer.

"Your phone rang many times while you were asleep."

I tense and turn to her. "Did you answer it?"

She smiles as she tops off my coffee. "It's not my place." She wipes her hands on a towel and rests a weathered hand on the table.

I notice a narrow sliver of light near the entrance to the tent. Sunlight. I'm about to ask how long I've been asleep when I look at my watch. Holy shit, I spent the night in a tent city.

"I can't believe I spent the night here." I notice the look on her face and shake my head. "I didn't mean anything—"

Dora pours a coffee for herself. "No offense taken. You were in no condition to drive and needed sleep." She takes a sip and grins.

I feel a sudden closeness to her. She's like a friendly tour guide in this real-life dystopian world. She feels like my mom from another universe.

My thoughts begin to drift. Jim knows I didn't come home last night, and I'm sure he read my note from yesterday morning. He probably thinks I stayed in a hotel and that I'll return for my things while he's at work.

"I know what it feels like," Dora says. "Our first night here—"

Loud knocking interrupts her, and I notice the small wooden door and frame built into their tent. A tall, bearded man enters and turns to me. "The mayor will see you now." Then to Dora, "Bring her and leave. I'm sure you have work to do."

She nods and rises. When this mayor beckons, people jump. I put down my unfinished bowl and grab my coat.

In the light of a cold but clear, sunny morning, the camp looks less ominous. Residents are going about their work. Some haul firewood in carts or wheelbarrows. One drives a small loader transporting bags of trash. Young people walk dogs on leashes. Some people nod or smile. It's not what I expected.

The ornately carved and painted totem pole is less imposing in daylight. The quality of the work impresses me. The eyes of the eagle seem to follow me wherever I walk. The painted wings give the appearance of feathers. Chiseled faces and carvings of animals adorn several sides of the pole. Sections near the top remain smooth and unpainted.

The daylight helps orient me to the camp layout. Dora and Tom's tent is in an area I hadn't seen yet, west of the picnic tables and the charred remnants of last night's bonfire. Tents and structures of all shapes and sizes line the path. Some are basic pup tents, while others are a jumble of wood, metal, canvas, and cardboard. One stands out from the others. It has a cute white picket fence, a rainbow-colored mailbox, and a sign that reads

"Number One Piney Lane." Ferns line a brick walk to the door, and cheery arts-and-crafts decorations adorn the outside walls. I spot cars on concrete blocks, camper shells, and discarded RV trailers.

On a slight rise immediately west of the picnic area, the three of us arrive at the mouth of a large outfitter tent with canvas walls and a framed wooden door. The chill returns to my bones as the tall, dour man instructs me to wait inside. I say goodbye to Dora, who walks away while I go inside. The tall man stands at the entrance. He has a large, sheathed hunting knife on his belt. Is he guarding me? Am I a prisoner? Anxiety creeps up my spine.

I pull out my phone; it shows all its bars. I was worried the signal would be weak or unavailable up here in the mountains and forest. I listen to my messages. Twelve are from the school, co-workers that grow more concerned and curious with each message. The last call is from Jim's cell. A hang-up. Typical.

What do I do if I don't find Danny? Crawl back home with my tail between my legs and dodge more projectiles? Move out and stay with a friend? How long would that last?

Do I stay at a hotel? I can't afford my own place right now.

I smile at the perverse irony that this worst-case scenario could temporarily cause me to be homeless unless I return home or request an order of protection. But Jim has never hit me, and the other night was the first time I ever felt scared he might.

Do I climb in my car and keep driving?

I unraveled the last strands of normalcy that held my life together by calling in sick for the week. This guilt will eat at me until I act on it. I must find Danny.

I look around in surprise at the ample living space I've entered. By no stretch of the imagination is it homey or even comfortable: the floor is dirt, it's out of the wind but cold, so it still feels like roughing it. Four haphazard rows of metal folding chairs, several weathered recliners, and a worn yellow sofa face a podium and table. An ironwood cross and plastic floral wreath hang on the wall behind the podium. To one side stands a large wood-burning stove with a flue that rises through the canvas roof.

I flip through a stack of weathered, worn books on the podium. Each of the gilt-edged pages of the tattered Bible is marked with notes written in a bold hand. Beneath the Bible are copies of the Koran and Talmud. Candles of varying colors and sizes fill a small table. A faded American flag adorns a long wall between framed pictures of the President of the United States and the mayor of Prodigal. I wonder what the Highlanders think of them.

I remember silently agreeing with friends back in Prodigal who mocked the homeless for being unemployed, non-taxpaying manipulators of the system who chose to live off welfare. Jim and I remained silent when our friends made light of the idea that health care is a right and that wealth should be redistributed to the lower classes. My father always said that if every homeless person and taxpaying resident of Prodigal were to live together and start the year with the same amount of money, after one year, the responsible and hardworking people would reacquire all the wealth and the homeless would return to the streets. It's a matter of character and willpower, he said.

Years after his death, I heard the horror stories and news reports about the Highlands being overrun by thieves, rapists, and the mentally ill, that people sometimes entered and were never found again.

Bulletin boards run the length of the wall opposite the flag. I walk toward them until I spot a rick of kindling near the claw feet of the stove. I kneel, position wood on top of the cold ash heap, and strike a match. Nothing. I burn four more matches, and still no fire.

"You asked to see me," a man's voice behind me says. A shadow moves toward me from the doorway. I turn and look up at a barrel-chested man, maybe in his early fifties, with a short salt-and-pepper beard. He wears jeans and a blue oxford under a brown bomber jacket. I rise and walk to him, wiping ash onto my jeans. His eyes are vivid hazel and quite striking. He's balding and not particularly tall, with patchy sprouts of black hair lining the back of his dome. Despite that, he's a handsome man who carries himself well. With backlighting from a lantern, his face appears framed by a blackened halo.

He extends his hand. "I'm Travis, mayor of the Highlands." His grip is firm, and his eyes remain on mine.

"Susan," I say. "I'm looking for my son. His name is Daniel Crusoe. He goes by Danny. At least, I assume he still does." I show him the photo. "It's the most recent picture I have, from two years ago."

"Why are you looking for him?"

I feel like I'm back under that leaky awning in Prodigal. "No disrespect, Mr. Mayor, but it's personal."

He smiles thinly and pauses while he assesses me. "You spent the night as an uninvited guest in our city. We welcomed you into our community with open arms. You ate our food and drank our wine. We know nothing about you. You collapsed, and we treated you. Dora thought you may be diabetic. We acted responsibly, out of concern for you. You brought several prescription medicines into the Highlands, some that are controlled substances—"

I forgot about my backpack when we left Dora and Tom's tent. "You went through my backpack? Where is it?" My face reddens with anger. "Where are my meds? You can't take away my prescriptions."

"I also have your money and credit cards." Travis reaches into his coat pocket and produces a sealed bag. Inside it, I see my prescription bottles and billfold. He hands me the bag. "Some of your medications have a street value of four dollars a pill. As mayor, I held these for safekeeping while you were incapacitated. Money and drugs are always a temptation—in here or Prodigal. Feel free to make sure everything is there."

Most of my cash is gone. I'm about to protest until I remember I stashed the lion's share under the front passenger seat. My credit cards, driver's license, and ATM card are in the same clear plastic sleeves as before.

"Oh, I almost forgot," Travis says, reaching into his jeans pocket. "Your keys."

"Thank you." I grab them and make sure the BMW keys are among the others on the ring. I need to check that my car is where I left it.

He reaches under a table and hands over my backpack. My prescription sunglasses are in the pocket where I left them, as are my lipstick, lip gloss, water bottle, towel, and assorted sundries. Everything's here.

He's saying, "I trust you would have done the same for Dora if the tables were turned. Would you and your husband have taken her into your home and provided aid if she passed out in your driveway?"

No. I would have called an ambulance. Dora and Tom *were* kind in my time of need, but why the attitude?

"Has anyone told you lately you are an impertinent man?" I say.

"Constantly." His voice lowers. "I'm glad you're feeling better. Now, if you want to remain a Highlander, you must abide by our one rule: respect your neighbors. I strive for us to be as drug-free a community as possible. Recreational alcohol and pot use are acceptable unless you're an abusive drunk. No hard drugs. If you truly need those prescription meds, you must see your doctor regularly and take them as prescribed. Above all, keep them in a safe place. Do not share or sell them. As I said, some have a street value and are potential drugs of abuse."

I smile at the thought that I would live in this tent city. "No, no. I'm not staying. I want to find my son. I'm told he lives here. It's a private family matter. I want to put his picture on your bulletin board with my contact information and encourage anyone with information about Danny to call me. I will look for him in the other two camps that Dora mentioned to me the first night before I leave."

Travis folds his arms across his chest. "I guarantee you won't find him at the other camps. And you will never receive an answer if you post a missing persons notice on our bulletin board."

"What harm is there if I post his picture along with my contact information?"

"You'd be surprised. Nothing good will come from it. Adults leave home for all sorts of reasons. Some don't want to be found."

"But I'm his mother."

"You may well be. You could also be a criminal hiding from the police and want to harm him."

"That's insane." I feel the aura of a budding panic attack invade my skin. He watches me dry-swallow three Xanax and close my eyes. I breathe in through my nose and out through my mouth to calm myself. When I open my eyes, his remain on me. Is he checking me out?

He smiles and clears his throat. He's blushing. "It may seem that way to you, but we live day-to-day, and our days here are most likely numbered. I'm responsible every day of the year for the lives of three hundred Highland men, women, and children. Winter is coming, and two pregnant Highlanders and several elderly, infirm, and mentally ill people live here. It's my duty to protect them as best I can from the perils of the outside world and sometimes . . . from themselves. You are a stranger. You come here asking many questions. Your driver's license says you live in Prodigal. You have all the trappings of the city that plans to shut us down."

"I understand everything you've said. I'm not here to cause trouble."

Travis' eyes widen. He rubs his jaw. "I've heard those famous last words in this very room. Outsiders with hidden agendas come here looking for people. Some are bounty hunters, some are owed money, others seek revenge—often more than a pound of flesh."

"Do I look like that type of person?" I say, exasperated.

"What does that type of person look like, Susan?" When I don't answer, he sits on a folding chair. "As you've probably noticed, Highlanders are as diverse as Prodigal is. But we are the invisible people, the vulnerable, the castoffs. People with no voice. As their leader, I need to know the truth."

I shift my weight when the wind kicks up and ripples the tent's canvas walls. "I kicked Danny out of our home. I've come to regret that decision. I want to meet him face-to-face, even if it's for the last time. I'm not certain what my reaction will be, but I mean him no harm. I have no quarrel with anyone here." I try but fail to keep emotion out of my voice.

His eyes soften. "You're not sure he's alive, are you?" When I don't respond, he asks, "Is he wanted by the police?"

"Not to my knowledge," I lie.

His arresting eyes study me so long it becomes unnerving. "Oh, to be a fly on that wall if you two meet again."

I raise the picture up to him. "Let's cut to the chase. Does this man, my son, live in the Highlands?"

"No."

The air goes out of me, and my hopes sink. Apparently, the giant with the teardrop tattoo was blowing smoke up my skirt to carjack me. I feel tears well as I ask my last desperate question. "Has he ever lived here?"

Travis smiles, but I see reluctance cross his face. "You are direct and quite singular in purpose. How's that working for you?"

"You think you know me, but you don't. Has he ever lived here?"

He almost looks sorry for me. "He has. For brief periods, off and on."

My breath catches. I chastise myself for not searching here myself, but I was terrified of this place. All prior leads had him in other states. I never imagined Danny would rough it in a tent city. "When was the last time?"

"Twice late last summer. Lasted a few days each time."

My voice rises an octave. "Did he look well? Why'd he leave?"

Travis rises and situates the podium between us. "The rule here is simple. Respect your neighbor. Drugs, alcohol, and crime are problems that can rot any city from within, even Prodigal. The safety and welfare of these people override everything. Without a jail and police department, we strive to handle major offenses fairly and compassionately. Danny consistently violated the rule and refused to seek help. I exiled him."

"You kicked him out?" I shout. As soon as the words leave my mouth, I regret them.

He walks around the podium to step closer. "I think you know the reason."

I take a deep breath and nod.

"He used and dealt narcotics to Highlanders. During both his stays, valuables went missing. We could never tie him directly to the thefts, and we think he used a confederate. He played residents against one another. Some sought revenge for his actions. Dealing is automatic banishment when the user refuses treatment."

I fall silent, realizing that Danny could be anywhere in the world.

Travis exhales a big breath. "I'm sorry to be the bearer of this news." After a quiet minute, he says, "Will you be leaving now?" The illuminated black halo above his balding head appears even more pronounced.

The wind moans in one long song around the tent. I despise this place and the cold almost as much as I despise myself. "He lived here twice, which means you allowed him to return. Has he been permanently banished?"

Travis touches his jaw again, reluctant to answer. "I keep an open-door policy in my camp. Anyone who needs a place to stay is welcome as long as they agree to respect their neighbors."

I consider my labors on the Great Wall of Danny and the fruitless searches of the PIs over the last eight months while I returned home from work and Jim sat glued to his police scanner. After I withdrew into the guest bedroom, living in my own little apartment, I sometimes felt single again. But on other days, I felt like a prisoner. Something had to give.

Home truly is a place I can neither leave nor stay in.

My thoughts drift to work and Jim and what our neighbors and co-workers will think if I stay. I fondle the jagged car keys, the temptation palpable. I could sleep in the car, but if I start the engine for warmth, I'll leave. I could go home and return to teaching until the guilt overwhelms me. I could start over in another state, which solves nothing. I could find the right tree or abutment. Each has its merits over freezing alone in a tent city on a mountain in winter. It's so damn cold, and I know nothing about outdoor survival. I've never felt this alone in my life. I think of Danny and the gnawing certainty that I've committed a monstrous act that caused all this damage.

"No. I'm going to stay and wait for him."

Travis nods. "You didn't come prepared. You can't start a fire in a sheltered stove, and the temperature continues to drop. Soon snow will fall, and the ground will freeze."

"I can do more than you give me credit for. What do you know about me?"

He folds his arms against his chest. "You impulsively stuffed a two-month supply of medicines in your pack, but no warm clothes. Unless you brought a carload of camping essentials, you won't last a week on the mountain without cold-weather gear and a plan."

I'm not worried about that for now. Dora and Tom will put me up for the night. I can sleep on their sofa. "I'm staying."

"Very well. I will send someone. All new residents receive a tent if they need one and the use of a hammer and tools. Several hours of daylight remain. You are familiar with camping?"

I feel panic set in, and he correctly reads my face.

"Did you expect to spend another night with Dora and Tom?"

I hold my head high. "Of course not."

"There's no shame if you change your mind. This life isn't for you."

Unless returning home empty-handed leads to the death of my soul. "If Danny knows he can return, I want to stay."

"He knows the drill, but you should know this. Homelessness is not a chronic issue for most. People drift in and out of tent cities as their circumstances change. Your son may be shacked up with friends, sharing an apartment. He could be . . .

many places. If you leave your phone number, I promise to tell Danny you want to meet with him if he returns."

"That's not good enough," I say.

For an instant, those bright hazel eyes seem to flicker. "Can *you* abide by our one simple rule?"

"Yes, and I want to be told the minute Danny returns."

There's a knock on the door, and the tall, bearded man enters to whisper in the mayor's ear. Travis nods, and the man leaves.

He returns his attention to me. "I can't promise that. I have a city to run. I don't recommend you post a notice, but I can't stop you. Are you certain Danny wants to see you?"

When I hesitate, Travis repeats himself. "Are you certain you can abide by our one rule?"

"Of course. How hard can it be?"

His look of doubt remains, but he shakes my hand. "Welcome to the Highlands. Someone will be here soon with your supplies. In the meantime, I suggest you practice your fire-making skills. Fire requires air. Scoop the ash into the bucket and start with paper, shavings, and smaller kindling. You should only need one match. We expect bad weather to roll in tonight. Let the awakening begin, Susan from Town."

He exits, and before the door closes, I see stray paper plates tumbling down the forest path as the wind soughs through the pines like a ghost train. I feel like one of those plates.

PUTTING DOWN STAKES

I start a fire with three matches. As the room brightens and begins to warm, a short, smiling man enters and introduces himself in an accented voice as Vidal. I wonder how many Mexicans live here and whether that contributes to the crime problem. He politely asks me to follow him. Outside stands a rustic wheelbarrow filled with cardboard boxes and tools.

We walk the unsettled grounds, and he asks where I want to pitch my tent. I point out several places, but he shakes his head, smiling. "Ground too low," or "at the mercy of the wind," or "too far from water," he says. I relent and ask for his suggestion. We pass several tents until he spreads his arms and flashes that seemingly constant smile.

"Here," he says. "Shelter from trees, southern exposure, not too far from water, and closer to others." The wind does seem calmer here. He removes a folded tent from one of the boxes, pounds stakes into the hard, rocky ground, and shows me how to assemble the rods and thread the polyester. He uses a box cutter to flatten the cardboard, deposits the pieces outside my tent, and hands me several large garden-sized plastic bags. By the time we finish, night approaches, and I'm hungry and sweaty. I thank him and hold out twenty dollars, which he declines.

"Welcome to the Highlands," he says with a broad smile and deferential nod.

I don't know what to make of this strange, smiling homeless man who refuses payment for a job well done.

I return to the Pit, which is what Highlanders call the main communal area, and eat around the bonfire with the others. Tonight's meal is last night's leftover pizzas donated by restaurants in Prodigal. I recognize a spicy pepperoni and black olive one from Pizzazz, my favorite Italian restaurant. The picnic tables overflow with cartons of food in town that bear today's expiration date. I eat two fruit cups and a salad with my pizza. At last, the wind dies, and the bonfire flames reach to touch the sky.

A fight erupts between two men next to me over the last slice of pizza: Bert, the man Dora chastised on my first night, and another burly resident. Their bodies barrel into me and upend the pizza box. I crawl out from between the scrum as quick punches are thrown, and the coveted slice lands in the dirt. Wilbur and others separate the men, who storm off in different directions. The chatter around the fire returns.

Tom plays his piano under the awning, and a bottle makes its way around the fire, followed by another. Tom plays well into the night, and I linger by the dwindling embers until the crowd thins and the warmth starts to fade. I toss a few logs on the fire, and Vidal introduces me to his wife, Maria, and their three children. Others come over as well. An older black man named Charlie welcomes me with an infectious smile and leaves a blanket by my side. I receive an oil lantern and matches from a middle-aged couple and learn from them that Flossie and Wilbur are expecting their third child. Strangers shake my hand and introduce themselves. More gifts follow. Tom closes with a song that invokes a cheer; people hold hands and rally around it.

"I hope you're feeling better," Dora says, giving me a hug, another blanket, and a dog-eared book. She leans forward, pats my leg, and offers a conspiratorial wink. "I cleaned up for you. They are a nasty reminder of our all-too-human frailty." When she sees the confusion on my face, she smiles. "Well, I better go scrape the old man off that rickety bench and walk him home before his scrawny bottom freezes to it. How he loves to play! I hope you find what you're looking for, Susan."

I use the porta-potty before checking on my car. No Bert pissing against a tree and no jumping bugs this time, but the same rhythmic chanting comes from the commode nearest the woods. I knock on the door. "Are you okay?"

The mumbling abruptly ceases. I use my phone flashlight and find the door locked. No sign of the used syringes and crushed beer cans I saw the night before. I smile.

Thank you, Dora. I wish my mom would have been more like you.

46

My car appears untouched, right where I left it. I grab my journals and Faraday bag and head back to the Pit, where I borrow a wheelbarrow to cart the gifts to my shelter.

Inside my little blue tent, I use the flashlight in my phone to fill and light the lantern. I learn the purpose of the cardboard—it helps smooth the rocky ground when I go to lie down. The sections work better as a temporary bed than one of the blankets. I rummage through the care package and find toilet paper, tissues, matches, a pen and paper, toothpaste and a toothbrush, bottled water, and gum. I'm out of the wind, but my teeth still chatter; I reconsider the car, but I'm exhausted, and it offers too many temptations.

If anyone told me two nights ago that I would be alone freezing my ass off in a tent in the Highlands, I would have called them a lunatic and given them odds of a billion to one.

All the trappings of suburban life flow through Danny's veins and mine. His words echo in my head from when Jim broached the subject of camping years ago: *I'd rather cut off my right hand than camp in the woods*. If anyone had had the audacity to tell me when Danny was fifteen—before the injury—that my son would become a chronic drug addict and spend time in a homeless shelter, I would have fought them until my dying breath.

The private investigator confirmed that Danny hasn't used his social security number or opened any lines of credit since I kicked him out. His name has not appeared on any jail, hospital, or morgue lists. The PI checked the Highlands twice (once in the middle of summer) and found no trace of him. The PI followed up on alleged sightings in San Francisco, San Diego, Big Sur, and later in Colorado, Nevada, and New Mexico. Danny slipped through our net outside a truck stop near Salina, Utah, like he had a sixth sense. Then came a month of no news until unverified sightings on the east coast, usually in cities with active drug scenes, and he never stayed in one place for long. He could be anywhere, above or below ground, but he called this place home twice.

A loon wails in the darkness, its cry eerie and mournful. It's a hauntingly beautiful and resonating call. Primordial in its essence, it shoots through me like an arrow. A reply follows minutes later, and the tears come. I feel small and alone and lost in this cold, black world where nostalgia and aspirations go to die.

By the amber glow of the lantern, I swallow a double dose of my antidepressant and anxiety meds. I throw back the blankets and organize my gifts and the inside of my tent.

I'm pleasantly surprised that my gift from Dora is not the Bible, but *Walden* by Thoreau. It's a very appropriate and thoughtful gift. I know the book and author well, having taught it for years. If Thoreau could live in the woods, so can I. He built his cabin near Walden Pond just south of Concord, Massachusetts, to concentrate on writing. It stood on fourteen acres of land owned by his friend and fellow transcendentalist Ralph Waldo Emerson, who lived a mile or two away. I've seen replicas of Thoreau's cabin: four walls, a roof, windows, a brick fireplace, chairs, a bed—the Taj Mahal compared to this flimsy tent.

I reacquaint myself with the book and, if not comforted, at least feel reassured. I find my journal and log my initial thoughts and impressions of the Highlands. I grab the second journal and write for a half hour while the loons wail and yodel back and forth. I plan to make entries in both journals every day, come freezing hell or high water.

No matter what position I try, the rocky ground stabs my back through the cardboard.

I think again of the electric seat warmers and heater in the BMW while I scroll through contacts on my iPhone, which still shows three bars up here on the mountain. With the touch of a finger, I could call any number, anywhere. My finger hovers over one, and I almost press it—but how can I explain my crimes and misdemeanors to Jim (or anyone, for that matter) when I don't know them myself? It would be like talking to a Martian. Besides, the person I most need to speak with has no known number. He doesn't want to be found; at best, he's off the grid. I shiver while

I consider the odds of Danny returning here. I question my sanity for choosing to stay.

I scroll through Facebook posts by total strangers hurling the vilest insults at each other over political affiliations. I read about the latest knockout crime in Prodigal, in which thugs sneak up behind a random person on the street and knock them unconscious with a blow to the back of the head. I watch videos of fatuous and dangerous fads—young adults who eat packets of laundry detergent or take blindfold dares inspired by a popular movie.

Maybe I was right to leave civilization after all.

To detox from Facebook, I read an article about education from the *New York Times* and play a trivia game of literary fiction. My battery drops below twenty percent, and I feel a tad less cold in my cramped new world. I return the phone to my Faraday bag.

I study my reflection in my compact and realize I've worn blinders regarding the depths to which people can sink. I failed to see the warning signs about Danny and my marriage to Jim. I blame myself as I douse the light.

Another thought rises from the darkness while I struggle to get comfortable. For the last eight months, I posted countless fliers on telephone poles in the town quadrangle, and bus stops throughout Prodigal. Dora said the Highlands' bus makes trips to town, so Highlanders must have seen Danny's picture, yet no one called.

I empty my backpack to use it as a pillow, adjust my ridiculous cardboard bed a final time, and curl into a ball under the two blankets. The weather develops an animal rhythm, as if the night were breathing in and out, in and out, and I lie trapped in its belly. I feel like the six-year-old version of me, afraid of the dark and the monsters hidden within.

Exhausted, I fall asleep to the wail of a solitary loon calling for its mate.

Tonight, I'm a hawk, soaring with other hawks. We circle and hover high above the tops of the tallest pines on Mount Prodigal. I land in our nest with fresh kill in my beak. My chick cries and squawks, refusing to eat. He pushes me away with his tiny beak and underdeveloped wings—or is it me pushing him away? He can't fly yet, so if he leaves the nest, he will plummet to his death. My mate is away, off hunting somewhere.

Pushing me away. Something else—a memory? A fear?—presses in on my dream, and my breath catches. I toss in my sleep, muttering, pleading. I can't pinpoint the memory, and it slips from my grasp. My heart races.

In the next dream that night, I look down at my human self in the house we lived in when Danny was a toddler. I catnap on our bed, but my eyes snap open when he screams from his playpen. I try every trick in the book and all the old wives' tales. It's the worst case of colic the pediatrician's ever seen. Jim sleeps downstairs to rest before work; he takes colic duty on weekend nights. The only thing that helps wasn't recommended by the doctor. My mom made hot toddies for me when I was sick and couldn't sleep. The rum and warm water, lemon, and honey would send me and—sometimes—Danny to sleep. When he dozes off, I clean up the dinner mess: mashed peas and carrots on the linoleum, highchair, and walls, a tiny plastic spoon, and spilled sippy-cup on the floor.

If the spoons had stayed plastic, I might not be here today.

I resume teaching when Danny starts school. He's an A student throughout grade school, but he shows no interest in making friends. We sign him up for sports and activities, but he refuses to participate or quits. The Boy Scouts ban him after he threatens someone with a stick. He claims the other boy provoked him, but there are witnesses, and the pack leader reports other instances of aggression.

As the years pass, he morphs into Evel Knievel. He lives to race down steep hills on his bike past dangerous cross streets, skateboards down steep stair rails, climbs the tallest trees, and orchestrates epic sled crashes. During this phase, he breaks his collarbone twice, a humerus, femur, wrist, and several fingers.

We take him to a child psychologist. His IQ tests are at genius level, but he exhibits a tendency toward impulsivity and acting out when not challenged. The psychologist recommends he skip seventh grade and start therapy while we search for a college prep high school that will engage his intellect.

During his sophomore year at a college prep school, the therapist recommends an antidepressant. Later that year, on a ski trip, we find Danny unconscious at the bottom of a cliff; he's torn an ACL and has a fractured kneecap. His recovery is arduous and painful. Months later, silver spoons go missing from my formal dining room set.

A crack louder than a gunshot wakes me from my dreams.

A BABE IN THE WOODS

My eyes flutter open, and I exit a bad dream to enter a real-life nightmare. Bolts of lightning rip through the black sky, and I sit up with a start. A thunderclap shakes the ground, its baritone rumbling directly overhead. The world is enraged and has come for me. Rain batters the tent roof, and gusts threaten to rip the fabric from the stakes. The pines creak and moan as if they are humans crying. The night pulses, and more lightning sizzles. Rivulets of water flow past the tent, and the ground trembles. I hear what sounds like an approaching train outside my tent. Never have I felt so small and helpless. I always wanted to control my death, but it's out of my hands now.

My ceiling bows inward when the jagged end of a pine branch thrusts through my tent flap. Water seeps up from the rocky earth and soaks my cardboard bed. I realize now that the plastic bags should have gone under the cardboard rather than keep my journals dry. I peer outside past the downed branch, but all I see is an ominous green hue in the black sky. The acrid smell of electricity fills the tent.

I close my eyes and count the seconds between the thunder and lightning, listening while the storm crawls east. I dry-swallow another Xanax. The downpour slows to a hard rain.

At last, my breathing slows, but I'm too terrified, cold, and wet to sleep.

Quiet returns in time to the mountain. I must have catnapped, for the sun is out when I open my eyes. I'm exhausted and ready to kill for a cup of coffee and a hot shower. My feet feel frozen, but pins and needles shoot through them when I move. Every part of me aches, and as I roll off my soggy cardboard bed, I hear a sickening crunch. My prescription sunglasses. I removed them from my backpack last night. The frame is broken, and a lens is scratched.

I stumble outside and pull branches off the tent. I stomp the tent pegs down as best I can. It takes all my strength to extract the large branch that fell through the tent flap and likely prevented the tent from flying off in the storm.

On my walk to the barbecue pits, fog hovers along the wet path like smoke. A paper-thin sheet of frost blankets the ground in shaded and low-lying areas, while water drip, drip, drips from the pines in fat globules. I couldn't find a dry match in the tent, so I dry-smoke a cigarette and work out the kinks in my back and neck. I miss my brand of bourbon. The bottles passed around the bonfire have been thirty-dime wines and pints of assorted flavored Schnapps. Gross, but at least they give a buzz.

As I walk the rain-swollen path, the earth seems on the same level as my nose, the air damp and sweet-smelling. Resin hangs in the fresh air. Nothing else moves. The world has an absolute stillness, like it's been scrubbed clean and hung out to dry. I reach a clearing and look up as vast coils of mist envelop the tops of the pines. Beyond the pines loom distant mountaintops like jagged teeth.

Wood smoke drifts to me on the wind, and somewhere in the distance, a raven caws. My stomach rumbles, and I quicken my pace. The slippery muck slurps at my feet, threatening to pull me into heavy sludge. A downed tree blocks the path ahead, and I shudder; it fell in the exact place I first wanted to pitch my tent. I look upward and say a silent thanks to Vidal.

A great swath of devastation now cuts through the forest in a zigzag pattern up the mountain. An uprooted ancient pine, two feet wide, leans against others. I look up at another towering pine whose charred and bifurcated trunk tore a gaping hole through the forest canopy.

At the Pit, Wilbur eyes me as he scrapes the grill.

"You're late. Didn't you hear the bell? Stragglers don't get a hot breakfast." A grin blooms on his stoic face. "But today, you're in luck. You survived a tornado. Happy first Tuesday in the Highlands." His grin vanishes.

I think of the locomotive sound and the eerie green glow, the wide swath cut through the forest up the mountain, the broken trees scattered like fallen tenpins. "We don't get tornados here. And at this time of year?"

His deadpan look says he's not kidding. "We do now. On a mountain, no less. Damnedest thing I ever heard, like a freight train or bomber." He pauses. "If I didn't know better, I'd say you brought it with you."

I don't know what to say to that.

"We got lucky. There are no basements here, so all we could do is pray. Coulda been much worse; a lotta folks could have died. One look at the forest shows it touched down briefly west of camp and moved north last night. Seven Highlanders lost all their possessions, and a dog is gone. Two were injured by falling branches and debris. A lotta cleanup work ahead—the church sustained some minor damage to the tarp, and many lost their tents or suffered tears in them." He makes a face. "It spared Prodigal."

I came close to dying last night and feel glad to be alive. I find no solace in a senseless death that's not on my own terms. "Got coffee?"

I hold out a mug from the table, and Wilbur fills it from a battered Coleman percolator on the grill. It could be hotter, but it's strong, just the way I like it. He moves a few remaining reddish-colored coals. "I found some heat." He opens a cooler and slaps the last ham steak on the grill. "One egg or two?"

"Two, please. Can you do sunny-side up?"

He wears two hoodies this morning and a Packers skullcap. A rag pokes out from the back pocket of his jeans. "I ran a diner in town for years. I can make any damn kind of egg you want, but there's not much heat left in the grill. Okay, if they're a little runny?"

"That's fine. You wouldn't happen to have any Woodford Reserve to spice up my coffee, would you?"

His grin returns while he adds lard and skillfully cracks two eggs at once. I think of Tom and Dora's tent. "Where do people get stoves and beds to make their tents halfway livable?"

He flips the steak and seasons the eggs. "Most, unlike you, bring all their earthly possessions with them. Some buy necessities in town, and others barter. A half cord of firewood in winter can be traded for anything—cigarettes, liquor, you name it—long as both sides agree."

"What if they don't?"

Wilbur's bushy brows knit together. "You met him."

I watch a young boy pick up after a wiry mutt on a leash and find it curious. In Prodigal, many dogs roam untethered, and owners who do walk their pets often leave dog shit on their neighbors' front lawns.

Wilbur transfers my steak and eggs to a paper plate and tops off my coffee. I add hot sauce to the eggs.

"The mayor's a powerful man, is he?" I say.

Wilbur doesn't answer. Instead, he stares, waiting for me to try the food. I take a bite and use a slice of bread to sop up the yolk. I close my eyes. "Mmm, incredible. You do know your way around a grill."

He smiles. "That, or maybe we appreciate the little things more up here, especially after a brush with death."

When the coffee kicks in, I start to feel half alive again. "You didn't answer my question about the mayor."

"We don't operate that way. You want to know about him, talk with him yourself."

"Okay. What happened to your diner?"

He sits across from me, the weight tilting the table toward his side. "Life. The economy. Mickey D's. You name it. Too few paying customers with enough time in their busy lives to sit down in a diner anymore. Death by drive-through. We fell behind on the rent."

"You and Flossie?"

He nods. "The landlord got tired of our sob story and evicted us after three months. Our cars and most of the furniture were repossessed. We were lower middle class. We had cable TV, cell phones, you name it. Floss worked for a cable company until they laid her off. The new owner lets me work shifts at the diner when I can."

I don't ask why they fell behind on the rent or where their two children live. I stop mid-chew. "Wait a minute. You still work in town . . . and live here?"

He raises an eyebrow and sips from his mug. "You *are* a babe in the woods. Most everyone here works in town. Some work two full-time jobs, especially adults with no kids. You know the cost of rent in town? Cheapest one-room apartment in Prodigal costs over fifteen hundred a month. I'd have to work three full-time minimum-wage jobs just to make the note. Not to mention the cost of food, utility bills, and no fucking time to sleep. Pardon my French."

"What about welfare?"

He cleans and wipes down his kitchen tools with the care and attention an artist would devote to his brushes. "The only government aid some here are eligible for is food stamps, which is a trip because the one thing we get plenty of is food donated by businesses, thanks to Pastor Frank and the mayor." He puffs out his chest. "If someone goes hungry here, it's their own damn fault."

I don't mask my surprise. They work in Prodigal, and the only handouts are donated food that businesses deduct as tax write-offs.

I watch Wilbur prepare for the next meal rush and shut down his workstation. I can see him running a kitchen staff in Prodigal with ease.

The steady whack of an ax striking wood to the north disrupts the quiet. It's coming from higher up the mountain. Closer and to the west, from the direction of my tent, men call to one another as chainsaws growl to life. I hear the distant drone of a helicopter that grows louder and performs a quick fly-by of the tent city before it gains altitude and heads higher up the mountain.

Wilbur looks up, and his eyes narrow. "The local news chopper here to show the good folks of Prodigal the damage the rogue twister caused to their mountain."

A feeling of unease hits me. "Will it land here to check on us?"

He turns to me, his mood darkening. "The land and lumber on the mountain have greater value to them."

I have many questions, but before I can ask them, he says, "Your clothes and mannerisms tell me you're from town. You don't look or sound like a crusader. Why are you here? Your husband throw you out? Gambling addiction? Lose your faith in humanity?"

I hold up my hand. "You see a ring?"

He squints and then smiles. "I see the pale space where one used to be."

A wave of sadness washes over me, and I suddenly miss my students. I have lost faith in adults, especially myself. Is it that obvious?

"I'm here to find my son."

A look of incredulity remains on Wilbur's face. "Nope. I'm not buying it. Only a crazy person leaves Prodigal to live here."

Now it's my turn to smile. "I never said I was sane."

Wilbur extends a hand, and we exchange a fist bump.

A procession of women and older men passes by, laden with buckets and headed for lower ground. "Where are they going?"

"To haul water from the river. That'll be you too if you stay. My money's on you leaving. And soon."

I curb my tongue.

He adjusts his skullcap. "We don't get enough bottled water to wash plates or clothes, so we boil river water." He must have read the expression on my face, for he says, "We work hard up here. The only ones who don't are the homeless by choice."

The people Flossie mentioned when I first arrived, which now includes me. I start to ask about them, but a nearby engine backfires and catches with a loud chug. My ears perk.

"Is that a portable generator? With a shower?"

Wilbur grins. "Yes, Susan from Town. We're not animals. Only homeless by choice, bring nothing with them but the clothes on their backs, especially this time of year. Some don't survive winter here. You probably noticed all sorts of tents and dwellings. Some bring old RV camper shells stuffed with all their shit. Some places have special little touches from home, fixed up real nice, reminders of past lives they hope to regain. Me, I'm not sentimental."

I long for the sensation of hot water flowing over me, at least metaphorically washing away my sins. My hair feels stringy and must smell like Flossie's sweater by now.

I remember something Dora said about a bus. "You said most Highlanders work in town, twenty miles away. How do they get there?"

"Any way they can. The pastor drives an old bus each day to pick up donations. He takes workers into town and brings as many back as his schedule allows, but he can't cover all three work shifts. Some take the bus that stops at the railroad tracks, and our backup driver shuttles them from there. Others rely on the kindness of co-workers. Those left thumb it to the tracks and walk."

He laughs at the confusion on my face. "Did you think we barter Prodigal with chickens and eggs and shit? Money still makes the world go around, ever since there's been civilization."

He tosses the grill scrapings into the woods for the chickens and birds to pick over as another group of women, and older men trudge back the way they came, pulling carts or pushing wheelbarrows loaded with water containers.

Seconds later, excited voices filter down from the direction of a northern path, and soon a cadre of men appears, dressed in camouflage and carrying three field-dressed deer, shouting to Wilbur.

A big man wearing a coat of skins points to a carcass. "You cook us up deer steaks seasoned like you did before, throw in bread and whatever greens the pastor can wrangle for my men, and your group can have the one here." He pats it with a meaty, gloved hand.

A second man grins with pride and points to the largest deer. "I dropped this big buck here with one shot. Right between the eyes. To hell with venison steaks. It's five pounds each of deer sausage and jerky for me. His twenty-point rack will fit right over the entrance to my cave." He laughs and points the deer's muzzle at Wilbur. "Doesn't this scruffy face remind you of Finn?"

The giant red-bearded man helping the second man shoulder the buck must be Finn. He says, "I don't look like any deer, Junior, but his ass dangling in front of me reminds me of your mother's. Besides, how do you know it's a twenty-pointer? You can't count that high."

I cover my mouth with my hand and whisper to Wilbur, "No way am I eating Bambi."

A grinning Wilbur answers, "Don't knock it until you taste my venison."

He asks the mountain men who made the other kill shots, and a fresh wave of claims and objections follow.

"The one mentioned a cave," I say when the men have passed. "They live north of us?"

Wilbur nods. "The north camp is all men. Due west of here lies the third camp. Mostly women and children."

I struggle to get the image of the buck's lifeless eyes out of my mind while I wash out the coffee mug. "When does the bus leave for town today?"

"You missed it. You slept in, but you're in luck. Pastor Frank arranged an extra pickup today at one and offered to drive ten shoppers to the town square while he makes his rounds. He needs the rest of the room for the donations." He looks at his watch. "It leaves in an hour and a half. If I was you, I'd buy a lottery ticket in town, surviving a tornado and not missing the bus."

Right. I'm so lucky.

The prospect of a hot shower beckons like a siren, but I thank Wilbur and hurry toward my car, using my iPhone's compass to orient myself. A second, louder engine kicks to life, and through the pines, I see Bert, the bearded man who urinated on the tree trunk and fought a man over a pizza slice, operate a small front-end loader filled with garbage to a dumpster roughly the size of a train car.

I retrace my steps to the lone entrance east of camp. It feels like weeks since I parked my car near the clearing at the end of the road. The BMW appears unscathed by the storm, save for a crisp blanket of pine needles and twigs over the hood and windshield. I climb behind the wheel, out of the biting wind, and close my eyes. After a night spent on the ground, the soft leather and lumbar-supported seat is a sensual pleasure. The engine turns over like a purring lioness, and I flick on the seat warmer. I plug my phone into the charger. The wipers tick back and forth, making the pine needles disappear like magic.

I can return to Prodigal and resume my career, make peace with my husband or agree to a divorce. I can face winter alone in a tent city while I wait for an estranged son who may never return. I could start a new life under a different name somewhere warm.

I recall a quote from the Thoreau book Dora gave me: *Not until we are lost do we begin to understand ourselves.* Maybe the key lies in getting away from the trappings of my old life while I wait for Danny. Or I could choose the easy way out—a darker, more permanent solution.

The heater kicks in. I turn on the radio, shift into drive, and start down the mountain. I travel several hundred yards and stop. My fingers nervously tap the steering wheel. I turn around and park in the same spot. The radiant warmth from the sun and heaters greets me like an old friend. My fingers finally warm, I sink into the cozy leather seat and close my eyes.

This time I am not a hawk; I'm just me. Flightless, all too human, and frail. I'm considering what to make for dinner when the landline rings late one afternoon, and Danny screams at me from the other end, talking nonstop and making little sense. He's been arrested but insists the charges are bullshit. He says we have to believe him because it's all a big misunderstanding. I hear a man say something indecipherable in the background, and he tells a cop to kiss his ass. He threatens to sue the entire department. A policeman gets on the line and says they apprehended Danny shoplifting. We can drive to the station and pick him up since he's a minor, but the store owner intends to press charges.

When we arrive, Danny remains agitated, and he's worn to a nub what patience the cops have left with him. I see a scrape under his eye and a budding shiner. My anger rises, and I ask him if he's been mistreated. He flies into a tirade, and when I start to protest, the ranking officer escorts us to a room and sits us down. We're told store security detained him and found stolen jewelry in his possession—three women's watches and a tennis bracelet valued at twelve hundred dollars—and that he resisted arrest. For the safety of all, security forced him to the pavement, which is how he obtained the minor facial injuries.

I call the officer a liar. Jim puts a hand on my arm as if to shush me, but I bat it away. The officer in charge presses a button, and time-stamped surveillance footage from outside the store appears on his computer screen before us. My son lands punches to the face of a security officer and tries to flee the scene. Two men take him down to the pavement and cuff him. I see how he most likely received his injuries. No excessive use of force. The next segment shows Danny exiting the store with an accomplice. The smaller person kept their back to the cameras at all times. The officer asks if we can identify his partner, but we never see the other face. Danny refuses to answer questions about his accomplice. I want to defend my son and protest his injuries, but the footage says it all. My heart sinks. Jim shakes his head and mutters *oh, boy* under his breath.

Danny maintains his innocence and continues to claim police brutality.

We post his bail and drive home. His story falls apart with each question I ask, which sparks more anger from him. He rages at the unfairness of the world, which eventually focuses on us. *I was never home, I always expect him to be perfect, and I was never satisfied with his accomplishments. Jim was never involved with his school; Jim was always in the background.*

Danny never speaks of friends, so we have no idea who the accomplice may be. I ask if the other person put him up to this, but he doubles down on his innocence. He's been coasting through his expensive prep school, earning Bs and not participating in extracurricular activities. We've never seen him drunk or high, but I ask if he's using drugs, which he vehemently denies. We confiscate his car keys until the court date. He storms to his room and slams the door.

Lab tests later confirm he's been taking his prescription medications; tests for illicit drugs come back negative.

He's right about one thing—Jim didn't say one word to Danny in the station or in the car. When we get home, Jim walks into the kitchen like he just returned from another day of writing insurance contracts and makes himself a sandwich.

I stare at him. "What are you doing?"

He looks at me like I'm daft while he spreads mayo on a slice of bread. "What does it look like? We missed dinner. I'm hungry."

"I don't care. We need to talk about Danny. That's what two responsible, concerned parents would do right now. He's getting worse, not better. I don't think this therapist is a good fit for him; maybe we should find a new one—"

He turns and walks into the living room with his plate, sits on the sofa, and turns on the television.

I follow him and turn it off. "We have to discuss how we plan to deal with our son before we lose him. There may be no coming back for him if he stays on this path—"

Jim rises, walks back into the kitchen, grabs a beer, and sits on a bar stool at the counter.

I can't believe this. He's actively avoiding a Come-to-Jesus moment about our son. My hands fly into my hair. I'm about to lose my mind.

I'm nipping at his heels again when it hits me. Our family is broken, Danny is broken, and our marriage is broken. I'm broken. Maybe all of us are broken in some way. Depending on who we are, those cracks either let in light or the darkness. Maybe the entire world is just a fragile construct built of paper-thin walls through which the past leeches into the present.

I stand across from him. I can tell he's upset about Danny, but his silence infuriates me.

"Danny's right," I say. "You never were involved with him. What kind of man just sits there eating while his family falls apart? This is the time to stand up to your son. We're in a fight for his life here."

Jim keeps chewing silently.

"You don't care," I say. "You disgust me."

Jim's face is suddenly crimson, and his fingers ball into fists. I stand closer, daring him. He rises from the kitchen stool and throws the plate into the sink, where it shatters. Shards bounce off the window and clatter to the floor.

God help me, I want him to hit me. I'd gladly accept the punishment for Danny's behavior if I could. So long as everyone performs their roles up to Jim's standards, our family functions smoothly, but he has no answer for this.

I think this marked the beginning of the end between Jim and Danny, when he began to distance himself. No son of his could act like this.

Jim points a finger in my face. "This is all on you," he says before he retreats to the bedroom. He slams the door so hard picture frames bounce along the wall that goes up the stairs.

I stare at my reflection in the kitchen mirror. I feel broken, and now I have broken another. The sudden unbearable guilt returns, for sins I don't recall committing. If I can remember, maybe I could stop our lives from imploding.

As I kneel to pick up the pieces of the broken plate, I flash back to when I was about four months pregnant. Each time Jim closed the garage door on his way to work, I rushed to a storage cabinet. I'd done this for months already, but what does it mean? Some dark recess of my mind tells me this is a key, but the memory evaporates like a mirage on the highway.

After I clean up the mess, I check on Danny. He's not in his room, and his bedroom window is open. He climbed out and jumped from the roof. His phone goes straight to voice mail. I consider calling the police but instead collapse on the sofa, numb.

A TRIP IN TOWN

A pinecone bounces off the hood and wakes me.

Shit! The bus pulls out in front of me. Given the note I left Jim and the possibility that I may have been reported missing from Prodigal, I don't want my car spotted in town. I grab my cash and ATM card from under the passenger seat and stow my credit cards and jewelry in the Faraday bag.

As it starts down the mountain, I run after the full-sized yellow school bus and frantically wave my arms. The bus screeches to a halt, and the bifold doors creak open. I thank the dark-haired, clean-shaven young man behind the wheel. He acknowledges me with a nod and a smile. "C'mon, there's always room for one more." I see that I'm the eleventh passenger and thank him for allowing me on. The lady nearest me says hello and returns to her paperback. Couples chat while the bus begins its meandering, steady descent down the mountain. I recognize some people from the campfire.

At the back of the bus, a man starts talking about treasure. The gravel road broadens to two-lane blacktop, then four when the road flattens after we cross the railroad tracks and turn south. If the bus has a heater, it's either turned off or broken. There's no sun on my side, and I'm cold again.

By now, it is painfully evident that the man in the back is having a conversation with himself, or maybe someone not in the bus. He grows louder and more agitated. He threatens to kill a man named Zeke if he comes near his gold again. I startle when he yells and pounds the bench seat in front of him.

I take a quick peek back and see it's the redheaded giant, the hunter from the north camp.

"Your treasure is safe, Finn," the young driver calls out, glancing toward the back through the rearview mirror. "Zeke doesn't live in the Highlands anymore, remember?"

Finn pauses and agrees that Zeke may indeed be gone. The other passengers pay Finn no mind. We approach the city limits.

Familiar restaurants such as Soiree and Billy G's Landing appear alongside chain stores like Sachs and Bed Bath & Beyond. The driver says, "Remember, be back here at the town square by three o'clock or find your own way home." He parks between the 7-Eleven gas station and the main quadrangle of open grass in the square, which hosts a swap meet today.

I make a point to allow Finn to go ahead of me. While I wait for the stragglers backed up at the front of the bus, the driver stops me.

"I'm Pastor Frank. Are you Susan?"

Frank has large brown eyes, bowl-cut hair, and a small white scar on his chin. He looks so young, maybe late twenties.

"The first days are the worst," he says. "It gets easier. You adapt. I post a weekly schedule at the church; it can help orient newcomers. Stop in when you can. We're a community. We look out for each other up here."

I remember approaching the bulletin boards when the mayor entered, but didn't get the chance to read them.

"*If* you are a person who likes community or at least the comfort of routine, that is. And you look like someone who is organized."

"Does it show?"

He offers a brief smile. "In the Highlands, it can keep you alive. Stop by the church, and we can talk."

I look at my watch. "I'm not religious."

"Everyone serves a master. You're here for a reason, and I suspect it's a good one."

"Excuse me, but I have a lot to do before three."

Hoodie and cracked sunglasses on, I feel a rush of shame as I step off the bus and walk head down through the quad. I turn west toward the bank Jim and I have used for decades. I cover the fish-eye camera on the outdoor ATM with a gloved hand and withdraw the cash limit: twelve hundred dollars. The sixty twenty-dollar bills prevent my billfold from closing; I prefer hundreds, but that would necessitate a walk inside.

Next, I enter the 7-Eleven, where I load a cart with toilet paper, personal packs of tissue, a toothbrush and toothpaste, mouthwash, Bic lighters, pens, coffee, duct tape, super glue, matches, and a small candle. They don't carry Woodford Reserve, so I place two-fifths of Wild Turkey in the cart, along with two cheap chardonnays to share around the bonfire. At the checkout, I ask for three cartons of Virginia Slims and ask the young cashier to double-bag the bottles. Now I know why the others brought cloth shopping bags, but I don't see them for sale here.

She shoots me a knowing, sideways look. "When I go through a bad breakup, I buy ice cream. You want some?"

I smile at the whimsical thought. The bill comes to over two hundred dollars. I pay cash and throw the receipt in the trash. My purchases are heavy and awkward, but I leave the cart in the lot. I return to the quad and hit the swap meet. I pay cash for underwear, shirts, and a wool sweater that I stuff into the 7-Eleven bags.

At one side of the quad is a section geared for outdoorsy people, with knockoff brands and irregular clothes from a local sporting goods store. From camo-clad dealers, I buy a dual-layer cotton-canvas sleeping bag, a heavy-duty flashlight, extra batteries, and a lace-up pair of snow hiking boots one size too large to accommodate the heavy, cold-weather socks I buy. I wonder how I'm going to haul everything back to the bus, so I stuff the socks into the boots and tie the laces together to drape around my neck. I draw stares.

I buy cups, plates, silverware, and a small coffee pot. On Main Street, I hear the screech of air brakes and look at my watch. I have ten minutes. I keep thinking I've forgotten something. Who am I kidding? I bought nothing to improve or winterize my tent other than duct tape. The Highlanders are forming a line to board the bus. Many push shopping carts.

I scan the far end of the sporting goods section and spot an essential: long underwear. I rush over and wait for the person ahead of me to finish, but he takes an interminable amount of time. The bell tower in the town square tolls three times. I toss two twenties at a slow-moving, morbidly obese man in a camouflage jacket behind the counter and ask for the smallest women's pair. I decline the offers of change, a bag, and a receipt and stuff the long johns in the sleeping bag. I take off at a lurching trot lugging a sleeping bag, three bags jammed with supplies, and a pair of hiking boots that flop around my neck.

The townspeople give me a wide berth. Most look right through me, but a few stare or frown. I panic when the bus pulls away from the curb. I scream, "Wait, wait!" I trip and fall, and my cups and silverware clatter to the sidewalk. My billfold skids to a stop before me, and twenty-dollar bills spill onto the concrete. I feel blood on my skinned knee and chin as I scramble to gather my possessions, talking to myself. I look up and see a man in a suit sidestep me, his look of disdain sharp as the crease in his pants and unsightly as the fat in his pasty cheeks. He utters something that doesn't register because I'm so panicked about the bus. I look up, certain it's gone, but mercifully it stopped. Two middle-aged Highlanders approach; each grabs a bag. As the man helps me up, he asks if I'm all right.

"I think so." I hadn't thought of buying Band-Aids, disinfectant, or basic medical supplies until now. The remaining wad of twenties protrudes from my fist; I hope I retrieved them all. The man's eyes widen when he spots it. I stuff the bills in my pocket.

A small crowd forms at a distance. I dust myself off. My knee throbs. The sweet, cloying smell of alcohol fills the air; the bag the man is holding drips brown liquid onto the concrete.

"We saw you running and told Frank to stop," the woman says. "We didn't want you to miss the bus."

I turn to her. "Thank you. I don't know what I would have done. Take a taxi, I guess."

Their mouths fall open as they regard me. "You're one of us," the man says uncertainly. He limps badly and wears special orthotic shoes. He shakes the bag and makes a sad face. "Sounds like broken glass; I think you got a dead soldier here. We remember our first days. They were rough. We better get moving. Pastor Frank has to make another run into town tonight."

I should have taken the shopping cart from 7-Eleven to the quad, but I didn't want to look like a homeless person. I feel mortified and stupid.

Back on the bus, now loaded with donations from town, the helpful couple introduces themselves as Judy and George. She gives me extra plastic bags to help keep my purchases dry. I repack my supplies—one of the Wild Turkey bottles has been reduced to shards, its puckered label at the bottom of the soggy bag. My underwear and cigarettes smell of alcohol.

I learn that Judy and George are my closest neighbors. They live a hundred feet down the path, farther west of camp, past the next bend and a stand of pine. We chat about our purchases and the tornado. George adjusts the ancient brace on his leg and invites me over to their place after dinner. I decline; I must organize my tent. Judy leaves it as an open invitation. George casts furtive glances at me during the ride back.

I stow my gear in my tent and search for a place to hide my money. For the time being, I stuff my bra with twenties and ready the ground for my sleeping bag. I throw out the soaked cardboard. My bare hands make little to no progress, even with the soggy ground. The Highlands rests on massive granite slabs, so I use the thickest shard from the broken bottle to dig out the rocks. I arrange a circle of granite stones near my tent and collect kindling and larger sticks from the forest, but the wood is too wet. I stack them near my tent to dry.

Exhausted, I skip dinner in camp and alternate between sweating and shivering in my sleeping bag with three fingers of Wild Turkey and a cigarette. I read my e-mails, check and delete voice messages from work, and scan the local news. No messages or other hang-ups from Jim. I'm down to twenty percent power and shut off my phone. It's my lifeline to the world; I plan to ditch it to make certain I can't be traced.

I read excerpts from *Walden* as cold wind howls again through the forest, and I'm colder than the night before. How can this be, since I have a quality sleeping bag and more clothes? I consider a walk to my car to recharge the phone. I could bask in the warmth and sleep comfortably, but I will never adjust here if I do. I resist the temptation of returning home.

Before I go to sleep, I log my impressions about the day in my journals. Now I remember the words of the businessman who sidestepped me like I was a pile of dog shit: "Fucking homeless alkie."

I close my eyes, but sleep remains a pipe dream for hours.

We're sitting around the kitchen table one day in my dream. Danny hates his new court-ordered therapist and refuses to talk with him. Nothing earth-shattering there. He thinks they're all stupid. History has taught us he tolerates the ones who don't challenge him, so we assume this one is qualified and cross our fingers for a sign of progress from the individual and family sessions.

We receive all sorts of diagnoses that increase in severity as the years pass: dysthymia; oppositional defiant disorder; major depression; Asperger's syndrome; autism; bipolar disorder; antisocial personality disorder; even schizoaffective disorder. We dodged an early bullet with Danny, as most preemies born at twenty-five weeks are blind, and we never received a definitive connection between his premature birth and his later behavioral issues.

After the skiing accident, he insisted on negotiating the stairs with crutches so he could remain in the third-floor attic rather than move to his old bedroom on the second floor. I wrote it off at the time as typical behavior for a teenager who wants to stay as far away from his parents as possible.

Two years before, Jim and a handyman remodeled the attic. It used to be my study. Now, posters of Tony Hawk, Bode Miller, and Danica Patrick adorn the walls while one of Lindsey Vonn, holding a pair of skis across her shoulders, smiles down from above his bed.

Dirty clothes litter the floor. I stopped doing his laundry about that time. I remember because it coincided with another call from the police.

This time he's charged with assault of a police officer, resisting arrest, and possessing narcotics with the intent to distribute. Twenty-five hundred dollars' worth of heroin, OxyContin, and fentanyl patches. When we arrive at the station, the left side of his face is purple, his eye nearly swollen shut, his lip split. The bust netted three men in their thirties from Prodigal, but they found the drugs on Danny. A policeman asks about his history of drug use, and we say he has none. The detective looks at us with a stone face.

He questions us, and I mention the skiing accident and the OxyContin the doctor prescribed. The detective stops writing, and the look becomes one of pity. "That's how it starts."

Danny cries setup, denies it all, claims police brutality, and refuses to snitch on the older men. Against Jim's wishes, I decide to let him stew rather than post bail again. I still remember his contorted face as he calls me a cunt and his father a fucking pussy. He spits at us when we leave.

During the trip home, Jim fumes about Danny until it develops into a full-fledged rant. His brown eyes fill with fury and fear. We hurl insults at each other born of frustration and resentment, reprehensible jabs that only longtime partners know exactly where and how to inflict maximum damage. I accuse him of mollycoddling Danny, of wanting to be his friend rather than his father. He resurrects my emotional issues after Danny's birth, which he attributes to postpartum depression—I never told a soul about my psychosis and paranoia during that first year—and to the extended NICU stay that he claims impaired my ability to bond with our son. I exhume the fact that his parents were inveterate alcoholics and gamblers, and the popular belief that addiction often skips a generation. We shoot each other with so many poison darts, and arrows that my eyes corrode and my face trips over itself.

Home, I climb up to the attic to get away from Jim. I lie on Danny's bed and look up at lovely Lindsey, who smiles down on me from the ceiling in her black bra, come-hither look, and tight white stretch pants. I want her to have mercy on me and fill in the missing pieces to the mystery that is my son. I blame myself for not knowing he was in such trouble. Maybe Jim is right. Maybe we both are. We—I—must have missed signs along the way.

I search Danny's closet and pull out every drawer looking for drugs taped to the bottom. I turn his pockets inside out, check under his bed, overturn the mattress. Nothing. Does he get high away from home? I scratch my head and pace the floor until a faint squeak sounds when I walk near one of the dormers. It squeaks again when I retrace my steps. I turn back one end of the rug.

I sit on the edge of the mattress and stare at the floor until it dawns on me why it looks different—one plank has no screws. The fit is too tight for me to pull it up with my hands, so I use the pocketknife on Danny's dresser. Underneath is a terrycloth towel atop the pink insulation. Under that is a steel box amid a cutout section of insulation. I recognize the old battleship-gray container. It once held mementos of happier times—handmade cards from Danny, a decoupage pencil holder he made for me in fourth grade, the tattered baseball card he put between the spokes of his bicycle the day I taught him how to ride, and a purple penguin he made out of clay. The box used to be in the basement, and I'd wondered what had become of it. Now a bag of cotton balls and cigarette filters lines the top. Tucked below it are lighters, small tinfoil squares, and Ziploc bags of brownish-white powder. On the bottom sits a row of syringes encased in clear plastic—and one of my good kitchen spoons.

Feeling defeated, I carry the box downstairs and sleep in the guest bedroom for the first time.

I wake with a start in my little blue tent with that familiar, sickening sense of worthlessness and self-loathing. This time another feeling appears: the fear of drowning, which makes no sense because I'm a terrific swimmer.

I unzip my sleeping bag to find my socks frozen to my feet. How can this be?

If I don't learn about living outside in cold weather, I will not survive here.

FLAMES

Something looks different when I return to my tent after breakfast—my sleeping bag's been hastily remade. My clothes are no longer neatly stacked and organized. I wonder if an animal, maybe a bear, wandered inside to scavenge for food, but my bag of supplies has been rearranged by human hands. Nothing seems to be missing; the surviving bottle of Wild Turkey and cigarettes are here. I have my cash with me. I drank too much last night; did I forget my morning ritual before I went to the Pit breakfast? No. Someone's been here and rummaged through my things. Flossie? George? I remember the look on his face when my cash spilled out on the quad. And neither were at breakfast this morning.

I read the local paper on my phone and check my mail. More concerned text messages from co-workers and an exasperated message from Jim: *Where are you? We need to talk.* The next day, two more terse messages from him: *Call me,* and *This is so like you.* My friends' rising concern leads me to conclude they may soon contact the police, which was inevitable once I decided not to respond to my old world. I don't want to explain my actions to them or Jim. Not yet.

I replace the phone in the Faraday bag. I will need to toss it soon because the longer I remain gone, the greater the risk each time I use it. I read online that my phone could be listening to my conversations and storing them while it waits for an internet connection. That, and the police may have other methods to track iPhones that are unknown to me. I add an item to my things-to-buy list.

I imagine Jim finds life simpler with me gone. Maybe he even fancies that life would be easier if I were to disappear and never return. Like Danny. I—we—have made an unholy mess of things.

I plan to hike and map the perimeter of the Highlands, visit the other camps, and familiarize myself with this vast area and its people. The camp I live in is the original camp, which Highlanders call Camp Thunderbird.

Besides being mayor, Travis is the creator, carver, and painter of the Highland totem pole. I find him up a ladder one sunny morning, chisel and hammer in hand, feathering the wings of a hawk. The ladder looks a bit unsteady, so I brace it for him.

"You've put a lot of work into this. What does it mean?"

He wipes his brow and glances down at me. "What does it say to you?"

I shield my eyes from the sun while I look up. "It scared the shit out of me the first day. The scowling eagle on top, the spread wings make it look like a giant predator about to swoop down on me. I took it as a warning to stay away."

He keeps his eyes on his work. "You were scared, out of your element, in a place with a bad reputation, and the light was fading. How about now, in daylight? What do you see?"

"Creatures of the forest. A bear, a two-headed snake, a deer, a wolf, fish. I see profiles of a man and a woman. The eagle on top looks different today. The mouth is odd—it's not exactly that of a bird of prey. Is it part human?"

"You have a good eye."

I point to other sections. "Four people hold hands by what might be a bridge. I see a cornucopia filled with fruit below a rainbow, and above that, over there, looks like animal skins. Such detailed carving and careful painting. You are quite the craftsman." I frown and point to a higher section I can't decipher. "Are the jagged lines up there flames or lightning bolts? I don't know what to make of that. It's quite beautiful, actually."

He descends the ladder and stands close while he removes his tool belt. "The totem is my tribute to our people and the animals we coexist with on the mountain. We share this land with them and should always remember that. The eagle atop it all is the Thunderbird. I borrowed him from totems of the Pacific Northwest, though we're far removed from that region. The Thunderbird is a legendary creature Native Americans believed to be a supernatural being of great power and strength. I studied anthropology in college."

His last comment comes as a surprise.

"And the lightning bolts?"

The corners of his mouth turn down briefly. "Flames. We had a fire. A resident fell asleep in his tent with a lit cigarette and died."

"I'm sorry."

He clears his throat. "Me too. Prodigal used the accident as the excuse to begin the process of shutting us down."

His words freeze me. "What? They're closing the Highlands? No. When?"

Travis takes a drink from a metal thermos and passes it to me. "The blaze spread to other tents and almost set the entire mountain on fire, but we contained it. Groups in town called us a firetrap and wanted us shut down immediately, even though Prodigal has more deadly fires per capita than we do. They filed a petition with enough signatures to put it before the city council for a vote. Community activists advocated for us, that we should either receive safer, more sheltered housing in town or remain autonomous where we are, but nobody wants a homeless shelter in their backyard. The next decision is what sealed our fate. The president of the United States recently decided to allow each state to determine what to do with their homeless encampments. The city council doesn't want to solve the problem; they simply want to push us farther down the road. Our legal options and continuances have been exhausted. We have ninety days. I need to find alternative housing for everyone by then."

I remember signing that petition. Jim did the same.

I take a sip of what turns out to be hot coffee. Danny has less than three months to return here. I may never see him again. I feel like I've been punched in the stomach. "Do the Highlanders know?"

Travis nods. "I told them right away. There are no easy answers. The nearest shelters are hundreds of miles away on the opposite end of the state."

"Can Frank drive them to the shelters?"

Travis produces a wooden box and opens the lid. Inside are tubes of paint and a palette. He returns his attention to me and smiles. "It's not that simple. Most of us grew up in Prodigal. We work here. Want to help mix the colors?"

I nod. We remove our gloves.

Travis organizes the tubes, giving me instructions. "Many of us have lived in shelters before and want no part of them."

"Why not?" I say, shocked. "It's better than freezing to death on a mountain."

"You think like someone from Prodigal. Do you value your privacy?"

"Of course."

He tells me to add more red and to open a black tube. "In a shelter, there is no privacy. If you have a dog or cat that you love, who may be your only companion, you have to give it up. Couples are separated—shelters are unisex. Many people view them as jails. You leave during the day, but there are curfews, wake-up calls, and staff often talk down to you or talk tough."

I didn't know that. "But the idea of a real roof over your head, regular meals, and a warm place to stay seems to me—"

Travis leans close and places his hand over mine. "You need to exert more pressure to mix colors. Like this."

It's been months since I've felt a man's touch, even on my hand. Our eyes meet until I eventually look at the pallet. I follow his lead.

"Good. Just like that." He releases my hand and clears his throat. Is he blushing? "That's it. You got it."

We sit in silence for some time until he opens another tube and clears his throat. "At least a tent city provides some security that people's belongings will be safe and undisturbed when they return from work."

I think of the uninvited guest who rifled through my belongings earlier. "What happens if items go missing from my tent here?"

"I try to find the guilty party. If the theft is serious, the thief will be exiled." He tests the brushes for suppleness. "So far, everyone here wants to stay as long as they can. That may be why you haven't heard about it until now. I'm fighting an uphill battle."

I can relate to that. "And when this place is shut down—?"

"Unless the powers that be agree to give us a building to rehab or place us in subsidized apartments as promised, most will return to the streets of Prodigal."

"Is that worse, to return to the way it was?"

We've opened and mixed all the tubes Travis wanted. He chooses a number of brushes as he answers. "Imagine a world where it's illegal to sit down, where there's no place you're allowed to fall asleep. I'm sure that seems ludicrous to you, but it's not when you're homeless in Prodigal. You're rousted from the park, from bus stops, from storefronts with an awning or overhang. Street life is an endless series of moving from an unsafe corner to a cardboard box under a bridge until they roust you again."

"I hear you work in town," I say. "What do you do?"

He drains the coffee and seems to weigh his words carefully. "I'm a home and building inspector." He laughs and smiles. "Ironic, isn't it? I've also worked as a general contractor. I'm pretty good with my hands."

"You don't seem like the others. Are you homeless by choice, like me?"

His eyes narrow, and the smile vanishes. "I'm not going down that road." When he stands, I do the same.

He intrigues me. I admit I feel a strange attraction to this mysterious stranger, who seems to be devoting his life to these castoffs. Highlanders are to him like my students are to me, which sets off another wave of guilt. I buck the ladder and look up at him while he climbs. "What do the other carvings represent?"

"The cornucopia represents the fruit and vegetables harvested in our west camp. The hides and deer above that symbolize the rugged north camp. You were right earlier; that is a bridge with four figures near it, linking hands in a circle."

I shield my eyes from the bright sun. "Why four figures if there are three camps?"

"It's a symbol of hope for lasting peace between the camps and Prodigal. Living in the spirit of harmony and coexistence."

"What about the unfinished sections below the Thunderbird?"

He shields his eyes. "I hope they remain that way. My dream is that one day soon, we may return the mountain to its rightful inhabitants, the animals, and nature. One day I hope the Thunderbird will rise from his perch and join us all in the valley below to live together."

Maybe my first impression of the mayor needs revision. "This place isn't as awful as I expected."

His smile returns. "Oh, it is. But it's more than that." He tilts his head sideways and smiles. "And you're quite the unexpected guest, Susan from Town."

THE OTHER CAMPS

Despite Travis' insistence that Danny does not live in the other camps, I fill my backpack and head out on the western path. Highlanders call the main camp I arrived in Camp Thunderbird, not Camp Travis.

My journey to the nearest camp necessitates I cross the river that flows down the mountain and is the Highlands' water source. The path runs a quarter mile past Camp Thunderbird, with a gradual downhill slope to the river. Today I walk past the watering hole trail and follow the western path until I come to a bridge.

I've heard Highlanders say most months, the river is easy to ford, but with the heavy fall rains, the stones here are submerged, and the river runs wide and fast. Some also said there's a bridge. What no one mentioned is that this bridge is hardly more than symbolic. The rickety thing sways in the breeze and looks ready to collapse.

I see two dangerous options. I can try to wade waist-deep in swift, freezing water or negotiate the suspension bridge. I choose the bridge. Looking at it resurrects terrifying memories of a day hike we took on a family vacation to Belize when Danny was nine. I had to zip-line high above a lake at sixty miles an hour and fit through a small hole in the thick jungle canopy. I remain terrified of heights, and this bridge has no safety harness. Panic sets in with my first tentative steps on the weathered wooden slats as the flimsy bridge bounces and sways in the breeze. I scream and look down. The handrails and netting are made only of rope. Some slats are slick with moss; some are missing altogether. If my feet slipped, the netting would keep me from falling into the river, but it would be a struggle to stand up again. I try not to look at the turgid water and focus on the boards as I place one foot in front of the other. My arms tremble, and I white-knuckle the handrails as I inch forward. I make it to the other side and fall to my knees, gasping. I may hit Travis the next time I see him for not warning me about it.

I follow a winding path through the pines until it deposits me smack in the midst of the western camp. There are women at work hauling water and firewood with quiet efficiency. Nearby but out of sight, the steady pounding of a hammer strikes wood. Rings of tents similar to mine but larger radiate from the central gathering place in a stepped arrangement that reminds me of the ancient Coliseum of Rome. The ground slopes down toward the picnic tables and the winding river beyond. In the center stands a flagpole with a banner of many colors that flutters in the wind.

From the picnic area, three women advance toward me. The one in the lead is nearly six feet tall, with dark brown hair marked by a shock of white at the part. The woman on her left is short and tiny, and the one on her right is of medium height and stocky build. Both carry kitchen knives.

The skunk-striped woman reaches me first and extends her hand. "Welcome to the Rainbow Camp, Susan. I'm Barbara. I run things here."

My radar goes up. "Have we met?"

She smiles briefly. "A rather one-sided meeting. I evaluated you after you blacked out the other night. It's good to see you up and about. I trust you're feeling better."

"Evaluated me?"

"For a concussion and other injuries. I'm a retired RN."

The women at her side sheathe their knives and wipe their hands on worn jeans. The larger one steps forward and shakes my hand so hard my fingers nearly fuse. "I'm Penny, and that's Kim." Luckily for my hand, Kim's grip is weak.

"Are you thinking about joining our camp?" Kim asks in a soft, high voice.

"Just a tour for now."

Barbara waves an arm, and we follow her toward the common area. "How are you adjusting to Highland life?"

I chuckle. "I have a lot to learn and much to do before winter hits. I wanted to see how the other camps live."

Kim smiles at my answer, but Penny lets loose a snicker. "Stay at Travis' camp long enough, and you'll find it's much safer here."

"Now, ladies, we're all in this together," Barbara cautions. "Be kind. She's a newbie and alone."

Kim and Penny exchange a quick glance while I turn to Penny. "What do you mean by that?"

Penny's grin disappears. "I shouldn't have said that. I'm sorry."

"Would you like something hot to drink? Coffee, tea?" Barbara asks.

"Coffee would be nice. Thanks."

Barbara orders Kim and Penny to the grills to make a fresh pot. "And while you're there, cook up something for Susan while we walk.

We approach the grills, which are smaller than Wilbur's. Weathered park benches wrap around the bonfire in a semicircle. Barbara waves her hand at the layout. "Our main community center and meeting place is next to the kitchen."

"Negotiating that rope bridge certainly didn't give me a feeling of safety."

Barbara looks surprised and smiles. "Had you remained on the path, it would have turned south and then west to a much wider bridge made from reinforced railroad ties that can bear a small car. It adds a quarter mile to the walk, but it's worth it, as you found out. Didn't Travis tell you about that?"

Now it's my turn to grin. "No, he did not." I *will* punch him on the arm.

Penny and Kim hustle to the grills while Barbara takes me on a tour.

"We're almost equal in number to the original camp, but ours comprises women, children, and a few elderly men. During growing season, we provide vegetables and produce for all three camps. We also tend to the apple, pear, peach, and cherry trees planted generations ago by prospectors and sawmill workers on the mountain. It's hard work, but we continue the tradition. We sell the surplus in town."

We pass the semicircle of tents and come upon a clearing where the fields lie fallow, and beyond them stand long rows of fruit trees devoid of leaves. We circle back along several paths until we arrive at a large brown canvas tent. Barbara holds the door open for me, and we walk inside. A group of women huddles around two card tables placed end to end, sewing the border on a rainbow quilt. Others sit chatting on sofas near a small Franklin stove that warms the room. Two young women hold hands, their faces tilted toward one another while they talk in hushed tones.

In a subdued voice, I say, "Why does Penny think I'm in danger in Camp Thunderbird?"

She moves closer and whispers. "Given your unique position and the different compositions of our communities—"

"My unique position?"

"You're the only unaccompanied woman in that camp. Haven't you noticed?"

Now that I think of it, the other women do have male partners or husbands.

"In the Highland's first year, there were so many reports of unwanted advances and sexual assaults that some women returned to the streets and others considered following. It threatened to destroy what Travis had built. I suggested a second camp, run by me, with the river as a natural barrier and that we'd restore the gardens and orchards to pull our weight. We're almost exclusively women, some straight and single with young children, many forced here by a history of abuse. We also welcome LGBTQ residents whose families kicked them out to the streets, where they struggle to stay alive in Prodigal. Some of them arrive with their children."

Part of the darker side Travis alluded to.

"In the Rainbow Camp, a tribunal of five women and two male elders decide disputes. If the tribunal deadlocks due to an abstention, Travis casts the deciding vote, which has yet to happen. I think you'll find our camp very female-friendly and welcoming. We work hard here to foster a sense of community with a female emphasis, free of the inherent conflicts that arise from males and females living together."

Barbara continues her sales pitch as we exit the tent and circle back toward the bonfire.

"We don't have a laptop or library, so we use the facilities in the original camp. Kim and Penny are but two of the many women who share cooking duties. We receive the same food and supplies Pastor Frank obtains from Prodigal."

"You mentioned elderly males. Two serve as part of your decision-making body?"

"Certain select men reside here. They have either lived past the point of caring about sex or are homosexual and appreciate life in a progressive community such as ours. Their sexual orientation often made them targets and victims in Prodigal and the original camp."

We round a bend in the path and return to the picnic and bonfire area. She asks if I have any questions.

I hold out Danny's picture, now spider-webbed with creases. "I'm sorry if I gave you the wrong impression. I'm touring the other camps because I'm looking for my son. Does he live here? Has he ever lived in your camp?"

She deflates ever so slightly. "I knew him. This summer, in the other camp. Travis wanted me to evaluate him."

I return the picture to my backpack. "He's a drug addict. I kicked him out of our home a year ago. I want to see him again. This is the last known place he's been, so I'm waiting for him to return."

She locks eyes with me, and hers soften. "I worked twenty years as a psych nurse and another ten after that with alcoholics and people with other addictions. I'm no shrink, but I thought he fit the sociopath criteria to a tee. He uses people. Treats them as objects. He pitted Highlanders against each other. He pissed off a lot of people in a short time. Scared some of them. Your son is in his mid-thirties but looks fifty. I know the cliché is to never say never, but he's clearly chosen his path. Nothing and no one else will change that until he tires of the lifestyle. I imagine you had good reasons for what you did, and I know Travis tried his best. I've seen your son when he's using. It's like he's strapped to a bomb. You don't want to be nearby when he goes off."

I fight back tears. I felt the same way—waiting for him to explode—so many times. "Did he ever speak of me?"

Barbara puts an arm around my shoulder and gives me a brief hug. "Life during his short stays in camp revolved around his next fix, what he could steal or who he could con to get money, drugs, or sex. Such is the life of a street addict. I would never allow your son in my camp. Travis gives everyone another chance. It's an admirable quality I wish I possessed."

We hug again. It's been so long since I hugged another adult that the tears fall. Kim and Penny watch intently from a picnic bench. "Thanks. I appreciate your candor. Travis is so tight-lipped."

A sad smile appears on Barbara's face. "And with good reason. He lost someone he loved, and he blames those who run Prodigal."

We resume our slow walk to the picnic benches. We reach Kim and Penny, who hand me a hot coffee mug.

Barbara whispers to me and squeezes my hand. "I will leave you in their capable hands. If you want to talk, anytime, you know where I am. I hope you find peace."

I thank her again.

Kim waves for me to join them while Penny throws logs into the bonfire. Kim offers a seat near the fire. Luckily the wind is light today. I warm my hands near the flames.

Blue-eyed Kim wears her hair in a short bowl cut. "We're in between breakfast and dinner." She roots around the bonfire and produces a sharp, blackened stick. "We had brats and hotdogs last night. I could reheat one in the fire, if you'd like."

I notice a plate of burnt, wrinkled dogs but no leftover brats. Our brats last night were thick and spicy. We ran out of them, too. "That's very kind, but I'm not hungry."

"You're nice. I hope you move here. It's quiet and safe here, away from the Alpha Males up north and Camp Thunderbird."

Penny briefly rolls her eyes and takes a seat next to Kim. She skewers a dog with Kim's stick and heats it in the flames. She brushes her long, straight brown hair from her face with hands that are unusually large. She wears glasses with square brown frames. "Kim, don't be pushy with our guest." Penny turns to me. "Barbara laid her *one happy family* speech on you, didn't she?"

"Pretty much."

Penny notices me staring at her hands and briefly displays them. "I imagine every story in the Highlands is a sad one. I'm thirty-five years old and have already outlived my average life expectancy as a transgender person. My parents kicked me out on my eighteenth birthday. I lost track of all the beatings and times I thought I'd be killed on the streets. Nothing much changed when I came here until Barbara created this camp. I found refuge here." She brushes her hair back again. "But enough about me."

While Penny places the blackened dog on a paper plate and slathers it with mustard, Kim stares into the distance before she leans closer. "She's right. This is a safe place. Did you hear about the Prodigal High students who attacked a Highland woman?"

I nod. The rape made headlines a year or two ago.

She points to herself and then takes a moment before she can continue. "Barbara opened this camp after that, to help women here feel safer. I'm proud to be part of the lesbian community here." She looks to Penny, who bites into the hotdog. "We both found refuge here."

"What will you do when they close this place in three months?"

Penny touches Kim's arm, as if to say she will answer once she finishes chewing. "We try not to think about it. We should be allowed to stay. This is the only family that cares about us. Me, I've tried to kill myself so many times, maybe that's what I'll do. I won't go back to the streets or a shelter."

This time Kim squeezes Penny's shoulder. "And I'm considering the women's shelter. Maybe getting away from Prodigal will be a good thing," she says without much conviction.

I suggest relocating to a major progressive urban center that is more tolerant of alternative lifestyles. We continue to talk, but when I finish my coffee, it's time to move on.

"I do like your camp. I'm off to tour the north camp, to see if they know my son there."

Kim's eyes grow wide, and she touches my arm. "Don't go! The men up there are savages. Barbara has to supervise their summer forays into camp to trade their fish and game for our fruits and vegetables. They've reverted to the wild."

Penny snickers. "The Alpha Males camp—where men are men and sheep are nervous. Bring a knife, and don't hesitate to use it."

The trek to the final camp involves no heart-pounding river or bridge crossing, just a steep hike due north up the mountain. Massive boulders and a few ancient pines dot the stark hills. I walk toward the elaborate cave system that honeycombs throughout the uppermost section of the mountain, a result of the mining boom in the 1850s. A giant and perfectly straight pine towers above the others. It looks odd, too perfectly proportioned, and unnatural. It takes thirty minutes to reach it, and when I do, the mystery solves itself—it's a newly erected cell phone tower. This explains my strong signal and lends credence to the rumors that the mountain is about to be developed.

The men's camp greets me with curiosity and stares, the opposite of my first day at Camp Thunderbird. These hunters live alone or in small groups and seem to have no leader. Their numbers are hard to quantify since most live in caves, but some are in tents, and a few industrious souls have built elaborate treehouses in a stand of pines. One impressive structure employs an elevator system using ropes and pulleys. These men hunt and fish and live off the land, the campfires their only carbon footprints. All are armed with rifles, bows, or knives.

I recognize two of the men who carried the deer carcasses for Wilbur to prepare. Walking through this stark camp, I see no communal tent nor main bonfire, only individual tents, and fires. I recognize a few more inhabitants scattered here and there who occasionally venture to the main camp for food and clothes.

I introduce myself to a brawny man with a lazy eye dressed in animal skins and blue jeans, his long beard streaked with gray. "I came here from the Rainbow Camp. I'm looking for this man. Does he live here?" I show him Danny's picture.

He looks surprised and ignores the photo. "You walked here, alone, from the Land of Misfit Toys?"

"Crudely put, but yes, I did."

He laughs and locks his eyes on mine. "I see you aren't one of them." Now he glances closer at the photograph. "Don't know him. Looks soft. A boy like that wouldn't last long up here." He pounds his chest once. "That tornado the other day? I stood in the eye of that beast, and I'm still here. The men here are tough. If you're not, you die." He points to the photo. "He's a city boy. Try Prodigal." He spits on the ground.

Danny was a city boy at the time of the picture. "You mind if I show his picture around?"

"Won't do no good. You can walk around, though. It's still a free country, for now. Don't go into any caves alone, lassie." With that, he smiles and walks away.

I cringe. Maybe Kim and Penny were right to warn me. If this guy's Neanderthal views are the norm, it's Jeremiah Johnson meets *Deliverance* up here.

I walk the camp anyway. A few men smile and beckon me to their cave openings, but I give them a wide berth. I receive nothing but headshakes and a few ogles when I show Danny's picture to these men of few words. I learn nothing about Danny but come away with the understanding that disputes here are settled quickly and physically. If I could name this group, I'd call it Camp Lone Wolf.

I leave the Alpha Males and use my phone compass to chart a southeast course to the Highland entrance. Fresh snow covers this massive, steep wilderness. It *would* make an ideal layout for ski slopes and a lodge. Uprooted and twisted pines lay scattered atop one another like cordwood, marking the devastating swath of the tornado.

Before I head southeast toward the main camp, I spot a set of footprints headed north to the edge of the woods. Drops of blood mingle with the footprints. I follow them. Just one set of tracks, unlike the hunting party from yesterday. They take me up to the base of a sheer granite cliff carved into the mountain. The snow thins near the vertical cliff face, but I follow the tracks until they end at the mouth of a cave hidden between two massive boulders. The campfire is cold, the wood now charcoal ash.

Do I walk away or enter? After his second exile, Danny could have retreated into a cave. He could get high and deal drugs in relative privacy up here, plus be warmer in the winter than living rough in a tent. Dark, enclosed spaces terrify me, like the porta-potty my first night here. The prospect of entering this black, yawning mouth sends shivers through me, and I tap my thigh, debating. I find a sharp rock and ignore the big man's warning in animal skins, thinking of the Joseph Conrad quote: *The cave you fear to enter holds the treasure you seek.*

I cross the threshold. With each step, I feel the walls close in until the blackness surrounds me. The footprints and blood drops end. I turn on my flashlight and proceed. I force myself to focus on the positives instead of my fears. Fifty yards in, the trail slopes down, and support beams appear overhead and along both walls. I'm in a mine abandoned well over a century ago.

I come to a fork in the trail. "Hello! Is anyone here? Are you okay?"

I hear no response other than the fading echoes of my shaky voice.

I choose the right fork and find a narrow flight of timber stairs that descends into darkness. I can still find my way back, so I proceed with caution. Near the base of the stairs and a scant three feet to the left, a mine shaft plummets into darkness. I shine my light into the black abyss. The passage beyond it collapsed long ago. Its broken beams litter the floor like giant toothpicks. I walk straight ahead, where floor-to-ceiling timber cribbing lines the walls until the passage constricts severely. That sick feeling of entrapment worms deeper into my head, and then I come to a faded wooden sign that looms ahead. A crudely painted skull and crossbones above a warning: KEEP OUT OR DIE. The breath leaves my lungs at once.

I panic. I turn and run right into a solid wall of flesh. My phone falls to the floor, and my flashlight winks out. I wield the rock in my right hand, but a strong arm grabs my wrist in the darkness, and the stone falls by my feet. A brighter light from above switches on and blinds me, like an old-time camera flashbulb, and all I see is white. Strong hands grab my shoulders and lift me off the ground. I stop struggling when I recognize the beady brown eyes scowling at me over a full red beard.

"You scared the shit out of me, Finn! Put me down."

After a while, the giant releases me. He's wearing a miner's lamp, dirty jeans, and a filthy plaid shirt. A sheathed bowie knife on his wide cowhide belt grabs my attention. He must think I'm a thief.

I put my hands on my knees and let the fear drain from me. "Didn't you hear me calling? I saw bloody tracks that led me here. Are you all right?"

Finn's dusty brow furrows, and he looks to the makeshift bandage on his left hand, as if he's trying to recall whether he knows me or not. "Liar. You're with Zeke and the others. Come to steal my gold and lay claim to the mine."

"What happened to your hand?"

"Cut it laying a trap."

"You have any gauze? It looks like you wrapped it with a dirty shirt."

"I did."

"This won't do. It'll get infected."

"It was hard to do with one hand."

I unwrap the bloody plaid flannel and toss it to the ground, then irrigate the wound with water and apply antibiotic ointment from my first-aid kit. I wrap the wound tight with gauze and seal it with medical tape.

I pat his hand and say, "There. Have Nurse Barbara examine it tomorrow. It might need stitches. Keep it clean. Pastor Frank said Zeke no longer lives here, remember? And I don't give a damn about gold. The only thing I want from this mountain is my missing son. Danny Crusoe lived here last summer. Do you know him?"

Finn flexes his hand. The man who talks to imaginary people in public is blocking the only exit, pondering what to do. He could throw me down that vertical shaft or end my life any way he chooses. If I were bigger or more threatening, that knife might already be in my back.

I root in my backpack for Danny's picture.

Finn shines his miner's lamp on the photo. "I know him."

My heart races, and I grin up at him. "Where is he? Tell me everything you can."

"I liked him. He called me Bunyan. He used to say when I strike it big, I'll need a handler to manage all my money and that he's the man for the job. He said I'll be living the high life—a woman on each arm, a fancy new car, and a mansion. *If* I was careful. He warned me about Zeke and the others."

I feel a wan smile form in the dark of the cave. "That sounds like my son."

"He said I'd be able to make my own ox from solid gold and paint it blue." He laughs and makes a face. "Where'd he get a crazy idea like that?"

"Did he come here alone or with someone?"

Finn produces a rag from a back pocket and wipes his face. He squints as if he's trying to remember. "I don't know. Always had a woman with him. And new ones all the time. Called them his posse. He told me I should get one because they're useful."

"Where is he?"

"Gone. Travis banished him over a woman, I think."

And I thought it was only drugs. "Which camp did Danny live in?"

"He liked Travis. Said he was a straight shooter. He stayed in Camp Thunderbird because business was best there."

I play dumb. "What kind of business?"

Finn shrugs. "I don't like people, they cause me nothing but trouble, so I stay mostly by myself. Hunt, fish, and trap when I'm not working the mine."

He has no answers to my other Danny questions. He never heard him speak about his parents, just his posse. After much reassurance, I'm able to convince him that I pose no threat to his future fortune, and he lets me pass. I wish him safety and good luck. He issues a final warning not to tell anyone about the location of his mine. I think bandaging his wound helped earn my release.

As I return to the light of day, open spaces, and fresh air, a smile crosses my face. *Finn's the second giant I've encountered on my quest, and I fought for my life this time.* I also learned more about Danny from a paranoid psychotic and a retired nurse than anyone from Camp Thunderbird. I privately change the north camp's name from the Alpha Males to Camp Finn.

I continue east until the cliff forces me south and eventually returns me to an expansive forest recently marked with red and blue ribbons. Hundreds, maybe thousands. The rough path returns me full circle to the east entrance.

Exhausted, I pass the sign that marks the entrance to the Highlands, but I take the time to walk all the side paths past shelters, tents, RVs, even homes. Two residents own knockoff, miniaturized versions of tiny homes, one of the latest big-city innovations to combat the homeless problem. They remind me of a smaller version of Thoreau's house in the woods near Walden Pond. The two wood-framed homes here have shingled roofs, windows, and a living room/kitchen/bedroom area of about 200 square feet. Some tiny homes are welded onto steel frames with wheels and designed to be mobile with a trailer hitch, but these stand on stone blocks.

I'm in desperate need of a shower. On the walk to my tent to pick up shampoo, a bath towel, and a change of clothes, my thoughts drift to Danny and his likely customers. I need to learn more about each Highlander and the circles in which they run.

THE P WORDS

After circumnavigating the mountain, I sing praises to the inventor of the portable generator and revel in my first camp shower. The jets of hot water massage and needle the back of my neck as I thaw out from my first week as a homeless person. I never realized a hot shower in winter could feel so decadent. It borders on a sexual or a religious experience.

My stomach growls from the day-long, coffee-fueled hike. I warm myself at the Pit bonfire and eat a double portion of Wilbur's tangy spaghetti and grilled garlic bread.

After dinner, I walk west from the barbecue pits to the learning center next to the church. It has a laptop and printer, a library of sorts, and a community book bin. I meet a young man named Corey who runs the center when he's not at work in town. Everyone is welcome to use the center, but apparently, only people from Camp Thunderbird and the Rainbow Camp actually do.

The laptop becomes my new best friend. I use it daily to keep my phone safe from detection in the Faraday bag. I study how-to lists on camping and outdoor supplies while I keep current on the news from town. Nothing about me, but it's early. I learn the weekly Highland schedule and compile a list of items to buy during my next foray into town. The list swells to three pages. I post a notice about Danny next door on the church bulletin board, against Travis' recommendation.

The next day, I ride the bus into town. I don my hoodie over my cap, wear my taped sunglasses, and pay with cash. I move among the faceless crowd. No incidents this time.

I descend on a regular basis into the Highland dumpster, which is the size of a railroad car with no top. It's depressing to see how much trash three hundred people make and the amount of waste that ends up scattered in the forest by the wind. Like dogs that mark their territory, humans deface the world with their garbage, as if the vastness of nature compels us to leave our signature, and we do so with trash. Pastor Frank tries to keep the Highlands trash-free, but he's only one man.

I'm surprised by what some people discard. The garbage doesn't smell as bad as expected due to the cold temperature, but there's plenty of it, and the rusted metal sides and floor are slick from years of oil and grease build-up. It's a challenge to climb out alone, and today I slip and crack my head against a rusted cabinet.

I'm dazed and unsteady but luckily stay conscious; today is trash day. Travis brokered an arrangement with Prodigal's waste management company for weekly pickups and porta-potty maintenance. I construct a rickety makeshift tower of garbage to facilitate my escape.

Today's haul includes several waterproof tarps to double-line the floor of my tent and prevent seepage from the rocky ground. I salvaged yards of duct insulation and bubble wrap, plus a foam mattress. One man's floor is another woman's ceiling. The trash truck arrives while I lug my finds to my little blue tent. Had I lost consciousness, I'd be riding in a giant coffin.

Armed with printed instructions, I disassemble my tent, position the tarps, so they extend beyond the perimeter to keep out cold and moisture, and then reassemble my shelter over them. Two bucks at the Dollar Store bought me space blankets (the wrinkled aluminum foil in Dora and Tom's tent) with which I line my tent to retain heat.

I now understand why my socks froze in the sleeping bag. I need to wear fresh socks to bed and build a vapor barrier, since body condensation can freeze in the upper layer. Over time, the entire bag can freeze solid. I also no longer sleep with my head in the bag at night. I learn that my tent requires some degree of ventilation at the top to reduce condensation, so I open the vents at the top. I turn my sleeping bag inside out on sunny days and hang it on top of the tent to dry. My new boots have removable liners, which I place at the bottom of my sleeping bag so they're warm in the morning. Dora gives me a spare pillowcase to stuff with clothes for a pillow.

I buy towels, an LED lantern with a built-in charger that I hang inside my tent, lithium batteries I store in my sleeping bag, petroleum jelly to protect my skin from cold and wind, a quality thermos that would have come in handy on my trek to the other camps, a hot-water bottle to place between my legs at night, and a thick wool hat to wear while I sleep because a crocheted hat does a lousy job of retaining heat.

I cover my small stack of firewood with the smellier of the last two dumpster tarps and use the large one as a tent fly.

I heed Dora's advice and move my campfire farther from my tent, in a more leeward area. Tom suggests I dig a firepit a foot deep and five feet wide. It takes hours to make a dent in the frozen ground, and my nails are cracked, dirty, and bleeding. At one point, Vidal appears with a pick and shovel to complete the heavy excavation; later, I learn he came to my rescue after word of my struggles spread. I thank him, and he again refuses money. I hug him. Once again, this place at the end of the world amazes me.

Near the foot of my sleeping bag, where the two tarps overlap, I separate them and use a community trowel to dig a hole large enough to hide my wad of money in a resealable plastic bag. I cover it with plywood from the dumpster, but it sticks out like the loose board in Danny's room. I cover that with topsoil until it blends in, then reposition the tarps. My hidden piggy bank.

I clear the debris around my new firepit and line it with rocks.

I add work gloves, Band-Aids, and hand lotion to my next list of purchases. How frail and needy our bodies are. I must toughen my mind to survive in this hard world. I think of the pep talks I've given my struggling students over the years and apply them to myself.

An online article recommends three types of wood—dead twigs for tinder, sticks under an inch in diameter for kindling, and larger logs for fuel. I also need a bucket, water, and a shovel on hand. I learn the various types of fires—the teepee and lean-to are better for cooking, while the log cabin and crisscrossed kindling over tinder yield longer-lasting fires. When I light my very first campfire with a single match and gently fan the base of the flames, I feel a joy similar to learning that a student has earned a college scholarship. I squeal in delight like a contestant on *Survivor* winning a fire-building contest.

Vidal returns hours later with his wife and children bearing churros she baked with eggs from his chickens. They're still warm, sweet, and delightful as we enjoy them around my first fire. I have nothing to offer the kids except the pack of gum from my starter kit. While the children play around the fire, Vidal and Maria tell me they used to live in an apartment in town with seven cousins. Vidal's three children were born in the US and received a paltry amount in food stamps, but Vidal and Maria are undocumented, so they had no housing support. The eight adults worked in town as laborers or in food service—Vidal as a landscaper and Maria as a busser—until a cousin was stopped for a minor traffic violation eighteen months ago. They arrested him and dispatched immigration officials to the apartment.

Vidal pokes the fire with a stick. "This forced us to choose between deportation and the Highlands. The five of us and four cousins chose the mountain. Our two documented cousins soon joined us because they couldn't afford the rent on their salaries."

Maria wipes the face of their littlest one and shoos her off to play. "A local business bought the complex, gutted and dissected it into small units, and tripled the rent."

The only poor people left in Prodigal either live with family or in dilapidated row houses next to the potter's field on the outskirts of town. The hundred-year-old row houses are the lone vestige of Prodigal's history as a lumber town.

Vidal shifts his weight. "I worry we won't have any place to go when the politicians and businessmen kick us off the mountain."

Dora and Tom join us, bringing dishes, towels, and bowls. I thank them and mentally cross those off my list. Flossie and Wilbur arrive, as do my new neighbors Judy and George. Wilbur gives me a few handy kitchen supplies while George pushes a wheelbarrow of firewood that he stacks under my tarp. Judy gives me a bar of her homemade bay rum soap. Their generosity astounds me.

I rummage in my tent for the last of the Wild Turkey as the logs pop and crackle, and Tom plays a lighthearted riff on his six-string.

"Oh, you got the good stuff," Wilbur says, eying the label and taking a drink before he passes it on.

A smile blooms over Vidal's broad, mustachioed face as he raises the bottle to his lips.

"Of course she does," Flossie says. "Woman comes here wearing those designer clothes and that fancy watch not gonna drink Mad Dog unless she has to."

I want to ask what I've done to piss her off, but instead of making a scene with children present, I thank everyone again for the gifts.

While the bottle passes, my visitors wonder what will happen when the camp shuts down. No one intends to enter a shelter. They prefer to stay until the bitter end and pray for a miracle.

In an aside to Wilbur, I say, "Why should I be afraid of the homeless by choice?"

He takes the final swig. "Some people don't give a damn about others and refuse to obey the one simple rule. They're users. They stay in the shadows. Sure, we have a crime and drug problem here. Same as Prodigal—"

"I'd keep an eye on that watch if I was you. I'm just saying," Flossie says, her eyes darting from me to Wilbur.

I glance at George, whose face remains stoic.

The bottle empty and the churros eaten, I ask about the mayor and Pastor Frank. Vidal looks at Wilbur, who, in turn, glances at Dora. Maria breaks the silence by announcing that it's getting late and the kids are tired.

I look at my watch and see hours have passed. Vidal scoops up their youngest, and the others stand. I do the same. The women offer hugs. I thank them again, and they depart for their tents.

As the dimming light arm-wrestles the sky, I store my gifts. I'm about to douse my campfire when the last visitor of the day arrives. He wears a heavy pea coat, scarf, and matching wool cap.

Assessing my setup, the mayor brings no gift other than this: "I was wrong about you. I didn't think you'd last a week."

I sit down near the fire when he does.

"I know," I say. "I like proving men wrong." I light a cigarette and inhale as we gaze at the valley below in silence.

He reaches into a front pocket and proceeds to roll a cigarette.

"For months, I left Danny's picture on fliers all over town, many in the town square. Highlanders must have seen them."

He doesn't respond. It hits me that I didn't ask a question.

I watch the orange arc of his cigarette in the gloaming. "Why didn't anyone call me? Did *you* see them?"

He takes a puff and exhales. "I'm in town sixty hours a week. I work a full-time job there. I constantly advocate with city leaders for these people. I fight for them. I help them apply for the subsidized apartments the town promised us and mediate on their behalf when the lucky ones become candidates for apartment living. Ask a question you don't know the answer to, Susan."

Hawks circle the graying sky as the dark comes in pieces. I light a second cigarette off the butt of my first. I count to ten to calm my rising anger. "So, you and others saw them. I could have met with my son last summer had it not been for your goddamn Highland *omerta*."

"I doubt that. If he had been an underage runaway, I would have contacted you or the police immediately, based on his responses to my questions. We see fliers for missing people and children all the time. We pay attention to them far more than the general public because we've been separated from people we love. Go into almost any bulk-food store in Prodigal and read the corkboards at the exits. Missing persons notices often outnumber help-wanted ads." His voice softens. "He saw your fliers."

I think of how quickly the welcome committee disbanded when I asked about Frank and Travis. "The others left so quickly just now. They see me as an outsider, someone from the town that plans to tear down their homes, don't they?"

Travis pauses to take another drag. "They're coming around. They threw you a welcome party. Your presence here confuses most of them. I have an idea why they left abruptly. Would you like to know why?"

"They saw you coming?"

He smiles. "You are tenacious. No, they didn't. Let me tell you why we hold ourselves to a code, as you call it."

He rolls a second cigarette and licks the edge of the paper. "Every so often, usually in the summer, packs of kids from town drive up here to drink, smoke weed, screw, and act like bored, entitled idiots. Last summer, a group of high school seniors raped a Highlander in our woods. When two Highlanders tried to intervene, their friends beat them bloody with baseball bats. These recent grads, sons of respected leaders and businessmen in town, already had their tickets punched to Ivy League colleges in the fall."

Travis' jaw muscles work overtime as he lights up.

"When I called 911 for ambulances and the police, the seniors called for reinforcements. Their friends arrived before the first responders. I had a full-scale riot on my hands. By this time, everyone was armed. I demanded justice for the assault, the rape, and the beatings. The kids claimed that the victim initiated the sex and that it was consensual. Words can't describe what they did to the girl and the trauma she relives every day. The police chief promised a full investigation and said if the kids were guilty, they would be punished to the full extent of the law. We let them escort the boys off the mountain. No charges were filed. They accepted a misdemeanor plea of reckless endangerment, completed a hundred hours of community service, and their records were expunged in time for Ivy League classes in the fall."

"I met her when I toured the west camp," I said. "She's so young and tiny."

Travis raises an eyebrow in surprise. "We're out of sight, out of mind until an incident occurs. They wanted to shut *us* down, even though the students trespassed and were the aggressors. Prodigal held us accountable for the 'misunderstanding.' They admitted maybe things 'got out of hand,' then insinuated the woman was a prostitute. The fact that she's a lesbian didn't matter to them. Others drive by at night to destroy tents, bully the weak and elderly, shout foul insults, and speed away in sports cars. Once I found a noose hanging from a tree near the entrance with a note that warned us to go home before it's too late."

He laughs. "Go home. The ignorance and hate comes from somewhere. They see us as less than human."

Travis exhales as a loon calls for its mate somewhere in the valley below. "I think the truth is, deep down, they know we aren't any different, and it terrifies them."

I poke the waning fire with a stick. "I hear you established the Rainbow Camp because unattached homeless women felt unsafe, that male Highlanders harassed them."

He flicks ash into the dwindling fire. "You've been a busy camper. You heard right. Anyone who wished to move west was allowed, no questions asked. Homeless women, especially homeless single women like you, are at far greater risk. Those are some of the reasons we keep our business to ourselves."

"I feel bad for every Highlander who's been hurt by people from Prodigal," I say softly. I toss my cigarette into the fire. "But someone should have called. I'm his mother. It was the right thing to do."

The mayor smiles sadly. "On that, we disagree."

Owls call to one another. We spend some time sitting in silence until I turn to face him. "Do *you* see me as an outsider?"

Travis thinks a moment and nods. "You're definitely not a Highlander. You're not like anyone else here. I find you a breath of fresh air, albeit a stubborn one. Give the others time. To them, you're a strange hybrid of the homeless by choice and a Prodigal mom from the suburbs. The worst of both worlds, in their eyes, so to speak. They've lost far more than you, and you possess far more than they ever will. You'll either earn their trust or you won't."

I think of Flossie's strong reaction to me and my accouterments. And the looks on George and Judy's faces when I blurted out that I would've taken a cab had I missed the bus. I relive what the businessman said as he sidestepped me on the quad. I remember my house on College Avenue, the place where I cannot leave and cannot stay.

"I suppose you have me figured out."

He shifts his weight and lowers his voice. "Since you asked, I will tell you what I know and what I think. I know you're an intelligent, strong-willed, educated, attractive woman who can climb into that BMW parked outside camp and return to your life at any time, yet you don't. I know you are a serious person, that you are too hard on yourself, you use your intellect to distance yourself from others, and from that, I infer you struggle to make and keep lasting friendships. The last two may be intentional, but I'm not certain. I think you have—or had—a professional career and a husband, yet here you remain. If I didn't know better, I'd say it was *you*, not your son, who is running away from something, or someone. A talk with Pastor Frank could help, for your presence here smacks of penance."

His words chill me. I don't care that he knows about the car; that was a matter of time. His intuition and those eyes unnerve me. Do I truly want to discover my memory fragments, or am I running away from them?

"You couldn't be more wrong," I say. "I'm looking for my son. It's as simple as that."

He stretches out his short, stocky legs and nods. "You may be searching for something, but I don't think it's your son. Actions are motivation-based; sometimes, we're not fully aware of them."

Anger from an unknown source bleeds into my response. "Sounds like you took a Psych 101 class in addition to anthropology. A little knowledge is a dangerous thing."

Travis leans closer. "There's that intellectual distancing. Here's some free advice that could save your life: street smarts trump book-learning every day of the year in the Highlands. You're in more danger here than you realize."

I face him and cross my arms. "I'm adjusting. It's not like you have to be a rocket scientist to be homeless."

A smirk appears. "There it is again. You asked for my opinion, and I offered it. I don't want you to get hurt. And I think that's inevitable the longer you remain here."

Travis inhales and gazes south toward the city. "You have a life down there, and now you're Can-Do Susan living in a homeless tent city. Waiting for a pot to boil can play on the mind. What happens when that kettle starts to whistle? What if it never does?"

Those hazel eyes seek mine, but I turn away.

"You need a purpose to accompany that new can-do attitude." He rises to leave and tosses the end of his cigarette onto the coals. "Think about it."

I watch his back recede into the darkness down the path. I suddenly feel cold and hug myself as the call of a mournful loon echoes through the forest.

The clear sky brings with it a half-moon and the coldest, windiest night of the year. Tonight's forecast is for a low of thirty in town, which means twenty up here.

Before I douse the fire, I use my pee bottle and burn the toilet paper rather than trek all the way to the outhouses. Once I can safely handle two hot stones, I wrap them in a towel and place them in the foot of my sleeping bag. I flip my water bottle upside down, since ice forms at the top.

A twig snaps outside, and I hear light footsteps. I open the tent flap and see nothing at first until a blur of movement near my firepit reveals the thin blonde in the green wool cap. She's mostly shielded behind a tree, but she watches me intently. I call for her to come closer, but quick and silent as a fox, she darts down the path, out of the moonlight and into the darkness. I wriggle into my toasty sleeping bag, update my shopping list, and log my thoughts for the day.

Settled in, my musings circle back to Travis. He doesn't know me. He doesn't know what he's talking about. I don't push people away by being emotionally distant, not most of the time. A desperate mother distributed those fliers, a cry for help to find her son. To hell with this Highland *omerta*. I'm not running away; I'm trying to find my son and remember the past. And the idea of penance . . . absurd!

Another panic attack hits, like hell unleashing pandemonium inside my skull. I dry-swallow a pill, close my eyes, and do my grounding exercises.

During the worst of it, I imagine myself driving, choosing the right tree or bridge. Why haven't I done this? Why *am* I still here, hoping for snow and ten-below-zero temperatures? Travis has some nerve, saying I need a purpose. He's smart but not that smart and has short-man syndrome. He's on a power trip. He's the mayor of a shantytown.

I remember now something that happened around the bonfire tonight, so subtle and fast I almost missed it. Flossie took two furtive swigs of Wild Turkey.

I turn off the light, bury my face in my pillow, and scream.

I see myself years ago in a stuffy room, when my hair was wavy with blond highlights and fell below my shoulders. Jim sits next to me with his eyes glued to the floor, arms folded. Once a week, we sit in a circle in these hard plastic straight-back chairs, and my back protests. We face a blackboard filled with sayings such as *Everything happens for a reason*; *What doesn't kill us makes us stronger*; *When God closes a door, He opens a window*; *When life gives you lemons, make lemonade*; and *Every cloud has a silver lining*.

Other couples and a few single moms sit captive around us. None of the women seem to know what to do with our hands. I catch myself digging at a cuticle and fold my hands in my lap. Jim and the other dads remind me of the stone statues on Easter Island. Through the prism of my memory, the light in the room is diffuse and blurred, the voices from the past echoing like mournful ghosts. The scene reminds me of an old-style sepia portrait; the mood is reminiscent of a wake for the living.

A mother who looks fifteen years older than she is speaks in a voice so tiny and wounded I see her fight with herself as she speaks, like this is the last thing she wants to admit. "Pete tested positive again this week, Bill," she says, acknowledging her husband, the bald man to her right with the paunch and stiff upper lip, "had to pay Pete's child support and truck payments today. Bill's chemo makes him weak, but he went back to work because we need the money." She rubs the handle of her purse like a worry stone. "I start a factory job this Monday."

The counselor glosses over the content and emotion in the woman's words. Instead, she asks how Pete has been doing at home since the last meeting. I frown.

The mother scans the room. "Same as last week. He lives in our basement. He watches television and plays video games at night. He says he applies for jobs online, but no one is hiring. He needs money for gas and cigarettes, which we give him."

She looks to the counselor, who remains silent. She rubs the handle of her purse faster. "I mean, if we don't gas up his truck, he can't get to job interviews, right? We can't kick Petey out on the street. We're his parents."

She reminds me of a balloon that's slowly losing air.

She tells us her son turns forty next week. I squirm in my seat as a great sadness overcomes me.

For the next three weeks, Jim and I hear the same story in various forms and degrees from other parents and spouses, their shoulders slumped, eyes downcast. After each tale, the counselor nods and pastes an attentive, concerned look on her face. Sometimes she asks the speaker how that makes them feel. This results in more hunched shoulders, averted eyes, some tears, and occasional displays of frustration. My anger grows with each group.

I feel like an emotional hostage, same as at home.

One night the counselor asks us to "share," which seems to be her favorite word. Jim recaps Danny's failed court-ordered inpatient stays, the failed intensive outpatient treatment centers, the arrests, the jail time, and the behavior issues—stealing, verbal abuse, bouts of anger—as if he's condensing an article from the *Wall Street Journal* for a colleague.

When the counselor asks Jim how that makes him feel, he says, "Bad."

I close my eyes and wish I could fly out of the dirt-streaked window. Then the counselor swivels her chair in my direction and smiles. She asks her default question.

"How does it make me feel?" I respond. "I'm a teacher. I motivate high school kids for a living, and I'm damn good at it. I get them excited to learn; I challenge and push them to be smarter, better people. For the life of me, I cannot do the same for my son. I have failed him, and I'm mad and frustrated as hell."

Jim offers his hand, which I swat away.

I turn to the counselor. "You're in contact with Danny's therapist. Family therapy hasn't done any good, and . . . whatever this non-directive shit is supposed to accomplish only makes me feel worse. You heard my husband—every intervention has failed." I wave my arm to those in the circle. "Everyone here knows exactly how we feel. We all feel like shit because we're trapped in the same nightmare." I divert my eyes to the chalkboard and then back to her. "What practical suggestions do *you* have for Jim and me, other than more of the same tired platitudes?"

The smile vanishes briefly; she purses her lips until it returns.

I feel like slapping her.

She clears her throat. "It's common for families to release pent-up emotion when they listen to and share their experiences with other parents going through similar challenges. It lends perspective in a safe, nonjudgmental atmosphere. Seeing another family farther along the road to healing and recovery gives hope to others."

I look around the stuffy room and find no hopeful faces, no parent near recovery. I'm about to call bullshit when she continues.

"Maybe you haven't discovered the right approach. Maybe Danny knows the right buttons to push. You need to see it through." She finishes in a reassuring tone. "Time will heal all wounds." She blinks twice behind her spectacles. Her smile broadens, as if sunshine and rainbows are filling the schoolroom.

What a crock. I turn away from her and smile at Pete's mom. "I'm sorry. What's your first name again?"

She looks as if no one's ever asked that before. She looks to the counselor, then back at me. "Donna."

"Hi, Donna. I'm Susan. How long have you and Bill been coming here?"

She again looks to the counselor as if asking for direction, but receives none. "Three years. And before this program, five more in another."

Christ on a cracker.

I ask softly, "I'm curious. Aside from the fact that Bill's cancer is now stage four, is Pete any different from last week? And the month before? And the year before that?"

Donna looks to the counselor for help that doesn't come. Her mouth forms a perfect O. "He kicked a hole in the basement door when I said I had no money. He tore the screen door off its hinges and drove away." She shakes her head and seems to bite her tongue before she says, "Now Bill has two doors to fix. And Petey's truck needs new tires."

I see myself in this dingy classroom after a twelve-hour workday, a week after Danny's sixth failed adult inpatient treatment. He gets high in all of them, and no one knows how he obtains narcotics while in treatment. This latest facility, seven states away, touted itself as the best in the country. It cost fifty grand, another hemorrhage of our retirement savings. He lasted four days.

I reach out to hold Donna's hand, which she tentatively offers. "Donna, I am truly sorry for what you and Bill are going through. I wish you both good luck, but happy thoughts and prayers aren't enough. You've been away from the workforce for twenty years, and your husband has advanced cancer, yet you both found jobs. Young, healthy Pete has not. What does that tell you?"

107

Her mouth forms that perfect O again, and she turns to the counselor.

I imagine the nightmarish scenarios that await Donna and Bill. And Petey.

I shudder. And us.

Our world is in shambles. I want to scream to the heavens, but my words would fall on the ears of a tone-deaf, incompetent group counselor whose lone talent seems to be a Mona Lisa smile. I've prayed to God, but maybe He's also tone-deaf and smiles as He looks down on us while our lives spiral downhill.

I scan the sayings on the blackboard and feel a sudden urge to send it crashing to the floor. Instead, I stand and hug Donna. She starts to cry against my shoulder and whispers, "Thank you."

I gather my coat and purse and leave, my heels on the marble floor the lone sound in the empty, dark corridor. My heartbeat throbs in my throat. By the time I reach the car, Jim has caught up with me and drives us home in silence.

While the garage door closes behind us, I say, "I'm not going back. She's useless. I can't go on like this."

He sighs under his breath, but when I glance his way, the corners of his mouth are upturned in the darkened garage. Like the happy day when you realize your parents can no longer force you to attend church.

I wake from this dream at four a.m. in my tent, shaking from the cold. It's the coldest night of the winter so far, fifteen above with howling winds. The stones at my feet are cold, and the radiant heat is gone. I take Dora's advice and do jumping jacks and squats, then mix sugar packets with a cup of water for a glucose rush. Until I can buy a Coleman catalytic heater, this will have to suffice. Between the exercise and sugar infusion, I feel warmer after fifteen minutes and drift back to sleep.

Travis appears in my final dream of the night, but I don't recall the details.

A CANDID PASTOR

With Thanksgiving looming around the corner, I attend Pastor Frank's service. I'm late to the big tent, where adults on folding chairs and threadbare sofas display variable levels of attentiveness. Some eat, and others doze off and on as Frank continues.

"And we thank you, Heavenly Father . . . for another day of your kind blessings. For last night's sunset and the beautiful sunrise . . . for the bounty you put on our table . . . for the caring community you have bestowed on us here in the Highlands."

He pauses to place his right hand over his heart. "It's easy to become despondent this time of year. To feel hopeless and forsaken. To feel alone during what is supposed to be a time for giving thanks and praise for His divine mercy. But let me tell you one thing: God *is* in the house, and God is about fairness. God is about justice. God knows that all men are created equal."

He raises the Bible in his right hand. "He teaches us that everyone is to be cared for. If we have faith in Him and our fellow man, we will inherit the Kingdom of Heaven. But He also tells us something else: the rich and powerful will be judged alongside us."

He places both hands on the lectern. "May He help the people of Prodigal understand that the hard workers I see before me—the same people who serve them in restaurants and mow their lawns and care for their elderly—cannot afford housing on minimum wages. May He help the politicians understand that human beings cannot be *illegal.* They can only be temporarily undocumented. Heavenly Father, we pray for you to hear our plea."

Heads bow in reflection. An older man in the back snores softly until his elbow slips from the arm of the sofa, and he wakes with a start.

Pastor Frank concludes the service with announcements. "The new weekly schedule is out. As many of you know, I will drive the bus to Prodigal Tuesday at three for the quarterly giant

109

tent sale in the quad. Those who wish to participate are encouraged to bring their wares to sell at our designated tables. Mayor Travis graciously paid the fees this year, so I urge you, sellers, to thank him in person. Many local businesses will also be selling items at discount prices. May God bless us all and help us bring His light to those we meet each and every day."

Nurse Barbara is the first to chat with Pastor Frank and shake his hand. I hear her express concerns about supplies and the children in her camp, but I can't hear the specifics. After the others file out, Pastor Frank greets me with a smile and a handshake. "Glad to see you, Susan. First-timers are always welcome."

I smile and search for the right words. "It's the first time I've been in a church in over thirty years, so don't get used to it. Highlanders sing your praises. You look so young."

He grins as he puts away his notes. "I assure you, I am a pastor, albeit a freshman one."

I feel awkward before him. "Have you run the church and driven the bus here for long?"

He stows his Bible under the lectern. "You don't seem to be one for chitchat. If you're curious about something, ask your question."

I'm taken aback by his candor. My face flushes, and I produce Danny's picture. "I guess I am. Did you know my son? He lived here twice last summer. Travis exiled him."

He suggests I help him fold chairs and collect hymnals while we talk. "I knew your son."

I fold a chair and follow his lead to the far corner of the tent. "Tell me about his stays."

He grabs a second chair and hesitates.

"Look, I know privacy is paramount here, but I left my home and husband and career to move here and wait for my son to return."

Frank stares into my eyes and appears to weigh his words. "Be careful what you wish for. You might get it."

I fold a chair. "What does that mean?"

"I'm sure you have your reasons, but to leave your life and come here might not have been the wisest thing."

"Why is that? Please tell me what you can."

Frank exhales as he picks up a hymnal. "Danny was quite the disruptive force. He sold drugs to all three camps, played residents against one another, stole, and sparked such animosity from other residents that Travis had no alternative but to banish him."

"Barbara said there was an intervention of sorts. Were you there?"

"I was. We tried several times. He refused. He threatened me. He broke Travis' jaw with a section of firewood. Minutes after Danny was banished, Travis' house was firebombed. No irrefutable proof pointed to Danny, other than the timing. Is this the Danny you remember from a year ago?"

I stop, and we stare at one another in silence.

Frank grabs a chair. "A month later, he returned. True to his word about the Highland's open-door policy, Travis welcomed him back, which I think surprised your son. In his own way, I believe he respected Travis for that. He walked the straight and narrow for a few days, but the old behaviors resurfaced. It was either exile, or the community would tear itself apart. The Danny I met is a very . . . hardened man. I would be amazed if he returns a third time, but you never know with addicts."

I thank him for his efforts with my son and feel horrible about what Danny did to Travis.

"If he returns, be prepared for the worst."

I lug another chair to the back. This one, like my mood, seems heavier.

Frank collects more hymnals. "You've given up much to be here, for no promise of a reward. I pray you have an understanding husband and place of work."

I consider opening up. He's easy to talk to, but I don't know him. "Let's say I have other reasons for being here."

Frank moves the lectern to a corner and moves a few folding tables. He offers me a stick of gum, which I decline, then places it in his mouth. "I first volunteered here during divinity school. Most new arrivals come in a state of shock and depression over how the world has treated them. Not Danny. He arrived like he owned the place. He came to make money and party. His lifestyle matched his personality. He was loud and bawdy but could be charming when he wanted something. If they become accustomed to life here, most new arrivals experience an emotional death of sorts. Their stories pound home the cold truth that man's cruelty to his fellow man knows no bounds. My instructors taught me that each person's deepest desire is to find meaning in life amid injustice and suffering. I try to help people rediscover that meaning."

I carry the final chair to the back, lean it against the others, and think, *If you had a time machine, I'd take you up on it.* "That must be a difficult job."

He nods. "These people have made me a better person. They may be at rock bottom, but most eventually cobble together a sense of community through shared adversity. Don't get me wrong, we have more than our fair share of bad apples. Every town does. After ordination, I used my networks in Prodigal to strike deals with local businesses for donations of food, clothing, blankets, and medical supplies. I bring back anything that can make life a little more bearable. Businesses are far more likely to donate items they can write off as tax deductions."

"So you live in town?"

He shakes his head. "Impossible to do and keep up with the needs. I didn't want to be just another pastor in Prodigal, so after my ordination, I moved here. When Prodigal shuts us down, I'm just as homeless, probably more so, than you."

I think of the new cell tower and the hundreds of pines marked with ribbons in the upper Highlands. I recall town gossip that these public lands may one day be earmarked for a ski resort.

"What will you do when the Highlands closes?"

Frank pauses a moment. "Hopefully, Prodigal will provide a building large enough for us to rehab into a shelter. I plan to follow these people. I make a difference here and want that to continue." He leans forward. "I sense you once felt the same. You can find that again."

I feel myself tense. "I have my doubts."

"To question ourselves—people in general, even at times those we love—means you're human. But we push through it and, in time, find peace."

I spot a stray hymnal partially beneath the old yellow sofa and hand it to Frank. "You said some tough words to the flock, but ultimately you turn the other cheek and pray for compassion from the rich and powerful in Prodigal. I think they worship a different god."

His smile turns rueful while he replaces used white votive candles in the stepped rack on the table with new ones. "If we shout and beat our chests, we surely lose. So we try every available legal means, push for the housing they promised, and kill them with kindness."

"*We* means you and Travis?"

"Pretty much. Along with our fledgling attorney."

I unwrap the individual candles for him while he scrapes the melted remains of the used ones from each red glass cylinder. I think of the poor side of town and the new construction underway there. "Isn't rehabbing neighborhoods, making them more attractive and livable, a good thing?"

"On the surface, it is, but it drives out the poor and lower middle class. Landlords buy up buildings with recycled tax dollars and renovate them. The rent skyrockets. Only those with high-paying jobs or wealthy retirees can afford the new housing." Frank struggles with the remnants of a votive candle and says he's going to have to heat it later. "Gentrification comes at a heavy price. It displaces people."

The faint smell of vanilla comes from each candle I unwrap. I remember delighting when the value of our house doubled.

Frank leans forward in emphasis. "The waitresses, cooks, grass cutters, and home health aides of Prodigal can no longer afford to live there. Without an affordable public transportation system, how can they be expected to move to the nearest town and drive forty miles each way to work for minimum wage?"

I open another box of votives and pass one to him.

"Economics has forced many workers to live here to fill those jobs. Evictions, divorce, job loss, or a health crisis may have been the trigger for others. The rest are the forgotten elderly without adequate income or family support, the mentally ill and drug dependent, and displaced veterans who struggle to reassimilate into society."

It used to be common to see homeless people sleeping on park benches or atop grates in front of stores. They'd try to sell fruit in summer or offer to clean my windshield when I stopped for a red light. Each time I would raise my window, make sure the doors were locked, turn up the radio, and pretend to look at my phone. The memory disturbs me now.

I hadn't realized until now that the lone homeless person I'd seen in town in two years was the man in rags squatting under that marquee begging for change the night I met the giant under the awning.

"Funny, now that you mention it, things are . . . different in town."

Frank acknowledges this but lets it pass. He uses a towel to clean the inside of a glass clouded by smoke.

"Business owners complained that the homeless pose serious safety concerns to locals and visitors, that we're bad for business. They paid for studies to corroborate their belief that the rising influx of homeless, caused by gentrification, serves as a stumbling block to new businesses. Then they made taxpayers pay for more studies that blamed the recent spike in crime on the homeless, without verifiable statistics to support the claim."

I grab the other towel and help him clean the glass cylinders. "I remember reading about that." I applauded it from my comfortable home in the suburbs. "What happened next?"

"The police rousted every homeless man, woman, and child from the streets of Prodigal. They did pickups in vans, mostly at night, away from the eyes of the media. Their only plan was to drive them, against their will, to the nearest shelter across the state. They drove some to the bus station and paid for a one-way ticket to anywhere, so long as it cost less than twenty dollars. The story goes that those who refused to board a bus escaped up the mountain and created the Highlands. It's an urban legend that happens to be true. Very few know this because no one reported it."

I hand him a cracked glass cylinder, which he carefully places in a trash bin. "Did anyone fight this years ago?"

Pastor Frank stands and walks to the yellow sofa, where he runs his hand over the worn, wrinkled fabric in a losing battle to smooth it. "Travis anticipated the gentrification push and hired a lawyer to fight for cost-controlled housing in town and a homeless shelter. We lost the lawsuit. The city council vetoed any expenditures for a shelter. No one wanted it in their backyard. Then they countersued the Highlands."

The door to the church creaks open, and an elderly Latino couple enters. They scan the schedule and light a candle. They kneel long enough to pray before they depart after acknowledging Frank with polite nods.

"What happened to the countersuit?"

Frank adds long matches to the brass well next to the candles. "Our first glimmer of success. A compromise. The town proposed a plan they said would fix the homeless problem once and for all—they set aside a million dollars in the budget for all eligible Highlanders to receive a year's worth of subsidized housing in town. That was six months ago, but I can count on one hand the number of Highlanders they approved. *Eligible* was not properly defined in the program. That's been their out."

"A million dollars is a lot of money." I remember complaining about it.

Frank smiles. "It is to me, but it's a pittance compared to the combined worth of the businesses and apartment complexes in town. The newly adjusted rent-fixed price of fifteen hundred a month would only provide fifty-six Highlanders with apartments for one year, roughly one-fifth of our population. And the eligibility requirement is so severe it's almost a catch twenty-two. After the subsidy year ends, each person must be able to pay the full rent and utilities on their own, which means they need to have a fairly high-paying job by year's end. In addition, they need to relearn the survival skills necessary to live in town. It may come as a surprise, but a return to apartment living after being homeless is a difficult adjustment filled with pitfalls and disillusionment."

I did the math in my head while I cleaned the final glass cylinder. "So the Highlands saves taxpayers over four million dollars a year for the other two hundred and forty-four."

Frank nods. "Yet Prodigal still plans to shut us down."

From the slant of the article, I'd assumed this was a case of people wanting free housing.

"Other countries have refugees and boat people," Frank says. "The homeless are America's forgotten people."

"Not forgotten by you. Or Travis."

"I fear Prodigal will break its promise, and we will have nowhere to go."

I nod and hug myself. "There's a new cell phone tower high up the mountain, and someone is marking trees for removal."

A crooked grin appears on his face. "Millions of future tourism dollars from skiers, I imagine."

I'm about to ask about Travis when Frank says, "Thanks for your help and your interest in our community. For someone who professes to be nonreligious, you know your way around a church."

I smile. "I'm a fallen Catholic. Like I said, don't get used to it."

"Do you plan to stay?"

I lean away from him. "That's a bit personal."

My comment doesn't seem to faze him. "I apologize if I seem forward. Life here has taught me many lessons. I'm more direct with people and think more in utilitarian terms, perhaps to a fault. I'm interested in your car. Specifically, what you plan to do with it if you decide to stay."

I hadn't thought about that. I feel my face redden. He speaks before I can answer.

"I may be a man of God, but this place compels me to be pragmatic. You met Charlie. He's our emergency driver. He's a veteran who lives in his car at the Daytona 500 Club."

"He's very kind."

"He's in his late seventies and sick. He donates his entire VA pension to the Highlands. He also transports people to doctor appointments or other town business when the bus is busy or down for repairs. He's an amazing man who decided to give back to his community in his golden years after being wounded overseas. Two pregnant women and other medically compromised people live in camp. I'd like to know we can count on another person in a pinch."

My face probably wore a look of shock. "So you want me to give my car to Charlie?"

Frank's brows knit for an instant. "No, it's no longer safe for him to drive. Would you consider being our emergency driver? Travis will pay for gas. You're one of us, at least for the time being, and your car is a valuable asset." His brown eyes remain on mine, unwavering.

I await an apology that never comes. The more often I go into town, the greater risk I run of being recognized, especially in my car. I keep telling myself that I've committed no crime, but I don't want to explain myself to a student or their parent why I abandoned them. I'm not there yet.

"You're damn right it is, and it's mine."

I leave without looking back.

I walk to the porta-potties. As my anger slowly subsides, I realize I've overreacted. The guilt from leaving my students remains an open wound. The car and iPhone are my lifelines to the real world, and the idea that someone has designs on my Beemer scared me. But the more I think about the car, the more I understand that it's a way to give back to the Highlands for taking me in.

The tinny sound of canned music from the stall nearest the woods breaks my train of thought. The same bass voice is talking to itself. The man yells twice, then mutters something about horses. It's the same chanting from the other day.

I call out from my stall, "Are you okay in there?"

He abruptly falls silent. The music shuts off.

"Are you sure you're all right?" I ask again.

The chanting resumes at a lower volume. I call out again when I finish, but there's no reply. I walk to the front of the last porta-potty and hear movement inside and soft mumbling. I knock and find the door locked. The noise stops. I'm so curious about this mysterious man.

MEMORIES OF THE ABYSS

The Tuesday before Thanksgiving arrives gray and snowy, and I climb into the bus with Dora and Tom, Judy and George, and others to attend the tent sale. I help Dora and Tom carry their items for sale.

Tom interrupts his constant singing to exclaim, "How ironic! We're leaving our little tents to go inside a great big one in town. We can't ever seem to get away from tents." With a devilish grin, he winks at Dora. "Does the thought of two tents make you . . . *too tense* . . . on a Tues-day, no less?"

Dora rolls her eyes and groans. "Leave your puns in camp, old man. You know the space heaters there make it comfortable." She fails to hide a grin as she settles by me. I think she added the last part for my benefit.

George frowns as he struggles to heft a loaded dolly up the bus steps and huffs in a contrary tone, "They picked a lousy day this time. Tuesday before Turkey Day, plus it's starting to snow. Many of the good townspeople of Prodigal will be home preparing holiday meals and desserts in their warm kitchens."

"I think people will shop today and cook tomorrow. All the better that Travis paid our table fees. He didn't have to do that," Dora reminds George. "We need to thank him."

Tom carries duffel bags full of scented pinecones of various colors and clusters from the forest. Judy carries a box of homemade soaps like the one she gave me. George lugs rustic clocks he carved from cross sections of trees he cut and stained to a glossy shine.

Kim and Penny from the Rainbow Camp carry homemade jewelry. They invite me to their camp for a girls-only slumber party the day after Thanksgiving, a kind offer but one that makes me feel old. I tell them it sounds like fun, and I will let them know.

A bearded man who looks like a resident of Camp Finn sits across from us. On his lap, he balances a plastic case full of arrowheads and polished stones in clear baggies. At his feet are three circular-shaped things in large plastic bags. The mysterious blobs are washed-out gray in color. They don't seem to weigh much, but he handles them carefully. Do I see bits of mud, crumpled paper, and sticks in them?

He notices me staring. "Hornet nests. Don't worry, ain't no hornets in 'em. I shellac the nests. People use 'em as decorations. In basements over pool tables."

I had never heard of that one before. "Good luck to you." I smile and return my attention to a dog-eared copy of *Lord of the Flies* that I checked out from the learning center.

Me? I'm not crafty. I'm here to shop for things on my never-ending list.

I peek in the cloth bags at Dora's feet and flip through floral paintings and nature sketches on canvas and poster board. "They're beautiful. Did you make these?"

Her eyes seem to grow distant while her fingertips fondle the wooden handle of a flowered bag. "I worked in graphic design for twenty years."

Tom ceases whistling. "The company downsized and let her go after the bosses made millions with her designs."

She nods. "Two of my designs went global. The CEOs took the profits and sold the company piece by piece to corporate raiders. The workers lost the class action suit." She shifts the bags at her feet to give herself more legroom. "And Tom worked as a music therapist until hospitals decided music therapy was an unnecessary luxury and eliminated his position."

I'm flabbergasted. "You both have gifts. It's good you still use them."

That gets me thinking.

Once we settle in, a peeved-looking George looks around and stands up. "We're all here. Where the hell is Frank? It's cold." Only then do I realize the bus is full, we're ready to go, but there's no driver.

Minutes pass, and George disembarks to look for Frank. Judy rolls her eyes and starts the chain of knowing smiles about her husband. Just then, I see a lean figure jog down the path toward the bus.

"Sorry for the delay, folks. I thought we had a budding emergency, but everything's okay. I'm sure everyone's eager to get a move on," Frank says, shutting the ancient bifold doors with the hand crank.

No one asks about the emergency, which bothers me. Are Highlanders so inured to suffering that they act like it doesn't exist? "What was the problem?"

Frank turns to make eye contact with me. "Nothing to worry about. False alarm." His tone is both lighthearted and brusque.

That does little to reassure me. Are we being kept in the dark about something, or did I violate the code again?

Dora pats my knee. "Trouble finds us all in time. Best not go looking for it."

I return her gentle smile with a hesitant one of my own and sink into the battered seat while the hornet-nest monger stares at me. I return my attention to Jack, Piggy, and the other boys marooned on the deserted island.

When we arrive in town, I pull my wool cap down to my eyes, put on my jury-rigged sunglasses even though the overcast sky is spitting light snow, tie my hoodie tight under my chin, and grab my new cloth bags.

"You look like a different person," Dora rasps under her breath, offering a covert thumb-up.

Her intuition is off the charts.

The bus glides to a stop in front of the quad. Frank announces we have four hours and imparts the same warning about missing the bus.

I help my friends—yes, the realization hits me that I have friends here—carry their things to their assigned tables. I wish them luck, then exit the main tent.

Before I enter the stores, I cross the crowded street and walk the lake that borders the town square. A walkway leads to an island that houses a gazebo with a shiny copper dome. Bright green benches encircle the structure, where a mother watches her two young boys chase each other in and around the gazebo. The kids laugh and squeal, their cheeks round and cherry red. I walk to the railing, and when the mother's back is turned to wipe a runny nose, I remove my iPhone from the Faraday bag and throw it in the deepest end of the lake.

My entire life was in that phone.

All my contacts, pictures, schedules, recipes, important dates, and addresses sink to the bottom of the frigid lake, soon to be covered in silt and muck. In a few weeks, the lake will be a solid sheet of ice for Christmas skaters.

Aside from loss, I'd like to think I feel relief, but that doesn't sound quite right. Maybe a sense of finality . . . or dread. Maybe all of the above. One lifeline gone.

I pull my wool cap down near my eyes and enter the shopping district. At Prodigal's largest electronics store, I pay cash for a prepaid burner phone and charger. I walk across the quad to the sporting goods store and buy an old non-propane catalytic heater and a can of the fuel recommended by the salesman. Next stop is a home goods store for a small cast iron skillet. My final stop is the 7-Eleven for Wild Turkey, cheap wine, cigarettes, and packets of candy.

The same young checker greets me at the counter. "Guys are pigs. Getting over them sucks. You sure you don't want any ice cream? It always works for me."

I decline the offer, stuff the bags of candy between the bottles to act as cushions, and then pay with cash. I keep the shopping cart this time when I head to the big tent. Those who look at me quickly avert their eyes like I'm invisible. A few frown and turn away. I've done the same countless times. And I was worried about drawing attention to myself. It's too early for the bus, so I walk over to see my friends.

I store the cart behind their tables. George complains that he hasn't moved a single clock. Judy says she sold a few seasonal bars of soap, mostly pumpkin- or sage-scented. Tom plies his considerable charms to sell a cluster of aromatic frosted pinecones to an elderly lady who doesn't need much convincing that it will make a distinctive Christmas centerpiece. Most of Dora's paintings have sold; only a few small charcoal sketches remain. At five dollars apiece, the quality artwork is a steal.

The moment I think this, a lanky teenage girl in a white parka saunters past Judy's table and pockets a bar of soap.

"Hey!" I yell. "Put that back!"

All eyes turn to us, and the girl takes off running.

"Shit!" I chase after her.

She's lightning quick, and her long legs dart between the holiday shoppers that congest the aisles. She bumps into a large man near the entrance, which slows her down. I catch up to her outside the tent in the open quad.

"Hey, young lady in the white coat! You have to pay for that soap."

A crowd forms. Over half a foot taller, the girl glares at me, defiant. An elderly couple catches the attention of a police officer on the sidewalk below, who walks quickly up the rise toward us.

"Give it back," I tell the girl. "Do the right thing, and you're free to go, before that cop gets here."

The girl sees the policeman and bites her lower lip. "Fuck you, bitch," she says and throws the bar at my face with such force it knocks my glasses off. I slip and roll down a gentle snowy slope. When I right myself, my cap is in the snow, and I push my hoodie back. I'm scrambling on my hands and knees for my glasses and cap when someone calls my name from the growing circle of onlookers.

I freeze because I recognize that high-pitched voice.

"Susan? Susan Crusoe? Is that you?"

Marjorie Keller, recently hired freshman math teacher at Hudson High. She observed two of my classes during her first week and often sought my advice on teaching her first year.

I cram the cap on my head and reaffix my hoodie while the portly cop makes his way through the mass of bystanders. Marjorie is pointing at me and repeats my name like the mere mention of it is a crime. The teenage thief is gone. Now the cop turns my way.

I run back toward the main tent and see a welcome sight: Frank is easing the rickety bus into a parking space next to a mound of dirty snow. Figures stand along the walkway and watch me run past, their confused faces a blur as I whiz by.

I hurry inside the tent, yank my cart from behind the tables, and rush out the other entrance near the parking lot, ignoring Judy's shouts.

"You're early," Pastor Frank says while I repeatedly rap on the bus doors. "I didn't expect you to be first in line."

"I didn't want to be late again," I say, out of breath. I slide my full cloth bags across the floor and lift the heater into a seat before I park the cart against the curb. Peering out a window, I brace for the worst. I imagine the police officer walking toward the bus with Marjorie in his wake, still yammering my name, then rapping on the bus doors with his baton and calling me out.

But there's no cop and no Marjorie. Nothing out of the ordinary. I close my eyes, hunker down in the seat, and take deep breaths.

Pastor Frank eyes me in the rearview mirror. "Shopping in town. It's not just a job; it's an adventure."

An eternity passes while I wait for the others so we can leave. My friends are the last to load.

"Why did you run out in such a hurry?" Dora asks under her breath.

"Sorry. I was sick."

"Did you get my soap from that thief?" Judy asks loudly.

Frank's eyes meet mine in the rearview. No clever grin this time.

In my panic, I left the soap in the snow.

I remove eight dollars from my billfold. "Here, I almost forgot. You're in luck. She paid up."

"Thanks, Susan. You did great." Judy hands the money to George, then says to him, "Hon, take this since you didn't sell anything today."

"Isn't it nice when things work out?" Frank says with a smile, and our eyes meet once more.

That night I boil water alone at my campsite while piano music and singing drift to me on the wind through the pines. If someone saw me board the bus, they know where I am. Though I've broken no law, I worry that the police will find me since I read in the *Prodigal Gazette* this morning that I'm officially a missing person. This was inevitable, but the timing couldn't be worse. Now that I think of it, I didn't anticipate the different interpretations of the note I left Jim. I had no idea I'd be living here when I left to see if Danny lived in the Highlands. I feel for him, but I don't want to be pressured to leave before I find Danny and recover my repressed memory fragments with his help.

I look at my reflection in my compact. The face I look upon has not touched makeup, moisturizing cream (other than petroleum jelly), eyeliner, hair color, or lipstick for weeks. The person I see looks haggard and old, with crow's-feet around her eyes.

I look familiar, yet strangely not.

I'm disturbed by what looks back at me.

I feel emotionless yet remain quick to anger and slow to calm.

I feel as if I'm outside my body as I search for the missing piece of what once made me a happy, productive human, beneficial to society. If I find Danny, will that help or hinder my hope for salvation? Is it realistic to think that meeting with him will right my ship and correct my downward spiral? Frank and Travis have their doubts, but they don't know my full story. What if I never find him or the trigger to my lost past? I shudder at the thought of Frank's second phase of homelessness—emotional death.

My thoughts drift to Travis and his attractive hazel eyes. I recall bits of a dream about him from which I awoke aroused. I hadn't seen that coming. His investment in these invisible people reminds me of my feelings toward my students.

I miss them. I miss the impact I had on their lives.

I close my eyes and take deep breaths. Being recognized in Prodigal and the fact that I took the last of my meds today has thrown me into a black mood. I can't get any refills without my doctor's approval. I walked into the woods to find myself. If I return to the city because I'm out of meds, I'd have to admit defeat and invite detection. How can I function without Zoloft, Lorazepam, and Ambien? I need them to make it through the day and to sleep at night.

One thing I know, my dreams have increased in frequency and intensity. They've expanded into a bizarre new realm on this mountain. I remember bits and pieces of the past, disjointed snippets of long-forgotten events that don't connect. It's maddening. Some of the flashbacks disturb me and carry the portent of a darker truth.

I plan tonight to heat up some instant soup and self-medicate with Wild Turkey until I pass out. I can't be depressed and anxious if I'm unconscious. Do your worst, dreams.

While the water boils, I think of what Travis said that set me off. As much as I hate to admit it, he could be right. It's what kept me sane and functioning. I think of Vidal's children and Barbara's talk with Pastor Frank. I need to quit running to the bulletin board twice a day to check for word of Danny. It ratchets up my disappointment and despair. The watched-pot conundrum. About needing a purpose. Perhaps even the part about penance.

Maybe.

On the night before Thanksgiving, I sit alone on a rock surrounded by fresh snow and listen to the call of the loons. Such a sad, primordial sound that echoes through the valley. I stare into the fire and try to empty my head of worry.

Behind me, I hear a faint rustle in the forest and think of bears. I'm scared to death of them and haven't seen one yet. An uneasy feeling washes over me: just because you're paranoid doesn't mean someone's not out to get you.

Then it hits home. It's not a bear. Someone is watching me. Again.

"I know you're out there. Show yourself," I call out to the darkness. I swallow the lump in my throat.

Nothing.

I toss two Snickers Minis near the winding path. After a minute, they disappear behind a tree trunk. The waifish blonde in the green cap materializes at the edge of the clearing. Holding and chewing the mini-bar in both hands like a fox, she whispers a barely audible *thanks*. Her eyes never leave my face.

"You're welcome to sit with me and warm yourself by the fire."

Silent, she stops chewing and stands her ground, staring at me like before. Wary.

"I don't bite. I have hot soup." The company of a total stranger seems welcome tonight.

She takes a few tentative steps into the firelight. I see her sallow, dirt-streaked face. She has that deer-in-the-headlights look of wanting to walk and not walk simultaneously. She must be rail thin, for she seems to be all coat. Her gloves are black and open-fingered, not insulated.

"C'mon, let me get you a bowl of soup. You look like a bag of bones. It's chick—"

When I turn back, she's gone. Somehow, she slipped through the pines without making a sound. Two candy wrappers lay crumpled on the snow.

She spoke her first word to me. That's progress. Like a student stepping out of his or her shell for the first time.

Oh well, she had her chance for a hot meal. Maybe next time.

I prepare for my night of self-medicating, which will include a warmer tent tonight. I fill my new catalytic heater with fuel and pour a generous amount on its domed top. When I bend and ignite it, a sudden *whoosh* of fire shoots four feet high, setting my cap, hoodie, and hair ablaze.

127

Blinded by the flames, I panic and stomp and flail my arms. I stumble over the stones around the campfire. Pain hits my face like a wave until I find my wits and drop and roll in the snow.

When I muster the courage to rise, my cap smolders. I crawl to my compact mirror and find my left eyebrow missing; the right is burnt to a whitish crisp. I treat my facial burns with snow and petroleum jelly.

My little blue tent is unscathed.

I read the instructions and learn that I added way too much fuel to the dome of the heater. The salesman urged me to spray small amounts from a squirt bottle, but I chose not to buy one.

In half an hour, the flames in the catalytic heater die down like the instructions said they would, and the top glows orange with clean, even heat.

I douse my campfire and carefully position the heater in the center of my tent. I open the Velcro flap at the top of my tent for a vent.

My face feels like it's been stretched taut as a drum by the burns to my forehead, nose, and cheeks. It hurts every time I move my face. My eyes are red and sting from the fumes.

I pour three fingers of Wild Turkey and start to laugh. What a sight I must have been! A tiny bride of Frankenstein staggering around the tent, screaming and raging against the fire. If the little blonde woman was watching from the cover of darkness, she caught quite a show.

In no time, the tent is cozy, warm, and I lower the setting on my new heater. My thoughts drift back to the teen thief and Marjorie Keller. The cops now have a confirmed Susan Crusoe sighting. More than anything, I want to stay here and work on myself while I wait for my son.

Exhausted and in pain, I drink and eventually drift off.

Some dreams are amorphous and fleeting, faint vestigial memories of another time long ago when we were different people than we are today.

We all see the past through the prism of our flawed perception, so why should our dreams be different?

The recurring dream/memory tonight is no stranger. It's seared into my brain with a branding iron.

Danny comes walking home one hot summer day, head down, seemingly lost in thought.

"Where's your car?" I ask.

He uses a shirtsleeve to wipe his brow and downs a Coke in a gulp or two. Ever since he was young, he always drank and ate like he was in a race. He belches and finally says, "Somebody stole it."

He's so nonchalant that, for a moment, I think he's joking. He always had a quick, dry wit. Then I realize he's serious.

"What? Why didn't you call your dad or me? Did you report it to the police?"

A head shake. A second can pops open.

"Why not?"

A quick shrug and an eye roll. "Gotta go." The screen door slams behind him.

I do what I feel like I always do with Danny: I chase him. I grab him by the arm and spin him around in our front yard. He wheels on me before I can speak, his right hand cocked in a fist. He squeezes my arm with such force it leaves a bruise later. I stare into his dark eyes, now two angry slits.

"Go ahead, hit me," I say. "You've always wanted to."

He relaxes his grip on my arm. "If I'm late, I'm good as dead. You'd probably like that, wouldn't you?"

Fear replaces the rage in his eyes as he lowers his hand. For an instant, the frightened little boy in him returns, then vanishes. Something in him refuses to be tamed.

"What is going on, Danny? Let me help you. Whatever it is, we can work it out."

All the years of feeling helpless with him are coming to a head on our front lawn. Any hope I have to regain a semblance of control over my son is in danger now, and I want it back. I sense a nearing abyss, and beyond that, doom.

"Leave me the fuck alone. I mean it."

God have mercy on my soul. I've dreaded and looked forward to this day. "What do you mean, dead? You're scaring me. No problem is too big to overcome together. Please talk to me!"

He pauses for a heartbeat, then wrenches my hand from his arm.

"Who do you need to meet?" I ask. "Let me take your place!"

He gives me one final anguished look before he turns and runs. I sprint to the garage and start the car. Frantic, I cruise the neighborhood but find no trace of him. I call his cell, but it goes straight to voice mail. I plead for him to pick up, to come back home. I phone the coffee shop near home where he works, but he's not scheduled to work today, and no one has seen him.

I call the police and report that our son is missing and his car has been stolen. I clarify that these were two separate incidents. I command their full attention until I mention his name. The Prodigal police know him all too well, and they remind me that he ran off twenty minutes ago. I insist they file a missing persons report and describe in detail the clothes he's wearing.

I've filed reports before, so I know there's no mandatory twenty-four-hour wait period. The police seem more interested in the stolen car than him.

During the drama, I forgot to ask where the car was stolen or the circumstances, but they make note of the license plate, make and model, color, and VIN. It's not a valuable car or particularly new. The cops try to be reassuring and say most likely kids saw keys in an unlocked car and took it for a joyride, or a friend borrowed it without permission. I tell them about my last conversation with Danny and what I fear it means. They promise to place a be on the lookout, or BOLO order for him and his car.

They expect he will return home soon, safe and sound, with the car.

I hate being patronized. I'm so upset my teeth itch.

Two days pass with no contact from him or the cops. Sad to say, this isn't the first time. I'm out of my mind with worry.

On the third night, Sergeant Collins of the Prodigal police calls to say they found the car.

I feel relief. "What about my son? Where is he?"

"The car wasn't stolen, Mrs. Crusoe. The driver bought the car from your son. The new owner produced the title when the officer pulled him over. Your son's car has been properly and legally transferred to its new owner."

"I want to speak with that person."

A brief silence on the line. "I'm afraid you can't. I spoke at length to the new owner. I'm convinced he knows nothing else about your son."

"We bought the car for Danny. How can this be?"

"His name was on the title, Mrs. Crusoe."

I'm at a loss for words until I hear my voice lower and ask the next dark question that comes to mind: "How much did he sell it for?"

"Four hundred dollars, cash. I'm sorry, but there's nothing we can do. The new owner insists he doesn't know your son or his whereabouts. Meanwhile, the department continues to look for him. We'll contact you with any more news." The line goes dead in my hands.

We recently helped him pay for a brake job and new tires. I look up the Blue Book value of the car, and given the mileage, it lists for $3,500.

I'm transported back to that stuffy classroom.

With the incompetent counselor.

And the platitudes on the chalkboard.

And that poor woman with a voice so tiny and wounded—Donna— as she bares her soul to a group of strangers.

I cover my mouth and want to scream.

I enter the bedroom to change my work clothes and notice my open jewelry case. I start to shut it, then look inside. My diamond necklace, tennis bracelet, and my mother's heirloom wedding ring are gone. I search around the dressing table in the bathroom and crawl on my hands and knees along the baseboards until it dawns on me.

I'm so stupid.

Jim returns home five minutes later in a rant. He wants to know why I took all the cash from his wallet, which forced him to use a credit card to pay for a latte on his way to work that morning.

I cross my arms and wait for him to finish. "How much money did *you* have?"

His eyes narrow as the realization hits. "About two hundred . . ."

I summarize the call from Sergeant Collins and mention my missing jewelry.

Danny still doesn't answer his phone. I call the coffee shop and learn he was a no-call, no-show today and that he has been fired.

I remember thinking *He better be dead because if he's not, I'm going to kill him.*

We discuss how to handle him. Neither of us knows what to do. We're beyond frustrated and angry. I'm out of ideas. All the interventions, the out-of-state treatment centers chosen in part to distance him from his suppliers. Change of scenery accomplished nothing. He found a way to get kicked out every time.

Jim and I have been living separate lives since I learned Danny is an addict, and Jim gleefully reminds me that was my choice. He says I never should have let him leave the house two days ago. I ask, how was I supposed to stop him? He parries back at me, and I counter with another thrust. When Jim mentions my difficult bonding after his birth, my mind flashes back to the delivery room. I look down at a clump of hair in my hand and shut my eyes. This is a new twist. We've been arguing for hours. We spin our wheels and argue in our familiar loops until midnight, when Danny strides through the front door without a care in the world. Jim freezes and looks to me for direction.

I stand up. "You sold the car we bought you, you're stealing from us, and you're using. How much trouble are you in? Who do you owe, and how much?"

Danny walks to the refrigerator without a word. I look to Jim, who says nothing, so I follow. As he opens the door, I slam it shut. He sighs and shakes his head. "Leave me alone."

"Wrong answer. Try again."

When he doesn't, Jim enters the kitchen, pointing at him. "You're going back to treatment, right now." His voice is unsteady. He sounds scared.

Danny doesn't acknowledge his father. He glares at me. "No. How many times have I told you that I like getting high? You just don't get it. And you're supposed to be this intelligent and great teacher. Nobody listens to what I say. I fucking love the rush. It's the only thing I look forward to. So leave me . . . the fuck . . . alone!"

He yanks open the refrigerator and pulls out a drumstick from the dinner he missed last night. He glares at me and tears into it with his teeth, defiant.

I'm about to remind him of his age, his inability to abide by the most basic rules, and how we didn't raise him to act this way. I want to recap everything he's put us through over the last eighteen years and how much pain he's caused, when I realize the pointlessness of it.

I look to Jim, who remains silent, so I turn back to Danny and step into the abyss.

"You keep telling us you're an adult. Act like one. You lost your job and sold your car to support your drug habit. If you want to be left alone, if all you want to do in life is get high, pack your bags. I want you out of this house."

This thirty-three-year-old man-child of mine points the chicken leg at me as if he's the conductor in some macabre symphony directing me to shut up. The world freezes for an instant. He hesitates. Is he reconsidering?

"Fine," he says and storms out the front door.

I startle as something hits the screen door hard. The drumstick bone.

He never returned for his things. That was over a year ago.

A MEAN DRUNK

The loon's call gradually lifts me from sleep, and I stretch in my sleeping bag. The temperature in the tent remained pleasantly constant through the night. I wake later than normal. I look up into my own wrinkled aluminum foil sky and say to myself: Happy Thanksgiving, dumbass. My burns still hurt, so I apply more snow and jelly.

For some reason, I have a fleeting thought of Danny in the delivery room, but the more I try to force the memory, the quicker it disappears.

The morning breaks clear and cold. The falling snow blankets the frozen earth for miles. It's pristine and beautiful and silent. I feel tucked inside a giant snow globe. I breathe in the brisk air like a draft of clear fresh water. My senses on alert, a stillness of perception settles in me as quiet as the snow, and I think of Thoreau. For the first time in years, I'm taking pleasure in solitude. Maybe he was right, that the luxuries and comforts in life are actually hindrances to our elevation.

Thoreau walked into the woods to drive life into a corner, reduce it to its basest terms, and to learn from experience whether it was cruel or sublime. I drink in the world around me as I walk to camp through the fresh powder of snow.

Out of habit, I check the bulletin boards, then chastise myself for doing so. Part of me is clinging to an irrational Hallmark moment, a Thanksgiving miracle, the return of my prodigal son. I paste on a smile and sit with my group as they wish each other Happy Thanksgiving. They take one look at my face and ask what happened. I downplay the damage and joke about how I must have looked. Dora says to come by their tent later, that she has a salve that will help. Talk returns to anticipation of tonight's feast. I drink black coffee and nibble on a sausage and egg breakfast patty Wilbur grilled.

I think of my mixed feelings for Travis. The image of a kettle on a stove reappears in my mind, and I realize that my voice is the only subdued one around the tables. I can never seem to get out of my own head for long. I'm a jumbled, screwed-up mess, and I wish I could remember why.

Who am I kidding, acting like a half-baked philosopher in the woods?

I need my meds. My brain chemistry is slipping more out of whack by the hour. I've never gone cold turkey before, and the thought starts a panic attack.

I excuse myself and tell the others I'll see them at dinner. My grounding exercises help some. I hike the camp perimeter to clear my head. Thoreau spent two years in the wilderness finding himself, but when I walk into the woods, it drives me up a wall, reducing me to my lowest animal terms. I recall some of the transgressions and failures my son and husband have committed over the years, but not my own. Tenuous connections appear to me during dream states but disappear like mirages when I wake. It may take a miracle to lead me to them.

I'm the worst possible creature: a failed mother. Mothers are supposed to be nurturing and caring, though mine never was. You see it in movies and read it in books—mothers never give up on their children. They would rather die first. But what did I do? I kicked out my son when he feared for his life.

Not far from the north camp, I see a herd of deer flushed into the clearing, chased by what looks like a wolf. Their silent and deadly game of hunter and prey proceeds up the mountain past my line of sight. All that remains are tracks in the snow. Minutes later, my head snaps in the other direction when a crack echoes across the valley below, followed seconds later by six concussive reports, each a second apart and of a slightly varying pitch. A few seconds later, one last shot echoes with a kind of finality.

I hike in the direction of the noises and crest a gentle rise. I hear the voices before I see them. Alpha males with shotguns slung across their backs kneel in the snow to collect their kill, a rafter of wild turkeys. They joke and laugh as they trek north back toward the catacomb of caves.

I consider moving north into one, maybe Finn's abandoned mine. Maybe I could bait him into completing what the giant in Prodigal could not, but I'd probably fail at that, too.

I could keep on walking aimlessly until I drop from exhaustion. I've read that freezing to death isn't painful; much like going numb and then to sleep. The wolves can feed on me when I'm dead. I'd live on in them and their offspring.

I fall to my knees and cover my ears with my hands. Beeps blare in my head, and flashing lights blind me. My hands tremble, and my heart throbs in my throat. This one's so bad I can't focus on my grounding exercises. I try to slow my breathing and ride out the storm.

When I can stand, I think: *Maybe a purpose is a first step.*

I return to camp late afternoon and wait in line for the showers. Dora squeezes my shoulder and urges me not to lose hope. Her intuitiveness again staggers me. There are two sides to every story, but I wonder how their adult children could reject them. The hot water lifts my spirits, but the shakes return. I check my skin, but I'm not crawling out of it. Going off meds cold turkey is pure hell.

For dinner, we eat donated turkey with all the trimmings. The stuffing is an instant mix, and the packages are at their expiration date, but Wilbur chars my turkey leg to perfection. Walking the mountain for miles in heavy snow burned thousands of calories, and I need the nutrition. My clothes fit looser now. I start in on a piece of pumpkin pie and canned whipped cream. Irish coffee helps combat the shakes, so I mix my third one. I sit near the bonfire and listen to the chatter.

Between bites, Flossie says, "You all know that wild-looking crazy white dude who talks to himself? Looks like a Viking on steroids?"

George has a blank look on his face, and Tom says to him, "You know him. Great big burly guy with a red beard. Looks twice as big as the man on the Brawny towels."

George still doesn't show a sign of recognition.

"He prospects for gold in the abandoned mines near the top of the mountain. Lives in the north camp. Always thinks people are stealing from him. His name is Finn."

Judy shivers and mentions a brief past encounter with him. "What about him?" I ask.

Flossie leans back and cradles her belly with both hands, eyeballing me. "Travis exiled him today."

Dora puts down her fork. "Oh no. On Thanksgiving?"

"Uh-huh," Flossie says. "Dude went batshit crazy and hurt two old men who live in that stretch of camp named for some car race."

"The Daytona 500 Club," I say.

Flossie looks past me. "Vidal, you were there with Travis. Go ahead, finish the story."

Vidal looks around, I think to make certain the kids are out of earshot. "Finn claimed the men stole his gold. Said he found two bags of it in their cars. Phil and Paul say they were only kidding around, but Finn lost it when they laughed at him. He broke Phil's nose, and Paul may have broken ribs. He pushed poor old Charlie down when he tried to act as peacemaker. Charlie fell on a rock and cut his leg, the one that may need an amputation. Barbara's with them now. Sounds like they need to go to the hospital."

I'm unsteady, but I stand up. "The man is mentally ill. He was psychotic on the bus. How could Travis exile a sick man like that?"

No one answers my question, and I roll my eyes.

Vidal turns to me. "We tried to get him to the hospital this morning. He thinks we fly government drones overhead to steal his gold. He overpowered Travis, Frank, and me. He ran down the mountain with bags in his hands. We lost him at the train tracks."

George's ears perk up. "Surely he didn't have bags of gold."

Flossie shakes her head. "Travis found two bags in the old dudes' cars. Phil and Paul admitted they filled two empty tobacco pouches with granite and quartz chips spray-painted gold."

"Finn left the fake gold and escaped down the mountain with different bags?" I say.

Vidal thinks about it some, then nods.

Flossie laughs. "The moral to the story is: don't fuck with crazy people."

I drain my mug as the warm liquor hits my belly. My eyes lose focus, and I'm unsteady. "It sounds like they got what they deserved."

Corseted smiles greet my remark.

"What? I don't mean Charlie. Don't you think there's some level of karmic justice to what happened?"

Vidal looks at the ground, and the others remain silent. I turn to Flossie, who doesn't follow up on her comment.

"C'mon, we're all adults here." I refill my mug and drink during the silence. Then I describe the mysterious blond woman in the green cap to those gathered around the crackling fire.

I receive headshakes in return. I tell them where I've seen the woman and describe her clothes in elaborate detail. Silence.

"Well, I didn't imagine her out of thin air. Surely someone else has seen her." I look into the faces hunkered around the Pit. "Dora? Judy? Flossie?"

Still no reply. I drink more Irish coffee and turn to the group. "How many of you bastards saw the fliers I placed all over Prodigal about my missing son and didn't lift a finger to dial my number?" My voice rises to a near shout, and I slur some words. I slip but don't fall as I reach for more whiskey. "To hell with you all! I hope Finn escaped with enough gold to never return to this shithole."

I'm wobbling aimlessly down a path hoping Finn indeed struck gold when I get the sudden feeling of eyes watching me again. Thinking it's the blond woman, I wheel and see the mayor approaching. Fast.

"Follow me," he says in the same tone I use on students when I lead them to detention. He strides past me without stopping, his jaw set, eyes fixed straight ahead.

"Slow down," I call out. I try to keep up but fail. I follow him into the learning center, where the mayor is standing by the computer alongside Corey, the young man with a patchy beard who runs the center and oversees the Highland website. Corey relinquishes the computer at the mayor's request and exits the room.

Travis tells me to sit at the laptop, which I do.

He stands over me. "When you chose to stay, I asked if you could comply with our one basic rule. Remember?"

I feel my cheeks redden and my anger return. My eyes struggle to focus. "Sure. Three little words. R-E-S-P-E-C-T your neighbor," I sing off-key. I improvise the next line. "What could be easier than T-H-A-T?"

Those hazel eyes study me hard. There's no black halo above his balding dome now. "Aside from being a mean drunk to the others just now, why are you really here?"

"What do you mean?" I don a serious face and look up at him. "Have I been a bad girl?"

"Why did you run from home? What have you done? The truth this time."

I realize he's serious and straighten my posture. "I don't know what you're talking about." Then the hiccups start. When they stop, I say, "I told you. I'm looking for my son."

Travis' eyes narrow. He moves closer and clacks away at the keyboard. The *Prodigal Gazette* appears with my picture on the front page. My unsmiling and sterile driver's license photo. I read the front-page story a dozen times yesterday.

"Go on. Read it."

LOCAL TEACHER MISSING

In a baffling case with more questions than answers, a respected teacher has been missing for over a month, and police are turning to the public for help. Concerned co-workers reported Susan Crusoe, 60, of Prodigal County, missing after receiving no response from Crusoe or her husband for two weeks after she called in sick for a week. Crusoe has taught English at Hudson High School for twenty years and was recently identified as the recipient of this year's National Teacher of the Year award.

Crusoe's husband of 34 years, James Crusoe, 63, a financial officer and accountant for Miracle Motors, told police he and his wife had been having marital problems, and he assumed she had simply moved out. Police later learned of a note Crusoe addressed to her husband on the day of her disappearance, indicating she feared for her life.

Mr. Crusoe called in sick to work the same week Mrs. Crusoe did. He told police he took a drive to clear his head and checked into a hotel for the next five nights. Forensic analysis of organic material recovered from Mr. Crusoe's SUV is underway.

Nelson Morris, Superintendent of Hudson High, stated that Mrs. Crusoe had never before used a sick day in her twenty years at the school. Morris said, "Over the years, she has volunteered countless hours of her free time as a tutor to any willing student and is always eager to meet and work with parents. We are all saddened and bewildered by her disappearance. We hope no harm has befallen her. All the staff and students at Hudson High are praying for a quick and safe resolution to this mystery."

The investigation is ongoing; police have not ruled out foul play.

Mrs. Crusoe is five foot two and weighs approximately one hundred pounds. She has blue eyes and brown shoulder-length hair with blond highlights. Her car is also missing, a late-model blue BMW 2 coupe with license plate G3H-V8D. Anyone with information is asked to contact the Prodigal Police Department.

When I finish, Travis leans on the desk. "What do you have to say for yourself?"

My mind is racing. Marjorie Keller told the police. They will be here soon. If they force me to leave, can I return to my old life without changing the past? I smirk at the cruel irony: I'm in another place I can't leave and can't stay in. Just when I'm starting to remember more of the past. I feel so guilty I don't know where to begin.

"I'm waiting," Travis says.

I look up at him and bare my teeth. "Are you going to exile me, like Finn?"

"That depends on your answer. And what the police find."

I lean forward. "It's none of your goddamn business."

"You're not leaving me much of a choice."

I shrug. If he banishes me, I'll get behind the wheel one last time. "Do what you have to do."

Travis studies my face. "Maybe I was wrong about you after all. You're content to let your husband twist in the wind as the prime suspect in your disappearance. You need to put an end to this. You're right, your marital issues *aren't* my business, but this could shut us down immediately. For all I know, Finn is wreaking havoc in Prodigal right now."

Travis leans closer, his voice a conciliatory whisper. "If your husband is abusing you and you need help, I will arrange it for you. It doesn't have to be in Prodigal."

I've lied so much, what's one more? "I'm not going to harm myself or anybody else. He's not physically abusive."

Travis doesn't look convinced. "Tell me about the note."

If I say the words, it makes them real. I hesitate. "The night before I came here to look for my son, he said he wanted a divorce and told me to pack my bags. I may have mentioned that he wants me out of the way."

Travis' tone changes. His voice lowers. "You need to tell the police you're okay. Make up something, anything . . . say you left to care for a sick friend."

"Where's your damn Highland *omerta* when it comes to me?"

The corners of Travis' mouth start to rise, then stop. "It's the right thing to do. Whatever his shortcomings, he shouldn't be considered a murder suspect. You chose to leave Prodigal the way you did. Like you, cops can be singular and dogged in their purpose. A quarter of all confessions are coerced. Stranger things have happened."

My voice wants to catch in my throat. "You read the article. What was he doing at a bed-and-breakfast the week I left? Why didn't *he* file the missing person report?" I feel hurt and betrayed, but even that doesn't seem justified. Frank is right about emotional death.

"Don't change the subject. It's the right thing to do."

A kettle whistles in my mind. I close my eyes.

Travis drums his fingers on the shiny silver top of the laptop. "Have you thought about our last talk?"

"About a purpose?"

He nods.

I remember Barbara's whispered concern to Frank about the children in camp. "How many children live here?" I ask.

An eyebrow rises slightly, and for an instant, the corners of his mouth curve upward again. "At any given time, I'd say fifteen to twenty between the ages of seven and seventeen, maybe more depending on how many currently live in the Rainbow Camp. Like any city, the numbers fluctuate."

I'm about to vomit, but I force the bile down. "I have no resumé other than that paragraph in the paper, but each month the children remain out of school, they lag farther behind their peers academically and socially." I have a fit of hiccups. "I want to teach them."

Travis looks skeptical. He could call the cops on me to score points with Prodigal and take heat off the Highlands. He could exile me. I realize I'm not breathing.

I pat the laptop. "Monitor the *Gazette* to your heart's content, but I'm staying. I need to be here for my son. I spoke with Frank. You're right; I need a higher purpose while I wait." I find myself holding my stomach with both hands again.

Travis takes a breath, holds it, and exhales. "Let the police know you're safe and make sure your husband is no longer a suspect."

I laugh. Travis asks why.

The hiccups return. "It's the first time I've been offered a job while drunk on my ass."

He taps the laptop one more time. "National Teacher of the Year?" he muses, extending a hand. "Welcome aboard. You're on probation here. Don't screw up." He grins.

I hurry outside and vomit.

A ROUTINE

Sober in the morning, I remember bits and pieces from last night. My unrealistic hope for a Thanksgiving reunion. The shakes from medication withdrawal. Too many Irish coffees. I made an ass of myself. I challenged Travis to exile me and may have come on to him. Of that, I'm not sure. Despite everything, I think I landed a teaching gig.

I don't want the cops in the Highlands, so I drive two towns away and mail this handwritten letter to the Prodigal Police Department:

I read the article in the Gazette regarding my disappearance. I'm writing this to assure you that I am alive and well. I left home of my own free will, and my husband, Jim Crusoe, should no longer be considered a suspect in any foul play regarding me. There is no need to look for me; I am where I need to be for now. I have broken no laws. If and when I choose to return to Prodigal, it will be my decision and on my terms.

> *Susan Marie Crusoe*
>
> *P. S. Compare this handwriting to samples from Hudson High. They're the same. It's me.*

I feel less shaky and grateful to still be here. I use the laptop to download the core competencies that guide instruction in our state. To teach a class comprising of students aged seven to seventeen, I need to either individualize or teach thematically at many different levels of learning. Accessing separate online curricula for one-on-one laptop teaching would be too time-intensive. I meet with the children and parents to start lesson planning.

Over the next weeks, the class in the learning center grows from Vidal and Maria's three young children to nineteen students, eight of whom are teenagers. Most live in the Rainbow Camp. Kim and Penny bring their adopted African-American daughter, Brianne, to start grade school. Barbara's son, Theo, is six feet tall and sixteen. He's the only high schooler who demonstrates major college potential. His IQ tests at 140. He wants to write novels and teach creative writing. His dystopian short fiction is unrefined but shows flashes of brilliance. We focus on ways to hone his dialogue and streamline the flow between chapters. Two of his stories are almost ready for submission. He is so passionate about learning that I must ask him to leave the learning center at the end of each day.

After a few weeks, we outgrow the learning center and relocate to the church. The age range is but one of many challenges, along with the dismal scarcity of textbooks and supplies. The Highlands only has one laptop, but kids thrived in schools for generations without them.

The school schedule expands along with the class size until I'm working a full-time teaching job for no pay or benefits, unless you count spending more time in the better-heated church/school canvas tent as a perk, which I do. Travis builds benches and desks and rigs up additional lighting. Frank procures two more bulletin boards for class announcements. I post inspirational quotes from Thoreau and Emerson weekly below pictures of nature.

Travis provides a budget from his own salary. I compile lists of necessities, and Frank begs what he can from town businesses. I purchase the rest—reams of paper, pens, pencils, crayons, and printer ink—myself. As Christmas approaches, my twelve hundred dwindles to a few twenties and smaller bills.

I create lesson plans for every child on English, math, science, and history. For the high schoolers, I devote time to life skills and job training. Everyday skills like communication, problem-solving, creativity, how to balance a checkbook and manage money, how to sew on a button, how to use common tools, basic safety, and even how to approach the subject of dating.

Pastor Frank and Mayor Travis take turns as guest speakers for the older students on how to prepare for the workforce. Nurse Barbara speaks about careers in medicine and health care. I chat up Dora to offer art classes and Tom for music appreciation and lessons. Corey offers to teach computer training and journalism to the older students. He works in Prodigal in IT and has been on the subsidized housing list for months. I ask Wilbur to share his culinary knowledge and skills with the students, but he says, "What the hell difference does it make? Prodigal is kicking us off the mountain the first of February." His mood grows more unsettled as Flossie's due date nears.

Today Charlie, the backup driver who gave me my first blanket, gets fitted for a prosthetic after he's stabilized from an above-the-knee amputation he had weeks ago. Barbara didn't like the look of the gash when he fell during the tussle with Finn, and the doctors said the time had finally come. Tomorrow he starts a rehab stint in a VA nursing home, but rumor has it his stay will be permanent. Travis works more hours in town now to make up for the lost income, since Charlie's pension must go toward his care. I now double as the backup emergency driver when class is not in session.

I've driven Highlanders to town for doctor or ER visits, to meet with counselors, social service, or DCFS workers. I stay in the car wearing a hoodie and bury my head in a book, wishing I'd opted for tinted windows. When the car needs gas, I fill up quickly, pay cash, and leave. It's another reason my money is almost gone.

On a trip to the porta-potties one day, I see the door to the last one sway open in the breeze. Inside it, around the rim of a functioning commode, are a pair of worn shoes, a moth-eaten jacket, a dirty pillow, cheap radio, a bottle of orange juice, hummus containers, a plastic spoon, and an empty beer can. Two items catch my eye: an ornately carved walking stick and a perfectly crafted origami horse that rears on its haunches.

I can't begin to fathom what I see here. Never in my wildest dreams could I imagine a person living in a toilet. I place five dollars under the horse and write, *You have amazing talent* on the bill. I take care to close the door.

On the way back to my tent, I hear noise by the totem pole. Travis is on the ladder again, tool belt around his waist, hammer and chisel in hand, inspecting his work. I watch as he nods and exchanges the hammer and chisel for a small shop brush. He whisks shavings from the trunk of the totem. He shakes his head. Then the hammer and chisel return. He keeps chipping away at the image ever so slightly until he finally nods.

"Guess there's not much demand for a class in totem pole carving," I say, smiling. "You do good work."

He does a double-take from the ladder. "I didn't hear you come along. Thanks. Good woodworkers can earn a decent living. Do me a favor. Open that box and hand me the palette."

Amid the pine shavings in the snow sits a wooden box. Under the plastic palette are the tubes of many colors. I pass him the preloaded palette. "I can't quite make out this new carving."

He smiles. "Hence the paint, for contrast and definition. You should be able to in a few minutes."

He produces a painting knife from his belt and adroitly adjusts the colors to his liking. Next, the brush appears for a final clean. Soon a large green rectangle appears on this new totem section, followed by a thin brown border. Below that, a bright red square materializes.

He glances down at me. "I've never seen children respond to anyone like they do you. It's easy to see why people chose you as Teacher of the Year. I may do passable carvings, but you have a true gift."

I smile and watch as a small figure appears on each side of a larger one. They are holding hands to the left of the red square. He finishes by adding black lettering to the square. While he works, his broad back partially shields his work from me. As he descends the ladder, it all comes into view, and I gasp.

The pole displays a chalkboard, a red book, and me with two children.

"I can't read the lettering on the book."

Travis wipes his brow. "Climb the ladder until you can."

When I do, the word WALDEN appears in block letters.

As I climb down, my boot slips from the last rung, and Travis rights me before I fall. He maintains his hold on my arms, and I feel myself blush again. We stand there frozen.

I stare into his hazel eyes and feel a heat grow in me I'd thought long dead.

He leans forward—slowly, tentatively, his eyes seeking permission—and pulls me closer. I'm frightened and excited, but don't stop him. Our lips touch, and the kiss deepens, followed by frenzied fumbling. He buries his face in my neck, and his hands reach behind me to fondle my ass. He pulls me against his body and kisses me hard.

I close my eyes and hear myself moaning when I pull away out of fear. I cover my face with a hand and look at the ground.

Travis speaks first, sheepishly. "I apologize if I'm out of line. I have feelings for you, and I thought you did for me. Did I misread the signals?"

I remove the hand from my face and meet his eyes.

Not according to the desire I'm feeling. I can't recall the last time I felt wanted by a man. I move closer and gently touch his mouth with my fingertips. "No, you didn't." I pat his collar. "Waiting for my son is not the only reason I walked into these woods. I can't remember part of my past. Whatever it is I've blocked out, I must find it and come to terms with it. I also don't know about my marriage. Until I do, I can't be in a relationship." I've never voiced a word about my repressed memory, much less shared it with another person. "Does that make sense?"

He nods. "You are quite singular in purpose. I like that about you."

I pat his collar once more. "I think you're rather special, too."

I help him pack his tools and brushes into the box while he hoists the ladder off the totem.

He turns and smiles at me. "You're the first Highlander I've hit on. It's important to me you know that."

"What a coincidence. You're the first Highland man I've kissed."

Our coats brush against each other. "You're sure you don't want to come to my house? We can talk, keep each other warm. No sex."

I grin. "I know how the male mind works. I don't trust you that much yet." Or myself. "The totem is beautiful. I'm honored to be part of it. See you later, Travis."

I bounce down the path, humming a happy tune. At lunch, I eat two bowls of chicken and rice soup with cornbread.

As Christmas nears, red Santa hats appear on tent poles, and pine bunting drapes the main paths throughout Camp Travis. Clusters of holiday lights within reach of the generators wink on at night. Each day Vidal's kids build snowmen outside the church after a student snowball fight marks the end of class. The young children chatter about wish lists. The older ones say Pastor Frank solicits donated toys and clothing from stores in Prodigal and dresses up as an elf. On a sadder note, this marks the first year that Charlie will not be reprising his role as the world's oldest elf.

Teaching full-time, helping with camp chores, and driving others to town leave me tired and ready for sleep at night. I haven't had time to check the bulletin board in the learning center about Danny, and my mind has stayed occupied and engaged. The welcome high I experience from teaching returns. I follow the *Prodigal Gazette* for updates about Jim and me. My disappearance made statewide headlines, but there's no acknowledgment in print of my letter to the cops.

I still ruminate about what Jim did in that B&B the first week. I imagine what people in town must be thinking of him. He has his faults, but he doesn't deserve to be a murder suspect. The focus on him has intensified, but we share culpability for this. We've put each other through so much. Our lives certainly haven't turned out the way we hoped or expected, and when my fog lifts, I may well realize that I bear the brunt—or all—of the responsibility for that. Travis doesn't like that I wrote to the cops. He thinks they will want irrefutable evidence—me in the flesh—before they close the case. Is he right? Could the cops force Jim to confess to something he didn't do? Does that happen in real life? Why would an innocent person confess to murder?

Today the *Gazette* reports that *60 Minutes* may air a piece on me if I'm still missing in March for the Teacher of the Year ceremony. I hope the committee has a runner-up in mind. Let them bestow the award on someone else. More power to her, or him.

By night my mood improves. While I walk to dinner, the snowdrifts lie on the earth so peacefully, in air so fresh, that the world seems a silver-painted carnival left to silence. Even with a thin sliver of moon, I sense a pale radiance from the snow, from the very earth herself, and from the stars, tiny suspended drops of quicksilver.

I fix a plate and take a seat near the roaring bonfire. I'm glad Wilbur convinced me to try deer meat weeks ago; the venison tonight is grilled to perfection. I sop up juice from the baked beans with bread. I love Bambi's musky, wild game taste, but I still avert my eyes when the hunters return from the forest with their kills. The carcasses with their lifeless eyes hang so otherworldly when they have yet to be field-stripped.

My days of quinoa, steamed vegetables, kale, baked fish, and zucchini noodles are a distant memory. My increased caloric intake has been more than offset by hauling water daily, washing clothes by hand, gathering and chopping firewood, and other chores that modern technology everywhere else handles with the push of a button. I feel stronger, and my clothes fit looser than before, and to be honest, I always hated quinoa and kale. I don't miss the *de rigueur* food trends of the suburbs.

After dinner, I excuse myself. I want to see Travis and walk toward his tiny house, but I learn he's working late again. The thought of curling up with a good book and falling asleep in my bed (I've come to call my sleeping bag my bed) sounds like the next best option. I'm rereading *Of Mice and Men*, near the final scene with George and Lenny. It always makes me cry. Most books in the lending library are classics, romance, or dystopian novels. I love teaching the Highland kids, but eight hours of sleep sounds decadent. This Friday night feels like the start of a rare weekend off back in Prodigal after a sixty-hour work week at Hudson High.

I never would have thought it possible, but I feel settled here. I've adapted to the cold and possess the knowledge and resources to maintain a predictable and habitable temperature in my tent. No more frozen socks. No more jumping jacks or sugar infusions. That, but more importantly, I'm a teacher again.

Travis and Frank were right.

153

I make a pit stop at the commodes, and the door to the one nearest the woods is once again open. Maybe he keeps it that way for ventilation while he's away. The same few personal items, minus the walking stick, line the rim of the toilet; only the food wrappers have changed. I leave a note: *My name is Susan. I'm the new teacher in the Highlands. Your origami horse is beautiful. You are quite talented. I'd like to talk with you. Please join me for breakfast in camp, tomorrow at nine.*

AN UNEXPECTED VISITOR

I return to my little blue tent, unzip the flap, and scream.

A man is sitting on my sleeping bag, his side to me, hands on his knees, a yellow plastic flashlight beside him. He turns, and I look into the eyes of my husband.

"Hello, Susan."

He looks at me with a pained expression, then averts his eyes.

He looks scared.

I feel paralyzed, as if my feet are ankle-deep in the ground. I remove my wool cap and comb my hair with my fingers. I don't know why I do this, nor do I know what to say.

He looks thinner, paler, older. There are bags under his eyes. He rubs his left wrist with his right hand, a nervous tell since college. He looks up, and this time, his brown eyes linger on mine.

"Sorry to frighten you. I would have been here hours ago, in the daylight, but I got lost. You look how I feel. How are you?"

I have no reply for that. "Did Marjorie Keller tell the police about me?"

He looks perplexed, and with good reason: he's never met her. "I was shopping near the quad in Prodigal when I heard someone call your name. Maybe it was her. A commotion by the large tent drew a crowd. I saw someone in a hurry push a shopping cart toward the parking lot. I looked closer and saw you run past me, not ten yards away." His lips pinch together. "Imagine my surprise when you knocked on the door of that old school bus."

I remember running past shoppers. He must have been one of them. He waits for me to say something, anything, but I don't.

"The crowd shielded you from the cop. I approached him, ready to say you were very much alive and in the bus parked by the quad so the detectives would stop harassing me. They're certain I murdered you and buried your body in the woods. I tapped the cop on the shoulder, even opened my mouth . . . but changed my mind. I walked to my car and waited for the bus to pull out. I followed it to the base of Mount Prodigal and turned around—"

"But that was weeks ago."

Jim nods, looking sheepish. "To be honest, I was afraid."

"Of what?"

More wrist rubbing. "Of this place. What I might find."

That's Jim. That used to be me. "You should have driven up here earlier. It would have simplified things for you."

Now it's my turn to wait for him to say something. Anything.

He rocks on my bed and seems lost in thought, as if searching for the right words. "I'm not sure, other than it seemed like *I* should be the one to find you. If I told the police you were here, they might try to force you to return to clear up the mystery of your disappearance. The note said you were following a lead on Danny. I didn't want to put you in that position."

"I said other things in that note . . ."

His hand starts to move to his wrist, then stops. "None of which are true, but the cops think I buried your body somewhere in the woods."

"I didn't plan to stay here overnight, much less for weeks."

"We're *not* at each other's throats all the time. I *don't* hate you. And I certainly don't want you *out of the way*." He lowers his voice. "There is no other woman, and I don't want a divorce."

"I didn't intend for you to be a suspect. For something you're not guilty of, that is."

His eyes narrow as he tries to get a read on me. "Since you've been gone, I've had time to think about things and our time together. I want you back."

When I don't respond, he clears his throat. "When you didn't return, I tried to call—"

That pushes a button. "Three times. The first time, you hung up. Then two brief, angry messages. Not much of an effort after thirty-four years of marriage."

"I called many other times as the weeks passed. I wasn't able to leave messages."

He may be telling the truth. I didn't return his early calls, kept my iPhone in the Faraday bag, and then threw it in the lake. "Why didn't you file the missing persons report? My co-workers were more worried about me than you. Why?"

He looks down at his hands, then back up at me. "I wish I had. It might have taken some of the heat off me. I understand your anger over that, but the note said you were following a lead. You didn't indicate where and you didn't return my calls."

I mull that over. There's truth in it. "So, how did you track me here?"

"I never heard you talk of hurting yourself, but you wrote *If I don't return, your problem is solved*, and I began to think your words might have a . . . darker meaning."

"That doesn't explain how you found me."

"Your bedroom. Next thing I know, the cops are at the door, and I'm their suspect. They wanted to know the same thing—why hadn't I called? I said we had a fight, and you left to search for our son. When I admitted we've been having problems, that convinced them of my guilt. One of them found your note. They accused me of everything from spousal abuse to kidnapping to murder."

"Finding me must be a relief for you."

He doesn't reply.

"What were you doing in that bed-and-breakfast the week you called in sick?"

A wind kicks up outside the tent, and Jim hugs himself, clearly unaccustomed to the cold and ill at ease on my bed. He looks at me, embarrassed. "You read the article in the *Gazette*?"

I nod. "We have a laptop here."

He clears his throat and struggles to find a comfortable position. "The detectives questioned me in the living room, and I acted like an uncooperative dick to ensure they took me downtown."

"So they didn't go into my bedroom?"

"No. I had a hunch that might be the last thing you wanted. And I had no idea what you kept in there."

It makes sense. If they had, they would have known exactly where to find me. In his own weird way, Jim protected me.

"They kept me in that interrogation room so long I began to question what's real. They twisted my words. Painted the bleakest vision of what prison would be if I didn't admit my guilt. They threw out all sorts of wild scenarios. It continued all night; they asked the same damn questions a hundred different ways. I had no food or drink, no bathroom breaks. I wanted out of that damn room so much, I was ready to agree to anything. Thank God Larry arrived when he did. He gave me grief for speaking to them without him present."

"What kinds of wild scenarios?"

"Like I had something to do with Danny's disappearance." He's about to continue, but checks himself. More wrist rubbing. "They didn't have enough to arrest me, so Larry drove me home after the cops told me not to leave town. At home, Linda crossed the street and said two policemen had walked the perimeter of our house with a dog. She asked if you were okay because she hasn't seen you for so long. I didn't answer because it's none of her business. She looked at me like I was a monster."

"Linda is quite the nosy neighbor."

"I used a bolt cutter on your padlock. I didn't want them to return with a search warrant without knowing what you kept in there, in case there was anything I needed to hide. I would have kept it locked, but I thought I had no choice."

"I would have done the same if I were in your shoes."

Jim's face softens. "I had goosebumps. I couldn't believe my eyes. Notes written directly on the walls. State and country maps. Color-coded pushpins with strings linking sightings with timelines. Lists of verified and unsubstantiated sightings. Sticky notes everywhere, even on the ceiling over the bed. A box of case files from the private investigators, including one you hired without my knowledge. Then 'Mount Highland' circled in red ink. I removed every clue that could lead them to the Highlands and burned it.

"I read your notes," Jim says. "You drove to this place alone and had the new PI focus his search in Prodigal. Then months later, I see you run by on your way to that bus."

"How did you know this was my tent?"

"I followed piano music to a clearing where I met a woman I heard someone call Judy. I said I was a friend of yours. She was initially skeptical but said to follow her since you live close to her. She didn't like me entering when she saw you weren't here, but I was freezing and promised not to disturb anything. And I didn't. Disturb anything."

"You still haven't answered my question. Why the B&B?"

He cups his hands to blow on them, which shields his face from mine. "I was distraught. It was an emotional time for me, too. I walked around the house, but everything reminded me of you. I couldn't sleep. I had to get away, so I lied about the flu and called in sick. I climbed in the car and drove until I happened upon that little place on Overlook Road. The one we talked about staying in but never did."

That had been in happier times. It's a romantic place, a lovers' getaway. "You stayed there by yourself?"

He gives me a sideways glance. "You've been here two months, and you ask me that?"

"Yep."

He sighs. "I went there alone to think things through and returned to work the next Monday."

"So, did you?"

He looks confused, nervous. "Did I what?"

"Think things through."

He shifts his weight on my bed. "Before we get into that, tell me what you've been doing . . . and why you're still here."

I summarize Danny's time in the Highlands and my decision to stay.

A feeble smile crosses Jim's face as he looks around my tent. He picks up a corner of my sleeping bag and lets it fall from his hand. "You can't stand the cold. You must really hate life with me to stay here. I understand that part, but I'm shocked you walked away from your students and your career."

I level my gaze at him. "You threw a cup at my head and screamed for me to leave, remember? And don't use my students to guilt me into coming home. It won't work."

"I was angry. And wrong."

I don't answer. I let his apology sink in.

He breaks the silence. This time his tone changes. "What are you trying to prove with this, and to whom?"

I have no answer for that. Yet.

"I'm trying to find our son. This is the best way."

Jim shakes his head. "He's gone. If he's alive, he wants no part of us. We've had no contact with him since he left. Come home. We can't change the past."

I shake my head. "I have to see him one more time. Nothing's changed between us, other than you know where I am. In some weird way, I'm learning about myself here. Remembering more. Some good, some bad." I fold my arms. "I'm staying."

The uncomfortable silence lands between us with a thud.

From the look on his face before he turns away, it's safe to say he's frustrated and hurt.

"Earlier, you said you were thinking things through. In the B&B."

He nods. "I don't want a divorce. We share so much history. We've been through too much together. We love each other."

"That's not enough."

"When things were good, they were great. Let's not throw everything away after all these years. We made the decision for Danny to leave—"

"No, *we* didn't. You kept your mouth shut that day, like you always do. *I* was the one who told him to leave. And you've blamed me ever since. Have you any idea how shitty that makes me feel? It's been building up every day since. I hate myself for it. There are times when I *do* think the world would be better if I were gone." My face feels hot, and when I rub my forehead, I wipe tears from my eyes.

160

He reaches out for my hand, but I shake my head. "We've become two strangers who share the same kitchen and garage."

I shush him before he can say sleeping apart was my decision. "At first, we reached a weird sort of balance, similar to peace, but not quite. Then we became that couple in *War of the Roses*, but rather than try to kill each other, we ignored each other. Our house is divided, the Mason-Dixon Line runs through it. We inhabited different halves. We ate and slept at different times. We lost interest in the things we had in common."

He watches and waits while I root in my backpack for a tissue. "The emotional commitment we made to each other when we married changed. We hated each other on bad days and tolerated each other on good ones. I grew numb to survive, to exist. In a way, it's a relief to be exempt from feeling. But I have memory gaps."

Jim's ears perk. "From the hospital?"

"Don't blame me again for not bonding—"

He waves his arms like he's ready to scream, but stops. "I'm not. It wasn't your fault. It wasn't anyone's fault. You almost bled to death on your way to the hospital. It was an act of God—" His voice breaks with emotion. "I can't imagine what you went through."

I feel a dark presence behind a wall that stretches as far as my eyes can see, hidden in fog. The skin on my arms starts to crawl.

"You begged me to get help after Danny's birth, and I refused." I look down and see my fingers digging at a cuticle again. I lace them together. "I never said this to you or anyone else before, but I lived in terror for a year after his birth. It wasn't my regular depression. I saw and heard things that weren't there. The voices said you and the doctors were plotting to take Danny and lock me in an institution. I entertained killing myself or running away with him. The voices eventually stopped." I find myself cradling my belly again and raising my hands to wipe my face.

Jim looks down at his folded hands in his lap and expels a big breath. "I had no idea."

161

I dread what I'm about to say. "Did I do anything horrific to you, Danny, or anyone else that year?"

He pauses, thinking. "No, I don't think so."

I feel faint. I lie down on the bed and close my eyes. Try to regulate my breathing. Use my grounding techniques. I don't know how long we pass the time in silence. At some point, he lies down on my bed, and I can sense him looking my way, but he maintains our new Mason-Dixon Line.

I put an arm over my face. "Being up here, alone with nature, has given me time to reflect. It's been good for me. The big piece is still a mystery, but bits of memory are returning."

"I want to stay with you tonight," Jim says.

I bite my lip. I don't have to think twice. "No. I'd only ruin it."

From his side of the bed, I hear a soft sigh. "Then may I return tomorrow, and we can talk more?"

I look to the aluminum foil sky for an answer but receive no sign. Opening up about the postpartum psychosis lifted a weight. I nod. "How about noon?"

We rise to our knees.

I hand-comb my hair again and ask Jim to take my picture.

He looks at me quizzically. "You hate having your picture taken."

"It's for you to show the police."

I have no clue what type of look this bizarre situation calls for, so I paste on a Mona Lisa smile and flash the peace sign. Stupid of me, but I do.

He looks grateful before the flash blinds me.

"Do you want me to bring food? Something from home?"

I think of medication refills, then realize my body seems to be acclimating pretty well now without them, after the first shitty withdrawal days. Staying busy and active fatigues me, so I sleep okay without Ambien or melatonin. My anxiety and mood improved once I began teaching. My anger and self-loathing surface when I drink too much.

162

I think of the young woman behind the counter at the 7-Eleven. "A pint of Ben and Jerry's Americone Dream."

"Seriously? The woman who wears a sweater in seventy-two-degree weather wants ice cream."

"Something decadent sounds good."

"Deal. I will bring that and something else to help you remember."

Something tells me I must do this on my own. An awkward silence follows. He leans forward—does he want to kiss me?—and I turn away. He crouches to leave and takes another picture of me outside my little blue tent. I escort him to the main path that leads to his car, which he said he parked alongside mine. I tell him to take a picture that shows my Beemer's license plate while he's at it.

I didn't ask about the "something else."

WEARY TO MY BONES

On the walk back, the breeze carries the sound of music to me. I join about twenty Highlanders who have lingered around the Pit after dinner. I take a swig and pass the wine.

A grinning Dora sits down and gives me a wink. "A little birdie told me you had a visit from a gentleman caller."

A Judy-bird.

I make a face. "It's good to know that no matter where in the world one goes, there will always be gossip."

This time she takes a rare sip from the bottle. "I hear tell he's a handsome man." She gives me a nudge and adds in that raspy voice, "Any spicy details you can share with an old lady?"

I raise an eyebrow. It's the first time I've seen her drink alcohol. I warm to her good-natured banter. "No, but I'd like to hear your thoughts on sharing your art expertise with my students."

My students. The thought warms me.

Dora begins to share her ideas for art class while I eat cold leftovers. Tom resumes tickling the ivories after his dinner break. He reminds me of an old lounge singer who loves his gig. He leads a singalong, and Highlanders add logs to the fire.

The flames seem especially alive tonight. They dance and pop and flicker, alternating from yellow to red to orange. Showers of sparks climb high into the night, and smoke billows into the cold clear air, casting shafts of light into the darkness of the woods.

Thoreau was right to simplify life; the world is grander and wider than I ever imagined. We forget about other people and assume that the beauty and wonder of nature will always be present. I allowed myself to wallow in a stale marriage that turned so unhappy I lost myself in work. I had to escape to begin to understand me, even though I'm still a work in progress.

I look up at the sky and feel insignificant. Though it sounds negative, it doesn't feel that way. It's a matter of realigning my world perspective. We are not the center of the world, much less the universe, nor are we its master or mistress. Mother Earth may indeed decide to kick us off one day, and soon, if we continue to mistreat her. If she does, we deserve it.

Someone calls out a song request. A hush settles around the fire. Tom begins a solo in a slow, soft, somber voice. It's a song he's played every night, but each time my mind was off somewhere else. Now that I'm paying attention, I realize it's one of the few songs I know the words to. Dora continues to share her plans for art class. Her words mingle and fall into a natural rhythm with the lyrics.

As Tom sings about being mistaken and confused, Dora says, "I will ask each student what art means to him or her and then ask if they prefer to draw, color, or paint."

When Tom opines about being forsaken and misused, Dora says, "I can organize them by age, interest, or ability. I already have many supplies, so the cost would be minimal."

Tom's voice cracks with emotion as he sings of the weariness of being in a strange land, and then Dora says, "We can discuss the greatest artists of all time; I have illustrated books of almost all the famous paintings and sculptures man has created from past and present cultures."

When Tom croons about shattered dreams, Dora says, "At the end of the course, students submit their artwork, the camp votes for their favorites in each category, and we have prizes. All work can be shared later online in the camp newsletter."

As Tom's voice soars to a dream about flying, Dora's voice rises. "Eventually, we can have our budding artists sell their works in town. Think of the joy and sense of accomplishment that can give a child!"

Dora notices my tears and squeezes my hand.

"'American Tune' is our unofficial anthem, Susan. I used to love singing with that man before . . . we moved here. What do you think of my ideas for class?"

I can't imagine that gravelly voice ever carrying a tune, but the haunting lyrics hijacked my attention, so I pat her hand, turn to Tom, and we listen to the finish.

I wipe tears from my eyes and clap with everyone else. Some whoop and cheer, and others share knowing glances with friends. Tom receives cheers and pats on the back. The song becomes my anthem.

Before I can utter a word of praise for Dora's ideas, frenzied shouts from beyond the edge of darkness shatter the mood.

And then all hell breaks loose.

Highlanders run helter-skelter, some fleeing into the woods. Frightened voices shout warnings that the police are rousting people from their tents.

I lower my wool cap and tighten my hoodie, ready to sprint into the woods and circle back to the tent for my car keys. Dora gently places a hand on my arm to steady me.

Crisscrossing flashlights illuminate the picnic area just before the police arrive with barking dogs, and chaos envelopes the Pit.

Pastor Frank appears, hair out of place, his eyes wide and crazy. Every few feet, he steps in front of a barrel-chested cop to slow the man down. The cop grips the black handle of his steel baton and glares at Frank, who now waves his arms and shouts, "They're handing out fines for fire code violations. They say we can't burn wood in our own stoves!"

People stir around the Pit and form tight groups while others scatter. Some curse the police and shout for them to go back to town.

Frank stands in front of the cop. "Sergeant Decker, you can't stop us from using stoves in winter. I was there for the ruling in city hall. The court order exempts Highlanders." He's about to lay a hand on the cop's arm, but a police dog snarls and snaps at him, its hackles up and spittle dripping from its black muzzle.

Decker hands him a crumpled piece of paper. "Things change, Frank. This is public land, and you're burning a public

166

forest. Highlanders can no longer lawfully cut down the forest for fuel. The fire marshal ordered a sweep for any and all violations. We will write citations based on their findings. Each offense carries a one-hundred-dollar fine, plus court costs." He loops his thumbs over his wide black belt. "Remember the fire up here? Pure negligence."

"That was over a year ago. And fires happen in Prodigal," Frank says. The air between them is thick with tension.

Highlanders are shouting. *You don't have the right to enter our homes!* and *Go back to town!* Flossie's screams of police harassment precede ones of *Get off our land!* and *This is our turf!* There are chants: *Fuck the town! Fuck the police!*

The tight little groups swell into a mob that advances on the cops and firemen. The police draw their weapons and form a compact circle, the German shepherds their first line of defense.

Highlanders brandish knives and sticks; a few produce handguns and hunting rifles. Bert emerges from the forest wearing a coonskin hat and holding what looks like an AR-15. If someone panics and pulls a trigger . . .

An out-of-breath Corey appears with Travis. who waves his hands and shouts for the mob to stand down.

Decker points to the paper in Frank's hand, who passes it to Travis. "It's all there in black and white, Travis. If we return and find green wood being burned or evidence of trees cut down, we will write more citations, maybe shut you down early. It's that simple."

A man shouts to Travis that a cop stole his propane tank.

I read fear in Decker's eyes. I think he wants nothing more than to lead his officers and firemen down the mountain to safety. This could become a battlefield.

The hills, now dark and foreboding, are thick with timber as far as my eyes can see. We're miles from civilization. A feeling of isolation washes over me as the entire camp—over a hundred strong—collectively holds its breath, ready to act.

Travis strides closer to the circle of police. "If your men confiscate our property or damage our possessions, you are in violation of our Fourth Amendment rights of protection from illegal search and seizure under the Constitution, as well as the Bill of Rights for the Homeless Act of 2013. A nearby state won their case last month."

Decker pushes his hat back on his head and takes a step forward. "That's the thing, Travis. The Feds are now leaving it up to each state to decide how to deal with you people. And the Governor just turfed it to the city government in Prodigal to decide what to do with you."

"But we won a million-dollar court settlement for subsidized housing, good for a year. We have six months to go, and Prodigal hasn't honored their end of the deal."

"Take the matter up with the city council."

"You can count on it, Decker."

A sly grin spreads over the Sergeant's face. "And those abandoned warehouses on State Street you wanted to rehab? Sold yesterday to a developer."

Travis takes a step forward until a police dog bares its fangs.

"We burn only deadwood up here, and you know it, Decker. And there are hundreds of trees earmarked for removal with red ribbons. We can help pave the way for your goddamn ski resort by removing some of those trees and burning them for heat. Why confiscate propane tanks and criminalize using stoves in winter?"

"Every tank confiscated tonight has been deemed unsafe by order of the fire department."

"Don't be tools for Prodigal. Don't dirty your hands. Don't do their hatchet work."

"I have an order to carry out."

"The county has six animal shelters, two in Prodigal alone, but none for people. We need shelters. We have pregnant women here."

"That's not my problem."

Highlanders within earshot brandish their weapons and hurl more insults. Travis calls for silence.

"It's everyone's problem. Prodigal rousted us from the streets and the park when business owners complained. Fines

168

don't fix anything. Closing us down doesn't address the problem. Another tent city will pop up somewhere else. Close that down, and another will take its place, and so on until the government finally acknowledges we exist."

I wonder why Travis stays on this long soapbox. He has to know that Decker can't do anything about this, and it's not like him to whine. Then I see Corey off to one side, recording it all on a hand-held camera. The cops with their weapons drawn, the canines' fangs bared. Talk about bad optics.

Travis rips the notice in half. "You may think you and the good people of Prodigal are better than Highlanders, but you're not. You know why you look right through us on the street like we're invisible? Because you're scared. You're one job loss, one major health problem, one divorce, a couple missed rent payments, or an eviction notice away from being one of us."

"Look, Travis. It's nothing personal, but if you try to prevent my officers and these firefighters from doing their jobs, we will make arrests and use force if we have to—"

"The town agreed," Travis shouts, addressing the crowd, "to provide subsidized housing for one year, but only three Highlanders have moved into town housing in six months. The clock is ticking, Decker. What about all the others? There's enough settlement money to house fifty-six people—"

"Then I suggest you hire a better lawyer. How many residents have you sent to the homeless shelters on the other side of the state? *That* clock is ticking," the barrel-chested sergeant says, motioning to his crew that it's time to continue their sweep. His eyes dart to Travis, as if asking permission.

Travis smiles as recognition dawns across his face. "So that's what this is about. Trying to make life so unbearable that we give up our freedoms and agree to a forced mass move, over a hundred miles away. Prodigal never intended to keep their end of the bargain because they don't want us in their backyard." He turns to address the crowd "The town is also fighting in court to deny a building permit for an upscale retirement center because of the NIMBYs on the town council."

Travis raises a hand in the air and gradually lowers it one rung at a time while he speaks. "So in Prodigal, business profits come first, then animals, then the three Highlanders who've been approved, then, maybe, well-to-do elderly people, but nothing for the three hundred people of the Highlands."

Decker smiles and tells his men to holster their sidearms. "I see that camera now, Travis. Well played. Make sure your boy also gets a shot of your people drawing down on law enforcement, and I want to see permits today for every one of those weapons. We are going to do our job now and finish the court-ordered inspection. We don't want any trouble." Decker says, "I am serious. Tell your people to stand down, or they will face arrest."

"You don't have to carry out this order, Decker. It's wrong, and you know it. We want to live in peace, but we must have a place to stay. I will speak to city hall about this."

Decker puts his hands on his waist. "Go ahead. Tell them. They'll only listen to you."

I see Travis form a response, then think better of it.

Decker calls out, "Until further notice, no wood stoves are to be used in the Highlands. Not for cooking or warmth. Charcoal fires are permissible for cooking grills and outside fires. If your propane tanks have been modified or do not meet industry standards, Prodigal is within its rights to seize those deemed a potential fire hazard."

Angry voices fill the night air, and the mob begins to close ranks. The cops collectively step back and resume shooter stances.

Travis steps forward, waving his arms. "NO! Stand down. We will get through this. We will work out a compromise. Everyone with a wood-burning stove or propane tank, meet with me in the church at seven tomorrow. No violence tonight. Cooler heads, everyone."

Frank echoes the sentiment and spreads his arms. The mob stops.

"One other thing," Decker says as he reaches into a coat pocket to produce a photo. "A woman from Prodigal went missing a couple months ago. Her name is Susan Crusoe, age sixty, five foot two, a hundred pounds, blue eyes, shoulder-length brown hair with blond highlights. She drives a blue BMW, last seen in town the other day. We have reason to suspect this woman is here. Is she?"

Dora and Flossie watch as I angle toward the woods, away from the Pit.

He studies the picture for what seems an overly long time before he hands it back. "She is not here. If she was last seen in Prodigal, I suggest you search there."

"Our witness thinks she was in the company of Highlanders. If she is here, I need to be certain it is of her own free will."

"Now you accuse us of kidnapping? Do Gilroy's dirty work if you must, and leave the mountain. I have more than enough lives here to care for than to worry about some missing woman from Prodigal."

Decker's eyes narrow. "We're gonna ask around while we finish our inspection. Just in case."

The Highlanders reluctantly break ranks while Decker and his men circulate my picture and ask questions. The bonfire is now reduced to smoldering ash, the music has long stopped, and the temperature continues to drop. What do I do when someone rats me out? Flossie has been cool to me at best, and hostile at her worst. Will it be her? George?

When they find my car, I'm screwed. I feel like a fugitive, but I've committed no crime. I don't trust them. If I try to assure them no one is forcing me to stay here, they may insist on interrogating me at the station, asking all sorts of private questions about my disappearance and my marriage. I'm not ready to go back. I may not ever be.

I slip into the forest and circle back through the woods to my tent. As I'm about to run inside and grab my keys, I hear voices approaching. I retreat into the pines to observe from the darkness of the forest.

"Anyone here?" a burly cop announces before he opens my tent flap. He looks inside to find it empty, then moves on down the path toward Judy and George's. I keep watch for what seems like an hour and listen to voices fade until all I sense is the heartbeat of the forest. Then a sudden flurry of movement to my left makes me jump. I turn to see deer scattering into the deep woods. They must have wandered near my hiding spot when I was upwind of them.

It's too late to flee the mountain by car, so I hide in my tent. Someone else has been inside. The colored string I placed between the flap and wall is on the floor where it should have been after the cop peered inside, but others are moved as well. My Movado watch and a bag of Snickers Minis are gone. My car keys and cash are safe in my hidey-hole, but I was lazy; I forgot to stow my watch when I buried my cash and didn't want to disturb the ground again.

Flossie mentioned my watch on several occasions.

Are my initial fears about this place coming true? Have the Highlanders been conning me from the beginning? Will Prodigal make good on their threats to close this place early?

My anger festers, and it takes hours to fall asleep.

I float on a cloud and fly back in time again.

One of the seemingly endless parade of therapists over the years suggested we maintain journals. Danny and Jim penned their thoughts for a few days, then quit.

At first, I thought it a pointless exercise, but for some reason, it provides a small comfort. Journaling helps me grapple with the big picture microscopically, or maybe it places boundaries on my challenges with Danny. It strikes a blow against the powerlessness I feel when not writing. It works for me better than listening to war stories from other parents, which intensifies the sense of hopelessness I face with Danny. For the last year, my primary diary offers time to reflect on life in Prodigal, my marriage and relationships, what brings joy and sorrow, and my bucket list.

I plan to give the second journal to Danny. That one has proven more challenging. I threw out my initial attempts, which were angry and focused on the pain he'd caused Jim and me. Now I write to Danny about what he means to me, my hopes and fears for him, my own regrets and aspirations.

Both journals date back almost two decades and fill several white English comp notebooks in what Jim, in happier times, called my perfect teacher's handwriting. Palmer method, of course.

Tonight, a different nightmare recurs. In this one, Jim and I separate when Danny is fifteen, and he chooses to live with his father. It never happened, but the dream is always the same. Pulsating beeps echo in my ears while Danny accuses me of leaving him in the hospital after he was born. He complains I was never there for him. That I was too absorbed in my career to care about his troubles. That I never should have given up on him. Then he curses and pushes me away while the beeps pierce my ears so much that I cover them with my hands.

Misreading this as me not wanting to listen to him, Danny pushes me away. Pushes.

Don't push me. Please don't push me away! No! I cry.

Then the same sick drowning sensation recurs. I don't think it has anything to do with my son, but I'm not certain. A shadowy image tries to take shape in my mind, but I fight it. I'm afraid if I face it, I will die.

Danny slams a nondescript door in my face. I don't know where we are, but I sense water nearby, then I'm back in the NICU staring at him in the incubator. The beeps surpass human tolerance, and I wake up in a cold sweat, crying and holding my belly.

This time I return to sleep quickly.

In the next dream, I relive an exchange from last year with my former best friend. I remember the day well. A picture-perfect, resort-weather afternoon in Prodigal. We sit smoking outside the teacher's lounge after an easy half-day at Hudson High.

Sandy, a math teacher five years my junior, brags about her adult children and their Ivy League GPAs. She asks about Danny, unaware that I kicked him out the week before. I hadn't told anyone, and it was eating at me, so I spill my guts to my friend about the night that changed our lives.

She stiffens, and the area around her mouth tightens.

My radar goes up.

A frown forms. She looks at me, flabbergasted. "How could you do that?"

"What do you mean? You know what we've been through the last eighteen years. The treatment centers. The drugs, the stealing. The run-ins with the police."

Sandy crushes the end of her cigarette in the plastic ashtray we bring outside. She exhales smoke through her nose and holds her head high while she shakes her head. "I would never *give up* on my children like that. Where is he now?"

"I don't know. By the way, he's thirty-three."

Her eyes grow wide. "So he's out on the street somewhere? I could never do that to one of my kids, no matter their age or what they may have done." Her mouth falls open. "I don't know what to say, Susan. I'm shocked."

Her boys were straight-A students in high school who never posed a problem bigger than the occasional detention for impertinence.

I've felt like a bag of raw emotions all week, and now my friend has blindsided me. I feel like I've been slapped in the face.

Sandy has no such difficulty. "Let me get this straight. You put your only child, who has substance abuse and mental health issues, out on the street?"

It takes all my will to look at her. I don't answer. I remind myself to breathe.

She leans away from me; her face lemons in distaste. "I can't believe you did this."

I stand and say in a low voice, "I resent the insinuation that I'm a bad mom. You haven't walked in my shoes."

I grind my cigarette into the ashtray. "Your devotion to family obviously doesn't extend to husbands. You divorced a functioning alcoholic after five years of marriage for not seeking help sooner. You got what you wanted all along—the big house, primary custody of the kids, a boob job, and a fat alimony check every month. You dumped your husband. I remember *all* the events before your divorce. the man on the side. You put your children through a contentious divorce for your financial security. Everything so well calculated on your part, or so you thought. But the man on the side? Long gone for greener pastures. He didn't want to deal with your kids."

When she opens her mouth, I raise my hand to silence her. "When I told Danny to leave, it was after eighteen years of failed treatment programs and therapies. When you cheated on your ex and divorced him at the first sign of trouble, he was twenty-eight."

She lights up another cigarette and blows smoke into the air through pursed lips. Her arms are folded. "You're being so unfair. That's not what happened. You're bending the truth."

I stare into her eyes. "Does putting me down help you feel better about yourself? Don't ever preach to me."

I hear beeping as I walk to my car, battered by waves of guilt.

That was the last time we spoke.

A few neighbors have inquired about Danny's absence during the last year. We say he's living on his own now, but they've witnessed the police cars, the front yard scenes. Their expressions speak louder than words—the averted eyes, the halting voices—they want to know the whole story.

Did I commit a disastrous act when I ordered Danny to leave? Like Sandy did with her ex-husband, did I wash my hands of Danny too soon? The events of that day have swollen to such mythic proportions that they're blocking the sun.

Great storms of remorse and anger have washed over me since then, an ocean of sorrow, until the guilt seized control.

As a child, I believed monsters with sharp fangs and long claws were hiding in my closet at night and lurking under the bed, waiting to grab my ankle. I no longer believe in monsters, but I believe in ghosts. Not the cheesy ones in B movies or dime novels that rattle chains in Gothic mansions. Ghosts don't haunt places; they haunt people. We create our own ghosts. Each is a facet of ourselves, our guilt, our regrets, and our grief. We all have them. They may not all be of our own creation, but in the end, they find us just the same.

Is the ghost that haunts me one I created?

One thing I know: mine is here with me. I sense it behind me and in my dreams, but when I turn to face it, it flees into the shadows. The solitude on this mountain and partial return to nature help free my mind. In a world where success is mere survival, maybe I can drag my ghost into the light and, if not defeat it, at least make peace with it.

After I exiled Danny, teaching became more of a refuge, a safe harbor. My twelve-hour days at Hudson High kept me sane and functioning—until the ghost invaded.

I saw myself rattling around our empty house and thought of Danny. I saw his features every time I looked at Jim. Both became collateral damage, courtesy of my demon ghost. I didn't know what to do with his clothes and belongings, so I kept his bedroom loft the way he left it—after I flushed the drugs, replaced the insulation, and secured the loose plank.

I wake up in a sweat to see dawn break clear and cold on the mountain, wondering how I can go on like this.

BACK AND FORTH

It's the week before Christmas, and class is on hiatus for the holidays. I sit by my fire, sipping strong coffee made from boiled snow. A low fog hugs the treetops, and hawks circle the snow-covered valley in long, slow arcs. One spots prey and dives, its talons out like landing gear.

I'm on my second cigarette, writing in my journal about Jim's visit. In the one I keep for Danny, I reflect on my halcyon college days.

I have the rest of the morning before Jim returns and feel a sudden need for a woman's perspective. I choose to brave the rickety bridge that leads to the Rainbow Camp rather than the safer one and find it's not as frightening the second time.

The first people I encounter are two elderly men pushing wheelbarrows of charcoal toward the picnic tables. While they leisurely stack the bags near the firepit, I hear a shriek. I turn to see one of my students running to meet me. Brianne's arms are open wide. In one hand, she carries a piece of paper that flaps in the breeze.

I bend down and brace for impact. She almost knocks me down.

She's out of breath. "Miss Crusoe, Miss Crusoe! I drew this for you!"

Brianne's drawing is awash with vibrant, warm colors and depicts a small, smiling figure as the centerpiece, holding hands with two grinning women—her adoptive mothers, Kim and Penny. One has short dark hair, and the larger figure holds a rainbow flag aloft. In the foreground, a smiling dog jumps at the threesome, and a small row of tents occupies the background. A sun high in the blue sky sends slanted golden rays to the ground. The grass below their feet is vivid green.

"Thank you, Brianne! This is really good! May I hang it in our classroom?"

"Yes. I'm gonna be an artist when I grow up."

I straighten her cap and think of Dora. "Well then, I have just the art teacher for you."

"Okay."

She puts her tiny hand in mine, and we walk to camp, swinging our arms back and forth. "I think your idea to be an artist is a terrific idea."

Off to the right, I hear a guttural sound and see Barbara struggling with a two-person crosscut saw.

"Brianne, do you mind if I talk with Barbara for a while?"

Brianne dashes off toward a group of children swinging on an old tractor tire suspended from a pine branch. "Bye, Miss Crusoe!"

Barbara eyes my approach. "The children love you. From what Theo tells me, you're one hell of a teacher."

She faces a stack of trimmed deadwood trunks and hefts one onto a pair of weathered sawhorses, then pauses to wipe her brow and arch her back.

"Looks like you could use some help."

She nods and tosses me a pair of work gloves. "Only if you wear those. The saw handles will fill your palms with splinters in a heartbeat. Our damn chainsaw needs a new carburetor, and who knows when it'll be fixed. I told Travis at the meeting we can't constantly be buying bags of charcoal. Fuck Decker and the horse he rode in on. Travis didn't like it, but the decision of our council to burn deadwood was unanimous."

It takes time for us to develop a rhythm, since she's much stronger and taller than me. That, and the dull blade binds often, especially in the pine knots. We finish one length, and I stack the sections while she lubricates the teeth of the blade with a soaked rag.

"There's not enough naval jelly in the world to keep this old blade rust-free up here," she says as she slaps the rag on the end of a sawhorse. She motions for me to help pick up the next section. "But you didn't come to help me work or hear me wax poetic about naval jelly, did you?"

I almost lose my grip on the trunk, which would have landed on my foot. "No, I didn't. But I'm happy to help." Once we've situated it on the horses, I pat it and say, "I had a visitor last night."

Barbara turns to me. "Your son?"

"My husband."

She seems to deflate. "And you're still here. How mad was he?"

"Why do you think he'd be angry? Or that I'd be gone?"

She smiles. "You're not the only one who reads the Gazette." She points to herself. "Twenty-year subscriber when I lived in Prodigal. Still print the New York Times crossword and complete it every day, in pen. Tell me about the meeting."

Two women wearing matching white parkas walk by, holding hands. The four of us acknowledge each other.

I grab my end of the saw while Barbara eyeballs the next cut. The blade bounces off the gnarled bark until we establish a groove. I recap the highlights of last night's conversation while we work.

"It was awkward and tense. He was scared about coming here alone, especially at night."

I send the blade back to her, and she quickly sends it back.

"He didn't know what he'd find when he arrived. He wasn't angry. More hurt or disappointed. And not in a condescending or patronizing way."

I send the blade back her way as sawdust flies from the track.

"Did he rat you out to the cops?" she asks, sending the blade back with a longer, stronger stroke. I inhale sawdust and stop to cough.

"On the contrary, I suggested he take a picture of me to show the police that I'm alive and well. Travis wants Jim's name cleared. It's the right thing to do." I send the crosscut blade back to her side of the horses.

"You believe his story about the hotel?" With great force, she muscles the blade through the last of a stubborn knot.

179

I feel sweat on my brow, and my arm spasms. "All I know is the cops think he murdered me and disposed of my body."

I fail to keep the blade in motion this time.

"The picture will put an end to that."

Barbara hefts the saw back on her own power.

"How'd you feel when you saw him?" She quickly pushes the saw back to my side.

"He scared the shit out of me. I walked into my tent, and there he was." I grunt, now in a full sweat, and my biceps are burning. With one final push, the blade slices through the trunk. It lands with a thud on the frozen ground.

We drop the saw and remove our gloves to wipe our brows. Barbara hands me a bottled water and opens one for herself. We lean against the sawhorses. A real-life Mutt and Jeff.

"Did you have sex?"

The question surprises me, but she quickly outs my shock as feigned, and I laugh. "No, we just talked. But he asked to spend the night. The last thing I wanted was to have to shoot that down."

"When was the last time you two had sex?"

My laughter ends.

Barbara doesn't back down. "I know his stay at the hotel bugs the shit out of you. You're dying to know if he's having an affair. I assume you came here to get another woman's opinion, other than dear sweet Dora. My question's relevant."

"It's been a long time." I mention that I'd moved into the guest bedroom but deflect the question.

We stand in silence until she hoists the next trunk into position, and I don the gloves again.

"I think you need to get off your high horse about whether he fucked another woman in that hotel room. You're both adults. He's a man. Cut them off, and it's any port in the storm." She sends the saw hurtling my way with such force the handle pushes my hand into my chest.

"It's not like I'm shacked up here with another man."

I send the saw back to her with extra force.

She grins. "You could be."

180

I stop the blade and stare at her. My thoughts turn to Travis. I feel my face redden. "What's that supposed to mean?"

"I may be a heterosexual turned lesbian, but I'm not naïve in the ways of breeders. I see how Travis looks at you. He's a good man. The Highlanders are his life. He's been alone since his wife was killed by a drunk driver, an off-duty cop from Prodigal. He did community service and is still on the force."

I turn away to process this. He must hate dealing with the police.

Barbara tilts her head and winks. "A warm body to curl up with makes these long winter nights more bearable. You know he built those two tiny homes and lives in one of them? All the comforts of home, just smaller. He's good-looking and has his shit together. For a man."

"I'm trying to simplify my life, not complicate it." With a mighty effort, I grunt and push the saw back her way. It only manages to go halfway before the teeth bind in a stubborn knot.

She studies my face and smiles. "You can't simplify life."

We wrench the saw free, and she applies more naval jelly to the blade.

"Your husband doesn't know what you've been up to or who you've been with for months, either. He had no idea what or who he might find here. But the fact is, he entered your home— your tent—without permission. That says something."

I didn't think twice about it. "But he was cold and frightened."

She slaps the rag back down. "You were scared shitless your first day here, weren't you?"

I feared for my life and passed out. "A little."

"Did you walk into someone's tent uninvited?"

"Of course not, but he knew it was my tent. Judy walked him to it."

She looks from the blade to me. "You could have been sharing your tent with another man. A hundred bucks says he went through your things. Do you always make excuses for him?"

181

I have no ready answer, so we slide the saw back in the groove and find a rhythm again. We cut through two more sections in silence until only one remains. We hoist it up and my biceps lock in protest, burning.

We get a track established in the dead wood, and this last one cuts easier. We're both huffing and puffing, pleased to finish the job.

"Double or nothing on the hundred bucks. He wants you to come home and start over again."

I nod.

"Something compelled you to leave your home and come here. I'm not convinced it was your son. Remember: you are lucky. You have options. Think long and hard before you make that decision."

She tosses the saw onto the pile of cut logs, and the blade bounces with a twang before it settles on the ground. She curses it.

We stand facing each other, breathing hard and sweating, until she leans against a sawhorse. "Thanks for the help. I'd still be at it if not for you. Least I can do is offer that drink you mentioned after you braved the bridge that first time. Follow me."

I massage my cramped bicep through my coat. "It's eleven o'clock somewhere. Lead the way."

She takes off with such long strides I have to almost trot to keep up. She turns her head and whistles to gain the attention of the elderly men lugging water from the river. "Jeremy, that bunch is ready for tonight. And make sure the chainsaw is fixed ASAP. This about did us in."

He acknowledges with a slow wave.

We walk past their bonfire pit and picnic tables to the semicircle of tents. She invites me inside, one in the middle of the front row, slightly larger than the rest. A single bed takes up one wall of her tent; next to it sits a small table and two chairs, one of which she offers me. From a shelf, she removes two glasses and a bottle of Scotch.

"Want something to eat after that workout? I have today's English muffins but with real butter. My splurge. I draw the line at government cheese, however."

I smile. "Perfect, thanks."

We eat in silence, and she pours two fingers into each glass. She offers me a bottled water, but I like mine neat. Apparently, so does she. She takes the seat across from me and stretches out her long legs. I wolf down a muffin while she eats two.

The Scotch warms my belly. I raise my glass to her. "Nice and smooth."

"I developed a taste for single malts back in the real world, but Chivas is the best I can afford now. Life means adapting to change, doesn't it?"

Right now, I say life is pain. "How did you come to live here?"

She swirls her glass and settles it in her lap. "I put my common-law husband in a coma. After he inflicted an especially bad beating on me. Something in me snapped. He survived but needs nursing-home care for the rest of his life. The house was in his name. The state insisted it be sold to defray the cost of his care. I didn't want the damn thing, anyway. Too many memories. I got off with time served because of his abuse, but nobody would hire me.

"I willingly accepted and lived with the things that could kill me—a violent, gun-collecting, alcoholic male." She shakes her head and takes a sip. "I was young and dumb."

I'm grateful Jim never owned guns, or I would have killed myself by now.

"Growing up, I felt attracted to other women, but I forced myself to forget a major part of me. It took a lot of therapy before I could accept I was not the problem. So I unlearned all the bullshit people fed me and came out. I didn't want to quit my profession, but I couldn't find a job. I needed a place to stay, and this place welcomed me as their de facto nurse."

"I can't picture you as a victim."

She nods. "I was a different person then, looking for a man to care for me after my parents died. He was a con artist who preyed on my vulnerabilities." She puffs out her chest and laughs. "God help the fucker who tries it now."

We share a smile. "What did you do to him?"

"Hit him with a baseball bat signed by his favorite player. Shattered it in two pieces on his head."

She refills our glasses, and we drink silently until I break it. "The most dangerous thing at our house is what I see in the mirror. I destroyed my family."

She turns back to me. "How did you feel right after you kicked Danny out of the house?"

"Enraged, frustrated, scared."

She waits for more that doesn't come. "What else? Be honest." She draws out the last two words and stares.

I feel defensive. If I admit the truth, the world may crack open and swallow me. "Relieved. Like the weight of the world suddenly lifted from my shoulders."

A tiny grin appears on her face. "When I stood over my husband and watched the blood slowly pool onto the carpet, I felt enraged, frustrated, sickened, scared . . . and relieved. Just like you. From that night on, I knew he would never beat me again. Then I dropped the splintered bat and threw up. I thought I killed him. I found a pulse, made sure he had a clear airway, sat him up, wrapped a towel around his head, and applied pressure. I sat on the front porch with him leaning against me, called 911, and lit a cigarette.

"You didn't kill your son. You didn't ruin his life. He made his choices years ago, and he's living with them. If he overdoses and dies tomorrow, that's on him. Not you. You finally took off your momma hat long enough to face him, to challenge him to act like a thirty-three-year-old man. Congratulations. Conflicting feelings mean you're human."

I ask her the time. I have an hour before Jim returns.

"So, your husband visited last night. You sent him home, and he's returning?"

"With Ben and Jerry's ice cream."

Her eyes widen, and she laughs. "Of all the things to ask for."

"It's the thing I miss the most. That, and real butter now. Thanks to you."

We clink glasses. "To each her own. Your hubby plans to take another run at you. Convince you to return home."

I take another sip. "I imagine."

She studies me for some time. "There's something else. Kicking out your son is only part of it."

I feel my face warm. "I don't know what you're talking about."

She taps a finger against her temple. "Neither do I. Trust me, he will use your guilt against you. So you can go back to being chief cook and bottle washer."

I'm going to bring you Ben and Jerry's, and something else.

I frown. "It's not that simple."

I see a sly smile spread behind her glass. "Oh, so he's a complicated man."

"It's not him. We had a decent first talk last night. I can't remember parts of my past, and I hope he can help me with it. I think it has something to do with Danny, and that's why I feel so . . . fucked up."

Barbara puts her glass on the table and leans forward. "I'm sorry, I'm a cynical old lesbian. I didn't mean to impugn your husband's character when I haven't met him. Years of therapy and my anger toward men on occasion breaches the surface. What time period do you think you blocked out?"

I mention the placental abruption, Danny's difficult birth, and my psychosis. She asks all sorts of questions that trigger nothing in me.

"You and I both have PTSD," she says. "My trigger was obvious, and to this day impacts how I perceive and respond to men. I wish I could have helped. Perhaps your husband can. When you do remember, make sure you're not alone."

This gives me shivers. I look at her funny. "Jim wanted, almost insisted, to stay with me last night."

"He was right. I'm serious. It will hit like a tidal wave and drag you under."

I rise from the chair. "I need to get back. You make more sense than the therapists we hired. How'd you get so knowledgeable?"

She takes my empty glass. "Graduate of the school of hard knocks. It also helped to stumble onto an older therapist who didn't have his head up his ass. Thanks for the help today."

She gives me a hug.

"I'm here for you," she says. "Don't be so hard on yourself, or Jim. Do what you need to do to remember. And I mean it— don't be alone when it happens."

I grab Brianne's artwork and double-time it past their campfire, waving to Kim and Penny, who are helping to prepare lunch for the camp. I easily negotiate the rope bridge and follow the winding path east to my tent, my stomach growling in protest after a breakfast of mostly Scotch.

THE SOMETHING ELSE

When I reach my campsite, Jim is huddled at my cold campfire with his back to the wind as he sips a Starbucks coffee. Two paper bags are between his brown Timberland boots.

"You're early," I say.

"Can we go inside? It's freezing."

He asked this time. I shake out my sleeping bag and set it up inside. I'd like to change out of my sweaty clothes, but that will have to wait.

He hands me the ice cream and a plastic spoon. While he nurses his coffee, I take a bite and close my eyes. Civilization has its perks. He reaches into the second bag and passes me a Starbucks.

I sniff the air. "Chai tea latte?"

"With espresso. Sorry, it's no longer hot."

"Thanks." I close my eyes and transport myself back to Prodigal for a moment. To my pastime of reading in the recliner in front of the guest bedroom window while the sun's slanted rays warm the nape of my neck, three fingers of Maker's Mark, or a chai latte on the table beside me.

I sit in silence, enjoying my treats.

Jim shivers and rubs his hands together.

I'm halfway done with the pint when he disturbs my reverie.

"Can't people here contact you if Danny ever returns? So you can come home."

"He doesn't want to be found, and people here protect each other's privacy. Staying is the best way to see him."

"What if he won't talk with you?"

I've played out the scenarios a hundred times in my head. "Then, at least, I tried."

"After you do, will you end this . . . and come home?"

My hackles rise at his tone. I feel my anger well. "This what, Jim? What were you about to say?"

He doesn't answer.

"C'mon, you paused. Spit it out."

187

"Drama. There, does that make you feel better? Is that what you wanted to hear?"

"This isn't a crazy lark. I'm not being overly emotional." I shake my head. Barbara was right. "I want the truth, and I don't get it from you. I don't know where I will go when I leave this mountain. That is my truth." I throw the half-eaten pint against the tent.

Jim lets loose a sarcastic laugh. "What do you hope to prove by doing this?"

My father used to ask me that.

I close my eyes and take a deep breath.

Stupid me—I'd planned to tell him about our late-night rousting by the cops and teaching the children here while I wait for Danny.

"I am not coming home with you today."

He crushes his empty coffee cup and jams it into the bag. "Why would Danny return if he's been kicked out twice before? Have you considered this? Aside from our house, this is the last place on earth he'd come to." His voice rises to a shout. Condescension and patronizing. Nice.

"What do you know about this place?" I meet his sarcasm with my own, but in a soft voice.

He presses his lips together. He rubs his face with his hands and looks toward the tent flap.

"Go home. I know you want to. You got half of what you came for—proof to show the police I'm fine. Clear your good name. Why do you want me home? Did she dump you?"

He rises to leave, his jaw clenched.

When the anger ebbs from his face, he places the other bag in my hands. He says in a low voice, "Here, maybe this will help you remember. I should have insisted you get the help you needed. I should have suggested we both go, not just you. I shouldn't have . . . gone along with you on this. Nothing prepared me for what happened. I admit, you always were the strong one. What happened was nobody's fault." The emotion in his voice surprises me.

188

The something else he promised.

I open it and find a photo sleeve. One with three holes on the sides that looks like it was removed from a photo album. Inside is a single picture. A black-and-white taken with a soft-filter lens. A close-up of a tiny newborn wrapped in a white blanket. A small ribbon adorns its wrinkled head, the mottled skin. I remember this picture from a long, long time ago. The newborn is grasping an adult finger, but it's impossible to tell whose.

I turn to Jim. "Sure, I know who this is."

He stares at me, and the color leaves his face. He opens his mouth, but nothing comes out at first. He takes a step back and covers his face briefly. "You do?"

"Of course."

His eyes brighten, and he bites his lip. "Tell me."

I hand the picture back. "That's Janet and Jack's baby, Meghan. They used to live in our subdivision. We hung out together until Meghan was born, remember? They moved to New York years ago. Meghan is a veterinarian now. I miss Janet. She was such a good friend. It's sad how easy it is to lose touch with people we were once close to."

He studies my face. "I'm reminded of that every day."

"I hope Meghan's happy in the Big Apple."

Jim continues to search my face. "I want to stay with you tonight."

I clutch my arms to my chest. "No. I'm staying until Danny returns."

"I really want to stay."

This is some sort of trick. "No, you can't. Take this—"

I throw the picture at him. He gently picks it up from the tent floor.

"—and get out." It feels gratifying to say it to him this time.

He opens his mouth to speak, looks at me, and thinks better of it. As he exits, he says, "No matter what, you can always come home."

I zip the flap behind him. The satisfaction is short-lived. I didn't take Barbara's advice. I'm angry and unsure why.

I notice Brianne's artwork and start to wad it up, but I think better of it and smooth it out. I sit on my bed and pour two fingers of Jack while I replay the conversation. My Americone Dream landed upside-down on the tarp floor.

I wish I could call Barbara.

I'm too agitated to stay in my tent but too edgy to be around others. I throw the pint into the woods and start a fire to heat snow for instant soup. I finish my drink and add two more fingers while I wait for the kettle to boil. The alcohol hits my stomach, and I feel lightheaded and nauseous.

My vision blurs when the anxiety attack hits.

It's not frigid cold today, but fat snowflakes have been falling for some time now, and several fresh inches blanket the ground. The mountain is eerily calm—no loons or owls call out, no Highlander sounds drift to my tent.

I write a note to myself: Reconnect with Jack and Janet when this is over. Meghan blossomed into such a pretty, smart girl. I hope she's enjoying life. She deserves it. As something new tugs at the outer reaches of my memory, I hear a twig snap behind me, then a tiny voice.

"I know him."

I turn and face the thin blonde.

What happens next occurs so fast, it's like a dream.

My breath catches. "Who?"

"Don—Danny, right? Your son."

"You don't sound sure of his name. Where is he?"

"I don't know. I know he's alive and where he was a while back. I know somebody who can put you in touch with him, but it's gonna cost."

I take a step toward her. "Why?"

She backs away. "It's not for me." She sniffs and hugs herself tightly. A brief, crooked smile, as if to apologize. "This guy, he doesn't give away anything for free. Know what I mean?"

I feel a sudden urge to grab her, but she lingers near the woods, cautious, ready to bolt. "No, I don't. What kind of person does this?"

"It's better if you don't know, but he can deliver the goods."

I take two slow steps, edging closer. "So you know my son?"

She shakes her head and glides away from me, angling toward the pines.

"How much?" I call out quickly.

"Two hundred."

"So he'll bring Danny to me?"

"No. He tells me the location. After he gets paid."

"Why?"

"Some bad men are hunting your son, but I don't know anything more than that. The man's taking a risk, telling you where he is."

"How far away is he?"

"The man won't say until he gets his money."

"What kind of trouble is my son in?"

The woman shrugs and circles closer to the forest. I'm so close, but she's too fast.

"Meet me by the outhouses at six tonight," I say. "I'll have the money then, but I need to be certain. Let me show you Danny's picture."

I hurry inside my tent for my billfold and return seconds later with his photo. "Here he is. Look, if you want candy bars, you don't have to steal them, but I want my watch ba—"

I look around my tent. Elusive as the whisper of a dream, the thin blond fox of a woman is gone.

I stare up into the blinding snow and hear the roll of thunder. I have to get to the ATM. I grab my keys and billfold.

THE QUEEN OF AVOIDING

EMOTIONS

On my way to the car, Travis calls me into the church/classroom, where Pastor Frank and Corey sit casually drinking beer, joking with two other men. It's as if the raid never happened, and the last week of frigid cold and the bleak moods in the camp were nothing but a bad dream.

I appreciate that no one has expressed any curiosity or resentment toward me about my situation with the police and feel accepted into their strange club. If this happened in town, I'd be fending off nosy neighbors with a cattle prod for months. I understand their omerta now.

I expected somber faces hunkered around the table plotting strategy, but the mood is upbeat, almost euphoric. The men smile and pat Corey on the back as Frank motions me over.

"Did you hear the news? Corey's application was approved. He's getting an apartment in town the Monday after Christmas!"

I turn to Corey. "That's great news. Congratulations."

Frank offers me a beer, which I decline. The thought of more alcohol sickens me.

Travis smiles and drapes a hand on Corey's shoulder. "This gives my young protégé a year to build his bank account for next year's rent. I don't ever want him to return here, except to visit." He playfully pinches Corey's stubbly cheek.

I've heard that the chosen few who receive subsidized apartments either return each week for boxes of food, or Frank meets them in town with care packages to supplement their paychecks.

When the cheers die down, I whisper to Frank, "May I have a word?"

We walk over to a corner. "Are you making a run into town today?"

He shakes his head. "I was about to look for you. The bus is down. Vidal says it needs a new alternator. We have parts, but we need you to transport Flossie to her clinic appointment right now. They want her there ASAP so they can close before the storm hits."

Damn. If the roads are icy, I may not be back by six. "The clinic is open this close to Christmas?"

He looks at me funny "Is there a problem?"

"What time is it?" I ask after reflexively looking at my wrist for my missing watch.

"Almost one, I think. I told Flossie to grab her coat and wait by your car. She's counting on you."

I struggle to keep the tension from my face. "No problem."

Frank smiles. "Thanks. Sorry for the short notice."

Travis turns to me. "You need money for gas? I have cash at my place."

The tank is about half full, and I don't want to wait for him. "I'm good." I should have enough money left to fill the tank.

"I forgot to tell you, after Decker said they were looking for you, I told Barry to run to your car and throw a cover over it."

"Thanks." I haven't used the car since the raid. Barry is the tall man with the dour face and hunting knife who stood guard over me the day I met Travis.

"The cover should fit in your trunk. If not, leave it on the ground," Travis says.

"Be careful," Corey says. "The forecast calls for ice and heavy snow."

I give him a thumbs-up on my way out. I double-time it east down the path to my car—then slip and fall head-first on the snow. I force myself to slow down. There's enough time so long as the roads hold.

The wind kicks up. Some of the pristine drifts along the path are half a foot deep. I lurch stiffly, breasting the heavy snow like some tiny forest golem. I arrive in a sweat to find Flossie and Wilbur huddled together, backs to the wind, waiting. Wilbur pecks her cheek and heads back without acknowledging me.

"Frank told me five minutes ago about your appointment and the bus not running. I came as fast as I could."

After I unlock the door for Flossie and start the engine, I shake the snow from the car cover and stuff it in the trunk. I start to chip away at the stubborn ice that formed on the windshield before the cover was placed. I hear Flossie mumble a trail of incoherent words while she stares at me through the glass.

We set off and slide dangerously close to a precipice before I turn into the skid and regain control.

"Shit, that was close." Flossie glares at me and does a slow boil. "I better not miss my appointment, but I want to get there in one piece. You best slow down."

I look at her when I can risk taking my eyes off the road. I don't want to rile her, but I won't take her shit anymore. "Look, I just found out about this. I'm doing the best I can."

She huffs. "What'd you do to be wanted by the cops? Didn't make you to be a badass."

"I don't know what you're talking about."

"So it gonna be that way. Okay." Before we reach the blacktop, she says, "You can turn down the heat; my ass is on fire. Damn hot flashes."

I turn down the blower and press a button. "It's the seat warmer. I turned it off."

"Thought I'd seen everything until now," she says, the edge still in her voice. "The Highlands has a BMW taxi service with seat warmers, driven by a white woman wanted by the po-po. Never been in a BMW before, or any car with ass warmers." She faces the passenger window and raises something to her mouth in one swift motion before she pockets it.

I'm angry at Jim for pressing me to come home and mad at myself for throwing him out before I could ask whether my ATM card still works for our joint account. And I still feel like I'm about to throw up. I force bile back down my throat. The dizziness returns. I need food and a quiet place to calm my rising anxiety. No such luck here.

"I hate being cold."

Flossie snickers. "You hate the cold, but you choose to live up here with your expensive ass-warming car and your fancy watch. That makes you the craziest, most homeless-by-choice person I know."

I sneak a sideways look at her when she mentions the watch, and I crack a smile. "You're right. I have lost my mind."

We share a brief laugh, and then I focus on the roads. The two lanes become four, but the car continues to slide at times. The going gets steadier once we pass the railroad tracks and the road levels off. The dashboard clock reads 2:06. So far, so good. The snow continues to fall.

Flossie rubs her belly. "You seem awful nervous. You got some other place you need to be?"

"The storm's getting worse. I want to get you to your appointment and back home, is all." Home. I can't believe I said it. I take a deep breath while we pass an old truck stopped along the shoulder. "I'm not being judgmental here, but you shouldn't be drinking alcohol in your condition, even that small travel bottle in your pocket."

Flossie makes a face and rolls her eyes. "I hate doctors. They make me nervous."

"I feel the same, but what if they smell it on your breath?"

She pops a stick of gum in her mouth and faces me. "Better?"

"What if they find it when they draw blood?"

She shrugs. The northern outskirts of Prodigal come into view. I notice a muscle hard at work near her temple as she stares at the falling snow.

"Our two other kids . . ." she says, "live in foster care. I had a drug habit then. I'm homeless, and the baby daddy is a felon, also homeless." She faces me. "What you think is gonna happen to this baby when it comes into the world?"

I don't know what to say, so I keep my mouth shut.

If Jim and I were with friends in town and this arose in casual discussion, we'd have plenty to say. Then don't get pregnant, or Get your tubes tied, or You brought it on yourself.

Now those flippant remarks seem like spiteful platitudes, the flip side of the incompetent counselor's chalkboard.

I can't fathom what this woman is facing. I find myself holding my belly with one hand while I drive. A shudder runs through me when Flossie orders me to drive with both hands.

"We're doing what we can," she says. "We have a caseworker, and we're on a list for an apartment, but . . . it ain't ever gonna happen." The air seems to go out of her as she rests a hand on her baby bump.

I think of Wilbur, who is older. "He has a job. That helps, right?"

We slip and slide into the outskirts of town, and the snow keeps falling.

2:14.

"He made a mistake years ago when he was young and dumb, took a plea of involuntary manslaughter instead of a trial by jury. His court-appointed lawyer's idea. Even though he did his time and paid his debt, no one will hire him for a livable wage."

"Doesn't he work as a cook at the diner?"

Flossie laughs. "One shift, three dollars an hour plus tips. Diners and restaurants get away with that half-minimum-wage shit. His voc counselor tries to convince employers to give him a chance, but . . ."

I skid to a stop behind a black Mustang stuck sideways near a ditch. The northern roads in Prodigal have yet to be plowed. It takes four men to push the car back onto the road.

2:29.

We near the quad and pass the ATM because I don't want her to miss her appointment. We plod on toward the poor side of town and the clinic.

"I want to ask you this," I say. "You always seem pissed at me. Have I done something to offend you? Ever since I arrived in camp, you've put out this strange vibe."

She doesn't answer, but I feel her stare.

"Did you know my son?"

She turns away and stares out the passenger window.

At last, it dawns on me, and I connect the dots. "He was your supplier."

Flossie takes a deep breath. Tears well in her eyes. "I wish I never met him." Before I can ask my next question, she says, "I have no idea where he is or where he went after Travis exiled him. He didn't last long either time. Look, I'm sorry we didn't tell you that first day, but it wouldn't have changed anything. It might have given you more hope, and Highlanders know hope is a dangerous thing."

We. I'm sure that includes Wilbur. What about Dora?

The clinic appears on our right, and the lot shows signs of having been plowed earlier, but fresh snow has fallen so rapidly that we skid into the closest parking spot.

2:41.

"Is there anything you can tell me about my son?"

Flossie collects her belongings. "Travis exiled him for stealing and using, but you probably already figured that out, being his mother and all." She's about to open the door and stops. She keeps her back to me. "He's a lady's man, always had women around him. That's all I'm gonna say."

I describe the thin blonde in camp one more time.

"Never seen her. Don't know the bitch. Don't wanna know her." She glances back and reads the doubt on my face. "I swear to God on the lives of my children. I understand if you don't believe me, I'm just a homeless junkie to you. But I—we—could have ratted you out during the raid. I know you want to stay and wait for your son. I respect that, even though I hate your son."

She pushes the door open and glares at me. "You better pray I get seen, or we gonna have more words." Then she wipes her face, and her tone softens. "Come on inside. Get out of the damn cold."

"I have to go to the ATM. I'll be back before you're done."

Flossie looks to the sky and back at me. More thunder snow rolls. Now she wears a look of doubt.

I help her negotiate the slippery lot and steps. When we enter the empty waiting room, it's evident by the quick attention

197

of the staff that they've been waiting for their last patient of the day. They whisk her into an exam room.

Back in my car, the clock reads 2:48. Should I wait for her, or should I go? I should have enough time. I turn on the radio. The weather service now urges all vehicles to remain off the roads until tomorrow unless it's an absolute emergency. Reports of accidents are increasing, and there's talk of highway closings.

Back on the road, I weave past two abandoned cars. The ones parked along the streets are snowed in by earlier plows. The snow is falling so fast, the plows can't keep up.

I crack the window to help clear the windshield. By the time I reach the quad, eight-foot-high snowbanks mottled with soot and grit rise above the street signs. The clock tower chimes three. The going is much slower than anticipated. The blizzard has created havoc in the streets, even in a city accustomed to winter driving. A tall couple on cross-country skis glides past the quad and heads toward the park's rolling hills.

My thoughts return to the ATM as I near it. Will my card still work? Is there money in our account? Has it been frozen? What if the bank notifies the police the instant I try to withdraw cash? Damn, I should have asked before I kicked Jim out.

Shit!

A police car appears in my rearview mirror, advancing quickly. I negotiate a series of sliding left turns and hope for the best. He drives past me on the first turn. Back on Spruce Street, there's no sign of the cruiser when I pull into a spot near the walk-up ATM at the bank. Flakes are falling in fat, sticky globules from the gunmetal gray sky. A few stalwart Christmas shoppers with their heads down dot the sidewalks as holiday Muzak fills the quad. Near the frozen lake where I deep-sixed my phone, a small choir starts to sing, "Let It Snow! Let It Snow! Let It Snow!" while a few hardy skaters glide in slow arcs.

I tighten my hoodie, bury my face under my wool cap, and keep my head down. Almost immediately, I bump into a shopper on the sidewalk and realize that not only does the hoodie limit my peripheral vision and hearing, but I look like a tiny bank robber. A cop could call my name from behind, and I might not know it until he tapped my shoulder.

The Salvation Army bell-ringer who mans the kettle near the ATM is none other than Maurice, the chatty volunteer I've donated to for the last five years. His outgoing personality and unabashed singing have helped lift me out of depressions in past holiday seasons. Not this year.

I turn my back on him and assume an awkward place in line, almost facing the man behind me, who's clearly uncomfortable with my stance. The woman ahead of me takes her sweet time. With the sidewalk presently empty of foot traffic, Maurice sidles closer to the ATM and belts out the first lines of "Frosty the Snowman." His bell tolls loud and clear through my hoodie as he cheerfully proclaims, "Happy holidays!" to everyone within earshot. When it's finally my turn to use the machine, I have to face the machine and him. He stops.

"Hey, Miss Susan. Almost didn't recognize you there. Good to finally see you this season. Merry Christmas!"

I hope he doesn't read the Gazette.

I ignore him and talk to myself, keeping my fingers crossed that the machine will accept my card. It does. I request the maximum amount and wait, with my head down. The man behind me asks why I don't answer Santa.

C'mon, c'mon, c'mon . . .

Maurice stops ringing his bell. The silence is immeasurably worse, and all eyes are on me. He knows it's me, and he's staring, waiting for my response.

"C'mon!" I yell at the machine. "Work!"

At last, it whirs and spits out a stack of twenties. I breathe again and yank my card free.

The clock tower reads 3:19.

I bump into the man behind me, who mockingly says, "Merry Christmas, Miss Susan." I turn toward the lot and break into a run but stop in my tracks when I see the police cruiser parked alongside my BMW. Did he see me sprinting?

199

"Take care on the sidewalk, Miss Susan!" More laughter and bell ringing from jolly Maurice.

Do I act normal, walk straight to my car, or duck left into the quad and lose myself in the shops? I don't have time to run; I have to pick up Flossie. I walk to the car, reminding myself to breathe. The cop finishes talking into his radio and swivels his head to look directly at me.

Our coats brush against each other, and he watches me fumble for my keys with my head down. I see him grin and touch the bill of his hat in my side-view mirror. I stifle a nervous laugh and open the door clumsily.

"Nice to see you in one piece, Mrs. Crusoe."

Shit! "Excuse me, but I'm in a hurry."

He tips the hat back from his face. "I'm afraid you're going to be here a while."

I'd been too scared to look at him closer until now. He's a bearlike man, over six feet tall, with broad shoulders and a wide stomach. Ancient acne scars pockmark his ruddy complexion.

"You have no right to detain me. I've committed no crime."

"Your right rear taillight is out. I noticed it back on Spruce. That gives me cause to stop you and issue a warning—"

"I'm late to pick up a friend at the doctor's office. She's pregnant, and the roads—"

"Would you rather I write you a ticket?" He frowns now, his posture stiff. "We have a be-on-the-lookout for a blue BMW, so I ran your plates. Our database lists you as a missing person."

I poked the bear. Take deep breaths. "Your database needs to be updated. You found me, but I'm clearly not missing. I'm currently staying outside of town. I come here several times a week to shop, like today." I maintain eye contact with him. "My husband knows where I am. We met last night and again earlier today. If you want to ticket me, that's up to you, but I'd prefer a warning. I didn't know it was out. I promise to get it fixed." I glance at his badge. "Officer Gant."

He asks for my license and registration. "It's not that simple, Mrs. Crusoe. The sergeant wants to speak with you himself."

I look up at the tower. 3:34.

I close my eyes and count to ten. "I'm happy to talk with him on your radio, but I must pick up my friend. She's counting on me to get her home safely."

"Sergeant insists on a face-to-face."

I plead my case again when I see a second cruiser enter the lot. The same barrel-chested cop who led the raid at Camp Thunderbird slowly exits his car. He isn't much taller than me, and his pants and coat are far too tight for his stocky build. Last night he appeared much larger. He hooks his thumbs in his pockets and squints at me through the falling snow.

"I'm Sergeant Decker. You've been officially listed as a missing person for months now, Mrs. Crusoe."

"As I explained to Officer Gant, I'm not missing. My husband visited me twice during the last two days. He knows where I'm staying and why. The roads are a mess, and I need to go."

His smile seems a bit off, like it can't reach the left side of his face for some reason. He puffs out his chest, and I can almost hear the buttons on his coat groan in protest. "Your husband and friends are concerned about you. Everyone wants to be certain you are safe. That includes me."

Thunder rolls overhead, and the snow intensifies.

"Like I said, my husband knows where I'm staying and understands the reason. I assure you I'm fine."

A gust of wind almost blows the hat from his head, and he catches it in one sudden jerky movement. He glances quickly at his fellow officer and frowns at how that may have appeared. "We want to make sure you aren't being held against your will, that you are free to return to Prodigal whenever you wish."

"How could I be kidnapped when I'm here shopping by myself? I'm fully aware I may return home at any time. I appreciate your concern, but I need to leave."

The clock tower chimes four.

Decker's eyes narrow as he studies my clothing. That broken half-smile of recognition appears. "You were on the mountain last night. To Highlanders, you would be considered a woman of great wealth and means. An easy mark. You may not believe I'm on your side, but you will. I hope you don't learn this the hard way. You can become a missing person up there and not see it coming. People have entered that camp and have never been heard from again. Most of the people you're living among are opportunists with, at best, questionable morals and values."

"Am I free to leave, Sergeant Decker?"

"And now, months after you've been declared missing, my officer finds you here in a god-awful hurry at the ATM, stuffing your pockets with cash. Now is the time to tell the truth. We can protect you. Who is blackmailing you in the Highlands? Valuables up there go missing, and when the proverbial fur flies, you will find yourself alone, facing a pack of desperate criminals."

I think of my watch and the small vulpine woman in the green skullcap. There is a grain of truth to what he says.

"Would you be harassing me like this if I were staying with a sick aunt on the poor side of town?"

Decker pauses for a brief moment. "But you're not staying with a sick aunt, are you?"

"I've committed no crime. I'm late picking up my pregnant friend at her doctor's office. I need to leave now, the roads are bad. Give me my warning about the taillight, and I'll be on my way."

Decker perks up at this and nods to Gant. His cockeyed smile turns to a frown. Knowing I'm pressed for time, he draws this out. The short man is on a power trip.

"A pregnant friend, huh? How about we have a little talk with her and give you both a ride home? You can leave your car here. Officer Gant will make sure it's safe. After all, we aim to protect and serve."

I panic. Flossie must be livid by now. "My pregnant friend lives in the Highlands."

Decker makes a sour face. He freezes briefly when the thunder rolls again. He seems to enjoy dragging this out, deciding my fate when I've done nothing wrong. At last, he tips his hat. "You have a nice day, Mrs. Crusoe. Be careful on the roads. They are treacherous today. Especially on the mountain. So easy to lose control up there. Know what I mean?"

Gant scribbles on his pad. He hands a sheet to me, and the cops huddle while I climb into my car. I give the BMW too much gas as I back out of the space, the wheels spin, and I sideswipe a mound of snow.

I curse under my breath when I read the paper. Gant ticketed me.

The clock tower reads 4:17. Twilight fades, and the snow doesn't let up.

My car gets stuck in snowdrifts several times during my trek back across town to the clinic. Luckily, I'm able to rock it back and forth with quick shifts from drive to reverse. The only good news is the streets are almost devoid of traffic. I spot a cruiser in my rearview—Officer Gant. Decker must have ordered him to follow me.

Two blocks from the clinic, I nearly slide into a stalled truck and wait while two men struggle to push it off the road. Gant watches from his cruiser behind me. So much for serving and protecting. I didn't think it possible, but the blizzard gains strength. Visibility is almost zero, and the snow is falling sideways as darkness descends.

When I reach the clinic, one lone car is in the lot, and the building is dark. Shit. What would they have done with Flossie? It's 4:59.

I leave the engine running and hurry to open the clinic door, but it's locked. I pound on the door and finally see movement inside. A nurse frowns at me as she unlocks the door. Their power is out. Flossie emerges and raises her hand the instant I open my mouth. She refuses my help down the steps and shambles to my car.

I apologize to the nurse, but she too ignores me and is halfway to her car after she locks the door, her head down against the sideways wind.

Across the street, Officer Gant regards us from behind the wheel. His dome light is on while he talks on his radio. I flip him off.

I'm not sure, but I think he smiles at me.

It's going to take a miracle to get us back by six. I try to tell Flossie of my ordeal with the cops, but she's yelling over me. As we sit shouting at one other, a miracle drives by: a snow plow. Going our way. I throw the BMW into drive. We slide out of the lot and fall in behind the plow. We make better time. Gant, the pest, circles, to follow.

The tower reads 5:09 when we reach the quad. Flossie's tongue-lashing finally subsides.

The street crews have regained a semblance of control over the downtown roads. If the road to the railroad tracks north of town is plowed, we just might make it. I turn off Spruce and head north, where my luck runs out.

A jackknifed eighteen-wheeler demolished the pole at the three-way intersection, causing a power outage on both sides of the street. A crew struggles to secure a downed power line while two tow trucks grapple with the disabled truck. We sit idling until there's enough room on the shoulder to drive around the accident, but when we do, we find that the road north remains unplowed.

Gant watches us leave Prodigal and turns around.

The going is painstakingly slow. Whenever I veer out of existing tracks in the deep snow, the car threatens to bog down and stall. Blowing snowdrifts make it worse.

I'm so focused on the road, I almost don't hear Flossie's soft voice next to me.

"Baby's underweight. Something's wrong. This one feels different." She sounds dead inside.

I glance at her and return my eyes to the road. "What did the doctor say?"

"He said to take my vitamins and eat more." She shakes her head. "Been tough to keep food down this time."

"The baby's going to be fine. You'll be fine. You're experiencing nerves, pre-baby jitters is all."

"No. Something's wrong. I just know." From the passenger seat, I hear another travel bottle crack open in the darkness. This one, she doesn't bother to hide.

I keep quiet.

"I could use that seat warmer now." Her voice a near whisper, empty and defeated.

I maneuver around an abandoned car but bog down again and have to rock the car back and forth to regain traction. The low fuel light winks on as we finally rumble over the railroad tracks, and the grade rises. I can't remember the last time I prayed, but I do now, for the four-wheel drive to get us up this damn mountain.

"They're gonna take this one away, too. We're less than human to them. They're never gonna give us a chance to raise our kids. We'll never get an apartment, not even for a year."

"On what charges? Why do you say that? The caseworkers are doing their best. Wilbur will find a better-paying job. One day you'll have a real place to stay and, eventually, your kids back."

The car makes agonizing progress uphill. The gusts of wind help in spots by blowing the drifts off the crowned road.

The dashboard reads 6:17. I quell my rising panic and force myself to believe: If this mystery man wants his precious money, he'll have to wait for me. My arms are fatigued from white-knuckling the wheel.

I feel Flossie stare at me.

The words spew from her like bullets from a gun. "Your son got me high both times he stayed here. And I'm still chipping."

I glance at her. I don't know what to say.

She shakes her head and cradles her belly as we fishtail out of a turn. "That's not right. He didn't put a gun to my head. I wanted it. After his first week in camp, he knew every one of his customers."

"So he sold drugs to you and others?"

She nods. "He's slick. He could act like your best friend, flatter you, or be all business and in your face. Whatever it takes to close the deal. He moved a lot of speed to the hunters in the north camp. Like that big redheaded Viking dude who lost his shit the other day."

"Finn." The unassuming man Danny conned into befriending him. Did the drugs play a role in his break from reality, was it Finn's mental illness, or both?

"Yep, that guy. He was a regular. He said he needed all his energy to work the mines."

At last, we reach the gravel road. We're close to camp. The snow keeps falling. "Money's in short supply up here. Did customers pay cash?"

She freezes and stares off into the pines out her window. "Can't say. The only one dumb enough to discuss it was Finn. He bragged that he paid Danny in gold."

She avoids my gaze. I recall something Wilbur mentioned on my first day in camp.

"What about the others?"

Flossie bites her lip. "They pay for it in trade. Same as in Prodigal. Same all over the damn world." Her voice carries a cutting edge.

In a soft voice, I ask, "What about you?"

She looks down at her lap and, in a bare whisper, says, "Guilty."

We travel in silence while I ponder the implications and count the months in my head.

She turns to me. "You better pray your boy never returns. If he does, Wilbur will kill him."

Stunned, I feel a chill.

"You're an educated woman with an ass-warming car. Read between the lines."

When my parking spot comes into view, I see Wilbur waiting under a stand of pines, hunkered against the wind.

She glares at me, her teeth bared. "Keep this to yourself, or I will gut you like a fish."

The hairs on my back stand on end. "Why did you tell me this?"

Her tone softens as she watches Wilbur trudge through the snow. "It's been eating at me. And I thought you should know in case your boy returns."

"I appreciate that. Your secret's safe with me."

A hundred feet from my parking spot, the wheels spin, and we start to slide backward. I apply the brakes. Wilbur hurries behind the car and helps push us the last few yards.

The dashboard clock flashes 7:11.

Wilbur looks panicked as he opens the passenger door. "You all right?"

Flossie pops a stick of gum in her mouth and says in a happy singsong, "Just fine, thanks to our new chauffeur. Did you know this car has seat warmers? Isn't that the craziest damn thing?"

"I was worried, babe." He turns to me and bows his head. "Thank you, Miss Susan."

I nod. The hairs stand at attention on my back while I regard Wilbur in a brand new light.

I walk behind them and flinch when I hear Flossie tell him it's a girl. When they take the path to their tent, I double-time it to mine. I fall several times on the slick, snowy ground and feel my sweat-soaked clothes under my coat. I stash my money in my hidey-hole, minus the two hundred, and cover the space with the tarps. I set up my colored strings and grab the lantern. I don't know when I reach the outhouses because I have no watch. The echo of a loon wails, forlorn and primeval, from the river. No response tonight.

I shiver in the dark with my lantern as owls call to one another across the clearing.

I cringe when a heavy whump lands in the dark behind me. I turn to find a large snowdrift sloughed off a canopy of pines.

It feels like thirty minutes pass, and no one arrives. Maybe she tired of waiting. Maybe the blizzard made her late. The wind kicks up and howls through the trees, making them groan. They sound like lost and broken souls.

How long do I wait? For as long as it takes, I tell myself. Danny's in trouble.

I use a commode and listen to the wind rattling through its sides like the drone of a machine. The commode nearest the woods is locked and eerily silent. I knock on the door, but there's no reply.

I pace and exercise to stay warm. The last time I felt this nervous, I was standing under an awning, full of self-loathing.

"You have the money?" a tiny voice says behind me.

The thin blonde hugs herself against the cold. Her coat is too thin, and she's wearing the same fingerless gloves.

"I do. Where is Danny?"

Her large fox eyes regard me, and she extends an arm. "Money first."

I consider grabbing her, but hand over the cash. She steps back and keeps eyeing me as she counts the folded twenties.

"Where is my son?"

She stuffs the cash in the front pocket of her jeans and hands me a crumpled note with an address. "In town," she says, nodding toward the paper.

The address is in an old section of Prodigal. I recognize the street name but can't quite place it. "How long has he lived there?"

She wipes her nose against a sleeve and smirks. "Maybe half a year."

Danny's been in town that long, and I haven't seen him? That roughly coincides with the time of his last exile. "Is he safe? How is he?"

She turns and hurries down the path, quick as a fox.

"Wait! Come with me to my tent. I have hot food," I lie. I call out for her to stop and run after her, but I slip and fall again. Wet snow plasters to my face. I fumble for the lantern and race up the path to the picnic area, frantic and out of breath. She's gone. I find no fresh tracks in the dark, even with the lantern. How does she disappear into the woods like that? Did I imagine her? Am I psychotic again?

Every part of me aches, and I'm mentally exhausted, but I now have Danny's address.

I trudge back to my tent, eager to change clothes and crawl into bed, but the string that was on my tent flap is on the ground.

Someone's been inside. My sleeping bag, blankets, and catalytic heater are gone.

What's inside my cast iron skillet turns my stomach.

The square section of dirt-encrusted plywood.

I frantically dig out the soil over the hidey-hole with my hands. Nothing. The plastic bag that contained my billfold, credit cards, driver's license, and a thousand dollars is gone.

I search outside, but there's only drifting snow, no tracks. I grab a coffee cup and sit, resigned to drinking myself into a coma, but the last bottle of Wild Turkey is also gone. I start to laugh and throw cups at my tent. I attack the tent with such ferocity several stakes pull up, and one side flattens. I scream long and hard into the deep dark night.

She knew when I'd be at the outhouses. She was two hours late.

All I have left is a car with less than a gallon of gas, a burner phone, and an address.

The carton of cigarettes is also gone. I grab my last pack and walk to the church with the lantern. I drag the old yellow sofa close to the wood stove and build a fire.

A spider is weaving a web where the stove top meets the vent. I note the red hourglass stain on its abdomen. Her presence here is a miracle. Like me, she should be dead, but fate brought her here, and now instinct has driven her to spin a web from her own guts. She hunkers down in the shadows of her bleak realm and waits. I lean close and whisper, "Good luck, but I haven't seen a bug in camp for months."

The bulletin board contains the new camp schedule for Christmas week. I stoke the fire, taking care not to disrupt my new friend, and curl into my own little ball on the sofa.

Sleep comes instantly. I look down from a break in the clouds upon a lifeless bag of skin and bones splayed on an iceberg hundreds of miles from land. To my surprise, it begins to move in a halting, stumbling gait until I see that it's a starving polar bear. I look closer, and the bear has my face. Stranded on a nearby floe sits a second emaciated bear with my husband's face. The man who wears navy blue ties and suits. The man with equal parts gray and brown hair, a wry smile, and age lines on his face and neck. I always thought he allowed his hair to spill a bit too much over the tops of his ears for a man his age. Jim the conformist, except for the hair. Jim, the yes-man. The man who goes out of his way to avoid scenes and hates confrontation. Jim, the soft touch. Danny's go-to parent. Only now, he's a starving polar bear like me. Our ice floes slowly drift apart in the current. Before I lose sight of him as his tiny iceberg slowly rotates out of sight, I see another bear on his floe raise its head and regard me.

Across the vast expanse of ocean, flashing lights appear through the mist, coming closer, growing brighter. Impossibly, a school bell sounds and beeps blare around me. The lights sting my eyes, and the beeps stab my ears. I turn away and see Jim in human form, rocking a crib. The crib is empty, save for a blanket. He turns to me and says in a voice void of emotion: You were always too sensitive and overprotective. You pushed Danny too hard.

Don't push me!

Next, I'm a young girl playing with dolls while my parents sit in our old wood-paneled breezeway, watching television. My father turns to me, a distant look in his eyes. Disappointment spreads across his face when I look up at him from my tiny spot on the floor.

Don't push!

A silver flash hits me. Again. Then again.

An old, dented rowboat adrift on a glassy pond.

A voice near me says, Why wasn't it her?

Words from an aunt years later.

Now I remember the events in their proper order.

Now I understand why I buried this memory. The aunt was the key.

It's a hot summer day.

I wear my favorite little-girl bathing suit, pink with white ruffles. The sickly sweet cherry smell of his cigar hangs in the still air. Just the two of us at the farmer's pond. Mother doesn't like to fish. We share an egg or maybe tuna salad sandwich, and I eat an apple. I drink a soda that makes me burp. We're in the rowboat for a long time. He sits drinking a beer with his line in the water, trolling for catfish. The sun beats down, the chirr of locusts echoes like waves of heat in my ears. The ugly bugs fly in the air near us and make awful noises. I worry that they will land in my hair and bite me. He says they're good because they attract fish, and, sure enough, ones that land on the water soon become fish food. I complain about the heat. He tells me to swim to shore. The rowboat drifts slowly above the deep end of the lake.

My complaint becomes a whine, this one more shrill. "But I don't know how!"

He makes that sour face I know so well. "Hasn't your mother taught you?"

I shake my head and cross my arms. "I wanna go home."

He looks at his watch. "Go ahead. Swim. You swim to shore, and we'll go home. I'll teach you."

He leans his rod against the gunwale and stands. The little boat rocks from side to side, which scares me, and I grab the bench. A splinter stabs my palm, and I cry. His face puckers when he tosses me screaming into the lake.

I go under, swallowing great gulps of water. He shouts words I can't understand. I reach for the sky, but the lake pulls me back under. My nose fills with water. My eyes sting. I cry out and reach for the boat.

Something pushes me away. A flash of silver through the air?

"Kick with your feet. Keep your head up. Dog-paddle with your arms."

Even with water in my eyes, I see his stern face. "You're going the wrong way, princess."

I flail and go down once, twice more. I beg for help, choking on water. The silver glint in bright sunlight appears again to push me away from the boat.

"Sink or swim, princess," he calls out. I hear the mocking tone he often attaches to my nickname.

I paddle and kick. I spit and go down once more. Paddle, kick, paddle, kick. The shore seems a bit closer, or maybe it's my imagination. I'm too scared to look back. My legs cramp, but I fight through the pain. My foot scrapes the bottom and catches on a submerged branch, which pulls me under a final time. I wrench loose and breach the surface, finally able to stand. I run to the car in tears. Only then do I turn back to the water and see Father leisurely reel in his line and row to shore. I climb into the hot brown Plymouth and roll down the windows.

That silver flash? His metal landing net, with its moss-encrusted strings pressed against my terrified face, pushing me away from the boat.

Outside the car, he looks to the sky and says, "Why wasn't it her?"

I didn't know what the words meant at the time, but he didn't care that I heard them. I avoid looking his way while he drives.

He makes two comments on the drive home. "You learned to swim today. I'm proud of you." No veiled threats, no warnings of Don't tell your mother. That scares me almost as much as nearly drowning.

I walk in the front door and tell Mother I learned to swim today. "That's nice, princess," she says with thread in her mouth as she prepares to sew a button on a pair of Father's pants. I'm not certain she hears me until she says, "I thought you already knew how."

And the words from Mother's sister?

Uttered at Mother and Father's wake.

They were struck and killed by a drunk driver in a head-on collision. I was fifty-five at the time, and they were in their eighties. An aunt lamented that Mother was never the same after she lost two sons during childbirth. Their umbilical cords strangled them at birth. I pretended I knew about the dual tragedies all this time, while my stomach did barrel rolls. They robbed me of the memories of my two older brothers. Would Father have saved me had I not learned to dog paddle?

The summer day I learned to swim was the last time Father said he was proud of me. Not when I earned my M.A. or my Ph.D. in teaching. Not when Danny was born. He never attended my swim meets or soccer games. In retrospect, the bitter man probably blamed Mother for the dead babies. Mother had her moments of humanity, but they were rare and short-lived. Whenever I'd cry over some childhood injustice, she'd stand me in a corner and order me to stay there until I understood that crying, or anger, does no good. Sometimes she'd give me a cookie after my time-outs and offer a brief hug.

She could have drawn from her childbirth experiences to offer support and reassurance to me when I almost died giving birth to Danny, but she didn't.

A dour woman of few words, she was the Queen of Avoiding Emotions. When I entered my dorm as a college freshman, I felt happy as a released prisoner. During my Ph.D. training, Jim and I happened upon Father with his arm draped around another woman at a bar late one night. When he excused himself to the men's room, I sidled up next to the stranger, and we struck up a conversation while I ordered another round. She was plastered, drunk enough to admit she'd been seeing Father for the last six years.

On subsequent visits home, Mother always sat in her damn brown recliner like a stone Buddha, staring out the window as she watched the world go by. I can't recall when I last saw her smile.

I buried that fishing trip for five decades. After all, I am Mother's daughter. The new queen.

I wake with a start from this cluster of forgotten memories and prop myself on one arm on the ragged sofa. This explains so much about my childhood and my future choices.

Damn! I whisper to myself and drift back, this time to a merciful and dreamless sleep.

Someone shakes me, and I flail. My fist connects with something hard, and I hear a muffled groan. For some reason, Travis has his hands on me and is telling me to wake up. A fresh red strawberry is blooming below his eye. I see a thin shaft of morning sun between the door and the jamb.

He puts a hand to his face and says, "What are you doing? You put us—the entire camp—in jeopardy by using the wood stove. What if Decker returns? They can shut us down. You better have a damn good explanation."

My eyes struggle to regain focus. "I need money."

"What?" he says, looking flabbergasted.

"I said I need money, for gas. I'm on empty."

Pinching the corners of his eyes, he says, "Did you hear what I said?"

I sit up. "I was robbed last night. My sleeping bag, heater, and all my money—a thousand dollars. ATM card, driver's license, credit cards. All gone. There's nothing left." I describe the mysterious blonde and receive the standard blank response.

He sits next to me. "I'm sorry. You've met her, talked with her, and you're certain she's the thief?"

"She's been following me since my first day in camp."

"Did you see her enter your tent?"

I consider others—George, Flossie, and Wilbur—but doubt it's any of them. "No, but I know it's her. A thousand in twenty-dollar bills."

He studies me for some time. "We'll organize a search. It's a challenge since we don't know where to look. Barbara doesn't remember a woman who fits that description in the Rainbow Camp. She could be living in a cave, but I've never heard of a woman living up there. I'm concerned about you. How else can I help?"

If I tell you, you'll try to stop me. Or accompany me. This I do on my own.

"I need an advance, for gas money. And supplies. I have to go back into town."

He rubs the back of his neck, removes his wallet, and hands me a twenty.

I hold out my hand, waiting.

214

"More?" he asks, surprised. "You are quite singular in purpose."

"She took everything from me."

He doles out another twenty. "That's all I have until payday. What else can I do?"

I gather my hat and gloves. "Thanks for the other night—with the police. I understand and appreciate your code. I'm sorry about the stove. I wasn't thinking."

His hand rests on my leg. "It will take time to restock your tent. The offer of my house still stands when you return."

"Your house . . ."

He nods. "I built one for me and one for Frank. Mine's the one with the porch. We can talk about books, teaching, or anything you want in a warm little living area. No sex."

I touch his cheek where my punch landed. He moves closer on the sofa, and we hug. The rush of heat returns. It doesn't feel quite right, but I don't want it to end. Above all, I have to find and help my son. If everything goes well, this could be my last day here. I linger in Travis' arms until my thoughts return to Danny.

"I'm sorry I hit you. I'll think about the offer."

My eyes land on the school bulletin boards, on a picture I put up last week. A snow-capped mountain under blue skies with the Emerson quote: "What lies behind you and what lies in front of you pales in comparison to what lies inside of you."

If I could remember everything that lies behind me, maybe I could move forward.

PART TWO: THE EDGE

"The Edge . . . there is no honest way to explain it

because the only people who really know where it is

are the ones who have gone over."

Hunter S. Thompson

CHOOSE YOUR CHILDREN WELL

When he walks me to my car in the morning, Travis says it's eight o'clock. It's Christmas Eve. A few drifts are over a foot deep along the path. The blizzard ended during the night, covering the camp in a fresh blanket of white powder. Like yesterday, the temperature hovers around thirty, but it feels much warmer today with bright sunshine and no wind.

He offers to accompany me, and I remind him he has a city to run. If this works out well or goes south, I may not return.

The engine doesn't turn over, and the low fuel icon glows. Damn, I may be out of gas. He looks under the hood and scrapes corrosion off a battery terminal. The engine shudders to life, and I call to him before I start my descent. I pull his face to mine, and the kiss I plant on him lingers and deepens. I wish we'd met in a different place and time.

"What was that for?"

"For luck. You're a good man."

The confusion on his face morphs into a smile. "And you are a most singular, bedeviling woman."

"I'll take that as a compliment."

His smile remains but weakens. "How else could you?"

I look in the rearview as I head down the mountain and watch Travis' shape diminish until he is out of sight. I remove the crumpled note from my coat pocket and open it on the passenger seat. It takes half an hour to negotiate the slippery downhill roads before the train tracks appear. I must be driving on fumes by now. The main roads in town have been plowed and treated, so the drive returns to normal. The radio station says the back end of the blizzard swung east last night.

The only open gas station is the 7-Eleven, and I'm the lone customer in the store. The same young cashier sits eating ice cream, spellbound by a song on her phone. I take my time as I search the aisles and make no effort to conceal my face. I drop a large buck knife by the register and point behind the counter while I do math in my head. "This, two pints of Wild Turkey and a pack of Slims." I drop the two crumpled twenties on the counter. "Put the rest toward regular on pump number six. Oh, and a pack of matches, please."

The cashier looks up from her phone and sees me with the knife. Recognition dawns on her round face. "He must have really done you wrong. Men are filthy pigs, but they don't deserve to die. I keep telling you, try the ice cream."

For the first time, I notice the little blue oval on her smock. "Melanie—that's a pretty name. I tell you what, Melanie. No man can take anything from you unless you let him."

She looks at me with what appears to be awe. "Wow, I don't ever want to be on your shit list." She quickly rings up my purchases.

"Remember my advice. And choose your children well. Do that, and you have a fighting chance."

Melanie considers me warily from the corner of one eye. "You're like an avenging angel in a graphic novel. You know the kind? One that carries a grudge into the afterlife . . . but in a good way."

She walks to a nearby freezer and places a quart of Rocky Road and a plastic spoon in my bag. "On the house. Since our pig of an owner makes me work holidays for minimum wage, I will help myself to the odd snack here and there." She glances at the receipt. "You got four dollars and eighty-two cents of gas coming on pump six. You sure that's enough?"

"It's all I need." I smile at her. "I'm Susan Crusoe, like in the book Robinson Crusoe. You're going to be okay, Melanie."

"Hey, Susan. Seriously, try the ice cream. It works," she says with a wistful smile, holding up her own container. She returns her attention to the song.

Outside, it's a picture-postcard winter day for the residents of Prodigal. Smoke coils into the sky from nearby chimneys, and the earthen, oaky smell of firewood fills the air as I walk to my car. Wreaths adorn front landings across the narrow street, and wide red ribbons hang from gaslights and mailboxes. Rows of white, green, and red Christmas lights spiral around evergreens laden with snow. One yard displays a manger scene. In the front window, a Christmas tree topped with an angel is decorated with brightly colored ornaments and strings of lights.

It evokes memories of what used to be, if only for a few fleeting years. I pump gas and glance once more at the house. Two young kids run past the picture window in their pajamas, all smiles, the larger chasing the smaller. I grab my belly.

I pull onto Spruce Street. The address I'm looking for lies beyond the quad and the health clinic. I locate the side street and search for the numbers. This road on this side of town remains snow-packed and slick. I pass colorful row houses, tiny and crowded together, dingy fast food places, a church. A grade school comes into view when the road angles left. Ahead looms a cemetery in front of an apartment building in decline, a middle school, and snowy ball fields. I see the apartments and slam on the brakes, which sends me fishtailing down the empty street. When the address appears on a large white sign, I look back in disbelief once, twice, three times at the number on the paper.

The address on the paper matches the one for the graveyard. I feel like dying.

The little blond bitch led me to believe Danny was alive.

I ram my elbow repeatedly against the door until my arm goes numb. I negotiate a U-turn and park in the plowed cemetery lot. Mine is the lone car this morning. It's hard to breathe.

I wish Travis were here. I sit and think, working up the courage. I twist the cap off a pint and take a pull.

Does this all end now? She said he's been here about six months. So close to home.

I think back to the emergency room after Danny blew out his knee skiing, and they gave him morphine for the pain. While we awaited the test results, the overhead speaker announced a STAT. Controlled frenzy erupted in the ER, and a woman was rushed into a nearby room on a gurney. A crash cart followed. A cast of twenty-some-odd nurses, doctors, residents, and ancillary staff rushed in and out of the packed room, performers in an oft-practiced ballet. Jim and I couldn't help but hear snippets of conversation—found unresponsive at a party; mother and family here now; past treatment for heroin, fentanyl, and OxyContin; Narcan administered at the scene. The family physically supported the mother when she arrived and guided her to a chair. The distraught faces of that family burned into my brain as we watched them pray and bargain with God. A priest and social worker arrived to offer support.

Cheryl was the patient. She was twenty-five. Someone described her as pretty and smart. Later, a different voice said she's a grad student with a good job. I turned to see staff in the hall exchange quick, somber glances as someone called out "Clear!" for the third time.

They knew. The mother's terrified eyes darted back and forth until she could take no more and closed them. A few minutes later, a doctor in green scrubs talked to her, shaking his head. He placed a hand briefly on her shoulder before he left. The priest and social worker stepped forward.

I remember standing next to Danny's bed at that moment, squeezing his hand tight when staff confirmed Cheryl's time of death at 15:45. I look at Jim, standing on the other side of Danny's bed, and knew we shared the same thought: We're so lucky that's not Danny.

Danny slept through it all, thanks to the morphine.

I look up. The graveyard beckons. I place the knife behind my belt and grab the open pint. This is the older and smaller of the two paupers' cemeteries in this section of Prodigal. I've never had occasion to walk it before. I pound on the caretaker's cottage, but no one answers, and the door is locked. The narrow footpaths remain snow-covered. The first rows are old graves, and some limestone markers date back to when Prodigal was a logging camp. I read the names and brush away snow that obscures the plaques on the ground. Two hundred years of snow, rain, and wind have eroded the chiseled names and dates. I walk over the graves of forgotten people and want to close my eyes like Cheryl's mother did in the ER. I linger, confident these older rows are safe, but I walk each one to be certain.

One lengthy row in the potter's field marks the newer graves. A few have small granite markers, but the rest are made from wood, all legible and none Danny. Three markers indicate this year as the year of death. Two men and a woman. Neither male bears Danny's first or last name.

At the end of the row, I see a raised mound under the blanket of snow. A freshly dug grave. And leaning before it, a plain wooden marker.

My heart skips a beat, and I freeze. I close my eyes for a moment before I summon the courage to move. As I approach, I read through my cracked sunglasses the name on the tiny marker:

Doug Jones.

Near this last row stands an ancient witch's tree, its twisted and gnarled trunk rising thirty feet into the air and containing crevices too high and black to see into. The branches sway and groan against the wind that has kicked up. When I sit under it, the buck knife pokes my stomach; I remove it and lean back tentatively against the tree and drink.

All the graves have markers. The little blonde woman said he's been here six months. If so, his grave shouldn't be mounded.

Did Danny use aliases?

Is this another con, capped off with a cruel joke?

I have to know.

This must be why Travis discouraged me from posting notices. No matter where you go, there's always someone ready to take advantage. I didn't listen.

I'm never going to find my son.

There's four fingers left in the pint when I test the blade against my wrist.

As the knife breaks my skin, a deep voice behind me says, "What the hell are you doing?"

I turn and look up to see an old black man on a John Deere tractor.

I stash the knife in my pocket. "Are you the caretaker?"

His eyes roll. "No, I'm Idris Elba. Between movies, I steal old lawn equipment from graveyards." His voice a yell above the motor.

"I knocked on the cottage door. There was no answer."

He shakes his head. "Was out back in the shed, getting this old green bastard to start."

I study his weathered face. "Do you get many people from the Highlands?"

"'Course we do. And not a complaint from any of them."

"What about that fresh grave? Was he a Highlander?"

He revs the engine when it sounds ready to stall. "We reach twenty questions yet?" He's so loud I wonder if he's hard of hearing.

I meet the man's stare. "I have nowhere to go."

"Sure was."

"What'd he look like?"

He shakes his head and grimaces. "The dude liked long walks along the beach and dogs. His turn-offs were country music and talking to people like you who ask way too many damn questions. Look, lady, I just plant them in the ground. Stiffs give me the heebie-jeebies."

Great. I return his yell. "Thanks for nothing. You do know you work in a cemetery, right?" I take a swig and replace the cap.

"I like the peace and quiet, until you came along." He raises his voice another notch for the last few words.

"Go away. Leave me alone."

He eyes my bottle. "I might know a little something about that fresh one over there if you was to hand over the rest of that sippin' whiskey."

I walk over to him, reaching for Danny's picture in my pocket, but it's not there. I last had it in my billfold, which the little blond bitch stole. I hand over the bottle.

He grunts and shakes the bottle. "Not much, but a deal's a deal." He drinks half of it and smacks his lips. "Ah, that's what I'm talking about."

"All right, talk to me."

"Usually, I never see them beforehand, but I was downstairs picking up my check the day this one came in. Saw the dude before they put him in the box . . . was about forty, medium build, with a beard. Full of tattoos. Looked like a black parrot painted green, red, and yellow."

"Are you saying the man in the grave was black?"

He rolls his eyes. "Still is. I said fifty times I planted a dude. Dudes are black. Mandingo. African American. Negro. You gotta get outta the suburbs more. Expand your horizons, missy."

I laugh at the irony, and it takes some time for me to stop. He looks at me sideways while he drains the pint.

He wraps the bottle in a plastic bag and stows it between his legs. "Get back in your car and scoot. Sleep it off. Don't do drugs. The sun will come out tomorrow."

So Danny isn't here. I feel a ray of hope again. I thank him.

He leans forward on the tractor, and the edge in his voice softens. "Look, I been where you're at, tried what you're contemplating. As Winston Churchill said, 'Never, never, never give up.' You're alive for a reason."

I plaster on a smile. He doesn't know I'm mocking him.

He shakes his head and spits. "Whole damn world's gone crazy. Become too hard to find a reason to live these days. You still feel that way, get your ass to 224 Hebert. Remember the address. Two twenty-four. I live there with my son and grandson. We don't have shit, but we got each other and a roof over our heads." He points. "The red frame house one block east. Somebody always there. Someone other than me answers, tell 'em Hades sent you. They'll understand."

"The Greek god of the underworld? That's your name?"

"Hell no, but it feels that way sometimes. That's been my nickname the thirty years I been here. It's a lot cooler than Freddie, and it fits my personality, so I kept it." He narrows his eyes and studies me. "Not many folks know who Hades is. You a Highlander?"

"I don't know anymore."

He frowns and shifts the tractor out of neutral. "Seems to me that's something you should know by now, missy. I damn sure better not see you back here. Don't make me dig another hole. You do, I'll bury your skinny ass upside down. That's a promise."

I stand and walk toward my car.

Hades calls out, "Two twenty-four Hebert. Knock on the door any damn time."

The tractor revs behind me. I turn and watch him lower the plow blade and chug up the last path I walked down. Do I deserve to be buried that way? I still don't know.

I drive north out of Prodigal. The sun has melted some of the snow past the train tracks. When the road rises, the drive slows due to the slush. When I reach the outskirts of the Highlands, the gas icon blinks on again. At my usual parking spot, I turn the car around so it points down the mountain. I cut the engine and turn on the radio. I reach for the second pint and look down the mountain. I drink and listen to oldies music. My thoughts drift to the lyrics of "American Tune."

I'm weary to my bones. And drunk. The dark thoughts return.

I scribble an address on the other side of the note and consider driving back into town. I start to shift into drive and stop.

People say I'm here for a reason, but I've lost it. Two hundred yards down the road stands a thick, gnarled pine. My eyes fix on it. I write another line on the note and say to myself: Guess you'll have to dig another hole. I finish the pint, start the engine, and floor the accelerator. Tires spinning, I fight the wheel and the packed snow and gravel until the car straightens. I see three trees looming before me where there should be one. I choose the one in the middle and head straight for it. The car goes airborne, my head strikes the dashboard, and the world turns black.

I float above a gray waiting room that stretches as far as my eyes can see. Thousands sit nearby—white, black, most are elderly, many middle-aged, some in their twenties, and a few unattended children and babies. A gray plastic hospital band

224

encircles my wrist, a question mark in black ink the lone marking. I hover down gently onto a bench.

The floor slowly moves forward, as if we're on a giant conveyor belt. More people materialize in the air and float onto benches behind me as those in forward rows disappear down seemingly endless hallways. When I reach the front of the line, a voice I recognize calls out my name. Mr. Morris, our high school superintendent, curls a finger for me to follow. I try to speak to him but cannot.

"Follow me," he says, and we walk until we reach an arched entrance two stories tall. He opens the massive doors, bows formally, and directs me to enter.

I enter a darkened room, and the floor moves again. It picks up speed until I realize I'm hurtling through a tunnel. On the wall that rushes past me, I witness my birth and learn my father wasn't there. He went fishing. As a toddler, I watch my mother intentionally ignore my cries for help whenever I am hurt. Every dog we ever owned parades before my eyes, miraculously alive and happy to see me again. My first day of school ends with my mother not meeting me at the bus stop, so I get lost on the walk home and wander unfamiliar streets in tears until a policeman helps me home. I relive my first clumsy kiss with a boy named Harold, who goes on to become a multimillionaire in his forties. I see the deaths of my paternal grandparents and watch as my father fails to execute his parents' wishes in their last wills and testaments, pocketing the lion's share of the money for himself. My first prom in our high school gym plays back, followed by my first fumbling sexual encounter in the back seat of my date's car. I see myself graduating with honors, attending college, earning my teaching degrees, and meeting and marrying Jim. Then hazy images of Father appear as he returns home after midnight to argue with Mother and, on some occasions, beat her. I witness the crash that claimed their lives. Then many high- and a few lowlights from my teaching career; the bizarre call from the police informing me that my fifteen-year-old son tried to climb a ten-story building in Prodigal; the haggard faces of every therapist Danny pulled the wool over; the other dysfunctional families trapped in a cycle of support groups and self-flagellation; the angry, feral, and scared look in Danny's eyes the day I kicked him out; the escalating arguments with Jim; and every day I spent homeless by choice. The playback on the wall ends with me gunning the BMW toward the pine.

These moments of clarity breach my subconscious and enter the light.

The floor glides to a smooth stop, and another door opens. I walk into brilliant light, temporarily blinded. Above me looms an empty judge's bench. "Hear ye, hear ye," Superintendent Morris, as bailiff, announces from somewhere in the gray background. "Court is now in session."

My judge arrives and bangs his gavel. I look up into the impassive eyes of Danny Crusoe. He turns to me and flashes that devilish grin.

THE MAN IN THE COMMODE

"Heaven or hell?" I cry out, waking with a start.

I tentatively open one eye and find I'm back on the worn yellow sofa under a blanket in the church/schoolroom. Was the cemetery and crash another nightmare? Then I realize I'm in my underwear. Where the hell are my clothes?

Red-orange flames dance behind the smoky glass of the wood stove. As before, the sofa is pulled close to the warmth. My cheeks feel hot. I lift a hand to my face and groan. When I turn my head, it throbs. I feel gauze wrapped tightly around my skull. My tongue feels like it has hair on it; my lower lip is split and swollen. I turn and move my jaw and touch several loose teeth. My eyes refuse to focus. "Hell."

Two figures are slumped in chairs before me, asleep. For some reason, one is in a Santa suit. The white beard is on the table. He stirs at the sound of my voice and sits up.

He moves closer and takes my hand in his. "How do you feel?" he whispers.

"Water. I need water. What did you do with my clothes, Santa?"

"Barbara removed them to examine you."

Now I see it's Travis, and I say, "I missed you and Frank handing out presents to the kids. I have to put the fire out. I don't want to get you in trouble."

He helps me sit up on an elbow and holds a water bottle to my mouth. "The fire is fine. You need to be in a warm, quiet place, and Barbara had to examine you."

I gather the blanket around my body.

He glances at Barbara and lowers his voice. "Frank found you in your car. We brought you here. I found the note. No one else knows about it. What happened? Why'd you do it?"

"Do what?"

He squeezes my hand. "You scared the hell out of me." He pastes on a smile. "I don't want to lose my Teacher of the Year that way." When he reaches out to touch my face, Barbara stirs.

227

"Good, you're awake," she says, rising from her chair. "We were getting worried. How do you feel?"

"Woozy. Beat up. How long have I been out?"

"An hour, maybe two. It's hard to be certain. Lie still and be quiet." She checks my pulse and blood pressure.

"You're lucky to be alive," Travis says when she removes the cuff. He leans forward, waiting for my response.

I laugh, but that prompts a coughing jag, and pain shoots through my head and chest. My body feels like one giant open wound.

Barbara manipulates my head and neck and checks my eyes with an otoscope. "Your vital signs are good, but you have a black eye and facial contusions from the accident. You took quite a blow to the head and lost a fair amount of blood from a scalp laceration. You have a headache?"

"Yes."

"Is it sharp and stabbing, throbbing, or behind-the-eyes pain?"

"Throbbing."

She asks me my name, where I am, who the man next to us is, and many other questions checking for signs of confusion. I think I pass. I deny experiencing nausea, vomiting, and ringing in my ears, but I feel dizzy, lethargic, and fatigued.

"Your pupils are equal, speech is normal. Short-term memory seems intact. You're not disoriented."

"What do you think, Barbara?" Travis says.

She continues the exam and talks over her shoulder to Travis. "The only way to be sure is with a CAT scan." She makes eye contact with me. "The odds are in your favor—maybe a thousand to one—against having a slow brain bleed that could be life-threatening, but I recommend you get it. If you refuse, tell us right away if your headache worsens or those other symptoms I mentioned appear."

I turn to Travis: "Did you find the blond woman?"

Travis shakes his head and gently wipes my forehead with a wet washcloth. "You do possess a singular purpose. Frank thinks

228

he may have seen her on the bus once and a few recall seeing a woman who fits the description, but she rarely ventured out of the woods. No one else remembers her initiating contact, let alone speaking. Odds are she's long gone, but we're keeping a lookout."

Barbara orders me to lie back down and tells Travis to turn around before she removes the blanket to palpate my abdomen.

I wince.

She manipulates my extremities. "How did you cut your wrist?"

"In the accident, I guess."

She looks skeptical but finally says, "You're lucky it wasn't worse."" She wraps the blanket around me again and helps me rise so she can check my standing vitals. She instructs me to take deep breaths while she listens to my lungs. It hurts to breathe, but the pain is bearable.

"The good news is I don't think you broke any ribs, but three are bruised, and they're going to be tender. My recommendation is to stay off your feet and rest. You're going to feel beat up for days."

She turns to Travis. "Find me immediately if the headaches intensify or she struggles to stay awake. I'm worried about a concussion or brain bleed."

Barbara closes her medical bag and walks to the door. She turns around and says with a sly smile, "I thought there might be something going on between you two. I'm glad. Travis, try to talk your stubborn girlfriend into that CAT scan."

Travis shifts uncomfortably until she's gone.

I bunch the blanket around me and wince while he helps me walk the church's interior. "I bet my little stalker made a beeline for town with my money and credit cards. How's my car?"

"Totaled. Damaged engine block, shattered front windshield, and two flat front tires. Frank and Bert are towing it out of the ditch."

I groan. My head throbs more. "That's enough walking for now. I need to lie down."

229

He helps me. "Your car and that woman are the least of your problems."

I tense.

"You were headed straight toward a tree. You probably didn't see the ditch under the snowbank. There were no skid or brake marks the last hundred yards. Frank found you sitting on your fastened seat belt, and this was on the passenger seat."

He hands me the crumpled note with the address of the pauper's graveyard.

"I didn't write this."

"Your handwriting is on the other side."

"I don't remember writing this." I look down to avoid his eyes. I feel ashamed and small.

"Read the top line to me, please."

I look up, and the shame multiplies. Please don't make me.

"I can't. I was drunk. I don't remember writing this."

His expression is grave, his voice low and soft. "Yet you did. Something or someone compelled you to double-time it to the potter's field. News of Danny? The blond woman? I found these in your car—" He drops the buck knife and an empty pint on the table. "The knife has flecks of dried blood on it. Your left wrist is cut. You're right-handed. Barbara and Frank don't know about the knife. I know you've gone through hell. Do you still want to die? I need the truth."

I cover my face with an arm to hide my humiliation. "I don't know. That's as honest as I can be right now."

Travis takes my hand in his again. "Was Danny in the graveyard?"

I turn and stare into the flames. I hear the ticking of the clock on the classroom wall. "No."

He leans in, so close I smell his musky aftershave. "So he's alive. Have you come all this way to give up? Look at me."

It takes a lot of effort, but I sit up on the sofa and turn to him. "No. I want to find my son."

"It's a miracle you weren't thrown through the windshield. I think a higher purpose or fate wants you to see this through." He looks at the crumpled paper. "You also wrote, 'Idris Elba/Hades—224 Hebert.' A movie star, the god of the underworld, and an address in Prodigal. What's it mean?"

The old curmudgeon on the tractor. "The woman in the green cap led me to believe Danny was nearby but in trouble. I paid money for the address on the flip side. When I learned it was the cemetery, I thought for certain he was dead. Hades is the custodian at the cemetery, and he lives on Hebert. He saw me with . . . he was very kind. I didn't plan this, Travis. I got drunk and wanted the pain to end."

He massages my back and neck. His hands are strong and calloused. Not soft like Jim's. For an instant, I imagine what it would be like to let go of the blanket after I'm healed, but I hold it tighter instead.

"Let me drive you to the ER for that test. Vidal fixed the bus."

So you can have me held for a psych evaluation? Like you wanted to do with Finn?

"I want to stay here. I'd already be in the hospital if Barbara thought I had to have it. I promise to tell you if my headache worsens."

He frowns. "Will you tell me if you feel like hurting yourself?"

I nod. "I appreciate your concern. I've caused a lot of trouble. And the fire feels nice. Am I still welcome?"

A smile spreads across his rugged face as he squeezes my hand. He returns my nod.

Over the next half hour, Travis exhausts every blunt and cunning way he knows to convince me to have the scan, but I stand firm.

There's a knock on the doorframe, and Frank, Dora, and Tom enter. Dora places a mug of soup on the stove to heat while the others ask how I feel. Travis gives the okay for me to remain here for a few days. Frank offers to bring whatever I need from my tent.

"A fresh change of clothes and my green toiletry kit for tomorrow would be nice. Tomorrow's clothes are under the kit. Thanks."

Dora nods to Travis. Frank and Tom leave. She places the steaming soup and a bread roll in front of me on the table, next to a bottled water and two aspirin.

She sits down on the sofa next to me and pats my leg. Travis sits at the far end of the room, engrossed in his phone. She leans closer. "When I said I used to enjoy singing with Tom before we moved here, I saw the look on your face. I imagine you were thinking How can this box of rocks carry a tune?"

I start to protest, but she waves me off.

"I took voice lessons and studied art after high school. We sang professionally in our twenties, playing clubs and resorts along the northeast during the summer months. Between his playing and my range as a soprano, we made decent money and loved our bohemian lifestyle. I felt I was put on this earth to sing. When we clicked on a song, my soul felt like a bird flying over all things earthbound and human. Then we got pregnant and decided to settle down. Life was still good but different. We had responsibilities, and I don't regret any of them. Once the kids started school, I went into graphic design, and Tom worked as a music therapist. I told you our kids responded to our misfortunes with embarrassment . . ."

I was no better, I think. I often felt the same about Danny. Any response from me seems trite, but I feel a need to respond to the pain in her voice. So like the fool I am, I apologize. For what? Their children? Having the same negative emotions about my son?

She lets my comment pass. "I didn't tell you everything. I couldn't accept their rejection. I felt so depressed and mortified when we arrived here. On day two, I walked into the woods on a perfect summer day with a plan to never return. By sheer luck, Travis found me with the empty bleach bottle and rushed me to the hospital. After they saved my life, I fell into an even deeper depression. I was alive but could no longer sing. I lost all desire to paint."

She cocks her head toward the far side of the church. "That handsome man back there bore the brunt of my anger for some time. Foolish, pitiful me. He saved my life, and now I thank God for him every day. Poor Tom didn't know what to say or how to approach me, but in time he did. Focused on what I had lost, I was blind to what I have. I will never sing like a bird again, but I have my art, Tom, and a family here."

I reach out to hold her hand.

"You have a precious gift," Dora says. "The gift of teaching. I suspect you have more waiting for you in Prodigal. Or here. Maybe you can't quite see it right now, but you will."

I hug her, and my tears fall on her faded sweater that smells of the mud of poverty. I think of Jim, Danny, my co-worker friends, Travis, and Dora, my second mom.

"You're in limbo here. It's time for you to decide where to call home."

She's right. I know it in my head. But I haven't found what I came for.

And still, part of me wants revenge on the mysterious little blonde. The one most likely to have entered my tent. She probably read the message board about Danny and waited to pounce like a fox when I was most vulnerable. She's so waiflike—is she an addict? Does she know my son?

I take comfort in knowing the buck knife is here in case we meet again.

I reach for the aspirin and water. I sip Dora's hearty beef noodle soup. When I'm confident it will stay down, I eat half of it along with the bread. I dunk the roll into the broth and bite it gingerly because of my loose teeth. I feel less woozy. She's right, but there's still work to do.

"I'm really tired, Dora. I need to rest, if you don't mind. The soup is great. Thank you." I'm grateful no one said Merry Christmas today.

On her way out, she stoops to tend the fire, but Travis says he'll take care of it.

She turns back to me. "I'll bring you a hot breakfast in the morning." She winks at us.

Travis stokes the fire and retakes the chair Dora vacated.

"Does that door have a lock?" I ask.

"No."

"Will you buck up a chair against the knob and lie with me? I don't want to be alone tonight."

He fails to mask his surprise. He moves a chair and extinguishes the lanterns. He removes his jacket, sweater, shoes, and pants, revealing muscled legs. I stand with the blanket around me and let him lie against the sofa before I nestle down next to him. He drapes a strong arm over me.

"I'm sorry Danny broke your jaw last summer."

"Me too."

I squeeze his hand. "I heard about your wife. Dealing with the Prodigal police must be so difficult."

I hear him quietly groan. "Barbara has loose lips."

I arch my neck to face him. "That's not always a bad thing." I kiss him once softly on his shoulder.

"He was Decker's cousin . . . that's all I'm going to say. I don't want to talk about it. Not now. Maybe not ever."

We all have our ghosts. "Understood."

Five minutes later, he says, "I'm getting a bad feeling about the camp. They sent Decker as a warning. It's going to get ugly soon. I plan to tell all the camps tomorrow that it's time to choose one of the shelters across state. Before people get hurt, and that includes you. You have a home, a life, in Prodigal. You should go back."

"What about you?"

A brief shake of the head. "I'm committed to seeing this through."

"I'm staying. In case Danny returns."

"You are quite singular—"

"In purpose. I know. Just as stubborn as you."

He brushes a strand of hair from my neck. "How's the headache? Any dizziness or nausea?"

234

I wiggle back closer to him and stare into the glowing red embers in the stove. My lids feel heavy. "It's more of a dull pain now, nothing else. Thanks for being here."

I don't know whether he responds to that, for I fall asleep and enjoy a dreamless night until beeping wakes me.

Travis reaches across me to silence his alarm clock. I feel his morning wood and smile. I can't remember the last time I woke to that happy sensation.

"What time is it?"

"Six. I have to get ready for work."

"The day after Christmas?"

He's already dressed, his broad back to me. He walks over and kisses me softly. "Uh-huh. And Dora is bringing you a hot breakfast, remember? Take it easy and rest. How's the head? Any nausea or dizziness?"

"Headache's gone, but I feel like I've run through a gauntlet and been beaten with clubs."

Barbara's prediction is spot on: I am one giant bruise when I rise to dress once Travis leaves. My sweater is covered in blood, as is my shirt. It takes all my strength to struggle into my soiled clothes and coat. Something's been bugging me about my blonde shadow. I stoke the fire and inspect the empty spiderweb at the base of the flue. My deadly female friend is living a pipe dream. I know all about that.

I grab a lantern and the buck knife. I hurry to my campsite in the predawn while most of the camp sleeps, and before kind Dora brings my breakfast. I'm unsteady and move in slow increments. Barbara will kill me if she sees me.

My little blue tent is a crime scene. All that's missing is the yellow tape. It looks like a half-buried time capsule, insignificant and forlorn between massive snowdrifts in the dim light of my borrowed church lantern.

What I came for is curiously missing. I organize my clothes and toiletry kit for Frank but leave them since he offered to bring them to me today. I backtrack across the sleeping camp to inspect my BMW and gasp—the grill and panels look like an accordion with its bellows twisted into macabre folds. The hood is crumpled and must have flown open on impact. The front tires splay outward at awkward angles. Snow, glass, and pine needles litter the front seats, and a ghastly trail of antifreeze and oil stains the snow from the car to the ditch I landed in. It is a miracle I survived. Maybe Hades was right: I'm alive for a reason. Only now I'm marooned here.

Before I return to the church, I head to the porta-potties. Halfway down the path, something makes a noise in the dim light. I grab the buck knife in my pocket, hoping it's my little thief. I see a shadow, then someone limps down the path ahead of me. The person is small and nearly as slow as I am. I gain ground and grab the door to the commode before it closes. I stare down at a tiny, bearded black man in his sixties. Wide-eyed, he holds his gnarled hands in a defensive posture when he sees the knife in my hands. I put it away. He clutches a half-eaten sandwich in his trembling left hand.

"Found it in the trash. Didn't mean no harm," he says. "Mmm, mmm, mmm, mmm. Mmm, mmm, mmm, mmm. First horseman was white, second was red, mmm, mmm, mmm, mmm. Third horseman was black, fourth was pale, mmm, mmm, mmm, mmm. Mmm, mmm, mmm, mmm."

The chant I've been hearing.

The same items line the plastic toilet rim, with one new addition, another ornate origami horse rearing on its back legs, this one painted pale white. Exquisite in every detail. The smell of chemicals and feces assaults my nose. "You live here?"

The sclera of the man's eyes glows pale yellow in the lamp's light. "Will put it back if you want," he says, raising the soggy sandwich in his hand as he rocks back and forth on the seat. "Mmm, mmm, mmm, mmm. Mmm, mmm, mmm, mmm. First horseman was white, second was red, mmm, mmm, mmm, mmm. Third horseman was black, fourth was pale, mmm, mmm, mmm, mmm. Mmm, mmm, mmm, mmm. End of days. First horse—"

I stand stunned before him. "Does the mayor—does Travis—know you live here?"

He raises the remnants of his sandwich in what appears to be a peace offering. He never takes his eyes off mine. He smiles. Bits of wilted lettuce fall to the outhouse floor. "Second was—"

I wish I had more money. "Come with me. Travis and Pastor Frank will help—"

He grabs the door handle before I can enter, slams it shut, and throws the lock.

Sonofabitch. I pound on the door. "I can get you hot food and coffee. You don't have to live this way. Why do you?"

He raises his voice to a shout. "Mmm, mmm, mmm, mmm. Mmm, mmm, mmm, mmm. First horseman was white, second was red. Mmm, mmm, mmm, mmm. Third horseman was black, fourth was pale. Mmm, mmm, mmm, mmm. Mmm, mmm, mmm, mmm. End of days. First horseman was white, second was red. Mmm, mmm, mmm—"

I use the commode next to his and try to yell over his chanting, but it's no use.

The activity is too much. I'm dizzy and vomit in the commode. My head throbs. I pitch forward and nearly pass out. I support myself on tree trunks and rest along the way back to the church while dawn breaks and the camp slowly comes to life. I see the first stirrings of people through the pines and Wilbur at his grills, moving boxes, prepping for the breakfast crowd.

I return to the church, stoke the wood stove, remove my dirty clothes, and lie back down under the blanket. My head spins. Not long after, Dora enters, bearing sausages and eggs from Wilbur's grill. After she leaves, in lieu of a bug, I place an ort of meat and egg on the stove near the web for my spider friend.

Barbara stops in around nine to check my vitals. I pass her tests and don't mention my walk or that I vomited. She looks at the pile of clothes and seems skeptical. "Your boots are wet."

"You caught me. I wore them to stand outside and smoke." It's not a lie because I did that after breakfast.

Once I'm back under the blanket, Frank knocks and brings my clothes and toiletry kit.

I thank him. "Did you happen to see two hardbound white books wrapped in plastic in my tent?" I ask, already knowing the answer.

"No. Should I have?"

"It's not important. Thanks for bringing my stuff."

I ask about the recluse living in the outhouse. He says his name is Benny and that he wants nothing more than to be left alone in his home of choice. My concern falls on supportive but deaf ears. When Travis visits late in the evening, he maintains his omerta about Benny but admits it's one of the saddest things he's seen.

It takes three days to recuperate. Frank visits again on the second day. He turned my little blue tent upside down and couldn't find any white books. Travis returns with a sloppy joe and salad courtesy of Wilbur after my other visitors return home, and he stays the second night.

My mood lifts in conjunction with my physical recovery and spending time with Travis. I can't figure him out. At first, I found him smug and arrogant, but he's intelligent, caring, and quick to act on behalf of his people. I wonder whether and how the death of his wife played a role in his devotion to the homeless. During the second night, we discuss current events and books, but nothing personal. I appreciate that. We talk well into the night and spoon on the sofa with the lights out. He nuzzles my neck, which turns into kissing and light petting, but when I feel his excitement grow, I end it.

"I'm not ready for anything more than this right now. Not until I figure things out."

He says he understands, and I fall asleep in his strong arms.

On the third day, Frank comes bearing a gift. "I found it wedged under the front seat of your car. I thought the books might be there. Hope it still works."

My burner phone. It's about my last worldly possession here. That, and the copy of Walden Dora gave me. I wonder: Why would the little bitch steal my journals?

AN IDLE MIND

Though my hardworking friends stop in and visit occasionally, I spend most of my convalescence alone with my thoughts. When I think of my relationships with family, I believe that most human activity is utter folly. I have driven Danny away with my expectations of him, but with Jim, I think my very existence in the world now causes him problems. But the same doesn't apply to my students or my friends here—they need me, and they look forward to seeing me. That said, I feel like I'm back to square one: the day before I opted for homelessness. If I were driving my car daily, I'd still be sitting on my seatbelt. The dark thoughts linger in the shadows, waiting for the right trigger.

I'm going stir-crazy.

I have to get out of my head, or I'll go mad.

Up here, the world is silent and cold and bare, but its terrible beauty somehow lay in all that. Maybe that's progress.

At last, Barbara clears me to resume normal activities.

I wish school was in session, but that's five days away, and between now and then lurks New Year's Eve, another dreaded holiday.

During my three-day recovery, a warm snap with sunny skies melted most of the snow, leaving a brown, slushy mess across the mountain. Snow falling from branches protected by the shade makes it appear to be snowing.

Dora is right; the clock is ticking. I can make a call on the burner phone, leave this place, and go somewhere new. I can return home and try to repair my broken marriage. I can stay here and teach homeless children. Travis and I can become lovers and work together to make the Highlands a better place until Prodigal shuts us down. But what then? I question whether I have the energy and the will to start over now or when they force us from the mountain.

My unrest grows with each passing day. Travis and Frank work long stretches in town to convince city council members to lift the stove ban, make good on their promise of subsidized housing, or consider other options for the homeless in town. Travis won't admit it, but the stress is weighing on him. Each night he returns frustrated and exhausted.

My little blond con artist worms back into my thoughts. I conjure up ways to exact revenge. On the pretext of regaining my strength, I search the camps and woods for her with the buck knife under my belt. I keep to myself, eat cold food, and boil coffee made from snow.

I don't want to put the camp at risk for another citation about the stove, so when Barbara clears me, I return to my tent. Travis' offer of his home tempts me on many levels, especially now that I'm faced with the daunting task of starting over from scratch with no supplies. I summon all my strength to brush the snow off my tent, pound home the loose stakes and then set about fixing the inside. I gather the scattered kitchen supplies and discover some of my nicer clothes are missing. The blonde, I assume. I tape the torn silver lining and refill the moisture barrier with dry pine needles and branches when I hear voices along the path.

Vidal and Maria stop by with an old multicolored serape, and their children offer pictures they colored. I tape the cheery artwork to the inside of my tent while Vidal stacks dry firewood under my tarp. Dora and Tom bring assorted food packets and bottles of water. Barbara arrives to give me one last brief physical and a tub of real butter. Frank surprises me with a lantern and a checkerboard-patterned sleeping bag he claims was donated. Their kindness overwhelms me, and I hug them all. They possess such inner strength. They think nothing about starting from scratch because they're accustomed to it, and they look out for one another. My life in Prodigal was one of comfort and privilege compared to theirs. Hades said: Never, never, never give up.

My second impromptu welcome-wagon party.

Travis arrives after the others leave. He asks, "Are you having any thoughts about hurting yourself?"

"I have some dark thoughts from time to time, but they pass. I wish I could talk to my son, but I can't control that. The start of school will help. A lot."

"The odds of him returning before Prodigal shuts us down once and for all don't look good. You should start preparing for that." He takes a business card from his wallet and hands it to me. "My cell number is on the back. Call me at work if you need to talk. Day or night."

I lean forward and kiss him. "I promise."

We walk to camp together and eat battered fish filets that Wilbur has fried to golden perfection, along with coleslaw and hushpuppies donated from a local seafood restaurant. After dinner, Travis encourages everyone again to decide on one of the shelters at the opposite end of the state. The mood is subdued tonight. There's less singing, and fewer bottles make their way around the Pit. I stick to Wilbur's strong, hot coffee. I don't seem to be the only one whose thoughts turn inward.

When Travis escorts me to my tent after dinner, we kiss one more time before he returns to his home. He makes the universal hand gesture that reminds me to call him if I need to talk.

This has become another place I can't leave and can't stay in.

I toss and turn in my new bed, thinking about Travis and the camp closing. When sleep arrives, no forgotten memories emerge. I wake, and it's still dark. Arcane thoughts stir in my mind. I have no idea of the time as I have no watch and no iPhone. By my read of the sky, it's about an hour before dawn on New Year's Eve.

At sunrise, I walk to the deepest section of the river from which we haul water, where it makes a sharp bend before meandering down the mountain. The banks are swollen with snowmelt from higher elevations, and their sides are partially frozen, but the deep pool has enough flow to remain ice-free.

I sit on a log, burner phone in one hand, suicide note from the car in the other. This is the one mistake I won't live to regret. I consider writing beneath it I'm sorry, Travis, and tucking it in my wool cap. I see myself removing my coat, folding it neatly on the ground with the cap atop it, and slipping into the deep end like a seal in water, where my heavy insulated boots would take me

241

straight to the bottom in a brief, weightless plunge to welcome the cold sucking blackness.

If I can't remember my crimes, maybe it's time to pay for them.

And it's past time to end the pain and dark thoughts.

I turn the phone over in my hand. Do I call Travis?

I remove a pen from my pocket and think.

Animated voices approach quickly down the path and interrupt my thoughts. Vidal and three men I recognize but don't know by name appear at the river's edge. They laugh and joke and playfully bop one other with empty plastic water containers. They see me and grow silent.

Vidal gives me a quick, sharp look and asks if I'm all right. As I stand, the note slips from my fingers and lands near his feet. I grab it before he does. He asks again whether I'm okay.

"This is rather embarrassing," I say. "Every now and then, I like to jump in cold water. It's invigorating. A great way to open up the pores."

I'm not sure he understands, but the man dressed in a red plaid jacket and earmuffs says, "Like taking the polar bear plunge? I did that for charity. Be careful. The bank can be dangerous, with the ice and all."

"I've done it here before with no problem," I lie.

Plaid jacket says, "We'll just fill the containers and be on our way. We won't keep you."

"That's okay. I'll come back another time." I start up the path, avoiding Vidal's eyes.

From behind, I hear the man in plaid mutter, "When I did it, I brought plenty of towels for when I got out of the water."

I feel Vidal's eyes on me as I hurry along the path to my tent.

I call Travis and can tell he's busy at work.

"I'm okay. I just wanted to hear your voice. Have a good day."

He tells me the same.

People are hunkered around my tent when I round the last bend.

"We haven't seen you for days. We miss you." Dora regards the fading purple and yellow bruises around my eyes and adds, "The swelling is down. That's good." I catch her as she nudges Flossie, who steps forward.

"Wilbur's cooking your favorite tonight."

I'm out of cold food in my tent and down to instant coffee. "Fried chicken and mashed potatoes?"

She nods. "That man puts a helluva scald on chicken. We got pumpkin and pecan pie, with real fake whipped cream from a spray can."

"Tonight is New Year's Eve," Dora says. "The start of a new year for us all."

Great, another god-awful holiday. I miss my journals.

My New Year's wish is to make use of what's tucked under my belt. Maybe she'll be lurking nearby, waiting for the right time to raid the henhouse again. Then I'll drag her into the woods and threaten to carve my initials in her like a tree until she talks.

"Come, walk with us," Dora says.

I am hungry. A party might divert my mind from these dark thoughts—and draw the little blond thief from the shadows.

We pass the picnic tables where Wilbur toils over vats of bubbling oil and steaming pots to boil the cubed potatoes. Judy and George help lay out sides and desserts. My older students are lashing a trashcan lid to a pole in the clearing while the younger ones push and roll snow into a giant ball. Many from the Rainbow Camp are here.

Bert suggests a before-dinner drink and passes a bottle of Everclear around the fire. I see no sign of Frank or Travis. The mood turns festive; people laugh and drink. I feel more alone with each passing minute. I resist the first go-around but drink from the other bottles. Tom begins to play the piano, and an accordionist and guitarist join him.

Flossie is true to her word about the chicken. My wing and thigh are crispy, hot, and spicy. Hours pass, and my buzz from the

243

shared bottles enters the next level. Frank appears and makes himself a plate.

As midnight nears, the crowd hushes while Tom plays a slow, solo version of "American Tune." I wish Travis was next to me. I imagine the quiet comes from the reality that the new year is about to kick us in the ass, but that may be the booze talking.

The boys hoist their giant snowball, now spray-painted silver, onto the underside of the trashcan lid. They plant the affixed pole into a hole in the ground softened by river water.

Dora walks over to Tom and places her arms around his narrow shoulders as the camp sings along to "Auld Lang Syne." The boys start the countdown, and at the stroke of midnight, one yanks the rope holding the lid to the pole, and the giant silver snowball lands on the soggy earth with a dull thud.

How apropos.

Firecrackers explode. Wilbur bangs pots together. A few shoot handguns, and others throw confetti while couples cheer and kiss. Some cry, and others look pensive.

A man holding a lantern and scythe appears from the darkness beneath the totem pole. Dressed in a flowing white robe and beard, he raises his hands. The crowd quiets. He lays down the scythe and lantern and produces a scroll from a pocket.

I feel a rush when I realize who is about to speak. "A wise man named T. S. Eliot once wrote: For last year's words belong to last year's language. And next year's words await another voice. And to make an end is to make a beginning."

Travis, as Father Time, rolls up the scroll and returns it to his pocket.

"Last year challenged us with defeats and losses. We bid farewells to Doug and Frances. Their bodies are at peace, and their souls are free to roam the heavens. We wish Charlie, the world's oldest elf, a healthy rehabilitation in his new home. He is a fighter and will spread his unique brand of joy to everyone around him. We miss him every day."

Doug Jones, the dude in the pauper's graveyard.

"Last year graced us with three subsidized housing approvals. Edna and Max, and most recently, our own Corey. Proving there is hope where precious little may seem to exist."

Whistles, clapping, and shouts of approval interrupt Father Time.

"Last year also ushered in a surprise for our children when we welcomed Susan into our family. She is a gifted teacher eager to share her knowledge and thirst for learning with our children. She is proof that Highlanders and Prodigalites can do more than coexist. They can thrive together for the benefit of all."

Dora, Tom, Frank, Penny, Kim, Theo, and others clap. Barbara gently pats my back.

Travis looks haggard as he removes his beard and robe. "The meetings in town have ground to a standstill. I've tried every idea I know. Prodigal will close us down no later than the first of February unless a new voice emerges with a plan. A new beginning is my hope for us all. We will keep fighting for you. So once again, I encourage every Highlander to choose one of the two homeless shelters. I know they're on the other side of the state. For many, that means losing your jobs in town and some of the freedoms you enjoy here, but we face three more months of a hard winter. To face that alone on the streets or in the woods can break the toughest among us. I implore you to enter a shelter instead. Frank and I will guarantee you arrive safely, with an open bed."

Travis grabs the scythe and raises it above his head. "May this year bring a new voice and a new beginning for us all. And an end to the divisiveness and hate in the world. We are all brothers and sisters—Highlanders and Prodigalites—much more alike than we are different."

Travis makes his way to the Pit amid muted cheers and applause. He stops to speak with several people. I've had too much to drink again and stand.

More firecrackers explode in the night. The flames flicker and rise while people sing and dance around the fire.

I leave the warmth of the Pit to search the perimeter for the little blonde woman, buck knife in one hand and a third of a pint of Mad Dog in the other, which I claimed to have emptied when it made the rounds to me. Now is the perfect time for the fox to enter, while everyone parties.

I circle behind the grill and coolers, walk the path, check the edge of the woods, patrol the outhouses and church/classroom, and find nothing. No news about Danny on the bulletin boards, of course. I check on my spider friend. The web is in tatters. She lies curled into a lifeless ball on the cool stovetop.

Happy New Year. You're in a better place, girl.

I don't want the company of Travis, or anyone, now that I've been drinking. How I hate the holidays. I want to wallow. I return to my tent, lids heavy from drink and my mind overridden by rage. I pull back the flap and sense a subtle change. It takes a while to notice. This time things have been added.

The ornate origami horse rears on its hind legs atop my new sleeping bag. It has been painstakingly painted pale white. Fine details adorn its head now—eyes and whiskers, jets of cold air shooting from its nostrils. The fourth horseman. End of days.

Next to it, a wad of crumpled newspaper contains the half-eaten sandwich.

I finish the Mad Dog 20/20 red grape wine and fall into a deep sleep. I have another sex dream about Travis. Sometime during the night, I feel sick and throw up in my tent, then roll back on my side.

I hope this is rock bottom. Maybe the next world will be better, for this one makes no sense.

SOBER CANNIBALS OR DRUNKEN

CHRISTIANS

As dawn breaks on New Year's Day, a twig snaps outside my tent. I hear a faint sound like little fox feet tiptoeing on pine needles. Coming closer. A shadow looms near my tent flap.

The little bitch is back.

I grab the buck knife and wait, wait, wait for the perfect time to pounce. Once the flap moves inward, I spring, grab hold of a collar, and yank. The trespasser tumbles forward, and I slip the knife under the neck of the little blond—

But it's not her.

It's Danny!

"Hi, Susan," he says, unmoving, hands up, eyes wide and locked on mine. Through gritted teeth, he adds, "So, how've you been?" in his casual, flippant way, a distant memory returned.

Of all the scenarios I imagined for our first meeting, sliding a knife under my son's throat was not one of them. I drop the buck knife and release him. I nervously straighten his coat, pat his tousled hair, and help him sit up. I want to apologize but can't find the words. Or any words, for that matter.

Breathe, or you're going to explode.

He dusts himself off and sits up. He grimaces at the congealed brown goo clinging to his hands, notices the empty Mad Dog bottle, and sniffs the air. "Jeez, is that vomit?"

"I'm afraid so."

He frowns at the moldy, half-eaten sandwich Benny left in my tent. "You finally left him, for this? Christ, how bad did it get? You were a neat freak, and now you live in filth?" Incredulity fills his voice, which is deeper than I remember, and somehow strangely . . . empty? Maybe a better description is hollow.

He's thinner than I remember. No longer the strapping, handsome young man in the picture with black wavy hair. No more dimples in his cheeks. No dreamy, faraway look in his eyes.

Barbara is right; the man before me seems much older than I expected. His unkempt dark beard is stippled with patches of gray. Worry lines fan out under his eyes. A neck tattoo I can't discern serpentines its way under his camouflage coat. The tat is new since I kicked him out.

I can't believe he's here. I try not to stare as I take in every aspect of him. "How did you know I was here? Did you see the notice on the board?"

All the time I spent rehearsing what I'd say if I ever found him, and I blurt out this nonsense. I expected the beginning to be awkward, but not like this.

He wipes his hands on the serape Vidal and Maria gave me to replace my bed. "I can't believe you're here. You hate camping."

"I do, I did. You're a hard guy to find. I heard you had stayed here before, so I waited. I'm glad I did! We missed you in Boulder and Loveland Park, nearly caught up with you at Big Sur and San Francisco, then again in Albuquerque, St. Louis, Louisville, and Raleigh—" I stop rambling when he appears lost in thought.

His brow furrows. "You hired a private dick to hunt me. I thought a pissed-off drug dealer was on my tail the other day. That bastard drove me here."

That can't be right because the PI I hired before I came here is focused solely in Prodigal. "The only thing that matters is you're here. Are you—?"

"Damn," he interrupts. "What happened to your face? It looks like somebody beat you up." His tone is matter-of-fact, and I realize he's been staring at me in the dim light of the tent.

"I had a car accident. It's nothing."

"Don't tell me you left your happy house in the suburbs, your husband, and quit teaching to become a homeless mountain woman pining for her junkie son?"

I look him in the eyes and smile.

He looks flummoxed. "Shit. No way. Why would you do this?"

I want nothing more than to reach out and touch him, but I keep my hands at my sides. "To see you and talk with you again. I miss you."

Wariness replaces his surprise. "I don't believe it. Well, here I am. Warts and all."

"And I didn't leave your father. I stayed here to wait for you."

"Is he with you?"

I shake my head. "But he's been here, to visit."

"How long have you lived here?"

I hesitate but don't want to lie. "About three months."

He laughs. "Then I'd say you left him."

He smells his hand and makes a sour face before he rubs it across his worn black jeans. "You've been here three months, and this is all you've done to your tent?"

"It's a long story. I was wrong to kick you out. I should have given you another chance, especially when you were in trouble. I made a bad, impulsive decision in anger and frustration. I'm sorry."

I stare into his dark brown, almost black eyes and notice the premature crow's feet around them. My heart sinks.

He laughs so loud and long it feels like I'm the butt of a private joke.

"I had so many chances to get my shit together. Wasn't it obvious that I didn't want to? Those outpatient programs you sent me to? I got high in all of them. You'd be surprised how easy it is to buy clean urine. Wanna know how I managed to get stoned in every inpatient treatment facility? Flowers. I had women on the outside send me get-well bouquets in your name. LSD microdots aren't my drug of choice, but they're much easier to hide than heroin. And who would expect it in a package from a parent? Like I tried to tell you, I'm an adrenaline junkie. I live to get high. I fucking love the rush. It's the only thing that makes me feel alive. Especially now that I'm too old and broken to bungee jump down a river gorge or fly down a mountain and catch a ski edge or ramp-jump off a building on a motocross bike."

249

"Too old and broken? You're a young man."

The laughter returns. "I peaked in my teens. It's a miracle I'm alive."

"The doctors. They got you hooked after the skiing accident. They prescribed OxyContin, then—"

"No. It wasn't their fault. It wasn't even an accident. I love the feel of flying. I wanted to ski off that cliff. It was a great ride." Another brief laugh. "I just didn't know the drop was that goddamn long! I'm a thrill-seeker. Hell, escaping from what I thought was a pissed-off dealer last night was a rush. One day, drugs will kill me. I made my peace with that years ago. I've been clinically dead and resuscitated three times with Narcan. I've been to the edge and back. I'm not afraid of what's on the other side. It's either a void or something better than this world."

Tears well and spill down my cheeks.

He stares, emotionless, into my eyes. "There are worse things than death, Susan. Like not living," he says with no trace of judgment or emotion.

"I've reached the same conclusion since I've lived here." I want to tell him about rediscovering Thoreau and my personal walk into the woods, but now, isn't the time. I fall silent, flush with conflicting thoughts.

"You two completed college and expected the same from me, but that was the last thing I wanted." His face sours. "Trapped behind a desk the rest of my life. Working for some dipshit of a boss who knows less than I—"

"You had the world at your feet. You could have been your own—"

He waves me off. "I've seen the world. Been to places not drawn on any map. Real places never are. When I get the itch, I sign aboard a steamer and sail the oceans. I've traveled to every continent, climbed Kilimanjaro, and landed on barbarous coasts. I've been welcomed and accepted by all sorts of cultures and religions, met some of the most fascinating, bizarre people in the world, and experienced more than most in four lifetimes. I've shared beds with sober cannibals and drunken Christians to find I prefer cannibals. During my travels, I probably tried every natural and synthetic drug known to man." He shakes his head. "I don't regret a single day."

I stare at him while I sit back and light my first cigarette of the morning. I blow smoke at his face. "Is that so?"

He frowns and doesn't answer.

"Have you been in love?"

"Love," he smirks. "If that means finding the one person in the world meant for me and settling down, the answer is no. I have shared the same soul, the same spirit, with like-minded women. Each are a part of me. I yearn for them when they're gone. I imagine you'd label me a hippie."

"Are you a father?"

He brings his knees up to his chest and wraps his arms around them. It looks defensive. He nods and looks away. For an instant, that faraway, dreamy look from his picture returns. I notice jailhouse tattoos of letters below his knuckles that spell ACAB.

I feel my heart pound. "Boy or girl?"

His eyes lock onto mine. He doesn't answer, and the silence lengthens.

My throat is dry. I'm a grandmother but never had the pleasure.

I describe the thin blonde to him. "Do you know her?"

"How could I? I hopped a freight and hiked up the mountain last night."

"How did you know where to find me?"

"Travis walked me to your tent after I agreed to his rule."

"He exiled you last summer for drugs."

"I was really fucked up back then."

"And now?"

The wry smile again, the crease of the crow's-feet. "Less so."

My look hardens. "Does the name Flossie ring a bell?"

The look on his face answers my question. "Enough with the interrogation."

251

"She's pregnant. You were her supplier. And more than that."

He doesn't avert his eyes, but his features harden.

"Remember Wilbur? Her husband. Big man. Convicted felon. Did time for second-degree murder. He knows. He plans to kill you. Is that enough excitement for you?"

He flashes a wry grin. "It does get the blood pumping. Good to know."

I turn my head toward voices that seem to move along the path in the woods where it winds near my little blue tent. It sounds like Judy and George out on a walk and George complaining about something or other.

"What are you going to do now?" Danny asks me flatly. "Live here?" A trace of challenge now.

"I don't know. I might. What about you?"

He asks to bum a cigarette. He makes a face when he sees the crumpled Slims box, but he takes one anyway.

I lean closer to light it for him. "It's been over a year. We have a lot of catching up to do. A lot of water under the—"

"I thought we just did that. I'm not going back to Prodigal. No way."

"Did I ask you to?"

He smirks. "Just a matter of time. Wanted to nip that in the bud."

"What are your plans?"

"I don't make them. I go where the wind takes me. I appreciate the heads-up about the angry husband."

"What's the story with Flossie?"

He taps ash from the cigarette and doesn't answer.

"I think the first thing you did when you blew into the Highlands was recruit customers. I think you learned Flossie is a recovering addict and enlisted her. She had no cash, so you took it out in trade."

The frown returns. "I never front my product. Strawberries are everywhere, and this place is no different. She started turning tricks in her teens to get away from home and her perv of a father.

Did you know that's how she met the big man? I prefer cash, but her method of payment was her choice."

"Strawberries?"

The smirk again. "Someone who pays for drugs with sex."

"Is the tattoo on your hand a gang symbol?"

He laughs at the question. "I can't believe you're still alive after three months here." He proudly displays his right fist. "All cops are bastards. The big ink on my chest is a dragon. I'm especially proud of that one."

Charming. "Do you care that she and Wilbur have two children in foster care and that her relapse cost them a chance for an apartment in town?"

"Everybody has a sad story. No one held a gun to her head."

"She's pregnant, and you might be the father. How about I take you to her so you can be reunited?"

A muscle in his jaw works overtime, but he says nothing. He nervously taps ash onto my tarp.

"You sold speed to Finn."

"Who?"

I describe the giant, red-bearded miner.

He smiles. "I remember him. Good client. Gullible sort. Gotta visit him, see if he wants more party favors. Help get him through all the hard labor in that dark lonely mine."

"He's mentally ill. The last thing he needs in his system is amphetamines. He had a psychotic break and ran off before we could get him help."

He looks concerned for the first time. "My man's gone? Damn. Not my fault if he had a bad trip. Some ride it out; others can't. You know where he lives up in those caves?"

"Why the sudden interest if he's not here?"

He chuckles and leans forward. "Wanna hear something incredible? You'll think I'm shitting you. He paid me in real gold. The crazy fucker struck gold!"

"He hurt three elderly homeless men because you put the idea in his head that they planned to steal his treasure."

He exhales smoke and grinds the butt into the floor tarp. "I don't know. Maybe I did. But my product is premium. It's not cut or jacked up with dangerous shit."

"For a hippie, you seem obsessed with money and the trappings of the real world. You know, the one you thumbed your nose at all those years."

He shrugs. "It keeps the wolf from the door and also lets us flip product so I can hardline."

"Us?"

He seems to backpedal. "The sisters who share my world vision."

"You fancy yourself a leader, then?"

"Of sorts."

"Where are your followers?"

He seems exasperated. Did I paint him into a corner? "You are full of fucking questions."

I take a slow drag and stare into those almost black eyes. I let the silence linger until he starts to squirm. "And you're a fucking liar."

He freezes. "What did you call me?" His tone cold, borderline threatening.

I grind my cigarette into the tarp. "Your partner in crime stole my journals and gave them to you. Melville, Moby Dick. I teach English, Danny. Remember?"

That smirk morphs into a snarl. "I was just trying to make you feel better since you were a miserable failure as a mother."

"But you didn't stop there, did you? You directed your little friend to steal a thousand dollars and my credit cards. Was that meant to lift my spirits? Or when you both led me to believe you were dead? What kind of person does that?"

He moves closer, his face inches from mine. "What kind of mother regrets becoming pregnant and regrets giving birth to her son? What kind of mother feels elation and relief when she kicks her son out of the house? If those dealers had found me, I'd be in a landfill with my fingernails pulled out."

I start to speak, but he clamps a rough hand over my mouth. I resist, but he's too strong. After minutes of frenzied struggle, I go limp. I'm terrified. If he wants to kill me, I'd forgive him.

He's so close I feel his breath on my face and smell the cigarette. "What kind of wife sleeps in a separate room from her husband for years? How many times did you write that you wished he would die? For fuck's sake, get a divorce. You live to work, read, and drink Maker's Mark in the guest bedroom until you pass out." He laughs. "And you denigrate my lifestyle? What a hypocrite. At least I'm upfront with mine."

He removes his hand and pushes me away from him. I fight to catch my breath and gulp for air.

"You had no right . . . to read my private thoughts. I want my journals back. You mention a tiny fraction of fleeting thoughts . . . ones that I'm deeply ashamed of. At least I tried to address them."

When the strength returns to my lungs, I say, "You gloss over all the positive feelings I wrote about you and your father all those years."

His expression turns cold, determined. "I'll make it easy for you. You don't have to kick me out this time." He rises to his knees and grabs my face between his strong hands, his voice a low whisper. "I hope that trip to the cemetery hurt. I know what happened after. Finish the job."

I hold my head up against his verbal slap. "I don't know you anymore."

He drops two packets on the sleeping bag. "Wear 'em both. That'll do the trick." And with that, he's gone.

I pick up one, read the label, and drop it instantly. Fentanyl.

PANDEMONIUM

The flashing lights return to stab my eyes. The beeping noises pierce my ears, and I clamp my hands over them. I close my eyes and writhe on the tarp for I don't know how long.

When they finally recede, I sit and pull my legs up to my chest. I bury my head in my hands and sob. His last words tunnel through my brain like a bullet.

I rock back and forth with my eyes closed until a massive explosion shakes the ground.

I stuff the packets in a front pocket of my jeans and rise to see what happened. I grab my backpack and rush outside. Frantic voices ring out nearby along the path, screaming over each other. I hear shouts of fire. I run into the chaos to find Highlanders sprinting down the path with water containers. I follow them and race toward the thick black smoke as it billows through the canopy of pines and into the clear blue sky.

The only ones running the other way are Danny—and Wilbur, who is chasing Danny with a meat cleaver.

I round the final bend in the path and lock eyes with Flossie when I realize which tent is the destination of the bucket brigade.

"Dora!" I scream, "Tom!" I run toward the flames, but Travis grabs me in a bear hug and won't let me pass. I struggle with him until he wraps his arms around me. Precious minutes later, people arrive with buckets of water to throw on the blaze. It takes too much time to get to the river and back. The heat is too intense to get close enough to do much good. Frank empties the fire extinguisher from the bus at the base of the flames, and others work feverishly to douse brush fires before the swirling winds spread them to other structures.

"Are they inside?" I shout into the chaos.

I see Flossie, but she's not paying attention. She frowns and bites her lip while she stares down the path Danny and Wilbur took. Visibly upset, she cradles her belly and looks for a place to sit.

The fire diminishes only after it consumes most of the fuel in the blazing tent. What remains is a charred, smoldering mass of twisted and fused shapes. As the thickest of the smoke lifts, where the bed once stood now sits a pile of blackened charcoal on the ground, the plywood floor and carpet consumed by the flames. Two amorphous, charred shapes lie face-to-face. The acrid mix of burnt liver and a heavy, coppery smell mingles with a sweet musky perfume that makes me bury my face in my coat. The fabric doesn't block the smell.

Everyone stands in open-mouthed silence, exhausted, arms at their sides, blinking in disbelief. Some cry and cling to each other.

"Has anybody seen Dora and Tom?" I cry out.

Travis holds me fast and gently pats the side of my face while he whispers in my ear. "They're gone, Susan. I hope the smoke took them before the fire."

"What caused the explosion?" Frank yells.

Travis holds on to me and points toward Dora and Tom's stove. The pipe that used to run through the tent ceiling has been torn from the stove, which is on its side at least five feet from where it used to stand. The blast blew the door off its steel hinges. I look around for the door; it must have shot through the tent like a missile. Someone finds it along the path twenty yards away.

"That's odd," Travis says, pointing to where the stove used to be. "That looks like a propane tank. They never owned one, far as I knew."

"Wouldn't the propane tank have exploded, too?" Frank asks.

"Hardly ever. They build safeguards into them. More likely, the valve was left open and added fuel to the explosion in the stove," Travis says, still holding me fast.

I turn away and bury my face in Travis' shoulder. When I look up, I see Wilbur, the rage ebbed from his face, plodding toward Flossie. No Danny, no meat cleaver. I tense at the possibilities.

Flossie cradles her stomach, her back against a pine trunk. All heads turn to her when her frenzied screams for Wilbur shatter the smoke-filled air. Her eyes grow wide while she struggles to stand. Wilbur runs and quickly closes the distance between them.

She yanks hard on Wilbur's meaty forearm. "Oh shit, my water just broke! It's way too early! Something's wrong." She grimaces. "Goddam, it hurts like hell!"

People spring into motion as if Flossie were the conductor and the rest of us mere players. Travis releases me and huddles with Frank. Corey, here on a visit, races to the learning center. Others leap into action upon orders from Travis.

I'm shocked when Frank tosses the bus keys to me and hands me towels. "Get them to the hospital. We've got a lot of work and explaining to do when the fire department arrives. Good luck, and God bless you, Flossie and Wilbur! Susan, remember— the clutch is real mushy. Hurry, but be safe."

I turn and run. Wilbur and others are already helping Flossie toward the bus in the clearing. He helps her inside to a bench and holds her hand.

I climb in. "Were you having labor pains before your water broke?"

She turns to me, and I see fear in her eyes. "No."

"Are you bleeding?"

"I don't think so."

I see terror on Wilbur's face.

"Are you still in pain?"

She nods, sweating. "Hell yes, woman. Something's the fuck wrong!"

Wilbur rubs her back, his face riddled with worry. "Her first two deliveries were normal. No problem."

I call to him while I struggle to start the engine. "It's usually twenty-four to forty-eight hours after the water breaks until birth." I familiarize myself with the controls and test the clutch. The pedal sinks all the way to the floorboard until it catches. The gears grind once, twice as the bus lurches forward down the mountain. I take a glance at the massive pine that had been my target. I feel a shadowy presence when we pass. The road is snowy where the sun doesn't reach the gravel, but it's ice-free. "We have time; we're gonna make it."

They sit together, rocking. Flossie cries out every so often. Wilbur soothes her in whispers.

We rumble over ruts and bumps and skid around a bend in the road, but we're making steady progress. We're already halfway to town when Flossie lets loose a blood-curdling scream. I check her in the rearview mirror. She's looking at her lap, wide-eyed. "Blood! Oh, sweet Jesus, lots of it!"

Wilbur's eyes grow big as saucers. He says, "Oh my God! This can't be happening," as he distances himself from her on the bench. "Do something!" he shouts at me.

"How far along are you?" I ask Flossie.

"Twenty-five weeks."

Déjà fucking vu.

"Wilbur, have you driven this thing before? Are you calm enough to drive?"

When he answers yes, I bring us to a skidding stop. "Trade places with me. Take the wheel and drive as carefully as you can to the hospital. Safety first. It does Flossie no good if we all end up in a ditch. Everything's going to be okay."

Blood is soaking into the bench seat. I take the towels, gently move her to the floor with her back to the wall, and prop up her legs. It's worse than I imagined. I squeeze her hands. "Everything's going to be okay, Floss. Hang on, you hear me! I went through something similar. We're going to get you and your baby help." I get close to her face and whisper, "Does your doctor know about the heroin and alcohol?"

Sweat clings to her forehead beneath the do-rag. Her terrified eyes lock on mine in defiance. She grabs my wrist and says through gritted teeth, "They aren't taking this one!"

She's losing too much blood. I pull out my burner phone. When the dispatcher answers, I say, "I'm with a pregnant woman whose water broke, and she's bleeding. We're in an old orange school bus driving south toward Prodigal on Route One." I look out the window. "We just passed mile marker eighty-seven. We're on our way to the hospital, but we need an ambulance now."

The dispatcher requests Flossie's name and mine. I tell her: No, I'm not a nurse. Yes, she's a clinic patient in town. She asks more questions, some I can answer, others I can't or choose not to. "Look, I have to go. Just send that ambulance," I say, and hang up. I hold Flossie's hand and wipe her brow with tissues from my backpack. "Help is on the way. Everything's going to be okay."

"How's she doing back there?" Wilbur keeps asking from the front as he negotiates a bend too fast, and the bus skids close to a roadside creek.

"She's hanging in there. She's very strong. She's a fighter. Keep us on the road, Wilbur. We need you. I just called—"

"I heard," he shouts, goosing the engine.

Her pulse grows weak. I shake her gently. "Flossie! Tell me the names of your beautiful kids and their ages. Right now. Talk to me."

Her eyes flutter open, but her look seems far away. "Tamika . . . Prince."

"Good! How old are they?"

I pat her cheek when she drifts off again. "Flossie! What are their ages?"

She shakes her head and opens her eyes. "Six . . . four."

She's slipping into lethargy. I rock her and talk to her to keep her awake. Before we reach Spruce Street, sirens approach from town.

"Here they come!" Wilbur shouts, flashing the lights and honking the horn. The bus skids to a stop as an EMT van and police cruiser arrive. I slip on blood and fall hard on my face. I rise from the corrugated metal floor as Wilbur rushes to us and sees Flossie awash in blood. "Oh sweet Jesus, have mercy!"

The EMTs triage and load Flossie onto a stretcher. Wilbur climbs into the ambulance, and in a blink, they're gone. The policemen offer to escort me to the hospital but order me to move the bus off the road first.

A fire truck passes us going north with lights flashing but no siren, and my heart breaks again for Dora and Tom.

I slide onto the hard vinyl back seat. The cop in the passenger seat swivels to ask me questions through the cage, but all I hear is white noise.

Followed by beeping. And more flashing lights.

Twenty-five weeks. Déjà fucking vu.

My mind flashes back to the NICU.

I'm groggy and exhausted. The OB/GYN rattles off a list of possible causes, including alcohol and drug use.

I pass out. When I wake up, beeping machines and flashing lights surround me.

I remain in the hospital for weeks, receiving transfusions and fluids. I can't bear to look at myself in the mirror. I can't bear to look at Jim, who hovers attentively at my bedside and provides updates on baby Daniel. He speaks of other plans, but my vitals are out of whack, and I'm in a daze. Bouquets of flowers and get-well cards from family and co-workers fill the window ledge. I avoid looking at that side of the room.

A chaplain and social worker persist as thorns in my side, but I refuse to meet with them. Once I'm strong enough to drag my IV pole to the courtyard, I walk outside to smoke. My OB/GYN walks up to me shaking her head. She is thirtyish, a petite Asian with a pretty oval face and immaculate skin.

"As your doctor, I strongly advise you to give up smoking. If you don't, please minimize the secondhand smoke around your baby when he is healthy enough to go home."

I promise that I will.

"You've been through a lot. Speaking with our social worker can help. If you derive comfort from religion, our priest is also an excellent resource."

I nod and tap ash into the mouth of a trash can.

"You will likely stay here another week, but Daniel must remain in the NICU."

I'm shocked. I sit down on a bench. I ask why.

"Daniel is ten inches long and weighs a pound and a half. Babies do not develop a sucking reflex until the thirty-fourth week. He may need to stay in the NICU another twelve weeks. Babies born this early have a seventy-five percent chance of having deficits. With your son, it's too early to know."

I barely hear her as she rattles off the list of potential deficits.

"You and your husband may visit him daily. In fact, I strongly encourage it."

She updates me on my latest labs and vitals. I thank her for everything she's done.

On the walk back to my room, I round a corner and see Jim huddled in the hallway with the priest and social worker. When they see me, they stop talking and turn my way. That's when I knew. That clever doctor probably sent them to my room while she was with me in the courtyard. They're all in on the plot—

A voice shouts at me. A man calls my name. I open my eyes and snap back to the present. I'm in the back seat of a car. A police cruiser. Flossie and Wilbur. Blood from the bus floor covers my face and hands. I start to wipe them on my coat, which is also blood-soaked. Exhausted, I lean forward to rest my head on the back of the front seat, but the cop in the passenger seat says no, no. He hands me some tissues through the steel cage. "Sit back for me, Mrs. Crusoe. Use those to clean yourself."

Mrs. Crusoe. I told the dispatcher my name.

"Sure," I say and sit back, drained and defeated. I thank him and wipe my hands and face as best I can. He hands me a plastic bag for the bloody tissues.

The cop riding shotgun resumes his questions. I hear him say the Highlands. His tone is mildly curt and condescending. Is there a touch of smugness in his demeanor? I have no idea what I say. I'm afraid he can read my thoughts. Like after Danny was born. I want to get far away from them.

We inch along a row of ambulances at the ER.

"I have to check on my friends." There's no handle on the back door, and I tell the cops to let me go. They glance at one another as the car glides to a stop. Released, I run through the sliding glass door to the ER. An older lady sitting behind a glass counter asks where I've been hurt. "It's not my blood. Where's Flossie? How is she?"

The older woman who wears a badge that says "Admissions" asks for the patient's name, and I say it again. She asks for the last name, and I realize I don't know it. First names only in the Highlands. She asks if I'm family, and I say no. She says she can't help me.

"But she's a friend, and I brought her in! She's pregnant and bleeding!" People in the waiting room turn and stare.

The woman frowns. Her mouth puckers as if she bit a lemon. "No, ma'am, you did not bring in that woman. You weren't with her, and you need to lower your voice. You're disturbing the others." The admissions person casts sideways glances at me while she whispers to a young woman who wears an ER nurse's badge. The nurse who had been speaking to a tall man in scrubs now turns to regard me through the glass. The admissions woman whispers "Highlands" to the nurse, who exits the station and approaches.

The nurse is young and blond. She greets me with a warm smile and gently touches my elbow with a gloved hand. "I'm Sherry. I'm here to help. Is this your blood? Are you hurt, ma'am?"

"It's not my blood. You don't understand. My friend is bleeding, and she's having a baby. I need to be with her husband, Wilbur." The beeping returns to stab my ears, and I want to scream. I'm the center of attention in the middle of the ER. Their looks say it all—they know the monstrous things I've done. Their eyes judge me. Everyone but the young nurse, who leads me down a hallway.

In a soft voice, she says, "You did a great job helping your friend get here, and thanks to you, she's getting the best care

263

possible. I will help find your friend's husband, but first, do me a favor. Take some deep breaths and please lower your voice."

I'm trembling, so I lean on her. "Sorry, I'm upset. I didn't realize I was yelling."

Hospital security appears in the doorway. The two men watch me, hands on their holsters.

Sherry shakes her head at them and turns to me. "Follow me, Mrs. Crusoe. First thing we need is for you to wash up. You do that for me, and I will make sure we get you to the right waiting room."

The admissions person hands a clean pair of scrubs to the nurse.

Sherry reminds me to breathe while we walk to a private bathroom in the ER.

"Thank you. You're very kind. I'm Susan."

"It's a pleasure to meet you, Susan. Take as long as you need to freshen up and change. We won't have an update on your friend and her baby for a while. I'll be near the station." She hands me the scrubs and a plastic bag. "This is for your soiled clothes. After you use the towels, please put them in the hamper."

I close and lock the door. I remove my bloody coat and hang it on the hook. Next come my soiled shoes and pants. The smells of smoke and death fill the small room while I remove everything else. I take a whore's bath in the sink and scrub my face and hands. The warm water helps thaw my cheeks and fingers. The beeping noises and flashing lights lessen but persist.

I scrub and scrub, but the smell of blood and death remains. Did Dora and Tom lie down in each other's arms and choose to die? I hope Travis is right, that the smoke took them quickly. Did they decide they were too old to start over again? I had similar thoughts after Danny's accomplice stole all my possessions. Was the explosion an accident or something more sinister? I never saw a propane tank in their tent during my months in camp. Prodigal sent their experts to the scene, so we may never know the truth. I think of Tom's bright, elfish eyes and dry wit. I recall Dora's kind words of wisdom when she brought me homemade soup. She was the nurturing mom I never had.

I draw a deep breath and stare into the mirror over the sink. In the harsh fluorescent lighting, a stranger looks back at me, one with wrinkles and worry lines and graying hair badly in need of a cut and color. An older, thinner face. One that's been makeup- and lipstick-free for months. My cracked nails haven't touched an emery board, and scratches and bruises dot my arms and legs. My breasts sag, but my stomach is flatter and more defined. I'm stronger physically now than I've ever been. The transformation stuns me—I don't know what to say to this stranger in the mirror, much less where she should go or what she should do.

The smell of death pervades the small room.

I close my eyes and think of Flossie. Her reaction to Danny's picture my first day in camp, her initial distrust of me, sneaking drinks around the campfire at night, the travel bottles, the heroin she bought last summer from Danny and the price she paid for it, the just-below-the-surface tension between her and Wilbur, and the awkward conversation she may face when this baby arrives.

Twenty-five weeks in. It looked like a severe placental abruption. Just like mine. I nearly died. Danny almost died. Will Flossie? What about her baby gir—

My breath catches in my throat. My eyes grow wide in the mirror. Everything rushes back.

Baby girl. Oh my God.

My spine turns into a column of ice. I cram a towel in my mouth and scream.

Now everything makes hellish sense.

A nurse left the delivery room with a newborn wrapped in a blanket.

A pink blanket.

Danny arrived a few minutes later. A second nurse placed him in a blue blanket before Jim, and the staff rushed to the NICU.

265

It was I who insisted Jim lock that picture away in his desk, along with the others. He fought me on it, but I was so unrelentingly cruel to him that he finally caved.

I dig the two fentanyl packets from the front pocket of my bloody jeans, and my hands shake as I open them. A final parting gift from Danny. There's a certain poetic justice to it all ending here. The killer returns to the scene of her crime to accept her punishment. I place them on the lip of the sink and stare. I can wear them or chew them. It's a painful way to die, and I'm in a hospital. The staff could save me.

I reach for them.

Then I stop. I left home to find my son and recover my memories. I lived in a homeless camp and learned to survive winter in a flimsy tent. I faced my fears. I established a school for homeless kids and more.

I grab the fentanyl patches and read the instructions.

Then I flush them down the toilet as flashes of images return like ghosts to crush what remains of my soul.

NOW I LAY ME DOWN TO SLEEP

In the photograph Jim brought to the mountain, our old friend Janet is not holding their tiny infant Meghan. I have no idea where they live now and no clue if Meghan is a veterinarian happily living in New York City. For all I know, she could be a divorced, depressed blackjack dealer living in a trailer in Vegas.

I am the one in the picture.

Dressed in a gown in a hospital bed, I hold newborn Gabby for the one and only time. The Now I Lay Me Down to Sleep photographer posed us and moved in close to make Gabby appear larger. He folded her cold hand around my finger.

He took another with Jim at my bedside, holding her, both of us dead inside and trying to hide our despair long enough for the macabre shoot to be completed. In one, we gaze down at our tiny daughter, who never had a chance, thanks to me.

Photos, like ghosts, are the persistence of memory over time. People fade from our recollection or change, but photos carry the truth, if only the briefest cross-section of it. When the pictures arrived, I cringed and called them ghoulish, but Jim was adamant about keeping them. He cherished them.

He said the pictures were a way to keep her memory alive.

For me, the beeping noises and flashing lights took over. Until they were replaced by voices and paranoia.

There's one more ghost, one more cross-section of horrible truth that I buried. One last picture with me in the hospital bed holding Danny, with Jim at my bedside holding Gabby. The twins together. Danny seems to be staring at Gabby. It chills me now to think of it.

Now I remember times when I'd walk into Jim's study and see him quickly open and close a desk drawer. He kept Gabby's memory alive through the pictures.

For me to survive, I had to deny her existence.

During some of our toughest struggles with our son, there were times I wished that Danny had died. Have mercy on me for putting that to paper. And for Danny not knowing about Gabby.

I am my father's daughter, and I hate myself for it.

I stare at my naked self in the hospital bathroom mirror.

I'm intelligent. I knew the risks. I elevated my clandestine smoking and drinking during my early pregnancy to an art form. I traded Maker's Mark for odorless vodka. No one, not even Jim, was the wiser. And in the old storage cabinet in the garage I rushed to when Jim left for work? Water bottles filled with Stoli. Packs of Slims.

The pain I repressed all these years returns as fresh and persistent as a toothache. Is there a limit to how much moral injury a person can self-inflict before they break? I feel I'm being torn in two, and in my center lies a stone.

I'm just as guilty as Flossie; only this married white woman from the suburbs got away with murder.

My worst act on earth, and there's no way to walk it back. I should have let Jim stay with me that night in the tent. He damn near begged me. He and Barbara knew the stakes. I chose not to listen. I search for something—anything—in the bathroom to hurt myself with, but there's nothing. Is the smell of death coming from my clothing, or am I rotting?

While I don the scrubs and stuff my soiled clothes in the hospital bag, I hope Wilbur is the father, and I want to know whether Danny outran him and his meat cleaver.

When I exit the restroom, an aide walks me to the surgical waiting room where Wilbur sits with his head bowed. I pour two coffees at the counter and touch his shoulder.

He looks up through bloodshot eyes and accepts the Styrofoam cup. "I got sick in there. Too much blood. Don't know anything yet. She's still in surgery."

Time drags while we sit in silence. The lone background noise comes from a high television on the opposite wall. Gabby consumes my thoughts.

Wilbur breaks the silence without a glance my way. "Been sitting here saying every prayer I know for her and the baby. She was doing so well since she got pregnant last summer. Not drinking, not using." His voice sounds lifeless, and he shakes his head. "Until your son shows up."

"Speaking of him, is he somewhere on the mountain with a meat cleaver in his back?"

Wilbur sips the coffee. "He runs too fast, and I'm big and slow. If he knows what's good for his health, he best stay gone."

He could snap my neck right now if I asked him to, and given his mental state, he just might. My knees shake. I can't stop thinking that I killed Gabby. I'd welcome a firing squad. Instead, I place my hand on Wilbur's broad back as we sit silently and watch people come and go from the waiting room. Watching the clock on the wall.

The OB said Gabby weighed one pound two ounces and was almost nine inches long. Tears run down my cheeks, and I grab tissues from a coffee table.

Wilbur leans back in the chair and crosses his legs. "I used to think drugs were evil, sent straight to earth from the devil himself. I watched drugs and booze kill my old man when I was young. It was easier to blame the drugs rather than him.

"Flossie told you why I did ten years before we met. She was a dancer at a club. After three or four months, she asked me to move in. Found out later that she left home at fifteen, turned tricks to survive. She said the drugs and johns were behind her. She quit the club and worked as a cable installer. I worked at the diner full time then, even bought the place before she got pregnant with our first. Life was good. Then she lost her job. I wouldn't let her work at the club again. We fell behind on the bills, so I sold the diner. That kept us above water for a few months until we lost the apartment. I couldn't find a job that paid decent money because of my record. We stayed with friends, but nobody had enough room for us and a baby. I didn't know she started back at the club. Then she began to chip again. She tested positive for heroin when the first was born, and we were homeless. Family Services took Tamika, then Prince two years later."

He shakes his head and crushes the cup before he throws it in the trash. "I thought we moved past this bullshit. I know your son didn't put a gun to her head, but if he hadn't walked into camp, maybe things would be different." He turns his weary eyes to me. "And I know how she paid for the dope. Drugs aren't evil, but pushers like your son are."

I wish I'd accompanied her inside the clinic that snowy afternoon.

A voice calls our names. I turn to see Frank, Barbara, and a friend of Wilbur's from the camp whose name escapes me approach. "How are Flossie and the baby?"

Wilbur stands and accepts their hugs and Frank's prayers while he tells them we don't know.

I blow my nose and try to compose myself. I'm shocked to see them. "How did you get here if I drove the bus and my car is totaled?"

"Charlie's old Riviera. Had to jump-start it. Travis and the others contained the blaze and were occupied with the fire marshal and coroner, so he told us to come lend moral support." Frank takes one look at my face and says, "Are you okay?"

I hug myself and shake my head. "Can we go someplace and talk? It's important."

He clears it with Wilbur, who's content to sit with his friend.

He motions for Barbara to accompany us.

The three of us walk the hall to the hospital chapel. Light slants through narrow stained-glass windows high on the walls. The pews are mostly empty, save for a few people who kneel hunched forward and finger rosary beads. An elderly woman lights a candle in a back alcove and crosses herself. A nurse in scrubs on the last bench turns her head when we enter.

Frank directs me to an area near the altar, but I have another idea.

"I know you're not Catholic, Pastor Frank, but I am . . . or at least I was in another life. Can we talk in there?" I point to the ornately carved booth with red curtains on each side.

He looks to Barbara and then back at me. "You want me to hear your confession?"

I nod.

"This is highly unusual," he says. "I'm not a priest, nor am I properly attired. I smell of smoke and sulfur." His ash- and soot-streaked face lends him the appearance of a firefighter after a blaze.

"If there is a God, She'll know where we've come from and understand."

I pull back the curtain and sit on the hard, straight-back bench, hoping he'll do the same on the other side. Darkness surrounds me, and claustrophobia hits me one more time. My chest rises and falls with each ragged breath. A minute passes. Maybe two. Then the intricate latticework of the sliding panel vanishes with a whoosh, and I jump. Through the fine mesh, I see the dark silhouette of a man with a bowed head. I assume my position on the kneeler.

"Bless me, Pastor, for I have sinned. It must be forty years since my last confession." I take a deep breath and lower my voice to a whisper. I tell him what happened to Flossie also happened to me. "It triggered a memory I'd repressed for years. I smoked and drank for months while pregnant." I pause but fail to steady myself. "But I carried twins . . . and . . . our daughter Gabby died because of me."

Silence from the other side of the mesh. Please say something. Anything.

I'm sobbing.

"Susan, I'm so sorry. But you can't possibly know you caused this. It was a tragic accident. Many physical problems can arise during pregnancy. We cannot begin to fathom God's will."

A length of time passes before I can speak. "I began to hear voices. I convinced myself my husband was going to take Danny away from me. To deal with the guilt and self-loathing, I buried all memory of Gabby deep inside. I withdrew into myself for a year and established an elaborate delusional system that Danny was our only child. You're the first person who knows. It damaged my ability to bond with my son, and it damaged my marriage. It caused Danny's future problems . . ."

"You can't possibly know that. You did what you had to do to survive one of the worst traumas imaginable. Don't apologize for that."

My chin quivers. "I got away with murder, while Flossie has had three children taken from her."

He stirs on the other side of the silk screen. A hand touches the screen as if he wants to reach out to me. "Did you intend to kill your unborn daughter?"

"No."

"What about your unborn son?"

"Of course not."

His facial features press the screen forward. "Does it feel like you got away with murder, Susan?"

"No, but I have all this guilt. I'm a monster."

"You almost died in childbirth, you survived postpartum trauma, and you did your best to raise a troubled young man. When we met, I could tell you were far too hard on yourself. Now I know why."

He pauses a beat. "I found you in your car. You sit on your fastened seat belts when you drive. I saw the cut on your wrist when we pulled you out. You've inflicted enough self-hatred for your lifetime. It's good this is out in the open. It's time to begin to forgive yourself. Time to heal."

Organ music that sounds like the shouts of outraged angels starts up. I hear people shuffle past the tiny confessional and into pews. I recall sitting in similar wooden pews as a young girl and hearing the priest denounce suicide as a mortal sin. The tears keep coming.

"And you didn't fail your son. He chose his path a long time ago."

I try to tell Frank that I met with Danny before the fire, but I can't find the words.

He shifts his weight. "I'm prepared to hand down your penance. Are you ready to accept it, no matter the cost?"

I feel like I've swallowed a razor blade. I nod my head and clear my throat. What comes out is a raspy whisper. "Yes, I am."

272

"Your penance is twofold. No Hail Marys or Our Fathers. First, make peace with your God or your Higher Power. Make amends with your husband and any others you may have treated unfairly during your time of despair. I know this sounds overwhelming because it will take time, but Barbara knows the name of a wonderful therapist who will help you come to terms with your survivor's guilt. You must promise to meet with him.

"Second, you are an exceptional teacher. Use your gift. And when you do, keep this thought in mind: for each future student's life you touch, I want you to think of them as Danny, or Gabby.

"So, does it still feel like you've gotten away with murder?"

"I feel so bad for Flossie—"

"Flossie's situation is different. Everyone is unique. Answer the question."

"No."

The organ music builds in intensity and stops. The priest welcomes those present to the house of the Lord.

Frank says, "My heart aches for Flossie and Wilbur, too."

I blow my nose with a tissue. I tell him where and how Flossie obtained her drugs. "Travis needs to permanently exile Danny."

Frank sits back on the bench and groans.

His silhouette returns after a minute. "I will speak with Travis. Unfortunately, we'll all be homeless by the first of next month."

The chaplain leading mass instructs the worshippers to open their hymnals. The organ starts up again, and "Amazing Grace" fills the chapel.

Through the mesh, I hear the rustle of Frank's coat. "Promise me you will stay with Barbara and agree to see that therapist."

I'm out of tissue. "I will, Pastor."

"I'm serious about your penance. Recovery will take time and won't be easy, but you can do it. You have so much to give. When you're ready, teach for as long as you can. I have to go. I need to find Travis and help with the fallout from the fire."

The music and singing keep the beeping and flashing lights at bay for now. "Thank you."

We meet outside the confessional and hug, both of us in tears. With my consent, Frank updates Barbara, then hurries off to make a call.

A murmur echoes across the waiting room when we rejoin Wilbur and his friend. Fingers point, and heads turn toward the televisions. Flashing lights fill the screens as an EMT crew wheels a covered stretcher toward an ambulance parked in slushy snow. Police cruisers flank the ambulance, and a news van is parked in the background.

An elderly man in a faded cardigan shuffles over to raise the volume.

"—is a live scene recorded in the Highlands, the tent city north of town on Mount Prodigal, where tragedy has again struck this small homeless community in the form of a second deadly fire. This one has claimed the lives of an elderly couple. Some viewers may recall a deadly blaze here two years ago that nearly resulted in a massive forest fire. The cause of this latest blaze, rumored to include an explosion, remains under investigation. This is Jessica Rau reporting to you on the scene with my guest, Sergeant Decker."

The screen shifts to a close-up of Jessica next to Decker. "Are there any new developments you can share with our viewers about the fire, Sergeant?"

Decker tilts his cap back on his head and squares his lantern jaw to the camera. "The deceased male was a smoker, but early indications from the fire marshal point to the use of an accelerant." He sucks in his gut and throws out his barrel chest. "During a recent inspection, we found numerous fire and safety code violations, mostly concerning improper use of stoves and propane tanks. We confiscated several potentially hazardous propane tanks. The high drug and crime rate in this tent city is exacerbated by an influx of illegal migrants and the itinerant nature of the homeless population. It's more than just a few bad apples—"

Behind Decker and the reporter, the police take down Vidal and another Latino face-first. A cop plants a knee on Vidal's back to handcuff him as the shadows lengthen in camp.

The old white man who turned up the volume cackles with joy. "Ha-ha! Look at those two. Goddamn freeloading illegals. Dregs of society probably happy to be arrested, get three hots and a cot, and cable TV." He points a finger at the Latina seated next to him. "You know those two?"

The pudgy woman turns away from him and purses her lips. "That's a horrible thing to say."

The old man dismisses her with a scrawny hand and raises his voice. "Bunch of bums never worked a day in their lives." He glares at the woman and gives a thumbs-up sign to the television. "That's two less welfare cases my hard-earned tax money won't have to pay for." He shuffles off, stoop-shouldered, down the hall.

The camera pans back to the reporter. "What can be done to prevent future tragedies like this, Sergeant?"

"That's a good question, Jessica, with no easy answer. Something must be done, and soon. The conditions here remain dangerous. With the extreme winds we've had this winter, the blaze could have burned down the forest and spread to every tent."

Jessica is a pert brunette in her late twenties with a peaches-and-cream complexion. She sports a bright red scarf and heavy coat, and her face fills the screen while she touches the Bluetooth in her ear. She turns away from Decker to face the screen.

"Word just in . . . city council has convened an emergency meeting to come up with a response to this latest tragedy. As our regular viewers know, the first of February was the scheduled date for the tent city to close. Highlanders have been reluctant to enter the two homeless shelters in the state. A rumor is gaining traction that the council may hasten the closure for the benefit of all. How this impacts the hundreds of people who live on Mount Prodigal remains a mystery. The identity of the deceased couple has not been released, pending notification of family. Stay tuned for more on this breaking story. This is Jessica Rau reporting live from the Highlands."

"They're going to shut us down," I say.

Barbara stares down the hallway at the old man and folds her arms. "I wish I had that baseball bat again." She turns to me. "I wouldn't put it past the bastards."

The doors swing open, and a stern, gray-haired man in green scrubs approaches Wilbur. He holds up a hand to silence us. "I delivered a baby girl weighing just under one and a half pounds and nine inches long. She will need intensive care in an incubator for months. The mother remains in ICU on a ventilator. She lost a great deal of blood, and it's safe to say had she arrived a few minutes later, we would be having quite a different conversation. Mother will eventually transfer to a step-down unit here on the third floor. Your daughter is in the neonatal ICU, also on the third floor. That said, they are not out of danger. We have to hope for the best."

Wilbur heaves a sigh of relief, and as he starts to speak, the doctor raises his hand again. "That's the good news. The bad news is your baby was born heroin-dependent and requires weaning. Did the mother also consume alcohol?"

"Heroin?" Wilbur repeats. "That can't be." I watch his hands ball into fists. "No. No alcohol, doc."

The surgeon looks to the rest of us.

"I saw her sneak a drink a few times," I say. Wilbur glares at me before my eyes seek the floor.

The doctor's face turns dour when he regains Wilbur's attention. "It's vital that we know this to provide the best treatment. Alcohol and drug use increase the risk of premature birth and placental abruption. Each person is different, but it doesn't take large amounts of alcohol for a baby to display symptoms of fetal alcohol syndrome."

He answers a few questions from Wilbur and more from Barbara while I agonize over my role in Gabby's death.

A husky black man wearing a white turtleneck and name badge enters the room and hovers nearby.

The doctor says, "I have patients to attend to. I am required by law to report this birth to Family Services, and I'm told Mr.

Jackson here is your caseworker. I will leave you in his capable hands." The doctor turns and walks briskly through the double doors.

The caseworker stands his ground. He looks at the group of strangers gathered around Wilbur and remains silent.

With an edge in his voice, Wilbur reluctantly introduces us, then tells the caseworker, "Feel free to talk with Susan. She knows what's going on. Apparently, more than me. They all know about you."

The caseworker man-hugs his client, nods to the others, and offers me his hand. "I'm Curtis Jackson. I'm working with Flossie and Wilbur to help them obtain housing and employment in town, so they can eventually reunite with their children."

"Nice to meet you," I say.

"Is there any good news for us?" a distraught Wilbur says. He sounds like he already knows the answer.

"The good news is I spoke with the Carters. They're willing to accept the baby when she's ready. They will be trained to care for any special needs she may have. So all three children can live together under one roof, with foster parents that you know. And in time, with good care and prayers, Flossie and the baby will be okay."

Wilbur remains as stiff as his upper lip.

Curtis places a meaty hand on his shoulder. "It's a setback, I know. The judge will expect Flossie to complete treatment this time after she helps the staff wean your baby off the drugs. I have a promising lead for you on a construction job. The foreman is sympathetic to your situation, but the company hasn't decided whether to add more full-time workers. If it turns out to be seasonal or temporary work, that won't qualify you for housing, even with the government support for the children that the adoptive foster parents currently receive. If the job becomes permanent, that's another story. I will let you know the minute I hear, my man."

Wilbur shakes his head and shrugs in such a way that Curtis must remove his hand from his shoulder. "It's going to kill her to give up another child. This could send her over the edge. She hoped we could keep this one." His eyes red, he slams a chair onto the floor and looks my way. People in the room turn and stare. Then under his breath, "All because she got with the wrong crowd."

Curtis clamps a hand onto the back of Wilbur's neck. "Not true. Flossie is responsible for her own actions. She has an illness." He pauses for a brief moment. "Did you two decide on a name yet?"

"Jasmine," Wilbur says, sounding deflated.

"Pretty. I know this isn't what you wanted, but the Carters are the best option for now."

"When Prodigal shuts us down, how can we visit our kids if we're forced into different shelters a hundred miles away?"

Curtis has no answer for that. I see the heartache and defeat and frustration in his eyes. I know it well. Barbara takes my hand and squeezes it.

"By the time we're allowed to take them back, our children may not want anything to do with us, and the foster family will permanently adopt them." Hands balled into fists again, he mumbles the rest. "I must have been out of my mind to think she was ever gonna change."

Curtis continues his positive spin, but I think Wilbur is wrestling with his own demons. The caseworker offers to buy Wilbur a late lunch while he waits for a chance to see Flossie. Barbara offers to pay for Wilbur's friend and me.

In the hospital cafeteria, Wilbur picks at his food while Curtis sips coffee. I eat bland spaghetti with one meatball and stale garlic bread that Wilbur could cook better outdoors in his sleep. We ride the elevator in silence back to the waiting room.

Evening descends, and there's still no word on when Wilbur can visit Flossie. Tensions are riding high.

Breaking news interrupts a vacuous court TV show about a man cheating on two women who are cousins; Jessica Rau stands outside city hall.

"We have new developments in the aftermath of the fatal fire in the Highlands. In light of the myriad safety and health concerns, Mayor Gilroy and the city council convened an emergency meeting and have recommended the tent city be closed in one week's time, rather than the prior February first deadline.

"Human rights advocates and social service organizations condemned the decision, alleging their concerns are being ignored. They describe the decision as a knee-jerk reaction, one that is ill-timed and dangerous during one of the coldest winters on record. Advocates say they need the February first deadline to finalize placement plans for every homeless resident. A spokesperson for Mayor Gilroy who requested anonymity countered that the leaders of the tent city have had three months to complete the relocation of the homeless to one of two shelters in the state and have failed to do so, despite offers of transportation assistance from the city council. The same source indicates that vans to transport the homeless to shelters may arrive in the Highlands as early as tomorrow.

"A spokesman for the tent city counters that Prodigal has failed to act in good faith with their previous agreement—that the town agreed to provide a year of subsidized housing to fifty-six qualified Highlanders. The spokesman also contends the decision to renege on the agreement is a power play designed to begin construction on an upscale hotel and ski lodge on the mountain. Human rights advocates plan a march through downtown Prodigal to protest the new ruling, culminating with a demonstration at city hall to coincide with Mayor Gilroy's press conference. We will be on hand to follow this story as it develops."

The old man in the cardigan shambles back down the hall, grinning, and stands over the Latina. "Now that's justice! You people will have to work for a living or return to Mexico."

The woman looks frightened.

I move between them and glare at him. "You have no clue how hard these people work. Leave this woman alone, or you deal with me."

He averts his eyes and shuffles away.

279

A few people clap.

Barbara and Wilbur's friend round a corner after a trip to the vending machines at the same time Wilbur and Curtis return from the restroom. She catches the tail end of the cheers. "What did we miss?"

I nod toward the hallway. "Cardigan man experienced a sudden epiphany about bullying people who don't look like him."

Barbara grins and slaps me on the back. "Sorry, I missed it. You're going to be okay, Crusoe."

Wilbur groans about the latest Highland news and turns to Curtis. "What are we supposed to do?"

Curtis' silence says it all.

A nurse approaches Wilbur. "She's awake now." Then to us: "Just the father for now."

Curtis turns to Wilbur. "I have another client to visit, but we will continue the fight. Travis and Pastor Frank are talking with community organizers now. I have a contact at Catholic Charities who is pursuing whether the Fair Housing Act can be—"

"That's all very nice," I say, "but people need someplace to live now. It's winter. Those who refuse to give up their freedom in shelters will die if they're forced to move down the road with nothing but the clothes on their backs. They will return to park benches or the quad. The churches in town could help. They lock their doors at night and sit vacant: make them open up and put in cots and blankets. The only single building large enough to safely house that many people is the Prodigal Community Center."

Wilbur stares blankly ahead. "I'm gonna go see Floss."

Curtis pats him on the back, and we say to tell Flossie we're thinking of her. Head down, he follows the nurse.

Looking as frustrated and helpless as I am angry, Curtis says, "Surely Mayor Gilroy will allow Highlanders more time, grant an extension. That's not unreasonable."

"The writing's on the wall. They've been orchestrating this for months. They can't break ground for their ski lodge with hundreds of squatters on three sections of the mountain. Time is money to them. The fed transfer of power was their coup de grace. I think it's happening n—"

I gasp when I see a familiar face approach with caution. I turn and say, "How in the hell did you know I was here?"

"You forgot my hobby already?"

"The police scanner."

I ask the others to excuse me and move with Jim to a vacant section of the waiting room, which is now almost empty. We share a sofa. "What are you doing here?"

Jim speaks in a soft, low tone, concern etched across his face. "I apologize for showing up out of the blue. I know you went through hell rushing that woman to the hospital and that you'd rather wait with your . . . friends than with me. But I have to know how you're doing."

"I remember everything. I remember Gabby."

He looks relieved. "Oh, thank God. Were you with someone?" The look of concern returns when he notices the butterfly bandages near my scalp and my fading bruises. "Was I too late?"

"I was alone when it hit me, but a friend helped me."

I don't know when I last saw Jim cry, but the tears start flowing. "I didn't know how to help you. You threw out all her clothes. Everything pink, anything that lit up or made noise went straight to the trash. You shut down—for a year. But not when it came to Danny; you cared for him like a mama bear. I was wrong to say you never bonded with him."

"But you did."

He lowers his head briefly. "I was angry. I'm sorry. You fired your OB/GYN and changed pediatricians every few months. We tried home visits from social workers and nurse counselors, but you kicked them all out. Whenever I mentioned Gabby, you either flew into a rage or acted like you didn't know her. When I showed you the hospital portraits, you insisted she was Meghan. Every time. Never a crack in your armor. Over the years, you developed a plausible defense whenever I tried to remind you that our Gabby had ever lived. It tore me apart."

281

He lowers his head into my lap and cries.

I rub his shoulders and hug him.

I turn to see Barbara watching impassively from the far end of the waiting room while I weigh this. Jim only knows a portion of the dark roads of my mind.

I smooth the top of his hair. "I put you, and our marriage, through hell. I got away with murder because I was a white, middle-class, taxpaying citizen of Prodigal."

He raises his head. "You didn't kill Gabby. It was an accident."

I meet my husband's eyes and tell him of my clandestine drinking and smoking.

His jaw drops open. "I had no idea."

I am my son's mother, after all.

"I understand if you want to change your mind about me coming home. I won't contest a divorce."

The silence lingers until it becomes a gorilla in the room. At last, he says, "Did your friend smoke and drink?"

"She drank and did drugs."

"Did her baby die?"

"She's on a ventilator."

"It was an accident, Susan. I made my peace with God years ago. Nothing could have possibly prepared us for what happened when the twins were born. I was terrified and angry when Gabby died. I lashed out and blamed you.

"I should have been a better father and husband, should've done my share of the work around the house. I didn't support you when you needed me. I know I've disappointed you. I want that to change."

I am stunned and don't know what to say.

He breaks the silence. "I hear you met with Danny on New Year's Day."

Amazed, I stare into Jim's gaunt, lined face. "How do you know?"

There's regret in his smile. "You're not the only one who can hire a private eye. My man flushed him out of the Ohio Valley straight to the Highlands a few days ago."

My mood lightens a bit. That explains Danny's flight to a familiar place known for anonymity.

Jim runs a hand through shaggy hair that's curled in the back. "He travels with different women. He hooked up with another when he arrived here. My PI apprehended the one in Ohio, but Danny escaped. He uses female confederates to commit felony thefts. My guess is they're all addicts."

"How do you know he hooked up with one here?"

He reaches into his satchel and produces a folder. He shows me a four-by-six glossy. "The police kept the trace on your cards. I never canceled them, in case you needed money. They caught Little Miss Anorexic here maxing out your credit cards in Prodigal and arrested her."

I stare at a headshot of the thin blonde from camp, looking more like a caged rat than a wily fox, as she holds a prison board next to her body. "What's her name?"

"She's not talking."

I smile. It all makes sense. Danny's partner in crime knew I was an outsider from day one when she watched me walk into camp. She learned early on from the bulletin board messages that I was looking for Danny and must have contacted him. She was the one who kept entering my tent. She stole everything of value and handed it to Danny when he arrived. Danny orchestrated it all from a distance and delighted in his last act of cruelty—using her to make me believe he was buried in the pauper's graveyard.

Jim reaches back into his satchel. "She also had these."

My dingy white, weather-worn journals. She gave them to Danny, and he read my innermost thoughts. His final sadistic words still haunt me. Then the explosion. I'm certain he hightailed it out of camp once he realized the inevitable arrival of police and firefighters.

Jim misinterprets my silence and looks uneasy. "I swear I didn't read them. All I noticed was the date you began writing.

You really maintained the journals; I hope they helped." He clears his throat. "She was high when they arrested her. Had no ID other than yours. They're waiting on a fingerprint match, unless she starts talking." He reads my face and says, "Do you know her?"

I smile. Well played, Danny. Flossie was right from day one. I am a babe in these woods. "Let's say she knew of me."

He shifts in his chair and crosses his legs. "I told the police we want to file charges."

"No, they're my cards. I don't want her charged."

He's surprised, then shocked when he realizes I mean it. "I don't think that's up to you. Or us. She's probably a wanted felon with outstanding warrants in several states."

"Does Danny know about Gabby?" I ask.

Jim looks to the floor before he shakes his head. "I wanted us to tell him together. There were days I tried to talk to you about it, but you wouldn't hear it. I kept hoping you'd remember."

I think of the brothers I never had.

"How is Danny?" Jim says. "Can I see him?"

I describe Danny and recount snippets of our conversation. I keep the worst parts to myself. "He's gone."

Danny may share our DNA, but he's someone else now, too. I think of Dora's wish: the prodigal son will not return to Prodigal. We met, I said my piece, and so did Danny. A weight lifted and another took its place.

"Prodigal will start to close the Highlands tomorrow," I say, "because of the fire."

Jim rubs his wrist. "Does that mean you're coming home?"

So much has happened the last day, so many thoughts battle in my brain that it feels on the verge of shutdown. I close my eyes and realize how exhausted I am for the first time. When they open, I scan the waiting room. Curtis has left, Wilbur's friend is asleep in a chair, and Barbara is still watching us. I didn't introduce her to Jim, but she knows. I stare at the therapist's card she slipped into my hand on the way back from the chapel. I was so driven to forge a separate peace with Danny and myself that I hadn't decided where to go when the time came to leave the mountain.

Jim breaks the silence. "I want us to start over—with a clean slate. Please come home."

"When I left to search for Danny, you wanted a divorce. You wanted me out of our house. What has changed?"

Jim reaches for my hand, then pulls back. "I was wrong. This. This changes everything. You remember. We can move forward. It's all in the past."

I think of the famous Faulkner quote: The past is never dead. It's not even past. My brow furrows. He's done a one-eighty, and I wonder why. The Highlands will be a ghost town in days, my car is totaled, and my bloody clothes are in a bag. A burner phone and an origami horse are all I have.

"Let's go home, I guess. Give me a moment."

I tell Barbara.

"Call me tomorrow," she says. "If you don't make an appointment with that therapist, I will find you and kick your ass," she says with a smile. We hug. I say bye to Wilbur's friend, who rubs his eyes.

On the way to the elevator, I think of Dora and Tom, Travis and Frank, Flossie and Wilbur, and my students. I didn't have a chance to say goodbye. Night has fallen when we leave the hospital parking lot. A beep sounds in Jim's SUV, and I startle.

He turns to me. "Seatbelt."

I reach under and click the belt properly in place. A habit to unlearn. I look at my blood-stained hiking boots and the clear plastic bag that holds my bloody clothes and coat.

We pull into the driveway, and I see our house for the first time in months. Even though looking at it hurts, there is comfort in its familiarity. I accomplished what I set out to do. That should change everything now.

A familiar thought creeps nearer: that home is a place I can't leave and can't stay in. I wonder if there's enough hot water inside to wash away the past.

PART THREE: TO THE MOON AND

BACK

"The end of the human race

will be that it will eventually

die of civilization."

Ralph Waldo Emerson

THROWING TOMATOES AT THE

MAN

The first night back, Jim makes no comment when I sleep in the guest bedroom. I curl up on the carpeted floor with a comforter.

It feels like a guilty pleasure to wake up the next morning, walk a few steps to take a hot shower, and choose from a variety of clean clothes hanging off the ground in a warm, dry closet. It takes a while to decide on an outfit since they all fit looser. Water comes from a tap with the touch of a finger, and a refrigerator stocked with food and drink stands nearby.

At noon, two local media vans park in front of the house. When I open the door, Jessica Rau stands on the porch. She says I'm a person of interest in the developing Highlands story and wants to interview me. I decline. She suggests I might change my mind if I turn on the news.

I return to the living room with a heaping plate of mac and cheese, uncertain whether I want to. I turn it on and see roadblocks at the mountain's base by order of the Prodigal Police Department. The tent city is closed for relocation by order of the city council, and trespassers will be prosecuted.

Jessica stands next to a grim-faced man bundled in a heavy parka near the railroad tracks at the base of Mount Prodigal. She raises the mic to her face. "I want to welcome Mr. David Jensen, a legal representative for the Prodigal city council, with the latest update regarding yesterday's tragedy in the Highlands. Mr. Jensen."

Jensen adjusts his wire-rimmed glasses. "Thank you, Jessica. When police and firefighters responded to emergency calls of a deadly fire yesterday in the homeless tent community on Mount Prodigal, they expected to find two casualties. However, a third body was discovered—" A look of disgust forms on his face while he pauses for emphasis. "—frozen to death in a portable commode. The self-proclaimed mayor of the Highlands allowed this man to live in a public toilet for years. The only belongings in his 'house' were food wrappers, an empty beer can, and a cane." He shakes his head and looks to the sky. "This is beyond comprehension. It's an abomination to God, and in my opinion, borderline criminal. This most undignified life and preventable death will not have been in vain. It will serve to strengthen the city council's resolve that they are taking the right steps in closing the homeless encampment by week's end."

My breath catches in my throat. Jensen failed to mention the many times Prodigal Hospital placed Benny in a cab and dumped him back at the Highlands after psychiatric stays. The system failed this veteran. I think of his bass chant, the sandwich, and the exquisite origami horse. He chose the hermit life and refused to live anywhere else.

"Where will these people go when the camp closes?" the reporter asks Jensen.

"The city of Prodigal is coordinating the orderly transition of the homeless from these unsanitary and dangerous living conditions to more humane ones, for the mutual benefit of everyone involved. I don't have details at this time. If the deals on the table can be negotiated in a timely basis, I expect Mayor Gilroy to announce particulars by the end of the business day tomorrow."

No longer hungry, I click off the television and throw the remote on the couch. "Damn that smug Jensen. There are two sides to every story."

Jim looks perplexed as he stares at me from his recliner. He's given me space since my return last night. He knows I developed a fondness for the people, but little else. For that, I'm grateful, but now he says, "Is that true? Was that man living in an outhouse in the woods for years?"

I nod. "It's not that simple, but yes, he was."

He looks disgusted and starts to say something but stops.

"You wouldn't understand unless you lived there, unless you knew him."

Did anyone really know Benny?

Damn you for knocking on my door, Jessica.

"I need to buy a car. Today."

Jim puts down his fork and meets my eyes with a blank stare. "What, now? Can't you borrow mine?"

I reach for the Gazette and browse the classified ads. "You need the SUV for work. I need my own car."

That afternoon, I buy a used truck with over 477,000 miles on it and stop at the 7-Eleven. Melanie sits behind the counter. I place boxes of tea and two quarts of motor oil on the counter. "This, and two packets of Nicorette gum, please. Plus the gas on pump number . . . whatever it is."

It takes her a while to recognize me, but when she does, she perks up. "You look great—nice clothes, a new coat, and makeup." She glances out the window toward the pumps. "Hey, where's your cute little car?"

Mine is one of two vehicles in the lot. She spots the faded orange Toyota with rusted rear quarter panels and the driver-side mirror held in place with silver duct tape next to pump five and frowns.

"That's my new truck. Isn't she great?" I hand her Jim's credit card.

She looks confused as she rings me up. "I guess so," she says, tearing off my receipt. "Hey, if it makes you happy." She reaches for her pint of Rocky Road.

The bell over the door rings as a tall, thin man in a Stetson enters and strolls down the cold beer aisle.

Melanie lowers her voice to a near whisper and leans closer. "You know, if it wasn't for that blue Beemer, I would have sworn you were one of them."

"Who's that?" I ask, looking around the store with feigned gravitas.

"You know." She rolls her eyes and makes a face. "One of those Highlanders."

"There are worse things to be, Melanie. Do you know how many miles it is from here to the moon?"

She licks her spoon and shakes her head.

I chew a Nicorette square until the peppery taste starts, then place it between my cheek and gum. "Take a guess. How many miles would you say?"

"I don't have a clue. A million?"

More's the pity.

"It's not important. You can look up facts like that on your smartphone anytime, can't you? But if you learn one thing in life, Melanie, learn to forgive. No one on that mountain ever dreamed they'd be living there in a million years. That old truck at the pump is like me; it's been to the moon and back. You will encounter highs and lows as tall and razor-sharp as the peaks and craters on the moon if you live long enough. And you'll have stories to tell that are unique to you." I tap the counter twice and smile before I leave.

I'm curious and have some time to kill before my appointment, so I drive to the Highlands, but the police roadblock is forcing private vehicles to turn around.

I'm on time for my first appointment with Dr. Goodman, a trauma specialist, and Barbara's former therapist. He's a short, rotund, gray-haired man in his mid-seventies who sees clients in his home. I enter his office flush with skepticism, but his personality and calm demeanor put me at ease. He expresses a quiet confidence that he can help demystify my repressed memories and that I will eventually accept the past for what it was. He suggests we meet twice a week initially. He insists I write and sign a behavior contract with him, that I will not try to hurt myself. He gives me his private cell number and says to call him whenever I feel in crisis. I leave his home a bit washed out but with a good feeling. Maybe there's hope for my marriage.

At five that afternoon, Superintendent Morris calls to express his joy for my safe return. He says the door is open when I'm ready to teach again.

Jim suggests dinner at our favorite steak and seafood place as a welcome-home night out, but I don't feel like being stared at, so I ask for Chinese delivery instead. I'm jonesing for pot stickers, crab rangoon, egg rolls, and stir-fry.

290

My co-workers call while we're eating dinner in front of the television. They're happy and excited to learn I'm home safe and in one piece. Some share their fears about my disappearance, and a few pry into what my time was like on the mountain. One suggests I write a book. My response is a quick Hell, no. Not a one says a word about Jim or the speculation over my disappearance. I try not to read anything into that.

I think of the quaint little B&B we never made it to, and my mind wanders down that dark alley again. I kept busy during my first day back home—a recommendation from my new therapist—which helped keep the idle thoughts at bay. Now I finger the edge of Dr. Goodman's business card, but I work through the feelings.

Before bed on the second night, I tell Jim he may as well return to work because we need the money. He asks when I plan to do so, and he frowns when I tell him I don't know. Tomorrow will be another busy day, and I don't need him hovering.

The next day, I drive to the hospital to see Flossie. Wilbur intercepts me in the waiting room, where he has his own place laid out with two blankets, a pillow, and magazines. "She's taking it real hard. She doesn't want to see you. Or me, or anybody." He looks exhausted, and his wrinkled clothes look like he's been sleeping in the waiting room.

"How are you and Jasmine doing?" I ask.

Before he can answer, Flossie starts calling his name, louder and more insistent each time. Wilbur stares down at me, his bloodshot brown eyes deep and dark as graves, then hugs me. "Thanks for what you did, but you should leave."

A needle slides into my heart. I think I could help her. No one gets it like someone who's been there. But I wish them well and hand him a get-well basket for Flossie filled with lotions and creams.

On the long walk back to the truck, I try Travis, Frank, and Barbara again, with no luck. Straight to voice mail. I'm dying to know what's happening in town and want to help. Is Travis severing ties with me, or are they inundated with eleventh-hour plans?

I'm getting into my truck when a cluster of protestors marches past the hospital waving signs and chanting. Travis and Pastor Frank lead the group—I know or recognize most of the marchers. I drive past the protestors, park two blocks away in the busy quad, and backtrack on foot to city hall. By then, the protestors have arrived.

A mass of spectators gathers near Jessica Rau while her crew sets up on the steps of city hall. They ignore the protestors, who have stopped a safe distance from the base of the steps by metal barricades guarded by police. Travis spots me as I stand on the city hall side, cordoned off from the marchers, and stops in his tracks. Does the look on his face convey that I'm no longer a Highlander? The crowd fills in around me, and I lose sight of him.

A well-dressed elderly man steps to the podium. He lowers the mic and taps it once. "I am Clayton Gilroy, the mayor of Prodigal. Entrance to the tent city known as the Highlands north of town is now prohibited due to a host of dangerous and unsanitary conditions. I have convened with Prodigal's board of directors and business leaders. Together, we weighed input from several social, community, and law enforcement leaders about this issue. The decision to shutter was unanimous." A chill wind ripples his sparse hair and nearly blows his prepared speech from the podium.

The mayor stares into the cameras and then pauses to refer to his notes. "The city of Prodigal will enact the following steps immediately. Two local churches have agreed to function as temporary emergency homeless shelters at night, effective this evening. The local VFW hall has agreed to do the same once cots and blankets are obtained. And soup kitchens are being established at all three locations. My staff will provide members of the press with the names and addresses of the churches after my statement. In addition, the city council will grant temporary emergency placements for the remaining twenty-two slots from the court decision last year, to be filled as soon as humanly possible for homeless families with dependent children. Doing so will honor the spirit of the court decree and solve the homeless problem in Prodigal once and for all."

People on my side of the barricades cheer and clap.

From the opposite side of the barriers, I hear a familiar voice rise up. "LIAR!"

I see Travis cup his hands while Pastor Frank throws a tomato that arcs through the blue sky and splatters on the gray marble steps near the podium. Police close in on them.

I've slowly worked my way up during Gilroy's statement until I'm a few feet from Jessica Rau, who does a double take and grins in recognition.

Gilroy turns to an assistant. "That's it. I've had it with these people. No questions from the press. It's cold out here." He shakes his head and swipes at his tomato-stained pants. He creates a smear that looks like he has blood on his hands.

I look at Jessica. "You wanted to interview me yesterday. I can do you one better. Hand me a mic." She grins and does so.

"You're damn right it's cold out here, Mr. Gilroy," I say too loudly, which causes a harsh reverb that stings everyone's ears. I cringe. "Sorry."

Gilroy turns in his tracks. Surprised, frowning.

I see a glowing red dot as a cameraman follows me. "That's what it's like twenty-four hours every winter day when you're homeless. Living in the Highlands is a terrible existence. But it's better than living alone on the streets of Prodigal or any city. At least there's safety in numbers in a homeless community.

"Speaking of numbers, yours don't add up. Three hundred men, women, and children live in the Highlands. You dispatched the police to treat them like criminals and evict them from their homes in the middle of winter."

Gilroy returns to the podium, looking angry. "You're wrong, young lady. The vans and buses are bringing far fewer homeless than what you claim—"

"Buses? They were prison vans," Travis yells at Gilroy from across the barricades. "Your officers beat and arrested us. They threatened us with deportation. Many people fled into the woods rather than go to jail. You didn't solve the homeless problem. You confiscated and destroyed our homes—"

"That's a lie!" Gilroy's pale white face reddens, tugging at his thin white mustache.

Travis' indignation emboldens me, and I speak into the mic. "Like I said, Mr. Gilroy, your numbers don't add up. Last year's agreement called for fifty-six homeless people to receive subsidized apartments for one year. It's a year later, and only four people have been placed. Now you claim only twenty-two spaces remain. Twenty-two slots would shelter only the children. Do you plan to separate them from their parents? These numbers are accurate. Mr. Gilroy, you have a public relations nightmare on your hands. Do you have anything to say in your defense?"

Gilroy bangs his fist on the podium and points at me, shouting into the mic, "Can we get some security here?" An aide reaches him, turns off the microphone, and whisks his boss away. A murmur runs through the crowd. Across the street, the protestors cheer and wave signs.

Police close in on me as I return the mic to Jessica. "I can't confirm the apartment numbers, I heard them from Pastor Frank, but hundreds of people live in the Highlands, including twenty or so children and two pregnant women. They will resurface in the park or the quad, to sleep on benches or in bus stops like before, until Prodigal stops turning a blind eye. Report the truth, no matter what."

Jessica instructs the cameraman to continue filming when the police arrive. They keep their distance once they see the red light of the camera.

A struggle erupts across the barricades, and I ask to borrow her cameraman for a minute.

We cross the street and push through the barriers toward the growing circle where Travis and Frank are arguing with Sergeant Decker at the center of a fresh crowd of gawkers. When Decker and his men notice the red light of the television camera, he grudgingly lets them off with a warning. I thank the cameraman, but when I turn, Jessica is at my heels, speaking into a mic.

"We are live outside Prodigal city hall, where not all the news is good, but the happy and safe return of one of our own, missing Teacher of the Year Susan Crusoe, most certainly is welcome news."

I make a cutting motion for her to stop, but she ignores me.

"That was quite a passionate speech. We understand you've been living in the Highlands. What can you tell our viewers about your time there, Mrs. Crusoe?"

I glare at her. "That Corey Landry is a smart and passionate aspiring journalist. Just the breath of fresh air your station needs. I recommend you hire him."

Her eyes narrow when she signals for the cameraman to cut. "Who the hell is Corey Landry?" She turns to the cameraman. "The Gilroy exchange with Crusoe is gold. Eighty-six the rest." Then back to me: "Thanks for that. It looks like you kicked a hornet's nest. If you ever want to share your story—"

"I don't."

"Here's my card, just in case. Thanks, again." She walks off to the news van.

I feel a tap on my back and turn to see Corey.

"You were great!" he says, hugging me.

A grinning Travis approaches with Frank behind him. "Thanks for sending the fourth estate. I feel like I've been arrested and beat up enough this week to last a lifetime."

"That goes double for me," Frank says, offering his hand and a hug. He whispers, asking if I'm okay, and I nod.

I pull back. "Who knew you were such a rebel, Frank?" I say with a devilish grin. "Throwing tomatoes at the Man."

We share a laugh.

Travis sports a nasty shiner under his left eye and other facial bruises. I want to reach out and touch his face but stop myself.

"Defending the Highlands with fire and fury. You've come a long way," Travis says as his striking hazel eyes search my face.

I feel relief to find him safe. And arousal. And vexation. "And I'm here," I say.

"Are you back home with your husband?" Frank asks, breaking the mood.

I look self-consciously from Frank to Travis. I nod. "For now. We'll see."

"That's good," Frank says. "I pray everything works out."

An awkward silence descends, then Corey walks off to shake hands with a friend he spotted from the Highlands. Travis clears his throat and speaks of court fights for permanent housing. He punctuates his plans with the rather pompous phrase my people. I look at him and wonder if this is directed at me because I've never heard him use it before. Is he the one distancing himself now?

Travis and Frank look like they've aged years over the last few days. I hear other Highlanders say they've been working nonstop. The realist in me says they're tilting at windmills with another lawsuit against the ever-changing rules stacked in favor of city hall.

I update them about Flossie and Wilbur.

Frank asks what's next for me.

"That's a good question. 'To be determined' is the most honest answer."

I look at Travis and wish him the best.

His jaw is set, and he holds his head high.

A guard from city hall with a walkie-talkie appears and instructs Travis and Frank to follow him, that the next meeting is about to start without them.

Travis slowly backpedals toward city hall, his eyes on mine until Frank tugs on his coat, and they turn in unison.

I'm standing alone in the crowd feeling deflated and uncertain about what to do next, when Frank spins back to me. "In all the excitement, I almost forgot. I left something from Dora in your tent. The city closed the mountain. Maybe you can sneak in at night when they let the heavy equipment in. But don't even try that if you see workers. They already told Travis they don't plan to waste money and manpower guarding our stuff." A wall of people soon separates us.

296

The crowd swallows them, and I'm alone again in a mass of onlookers.

I toss Jessica's card in the nearest trash can and walk to my truck.

I resist the urge to drive to the Highlands. At home on College Avenue, Jim orders delivery from Pizzazz. We eat our slices in silence and watch the evening news. The station airs a truncated section of Gilroy's speech but plays the entire confrontation between Gilroy and me. Jim stares at me. Jessica reports an anonymous source indicates that none of the three venues are prepared to accept any dispossessed Highlanders tonight, nor are they expected to be ready tomorrow night.

Travis or Pastor Frank, I'm sure.

"Gilroy lied again. What a bastard," I say. Travis and Frank must be beside themselves.

Only a handful of Highlanders have agreed to relocate to shelters. The segment concludes with a brief shot of Highlanders returning to Prodigal Park and the streets, and a mention that others have appeared in Destiny, the nearest town north of Prodigal.

Once the segment ends, Jim turns to me. "You have the energy to run around town on this homeless crusade, but you can't go back to work? It feels like you wanted me out of your hair today. You seem different now. When are we going to talk about us?"

I bite my tongue and take the dirty plates into the kitchen. When I return, I sit facing him.

"You remember the three dead bodies carted off the mountain? Their names were Dora and Tom and Benny. I knew them; I cared about them. Many other friends are out in the cold and dark somewhere, displaced from their homes. They could freeze to death tonight.

"Yes, I had things to do today that didn't include you. I went to the hospital to see if my friend and her newborn were still alive and if so, how they were doing. The marchers to city hall filed past the hospital as I was leaving, so I followed. I didn't plan to be on the news or interrupt Gilroy's speech. It just happened."

"What about us? Now that you remember Gabby?"

"It doesn't end with that. I went into the woods ostensibly to find our son, but I was lost. I recovered from events from my childhood, the difficult ones that shaped me. I need to somehow make peace with it all."

He looks at me. "And how do you propose to do that?"

The Danny I knew, hitherto invested with my mortal soul, is gone. I realize now he's far beyond my influence. When I remembered Gabby, a deep, sucking blackness consumed me, followed by storms of remorse and overwhelming anger. "I started therapy. It wasn't an accident that I wrecked the car. I drove it straight at a tree.

I wait for him to respond, but he sits on his hands while the silence drags on. The look on his face seems to say he has no clue what to say. I clear my throat. "It wasn't all about Danny, or me. I also walked into the woods to learn if our marriage was salvageable."

Jim leans forward. "What did you decide?"

"I haven't. Maybe this therapist can help. We've grown apart, and I accept my share of the responsibility. If you still want a divorce, I understand."

He rises and kneels next to me. "Gabby's death shattered me, too. It took years to make my peace with God, and I'm not about to change that now. After she died, we were still the same people, but at the same time, we weren't. I expressed my grief by talking and yelling while you kept everything inside."

He offers his hand, which I accept.

"I know that now," I say, lowering my head.

"We grieved on different cycles. Sometimes I resented you for bringing me down when I was having a good day, and I'm sure I did the same to you." He searches my face. "There were days when I had to be selfish in my grief just to survive. I wasn't able to consider your feelings, only mine."

I squeeze his hand. I have no words.

"I failed to make peace with you. I took it as a positive sign when you threw yourself back into teaching, even though that meant your return to twelve-hour work days. I feel like a failure as a father and husband."

I don't feel absolved of my sins. They remain hunched in a dark corner of my mind and may linger there forever, but they no longer weigh me down all the time.

I fall into Jim's arms, and we hug silently for I don't know how long.

That evening, I remove the remnants of the Great Wall of Danny from the guest bedroom and putty and prime the walls. I recycle the last of Danny's fliers and discard the broken lock. I record an entry in my new journal. I chew Nicorette and drink tea like I own stock in both. My hands shake at times, but the anxiety so far is manageable.

I sleep with Jim in the master bedroom to escape the fumes. I didn't go to bed with the intent to have sex, but it's good to feel closer to him after being apart for so long, that I acquiesce. Our sex life was good years ago. Maybe we can regain that intimacy.

Sleep comes in bits and pieces. I'm still unaccustomed to a bed and the strange room, but feeling a warm body next to mine is a comfort.

I dream that Jim and Danny sit with me around the Pit. We sing "American Tune" along with Tom on piano. Dora sits nearby behind an easel, brush in hand. Flossie and Wilbur laugh and joke around the fire, happy at last. Two young children at their feet roast marshmallows while a baby nurses at Flossie's breast. Travis and Pastor Frank hand out keys, congratulating everyone on their new apartments.

Travis walks up to me with a smile. "Sorry, Susan from Town. I have nothing for you."

Pastor Frank touches my shoulder. "You no longer need our help. I hope that you find peace."

I look up from my stone seat and watch in wonder as Jim, Danny, and the three young children slowly vanish. Hovering above the flames of the bonfire, Benny raises a sandwich before he dissolves into the night. Dora hands me the canvas, a painting of me standing alone, defiant, one arm thrust out with Danny's picture in hand, wearing my backpack that first day in camp.

"Remember me," is all she says before she dissipates into fireflies that fill the night sky.

In the distance, the wail of a loon is answered by another.

Tom vanishes, but the piano continues to play on its own.

I wake up in the master bedroom and hear Jim snoring softly beside me.

It feels like home.

WARNING SHOTS

Two nights later, my phone alarm sounds well before dawn, and I take care not to disturb Jim. I dress in the dark, jeans and a sweater. Last night's late news said the Highlands would open to construction crews at dawn. The land has officially been sold to make way for an upscale ski lodge and hotel.

The morning breaks cold and clear as my little orange truck chugs up the mountain, belching blue smoke. Heavy equipment lines the street past the railroad tracks, ready to tear up the gravel and pour asphalt roads up the mountain. There are no workers in sight. I'm able to maneuver my truck around the Road Closed and No Trespassing signs with relative ease and park near my old spot. It blends in with the other rusted autos and my totaled BMW.

As I walk the path, the woods are eerily silent and cloaked in mist. I direct my phone flashlight at the ground to guide my way in the darkness. The sun will break over the mountains soon. The Welcome to the Highlands: Abandon Expectation All Ye Who Enter sign is smashed to pieces on the forest floor. The cars on Daytona Row remain, but there are no foraging chickens, the dog cages are empty, and the rabbit hutches swing open and creak in the breeze. Only Benny's commode is gone.

I walk the narrow path toward my little blue tent and hope it's still standing. When I round the last bend, I see it. A mourning dove coos its satisfaction nearby in the woods. What I find when I enter freezes me in mid-step. On a worn serape is a canvas painting with a note: "All my love, Dora."

In it, I stand presenting Danny's picture to the viewer. My jaw is set, and I'm staring straight ahead, a challenge in my eyes. Quite singular in purpose is painted in small black cursive letters above her signature. Travis' first impression of me. The painting is eerily similar to the one in my dream last night, and it takes time for the goosebumps to recede.

I continue along the path to Judy and George's tent. Out of habit, I announce myself, this time in a whisper. On their mattress rests a canvas with a note from Frank. "Dora wanted you to have this." The painting shows them on the bus, George with his stack of homemade clocks, his mouth open, and Judy attentive. I remove a pillowcase from their bed to protect the canvasses.

My head turns at the sound of a diesel engine breaking the early morning silence. I'm not alone. I turn and hurry outside to the path. A Caterpillar tractor with the orange Gilroy company logo topples saplings in the meadow. After a sharp turn, its metal scoop lowers and plows up a row of tents, forming a massive waste heap. Workers slowly materialize in the fog to begin their workday.

I hurry along the trail to the church/classroom, which stands in the tractor's path. I stuff Frank's Bible, Talmud, and Koran in the pillowcase. The laptop won't fit, so I cradle it against my chest.

Bulldozers converge on the Pit. From behind a tree, I watch Wilbur's barbecue drums get crushed and mangled, our picnic tables reduced to splinters. My stomach turns when the blade plows Jim's upright piano into the giant trash heap, smashing it to kindling along with massive sections of shattered wood, twisted metal, and tattered canvas from tents and homes. I stare in disbelief when a worker turns toward the totem pole. I want to run in front of it and protect it with my body, but it's too late. Smoke billows from the exhaust while the dozer rips it from the ground, roots, and all. I wish there was time to salvage items from Travis' house, but the workers start to converge on my hiding spot.

Sickened, I'm running toward my truck when I'm knocked down hard from behind. I protect the laptop in my fall, and my head hits the ground hard. Dazed, I turn on my knees to face my attacker, and a black Lab starts to lick my face, wiggling and barking and trying to curl into a ball on my lap. Her tail whacks my head with each circular turn of her muscular body. I feel her ribs through the bur-riddled coat. It's a struggle, but I grab her collar; the tag says her name is Pearl. No owner, no address. Have I seen a black dog here before?

A worker in a hard hat turns toward us. "Hey, stop! You're trespassing on private property!" He must have heard the dog. He chugs toward us in a bowlegged run, speaking into a walkie-talkie about a crazy homeless woman on site.

"C'mon, Pearl. Let's get out of here!" I shout as I scramble to my feet and race down the path.

I climb into my truck, which doesn't turn over on the first, second, or third tries. The man gains on us; I see the snarl on his face, his labored breathing. Fourth time is the charm. Pearl is on the passenger seat, her paws on the dashboard, barking at the man. Blue smoke belches from the muffler when I shift into drive and spin gravel in the face of the big-bellied worker, who waves his hands in the air, coughing. He shakes his fist at me before his hands go to his knees.

My heart races as I speed down the mountain, expecting angry construction workers blocking the exit, but they're in no hurry to give chase as we chug down the mountain. They don't seem to care about a trespasser here. I keep one eye on the rearview, but no one pursues us. "We made it, Pearl!"

I stop at the 7-Eleven for gas, a plastic bowl, a chew toy, and dog food. A gruff older man with a handlebar mustache and wire-framed glasses stands stoop-shouldered behind the counter.

"Where's Melanie?" I ask, reaching for my money.

"She quit," he says. "Inventory the other day. Lot of missing stuff. Refused to take a polygraph. You believe that? Can't find good help these days. Have to man the counter till I find a replacement." He hands over my change and notices my truck through the window. "You wouldn't be looking for a job, minimum wage, variable shifts, and no bennies—at least on paper—would you?" He winks.

Gross. I feign excitement. "Sounds like a great deal. Plus, I get to take a lie detector test, too? Pass."

He mumbles something unintelligible as the bell tolls behind me. If Melanie has to consent to a lie detector to keep a lousy minimum-wage job with no benefits, so should Mayor Gilroy.

Pearl damn near licks my face off when I climb back behind the wheel. I think she smells the dog food. That, or the chew toy.

She helps me rip open the bag of dog food and inhales a bowl so fast she almost chokes on it. I pet her matted coat and tell her a bath is in her future. When she finishes the bowl, she licks my face and burps.

"And something for that breath."

We pull into the lot of the VFW, where Travis, Corey, and others are unloading trucks. I give Pearl her chew toy, and she's perfectly content in the truck. I hand the laptop to Pastor Frank, who passes it wordlessly to Corey.

Corey's eyes widen. "This is great. The cops held Travis and Frank overnight before they could grab anything. It contains the camp directory. It's pretty basic, but this will help us reach out to next-of-kin. We've lost contact with so many people. Quite a few are missing. It's been a nightmare."

Over the next two days, I help them prepare for the influx by organizing kitchen supplies, food boxes, care packages, and dining tables. We arrange rows of cots with thin mattresses and blankets in the main room and hang several carloads of donated clothing from makeshift rods. Tonight is opening night, days later than Gilroy promised. There's been one excuse after the other for the delays. No smooth and organized process as Gilroy would have the public believe. There's much work to do and little time to talk. Travis doesn't speak to me, but he looks my way often. Tension is my middle name.

When we finish, Pearl and I follow the VFW caravan through rush-hour traffic to one of the churches that agreed to open its doors tonight. Frank spearheads the soup kitchen operation here and is pleasantly surprised to see me. The cots are in place by the time we arrive, and he's almost done organizing volunteers to help with food prep and service.

Frank, Corey, Travis, and I sit down to eat soggy deli sandwiches and drink sodas. Travis sits slightly outside the circle and avoids eye contact with me. Everyone's tired, but I think Frank picks up on the awkwardness in the air. Corey ends a phone call with an expletive and shouts to Travis.

"We got a big problem. An hour ago, the Alpha Males fired warning shots at the construction workers and ordered them to get off their mountain. Most of the Alphas retreated to the caves, but the workers are sitting ducks. No one's been hurt yet, but my source said Gilroy ordered a work stoppage and called the Governor. There's talk they may send a negotiator and mobilize the National Guard. My guy will call me back if they do."

Travis utters the same invective. "No one knows how much firepower the northerners have. Finn claimed he had dynamite. This could get ugly. I have to go up there." He stands and looks to an exhausted Corey. "Did you take the old logger trail to beat the roadblocks?"

Corey nods. "It's a bit of a hike, but you're in better shape."

While Travis stuffs a backpack with food and bottled water, I ask Corey why he had to avoid roadblocks.

Corey says, "Because I filmed the forced exodus. It was a far cry from what Gilroy and the news claim. I'm compiling my footage from the last four days. Our people were threatened, beaten, arrested, and treated like animals. Heads should roll."

Travis grabs his coat. Frank stands to follow, but Travis shakes his head. "No, you're needed here. Corey, show me how to work your camera."

Corey says, "I'll go with you."

"No, I need you to take my place at the VFW. We open tonight, and we're not ready. People will start showing up. I'll be back when I can."

Corey explains the camera functions to him, and Travis makes for the door.

"Be careful," I call to him. "Come back in one piece."

He regards me for a moment and nods.

We sit in silence after Travis leaves. Corey halfheartedly announces the latest total of a GoFundMe account he created for the homeless people in Prodigal. Frank tells Corey he plans to sleep at the church tonight; Corey will spend the night at the VFW. I learn Travis and Frank crashed at Corey's apartment last night after they were released from custody—Travis on an air mattress

305

and Frank on the sofa. Frank said if Decker saw either of them on the mountain again, they'd face thirty days in jail for criminal trespassing.

I ask if anyone remembers a black Lab named Pearl. Corey says he thinks he saw one, but isn't certain. Frank shakes his head. I wish I could stay and help, but Pearl's in the truck, and Jim will be expecting me. I say my goodbyes for the day.

Walking to the truck, I feel like a boat person with no land in sight.

Jim is already home when I bring Pearl through the front door. She rushes up and dances around him, eager to play. I explain how we met. I can tell he's not happy about the dog, but I'm too tired to care. I sprawl on the sofa. He brought home Italian takeout, but I'm not hungry after the deli sandwich. Pearl hops on the sofa and curls up next to me. Jim storms into the kitchen. I hear him mumble to himself before I nod off.

When I wake, Pearl and I get in the tub, and she gets a bath. The burs are another story; I'll have to deal with them later. I grab an old towel from the closet to dry her off and use others to form a makeshift bed for her in front of ours. Tomorrow I'll buy a leash even though she follows me wherever I go. The last thing I want is for her to wander the streets alone.

A thick packet arrives in today's mail with a return address of 1600 Pennsylvania Avenue. It contains my invitation to the Teacher of the Year Awards in March, a month away. Out of fifty teachers representing each of the states, somehow, I've been chosen the best of the lot. Another bizarre twist of life. All fifty teachers and their immediate families will have an audience with the President and Secretary of Education in the Rose Garden for certificates, plaques, and commendations. As National Teacher of the Year, I am invited to provide input regarding future school policy to the Department of Education and travel, give speeches, and represent teachers. The last paragraph cordially invites Susan, James, and Daniel Crusoe to attend the gala. The other pages include directions, recommendations for hotels, and instructions about attire and speeches. I am urged to confirm my attendance promptly.

The irony is not lost on me. I'm deeply flattered. There was a time, not long ago, this would have meant the world to me. I've accepted the penance Pastor Frank doled out, and an award ceremony is the farthest thing from my mind.

Jim sees the packet on my lap and asks how many days we'll be in DC. I don't look up from the pages.

"I'm not going."

He's astounded. "What? You devoted your life to teaching. The White House? The best teacher in the country. It's a prestigious honor."

"They can give it to someone else more deserving, and they will."

"Why on earth do you say that?"

"I lied. I called in sick when I wasn't. I abandoned my students for months to live on a mountain. I'm glad I did, but I can't have it both ways."

Jim throws his hands in the air. "I don't understand this. It's like you're a different person."

More's the pity.

While I watch the late news with Pearl, he drives off to drink at Marcel's. The news report tonight indicates that all three temporary shelters have been up and running since yesterday, as promised by Mayor Gilroy, providing shelter, food, and clothing to the homeless. There's no accompanying video because it's not true. When I left the shelters, people were still working hard in the hope of accepting people tonight.

Jessica looks into the camera. "Reports from an anonymous source at city hall state that most of the Highland homeless have been safely bused to the two permanent shelters at the other end of the state. Those who remain in Prodigal have entered one of the three temporary shelters in town while they await placement. Though our cameras have not been granted access to the mountain, a top member of Mayor Gilroy's staff assured us that the transition has been orderly and peaceful. The Highlanders our

307

viewers have seen returning to town will receive police escorts to the temporary shelters. We've heard unconfirmed reports this afternoon of isolated incidents in which a few holdout Highlanders have fired shots at construction workers before fleeing into the honeycomb-like system of caves cut into the mountain. There will be more on this story as it unfolds."

Orderly and peaceful transfer. Gilroy wants to bury the truth. Travis returned there alone, under threat of arrest. His beat-up face is proof that this transition has been far from peaceful.

Jim has not returned.

After a trip outside for Pearl to pee, I move her bed of blankets to the front of the guest bed. The fumes from the primer paint are gone. She jumps on the bed and, in minutes, is snoring softly by my side. Sleep arrives slowly for me. I'm worried about Travis. The garage door rattles open at four a.m., long after Marcel's closed.

First thing the next morning, I leave a message for Superintendent Morris that I'm ready to return to teaching as soon as possible.

My next call is to the DC number listed for the Teacher of the Year ceremony. I inform the woman in charge that we will not be attending and to give my award to another candidate. She voices her regret at my decision and asks for my name. After a brief silence (during which I assume she checks her list), she says, "But you're the Teacher of the Year!"

An hour later, Superintendent Morris returns my call and is eager to have me start next Monday. It hurts me to break the news to him that I decided not to accept the award. He does his best to change my mind, lavishes me with praise, and speaks of the school's pride in vicariously sharing the award with me. He tries but fails to conceal the disappointment in his voice once he realizes my mind is made up. I feel guilty because Mr. Morris and his wife were looking forward to the ceremony. I tell him my reasons why I couldn't in good conscience accept the award. I push my luck and ask him for a favor down the road.

After therapy, I drive to the VFW, where about fifty Highlanders are milling about, looking dispirited. The volunteers look exhausted.

"Any word from Travis?" I ask Corey.

He shakes his head. "We're in the dark. Every hour or two, a cop car pulls up and drops somebody off from the park or downtown. Frank has almost forty people at his church, and another thirty-five women are in the church Barbara oversees. That doesn't count the Alpha Males still up there causing problems. Damn few people went to the state shelters."

We grumble about the news coverage. I ask about Vidal and his family, Judy and George, Kim and Penny, but no one's heard from them. Every one of my students and their parents remain unaccounted for, except Theo.

Corey crosses his arms. "Gilroy's numbers have already been proven false. One thing I know for certain is the Rapture didn't take the others. It's just a matter of time before they round up—"

An engine backfires outside, and the Highland bus squeals to a stop in front of the VFW, its windshield cracked. Forty or fifty bearded men in fur coats and animal skins pile out. They stare at the nearby buildings on the block before they walk up the steps. I wait for the driver to appear.

At last, a smiling Travis emerges, clapping the broad back of the last northerner on the bus. "Let's get these men some hot food and coffee. They've been through a lot," he calls out. The volunteers get busy and direct the newcomers to tables.

Corey applauds, and I do the same. I want to run up to Travis and throw my arms around his neck, but I stay back. He looks exhausted and has a fresh shiner under his left eye. We find a table at the back of the hall, and Corey retrieves a pot of hot coffee and a tray of mugs.

Travis takes a seat and turns to Corey. "It went better than expected. The men didn't have enough firewood or food and water to outlast a siege." He looks around and lowers his voice to a near whisper. "I convinced them that hundreds of National Guardsmen had surrounded the caves with so much firepower and a no-nonsense negotiator and that snipers above the caves were prepared to pick them off one by one. Once they believed they'd lost their only advantage, higher ground, they agreed to surrender."

"I'm confused," I say, then lower my voice. "You're telling us the National Guard surrounded the place?"

Travis smiles at me for the first time in a week and whispers. "No. Let's say I'm a pretty good bluffer. When we pulled out, a few men asked where the soldiers were. I told them they retreated to the road because they didn't want any trouble with us."

I smile back. "You preserved their macho dignity."

His euphoria tempers a bit when he adds, "I brought them all back except one."

"How did you get the black eye?"

"Their de facto leader. He tried to convince the others to fight for the mountain. He thought I'd sold them out."

"Who's their leader?" Corey asks.

"A big man who calls himself Jeremiah Johnson. Dressed in animal skins. Has a bit of a lazy eye. Long gray beard."

The man who warned me not to enter a cave alone. The one who boasted he stood in the eye of the tornado and survived. I ask what happened to him.

"He fled on foot higher up the mountain. Said he was taking as many of the bastards as he could before they got him." Travis breaks a smile. "Old Jeremiah's going to be surprised when he finds no one to shoot. I hope he comes to his senses and comes off the mountain."

I think back to the Japanese soldier who didn't know the war had ended. "He'll have another story to embellish, as long as he doesn't shoot anyone first."

Travis' smile fades. "My bet is he returns to the caves. I have to warn the city council he's probably still up there and armed."

Corey shakes Travis' hand and says job well done.

"I need a shot of something in this coffee," he says.

A volunteer has just brought a plate of hot food over when Frank and Barbara stride through the doors wearing grins. Frank hugs Travis. "I heard the good news and brought Barbara in case anyone needs medical attention."

Barbara is already tending to the new arrivals. I hear her mention a case of mild frostbite.

Travis looks to Frank and silently holds out his coffee cup. Frank reaches into a back pocket and produces a flask that he tips into the cup.

I grin. "Pastor Frank, you surprise me more each day."

"There are many forms of spiritual and physical comfort in these times that try men's souls. This particular one happens to be of the southern variety."

People gather around Travis while he picks at his meal. "On the ride down, I heard the fire marshal determined the cause of the blaze in Dora and Tom's tent was negligence. Use of a faulty propane tank next to a stove." His shoulders sag. "The cynic in me believes otherwise. They didn't own a tank and only used the stove. Who placed it there and why?"

"I can't get the last image of them out of my mind," I say. I think of the paintings. "Did anyone get the sense they were giving away their possessions? Some people do that before they . . . die." My gaze lands on Frank.

There's a pause until Frank says, "A stack of them were by my front door that morning. I never had the chance to ask her why."

"I wonder if the camp closing was too much for them and they decided to die together rather than try to start all over again in some new place."

Frank bows his head. "Perhaps. But there's no villainous explanation for Benny's death. Other than we failed him."

Travis stands. "We may never know about Dora and Tom. We need to locate every remaining Highlander and make sure they're safe."

"Maybe this will help," Frank says, holding the camp laptop. "Susan smuggled it out of camp. At great personal peril."

Travis smiles and embraces me. The hug lingers.

When I open my eyes, Frank flashes a suspecting smile.

Travis breaks off the hug. "This is great. The directory isn't complete by any stretch, but it's a helluva start."

I help the others get the northerners settled in for an hour or two until I need to leave. Frank walks me out. On my way, I grab half a bologna sandwich for Pearl, who's been waiting patiently in the truck.

Frank flashes a knowing smile. "Travis is a good man. I dare say he's a great man."

I feel myself blush and say nothing.

"Well, stay strong and don't be a stranger, Can-Do Susan."

"I will. Still no news of anyone looking for a lost black Lab named Pearl?"

When he shakes his head, I find an extra bounce in my step on my walk to the truck. I placed an ad in the Gazette this morning after a trip to the vet revealed no chip. If Pearl's owners want to claim her, they'll need to find her in the paper. I also bought a leash, breath treats, and more chew toys.

Pearl inhales the sandwich in the front seat and burps in my face again.

"Such a lady. Let's go home, girl."

On Saturday, I paint the guest bedroom and, upon the recommendation of my therapist, free Gabby's pictures from Jim's desk. No beeps or lights. I feel ripples of sadness and what-might-have-beens, but the thoughts don't carry me away. I drive into town to shop and buy supplies, my new word for groceries. I throw a box of Frosty Paws in the cart for Pearl. Today I declare she's my dog, free and clear, and this is her new official birthday.

Near my parked truck, I see what I hope is the last weathered Danny flier on a telephone pole and slowly tear the pieces down. I look to the sky and give silent thanks to the man with the wing-nut ears who wanted to steal my car but instead suggested I search the Highlands. Without him, I likely would have crashed headlong into a bridge abutment on some desolate country road.

That reminds me: I call his number, prepared to mail the two-hundred-dollar reward as promised, but it's no longer in service.

An American Nakba

My first day back at Hudson High comes and goes with no speeches or banners, no school assembly. I thank Mr. Morris for honoring my request. The initial excitement of my return soon dies down. It's a relief to be with the students again, away from the house and Jim during the days.

Jim is happy I'm back at work because we need the money, but I know he resents me volunteering in the shelters since my return home. I crate Pearl during the day so he doesn't have to walk her, and I take her with me at night.

Monday night, Franks calls and suggests I meet him and the others at the television station. Jim doesn't look up from his paper when I tell him where I'm off to, but the corners of his mouth turn down.

When I arrive, Travis, Frank, and Corey are waiting to meet with Jessica Rau. Travis and Frank are solemn, but Corey seems excited, and I soon learn why. He's loaded with damning evidence against Prodigal and eager to be the whistleblower.

Jessica arrives, and the introductions are quick. "You said you have something to show me, Mr. Landry?"

"Call me Corey. You voiced on-air frustration to viewers about not being allowed to shoot footage of the forced evacuation of hundreds of Highlanders. I have it all right here for you, and more."

Her eyes light up briefly. "Okay, let's see what you got."

The first segment he plays is from the night when armed police with canines entered the camp for an unannounced inspection. It shows them confiscating propane tanks and issuing tickets for fire code violations. He freezes the film when Sergeant Decker and the police draw their weapons on Travis and the Highlanders.

"Oh my," Jessica says.

"Effective immediately, residents were told that night it was now illegal to burn wood of any kind, dead or green, in their wood stoves for warmth or cooking. Full disclosure here—when the cops drew their guns, some Highlanders drew theirs in response."

I remember Bert emerging from the forest that night in his coonskin hat, shouldering an AR-15.

The anchorwoman looks surprised. "There were guns in the Highlands?"

Corey looks at her, nonplussed. I almost expect him to say Bless your heart. "Shake a tree in this country, and a gun is likely to fall out of it. If you're homeless and live on a mountain, a gun would be a smart thing to own if you could afford one."

Travis shifts in his chair while the video continues to play. "This was in direct violation of the agreement we'd struck with the city council. We were allowed to burn dead or fallen wood in stoves and campfires. This was their initial attempt to weed out our residents." He points at the screen. "Do you see people fleeing into the woods there? That's because the cops were shouting about mass arrests and deportation."

"Okay. What's next?" Jessica says, frowning. She takes a seat next to Corey and leans forward.

He fast-forwards to the Pit. "The screen will stop bouncing soon. If I didn't seek cover and keep moving, I would have been arrested and my camera confiscated."

Corey raises the volume. "This was the onslaught of the evacuation when, as you can see, the police and deputies arrived in riot gear with police dogs and ordered everyone to leave immediately." On the screen, children cry, mothers grab essentials in a panic, angry men protest, wanting to resist. "This tragedy could have turned violent, potentially deadly. But these two men," Corey says, pointing to Frank and Travis, "prevented that."

The scene bounces again and shifts to one of the central paths.

"Here, Sergeant Decker is yelling at Mayor Travis, the man in the bomber jacket, that the evacuation is taking too long and the Highlanders have fifteen minutes to load into the buses before they're handcuffed and arrested. The man next to him is Frank, the Highland pastor. You can see and hear they are not being aggressive or using profanity. They are arguing their case for more time." Onscreen, Travis is following a group of officers. A moment later, they shove him down face first, and a deputy cuffs him, then kicks him repeatedly while he is down. I cringe. That had to hurt.

"Oh, my," Jessica says a second time.

"Now we see Decker wave frantically at the deputy, shouting for him to stop, which he eventually does." Frank rushes to Travis' side, is kidney-punched from behind, driven to his knees, and then cuffed. "Neither of them fought or resisted, which is what they were arrested for."

The screen bounces wildly as the camera quickly moves to the left before going dark. "Here we see the 'buses' are actually black prison transport vans marked POLICE, at the southeastern edge of the Highlands. The mayor and Pastor Frank are forced into the back of a prison van with other Highlanders."

In the background, my crumpled BMW sits under a stand of pines.

The screen bounces and lightens to show officers destroying Vidal and Maria's tent, poles and all, and we hear a deputy order them to proceed to the van, warning that resistance of any kind will result in immediate arrest. Maria is carrying their youngest, and all three children are in tears while Vidal gathers what he can before he's pushed along.

I'm so angry I find myself crying. Where are my students and their parents?

"They rousted this family with three young children, herded them like animals, and gave them no time to pack clothes or other belongings," Corey says, his voice cracking with emotion. We see a long line of Highlanders trudging down the congested path toward the prison vans.

"This clip here gives a better indication of the numbers of displaced people. There," he says, pointing at the screen, "you see people break from the line and run into the woods."

Jessica turns her head. "Why are they doing that, Corey?"

"Could be several reasons." His voice grows more animated. "Wait for it . . ."

A deputy aims a rifle at the back of an unarmed man fleeing into the forest.

"Oh, no," I say and close my eyes.

"Thank God the deputy doesn't shoot. Some people would rather take their chances on a snow-covered mountain in winter with only the clothes on their backs than be hauled to prison. They may have expired work visas or no paperwork. They may be plain terrified out of their minds. Imagine if this were you. How would you feel if you were forced to leave your home this way, in darkness, with nothing, in the middle of winter?"

The screen goes dark again, and Jessica asks, "How were you able to film all this without being caught?"

Corey adjusts his glasses. "I know the mountain well. I used to live in the Highlands until recently, when I qualified for subsidized housing. I used an old mining trail to bypass the roadblocks, plus I'm familiar with the woods around the camp."

Travis speaks up. "They drove us in police vans to jail. Frank and I were beaten and arrested for being leaders. They booked a few others with possession of unregistered firearms."

"Where are Vidal and his family?" I ask Travis.

He shakes his head. "They weren't in our van, and I didn't see them at the station. Maybe they escaped into the woods." He turns back to Jessica. "Those not arrested were processed and identified. Consider it a weird kind of triage. Immigration was present and detained a vanload of 'illegals,' as they were called. Anyone left was assigned to a shelter. The women were all sent to the church in old town Prodigal, the one Barbara oversees. Married couples were forced to separate. The pets who weren't lost in the melee were forced into animal shelters."

Frank speaks next. "Of course, Prodigal allowed you to film the bodies wheeled out on gurneys. It helped justify closing us down. We heard an explosion before the tent caught fire. The tent of the older couple. They were gentle and respected members of our community, accustomed to life in the Highlands, well-versed

317

in safety with their wood stove. After the blaze, we found a faulty propane tank in their tent. They never owned one."

Jessica's brow furrows. "But the fire marshal ruled the cause of the fire was negligence. Do you have evidence to the contrary?"

When he remains silent, she continues. "This is the second deadly Highland fire in two and a half years. An alcoholic man smoking in his tent two summers ago nearly started a forest fire—"

"Deadly fires happen in town, also," Frank says. "Families die in Prodigal and across the country in house fires that have smoke detectors with dead batteries."

"Okay, but what do you have to say about the third body?"

Travis fields this question. "There was nothing simple about the man or his situation."

She frowns. "He really lived in a toilet? And you, Frank, and everyone allowed it to happen?"

"He chose to live in a porta-potty near the woods. Like I said, he was a loner and mentally ill. Two years ago, Benny was the last known homeless person who slept on park benches or heating grates. When the town rousted him, Sergeant Decker personally dropped him off at the Highlands after he spent the night in jail for vagrancy. I offered Benny a tent, same as I do for every new arrival without their own form of shelter, but he refused. He was a veteran with no family and a long history of mental illness. Whenever he became psychotic and a danger to himself, we drove him to Prodigal Hospital for psychiatric treatment. I pleaded with the hospital's social worker to contact his VA case manager to find a halfway house or group home for him, but he was at the bottom of a years-long waiting list for housing. After each stay, Prodigal Hospital sent him back to the Highlands in a cab with no long-term plan. I filled his medications and urged him to take them as best I could."

"So this man fell through the cracks," she says.

I feel the hairs on the back of my neck rise. "No, this honorably discharged veteran was forgotten and abandoned by society. What happened to him is a goddamn tragedy."

I shudder at the thought of Benny's ghost haunting my dreams.

Her eyes harden while she studies me, then turns back to Corey. "You have anything else?"

He presses a button. "One more segment. Here, we see heavy machinery on the mountain yesterday." The sun is low in the sky behind equipment bearing Mayor Gilroy's construction company's logo. Caterpillars are pushing detritus from the Rainbow Camp into giant mounds of trash. We watch as the flagpole is bulldozed and the rainbow flag trampled. Dump trucks loaded with the skeletons of tents and twisted shelters.

"Okay, we knew this was bound to happen," Jessica says.

"Wait for it," Corey says.

The screen pans right to show workers carefully loading the commodes onto a flatbed.

Corey looks into Jessica's eyes. "To think that porta-potties possess more value than the homes and belongings of three hundred people sickens me. There are children's clothes and family photographs in that rubble. All the earthly possessions of the Highlanders thrown out as garbage. Should Benny have spent the last years of his life in a commode? Of course not. But these are crimes against humanity."

The screen bounces and shifts to another location.

"What's going on in the background there?" Jessica asks.

"People are emerging from the woods near the railroad tracks, walking south toward Prodigal. They have no other place to go, so history repeats itself. They're returning to the park benches and city storefronts because there is no plan for these people."

The figures are too distant to discern specific individuals, but they all look female, so I think they are Highlanders from the Rainbow Camp who escaped the police roundup. I worry that Kim and Penny must be reliving their old fears about Prodigal while they walk with Brianne into an uncertain future.

Corey pockets his thumb drive and looks to Jessica. "I have an anonymous source who claims Gilroy's construction company received a no-bid contract with an out-of-town private developer in exchange for multimillion-dollar tax breaks. My source projects that the jobs will be mostly minimum wage and that the development will call for an onsite hotel with its own restaurants, effectively shutting Prodigal from reaping any of the financial benefits. My source thinks the town stands to lose millions if this deal goes through and that it will cost Prodigal jobs, prompting budget cuts to the usual victims—schools, parks, and social programs."

"Sounds like more welfare for multimillionaires," Travis says. "And the pesky homeless people squatting on public land proved a real nuisance, didn't we? The truth needs to be told, Ms. Rau, and these people still need permanent housing. Desperately."

She finishes her notes, stands, and smooths the hem of her dress. "I agree with you. You've done amazing investigative work here, Corey. Susan is right; you have a future in reporting. You've given me a lot to take to my manager. Hang tight for a few moments."

We talk about the Highlanders who have returned to the shelters while we wait. Still no word of Judy and George, Vidal and his family, or Kim, Penny, and Brianne. And no update from the hospital about Flossie, Wilbur, and Jasmine. Before he sees it or hears about it from anyone else, I tell Travis they bulldozed the totem pole. He winces and looks at the floor. Frank places a hand on his shoulder.

The door opens thirty minutes later. Four beefy security guards approach, their faces void of emotion. The one in charge says, "Ms. Rau has been called away on another matter. If she wishes to pursue your story, she will be in contact. Time for you to leave."

"I knew it. I knew this would happen!" Travis says. He's so angry, Frank and Corey must restrain him on our way out.

Epilogue

Over the next few weeks after school, I use my truck to collect clothes, food, and supplies from restaurants and businesses for the VFW hall and churches. The police continue to drop off people, some familiar and some new, at the temporary shelters. Judy and George arrive at the church after a failed effort to reconnect with their adult son. Vidal, Maria, and their three children emerge from the streets, hungry and frightened. The couples are separated, and the children stay with Maria. I'm delighted to see them all safe and sound.

With the return of my missing friends, I call in the favor I asked of Superintendent Morris and ask the same one of Jim. He surprises me when he agrees so readily. He's been more understanding and eager to hear about my evenings at the shelters. I think he's resigned himself to it, knowing that it's temporary. I call Travis, Frank, and Barbara to tell them that standing job interviews wait for any willing applicants at Hudson High. Human Resources at Hudson High agrees to interview Vidal and others for potential mechanic/driver positions and any former Highlanders interested in food or custodial service jobs. Jim works as a financial officer and accountant for Miracle Motors, the largest automobile dealership in Prodigal. They always need administrative assistants and car salesmen, so I thought Judy, Maria, George, and others might want to apply. With jobs, maybe they can secure those last remaining subsidized apartments.

My therapist switches me to weekend appointments and says I'm making progress, but I still feel like shit turned inside out some days. Jim halfheartedly accepts Pearl as part of the family but leaves the care and walking to me.

During these weeks, the news shows newly paved asphalt roads that now serpentine up the mountain. Water lines and fire hydrants follow the roads. The television anchors focus on the positives that the ski lodge will bring to the area.

One evening, Travis, Frank, and I are allowed to drive onto the newly paved roads and find that the cars from the Daytona 500

Club have been towed, along with mine. The land where the Pit, the church/classroom, and the 500 Club once stood has been graded for a future parking lot. I hug myself and bite my lip; it's like the tent city never existed. The only buildings that still stand are the two tiny homes that Travis built. They use their keys, and we carry their clothes and valuables to our vehicles. The ski lodge plans to use the former homes as parking lot booths, and the city agreed to pay the Highlanders a lump settlement for the homes and the large canvas tents. Travis says the money will be given to those who lost their possessions in the forced exodus.

I attend the memorial service for Dora and Tom and Benny in the potter's field. Dora and Tom's adult children are no-shows.

Frank sleeps at the church often, and I hear Travis frequently stays overnight at the VFW hall. On quiet nights they sometimes crash at Corey's apartment, who's working nights at the news station.

Flossie discharges from the hospital without her baby, who remains in the NICU. We hear no word of her or Wilbur.

A co-worker tells me Prodigal suburbia dealt with double-barreled crises of their own while I was away. A man who lived in a house one street over from us barricaded himself and his family during a domestic dispute. The police shot and killed him after a tense, two-hour standoff. I used to nod or say hello to him on the street. I never knew his name and had no idea he suffered from depression. The second barrel concerned an elderly woman who lived alone in our subdivision. A home health nurse learned she was a reclusive hoarder living in filth. The Health Department condemned the house. She threatened to sue but eventually agreed to enter a nursing home. She had no family and paid a neighbor boy to deliver groceries, mow her lawn, and shovel snow. No one in the subdivision had a clue.

The Teacher of the Year awards come and go without me. I receive no requests to speak at schools, but the National Coalition for the Homeless, the National Alliance to End Homelessness, the National Coalition for Homeless Veterans, and the National Runaway Safeline contact me to be a speaker. I suspect my impromptu confrontation with Mayor Gilroy played a role in the requests. I accept every invitation.

After shopping for supplies at the quad one afternoon, I spot an elderly black man approaching people on the sidewalk. His coat is ragged, and his pants are disheveled. With bowed head, he reaches out his hand and speaks in deferential tones to passersby who ignore him. A teenage boy mimics him after he passes, but the old man perseveres. When he sees me, I cut across the grass, and he lowers his head again, "Anything, Miss. I'd appreciate anything you can spare."

I look in my bag and frown at my choices—spaghetti noodles, ground beef, sauce, a garlic bulb, French baguettes, and Snickers Minis. I hand him the bread and a bag of candy bars.

"This is the best I can do right now. Here's a dollar. It's all I have. If you buy coffee at the Quick-Mart over there, they'll let you sit inside out of the cold. If you need a place to stay tonight, Pastor Frank will be in the quad at six o'clock." I glance at the tall clock tower as I still don't own a watch. "That's in thirty minutes. He drives an old yellow school bus and runs a shelter at a church in Prodigal. He can drive you there." I point at the candy. "I assure you the church food will be healthier."

I'm not certain which is greater, his surprise or his smile. "Thank you, Miss. May our merciful God bless you." His fingers betray a Parkinsonian tremor. I notice stuffed newspapers that serve as lining for his threadbare coat. Spring has yet to grace Prodigal.

One of the surprising traits many Highlanders possessed on the mountain was an unshakeable faith in God, while I spent much of my adult life cursing Him. They also were quick to forget, forgive, and pull together. "God bless you, sir. What's your name?"

He looks stunned, and for an instant, the essential tremor disappears. "Why, it's Calvin, Miss . . ."

"Susan. Remember the bus, if you need a place to stay. Six o'clock. Pastor Frank will find you warmer clothes, too."

"You are an angel, Miss Susan."

"As are you, Calvin."

Every once in a while, I think maybe, just maybe, there is a God and angels.

I like to think Thoreau is looking down and smiling right about now.

When I arrive home, I take Pearl out and whistle a happy tune while I put away the supplies. I walk upstairs to the master bedroom and place a box on the bed. My other purchase today in the Highland spirit of forgiveness. A present to acknowledge Jim's understanding of my need to continue to volunteer until final arrangements for all are in place. We've settled back into our separate lives again, and I don't know if our marriage can be saved, but I feel a need to try.

Jim's SUV is in the garage, but I don't see him.

I take a quick shower, dab on perfume, and put on the red negligee from the box. It's a perfect fit. I return Pearl to her crate. Humming, I look for Jim, but he's not on the first or second floors. In the kitchen, I hear him outside on the backyard patio, talking to someone on his cell. As I'm about to turn the doorknob, the conversation becomes heated. I stop to listen.

"So, you still want to throw away last year? I thought we reconciled that week at the Overlook? You said we had something special."

He pauses to listen. He quickly glances over his left shoulder toward the door, and I reflexively step back, but the curtain screens me from view.

"Yes, I know she's back, but that doesn't change anything, Sandy. It's not like you two are still friends."

Another pause while he listens. I close my eyes and feel bile rise in my throat. I can't get air into my lungs fast enough. Now I know why he didn't return home until 4:30 that morning. Why he's been so understanding. I was a babe in the woods, and now, I'm a fool in the suburbs.

"So, what you're really saying is you're ending it because I have no money. If you loved me, money wouldn't matter. She was right about you: you are a gold-digging bitch. Go to hell!"

I return upstairs, change out of the negligee, and back into jeans and a sweater. This time, I fill the suitcases he placed next to the door of the guest bedroom months ago. When I load the truck with my clothes and Pearl and her crate, he enters the kitchen from the back patio.

His face is flushed with anger, and he's surprised to see me. "I didn't hear you come home. What's for dinner?"

"I heard plenty. You get your wish at last. I'm leaving."

He looks flummoxed. His hands go to his waist in a defiant stance. "What are you talking about? We're starting over."

"I bet Sandy dumped you when she found a younger man with money. I will return for the rest of my things after I find a place to stay, so don't change the locks. Don't try to close our joint account until I say so."

He tries to convince me to stay. The desperation in his voice rises with each attempt that I ignore. His words ring pathetic and hollow; he blames me for his affair. So predictable.

Undeterred, I gather my coats and gloves from the hallway closet.

Frustrated and angry, he changes tactics and screams. "Go on, leave, then. You'll never be anything more than a crazy bitch who killed our daughter and fucked up our son."

From the cab of my truck in the garage, Pearl starts barking in earnest when Jim raises his voice.

I turn to him and smile. I don't say a word.

I never saw it coming. He strikes me with a short, closed fist that sends me crashing to the floor. My head misses a sharp corner of the coffee table by inches and bounces off the hardwood floor. He kicks me once in the stomach, but the table leg deflects some of the blow. I see stars and nearly pass out, but I slowly pick myself up. My nose is bleeding, and I taste blood in my mouth.

"Wiped that smug smile off your face, didn't I?" he gloats. "Go kill yourself!"

I fumble for the garage door while Pearl's frantic barks turn to shrieks. I hope he doesn't grab me from behind because I'm no physical match for him. When I close the door to the kitchen behind me, his screams precede glass shattering in the kitchen. Then a loud thud—the kitchen table being overturned?

So much can happen in ninety seconds.

But I ended the argument loop, the last thing we had in common. I have a split lip, and I'm going to have a nasty black eye. I will file for divorce and return to the house with a cop for my belongings once he's served a restraining order. He won't get a second chance to kill me. He can have the house. All I want is my freedom.

I pet Pearl's frothy muzzle to calm her as she stares into my face. I think my new pup is an empath. She licks my face, and her tail wags after I reassure her everything's going to be okay.

A slow drizzle starts to fall when we back out of the driveway. The forecast predicts the start of spring next week in Prodigal. There's a cheap motor lodge on the highway outside the city that accepts pets. We head that way. I have school to teach in the morning, and I volunteer with Travis at the VFW soup kitchen tomorrow night. We drive into a red sky at night. Pearl, my fledgling navigator, places her front paws on the dashboard. She looks at me with those big chocolate eyes and smiles. The rain stops almost as soon as it began. It turned out to be one large cloud above the house.

I see no flashing lights and hear no beeps. In the motel later that night, there are no ghosts.

Best of all, I remember.

And I'm making peace with the past. And myself.

The world and all its possibilities await us.

The End

326

Acknowledgments

A book never writes itself, no matter what you've heard. There are so many people to thank each time I write a novel. Thanks go out this time to Sheri Williams of TouchPoint Press, to Kim Coghlan, main editor of TPP who kept me informed and somewhat sane during the lengthy process of publication with a company new to me, to Scott Bury, who was the initial TPP editor, and to all the ancillary staff, including Ashley Carlson. Unforeseen circumstances led to the book's re-publication by NYBP.

A special thanks go to my friend and editor Meghan Pinson-Moore who helped grow the story of Prodigal with her keen insights, to Matthew Arkin, who reviewed the plot specifics with a critical eye, and to 52 beta readers who provided insights regarding story readability. Thanks to Janet Muhm, illustrator supreme, for her careful and detailed work on the map for my fictional homeless encampment. Also, a hearty thanks to my former writer's critique group through the Missouri Writer's Guild that includes writers John Frain and Ed Protzel.

More thanks must be given to longtime friends who've provided assistance on prior novels as well as this one: Dr. Felix Vincenz for his expertise on all things of the mind; attorney Michael Schaller for his knowledge of the law and legal terminology; Mark Halfaker, a former police officer; and Lauri Chamberlain, a teacher who helped me address the inherent challenges of teaching kids of all ages in one classroom. In addition, to any service providers or temporarily homeless people that I spoke to, I owe a debt of gratitude to each of you.

To the newest additions of my writing family and friends, sincere thanks go to the New York Book Publisher's staff that include Lisa "Tokyo" Smith, Conner Stewart, Logan Walsh, Jessica Cohen, Emma Becker, and Jeremiah Hofsted. Thank you and all others for all your work on my killer new website, with this book, with Boundless and The Nostradamus Society, and in getting my early novels ready for re-publication and for the creation of my future audiobooks and book/video trailers. I almost wish it was a year from now!

Every one of you shaped Prodigal for the better.

Trooping the Colour

Testimonial

I have been asked by the author, an American I have known for thirty years, to attest my assurance that his use of the term "trooping the colour" to entitle this curious fiction is in no sense intended to be disrespectful to any soldier of the Sovereign who, as he recognizes, lies on hard ground and fights while the he sleeps in a warm bed and writes. Having spent my entire adult life in the army, serving with all manner of men, I do not claim solders are better than artists but only wish to delineate, with a nod to the Senior Service, the line of debt. If Drake's seamen fail to repel the Armada, we will never hear in an oppressed and occupied England, one word of Shakespeare.

Brigadier Robert ("Bobs") Assingham, MC, DSO.
Colonel-in-Chief, Worcester and Sherwood Foresters Regiment
(29th/45th Foot)

Trooping
the Colour

by
Page Nelson

Edited and Augmented
by
William Ruminant

Another
Sparrow
Press
2012

© Copyright 2012 Page Nelson

Published by Another Sparrow Press, the publishing branch
for fine arts and the humanities
of Passerine Inc., a global multi-media entertainment provider

Page Nelson asserts his moral right not to be identified as the author of
this work; any reproduction, transmission, broadcast or rebroadcast in
any form or by any means, electronical, mechanical, pastoral, including photocopy, recording or storage by any retrieval system without
prior permission of the publisher is permitted with attribution.

ISBN: 978-0615692388

Cataloging-at-Publication Data
Nelson, Page, 1952-
Trooping the Colour / by Page Nelson, edited & augmented by
William Ruminant.
    1. Man-woman relationships – Fiction. 2. Poetry – United States –
Criticism and interpretation.   I. Ruminant, William. II. Title
PS3546.E478T65 2012   2012
                    CAP/NOTCIP

Revised edition

Book design by Jo-Anne Rosen, Petaluma, California

Front cover art: "British Parade" (www.istockphoto.com)
Back cover art: Colour of the 76th Regiment of Foot (Wikipedia)

Passage from Walter Benjamin's *Ursprung des deutschen Trauerspiels*, translated
by John Osborne.

My opus ground to a halt of its own growing weight, all that comparing of subtly disparate secondary versions of the facts, and seeking out old newspapers and primary documents, and sinking deeper and deeper into an exfoliating quiddity that offers no deliverance from itself, only a final vibrant indeterminacy, infinitely detailed and yet ambiguous, as unsettled, these dead facts, as if alive.

— John Updike, *Memoirs of the Ford Administration.*

Fire control's deep-seated importance in the collective sub conscious of the army is demonstrated in the annual Queen's birthday parade on Horse Guards ("Trooping the Colour"), for the evolutions through which the Foot Guards are put in that magnificent hour — sharp, precise, emphatic — are a relic of the battlefield drill that got the serried ranks of infantrymen to deliver volleys in whatever direction was needed in the shortest possible time.

— Allan Mallinson, *The Making of the British Army.*

The best part of most books is the introductory epigraph.

— *A Wilderness of Monkeys*

Contents

Critical Introduction

Trooping the Colour is a book by method and mediation (described in detail in "William Ruminant and Page Nelson in Conversation"). Perloff's sexualized terms, "appropriation and constraint" are likewise descriptive if supplemented by "incrementation" since this is a bricolage of fiction, poetry, aphorism and interview. Its titular presentation is as a gestural fiction of a curious kind; as if an amateur prestidigitator attempting to pull a rabbit out of a hat forgot to supply the rabbit but also the hat so that the failed performance is redeemed as mimicry, soliciting the reader to the reconstruction of a faceted object that never was, the various verbal behaviors constituting a ceremony that is respectful, nostalgic of meaning if practically and unapologetically pointless, at best pageantry, a presentation of flags.

Its justification as the author claims (and all such foundation claims should be viewed skeptically and deconstructively) was the simultaneous perception and manufacture of an underlying horizon or stratum of meaning (see the eighth aphorism), an Imminence he is entirely disposed to leave unnameable — as if a constellation of concepts, the Forms, Deep Grammar, The Absolute, Kabalistic Logomachia, Imminence itself, transcendentally grounded discourse. This is likewise a horizontal or superficial *line* of reasoning. We detect a formerly sensitive ear, like that of deafened conductors, which has registered so many "voices" it has finally found its long coda of satisfaction in silence or indistinguishable din. The case is not quite Kenneth Goldsmith's "Faced with an unprecedented amount of available text, writing needs to redefine itself in the new environment of (super) abundance"[1] where words are not vehicles of expression but objects to be arranged. Nelson's project, not so positivistic, is more mournful, a rueful (in the Elizabethan sense) ambix of alchemo-kabalistic research, in some sense "Benjaminic,"

---

1. See "Uncreative writing: managing language in the digital age," by Kenneth Goldsmith, Columbia University Press, 2012.

and one least likely to receive certification by those stern, semi-resentful culturalists, the rear (not avant) garde of the new aesthetic order, Adorno, et al.[2]

"What does it mean?" is not a question we (and we all are, whether we know it or not) post-post modernists should be asking. Rather, our task is discernment of trace, of the aggregative micro-arrangements that are unfixed by the beam of our detection, itself composed and fluxious. I speak of life, but it will do too for the work in hand, its fore-knowing genealogical generators, Need and Hope.

William Ruminant,
Verver Professor of Comparative Literature,
Director, The William Ruminant Institute for Textual and Editorial Studies (WRITES)
Edmister University

---

2. Readers such as Raul Trembley who affirm Adorno's aesthetic progressivism are privileging his "open form" superstructure at the expense of his deeply conservative base. Photographs of Adorno in a full body swimsuit say it all, the puny escort of the aloof beauty, Diotima, who seeing him getting sand kicked in his face by the brute "historical materialism," desires "a real metaphysical man." But "Teddy" knows to clip the coupon, buy the book and soon, via aesthetic-judo, over throws the bully *by his own force.*

Textual Note

The peculiar taxonomy of this manuscript, at once pre- and succeeding *A Wilderness of Monkeys*, is described in "the Conversation." The text of the original novel ("Trio') and the word file of *"Trooping the Colour"* are housed at WRITES, where the manuscript was prepared for its publication by Another Sparrow Press. Various editorial variants exist and a final selection was made in remote consultation with the author. The editor wishes to thank the graduate students preparing an *apparatus criticus* under his direction (which will be available online, from WRITES) who brought to the project an inexhaustible energy and good humor that daily anointing the work in progress with fresh designations ("A Comedy of Eros," "A Commodity of Errors") much alleviated the editorial load. Nelson assures us his heterogeneous facetiousness is incidental, accidentally if not actually innocent, aimed at himself, not his readers and that may be. The tone is contagious.

W.R.

Trooping the Colour

Odds of Nightingales

Of flesh informed by intelligence and by prosperity that ultimately and tastefully throughout the 19th century (note the tone) absolutely historical, a university town. There more books than in all the surrounding thousands of nightingales trapped for the London market. In the words of one observer connecting counties, bodies and brains gently pressed, nourished sufficiently, "the birds take poorly to captivity. At certain seasons, the gutters of Holborne suppress or that idealism so that to the cynical, sober well being and wholesome Seven Dials were clogged with their felted bodies." Yet I doubt they were miserable, purpose seemed causal though no one would say which was the cause and which a decadent, quick dying. And to balance the equation, what enjoyment took place? Most professors lived a life the envy of any desert father, each so they bring to the old, the sick, the melancholic? Oh, you want a concrete conscious, scholium ad scholia as to engage in but behind the back, Ok, think Regency; Jennie the maid jilted by Jack the drover, buys a bird to sweeten the staleness of her attic mind, autumn days when squirrels gathered nuts with attention, when all creation looms. At night, it forgets the weave of wire and dreams it is free. Hearing it paused to tense, horns calling behind pyres of far maples as if the fall of soft throated notes and for a while so does she. But frankly, its hard to get worked up about winter, to see the brilliant young crossing the quad, one could well believe overloads of dead nightingales. Or the people. Everyone alive — pick a date, say "Many gifts but you lack that high seriousness. You will squander them." April 1868 is dead, she had said as he sorted the bales of letters, the skins. Tell me that makes you sad when really you're glad they are not around, old Virginia ladies who dutifully to the library where they were filed and ordered, competing for love, position of space. They are out of the race. And as to locks of hair stitched with dry rotted thread, no matter. Nightingales? Well I heard one once, one summer in Somerset. And if you didn't there's always "Audobon's

Big Book of Birds" with CD-ROM of song carried if the radiator was on, up and tacking light, galleons amid attendant pinnaces of dust sailing despite the pressure the urgency building (cyclotron) as the morning aged from the cosmic expense from one discrete moment of work to another to drink water or doing nothing until even greater because the work had atomized again so that by five, after thousands of years in the brain refused to move some little motor in your nostrils or under your arms that walking home the quick emphatic nods of routs of sparrows that had scattered and then split amid the various flights of melody more impression than fitful summer breezes against exhausted quarries.

Marshalling the Memoirs

At any hour of the day the ringing, the disynchronous clicking closed of a hundred jacketed books above the glittering debris fields, the Benz star rising, bands back in the beer halls, stocked shops and typed papers so the privy was preserved, the sugar bowels were plenished and the old academic hounds, wise, who strained at the leash and wrote from retirement's bungalows. The field marshals are maneuvering, straight, stiff with the "I" in the knowledge that I am lean, carelessly intellectual "Dear Colonel General, thank you for your letter describing the retreat of Army Group B" fumbling in my pockets, my penis swelling its blue red swilled water certifies my having drunk from the well. If you are ever in Kessel ... my account will appear in England with an introduction by Hart, their panzer man of wisdom, linear to whom all consciousness refers, a light upon the tracks. I was humbled and this the book I hold in hand, delightful with details and bluff soldierly descriptions, it is any wonder when — she had back eyes, one December afternoon, "Behind the in-leap saplings of the state collective farm, summers distant, deep in bed came Schubert's Ninth beginning and beginning on four notes, "Our Jaeger groups lay in wait" or "I knew of no crimes behind our lines" sonorous and low over and my oath I could not break." A good dinner rumbles in my gut over, broken, possibly embraced with another coupling, ponderous coaxing or some lunatic resolved which would not play fresh reinforcements but I nod off, all western civilization stuck on folded dark, the light backed up behind the spill when cicadas began to sing under the reading light's heavy siege, the wavering air and I wondered if that was why they cracked and bled a thin green cooler, pondering the legalities of words falling into letters, long black ranks on life's white page position, plead and pun "sic succubus Tyrannous" giving way at the sudden contracting chill, syllables of love or mockery stiffed, as the blinds half heaved in the weak meter of membrane against bone, like solders, like graves.

Setting the Rotors

Burning with desire to say something and finished and he glanced at her and past to a voice behind Cloud shuttered light and slaps of wind, the rippled pond and one cold swan, these we accept as they were beginning to boil and bubble, to leave the bottom of the pot but they crested-subsided nature's clear text. We interrogate the rain-pooled drive that once was thronged with official cars into the late afternoon corridors but for the sentinel humming of fountains, exiting as the vacant mansion, echoing in our footfalls its memories of generals and boffins, the huts that were philosopher, I use the term, directly, jostled into formation in the same way I had clutched my desk upstart, pungent with pitch, dilapidated into a barrow like belonging corner, rejoicing it is rough it is real, dragging the floor, her slow walk if not meditative and should I stay back, deciding she will in this cloistered context, in the brightness intensified, behind the blackout curtains a man, a woman stared at randomized letters that it is just that for her ears, tuned to semitones, conscious of crowding her course, looking for a way in, an intuition almost touching our steps in time then breaking as if playing chess against a master, one long line of stalls that reminded one by each a small lamp sent a tartared light through clouds of various densities that has this weakness, faced with one correct attack his moves become predictable, this then that, drifted when like cattle really so that the light also appeared in that uneasy period when you have decided but no one has forsaken, a position cracked as decryption machines clatter. A soldier in the graying dawn, she had finished her cigarette, timing it exactly, crushed it in the tray and dawn leaked in, the day watch entering said in that terrifying composure a cat's step propelling the body of her thought she was ready to speak. Now a half century of commentary sentimentality and critique because he had trailed off lost as the wind changes so that although he had ceased the whole effect one of perfect cueing. The best minds enjoyed anagrams, chess and amateur theatricals, accelerated in their sentence. And we exchanged glances, keepers and old ladies who ran gift shops observed comprehending what can be read in any book or learned from guides though today she was pointing as gently the fact that he did not speak as I sometimes did or with that curious fluency, their words wind blown, scattered as magpies shelter under eaves chatter.

From the Affairs File

Now from an excess of intimacy, beyond all discerning music or painting from long acquaintance in a rush of masculine desperation and breathless from the stairs, he ran to her office to find her acquired, our indifference to become a mere possession in the bathroom mirror beyond recognition and dispossession, not there. "Despite all marriages I must see you" read his jagged note, later playing with her reply I could read nothing in this face or only a Queen of the Portal Royal comprehending only their Romanesque eyes focused into abstraction, lips sensuous., she looked from her

May Fair window, saw in the root lap of a London Plane. I concluded you were thinking nothing, we had come to "I love you," "I want to" midwives meaning that we could not conceive the other, a blaze of unmown green. This is the good and bad of it, a total trust where noticing the next day her letter, blank paper, two grass blades touched with perfume, your subdued manner, your lips pursed but would not think it, in terror of your good. He grasped its sexual yes, later the expectant room of lust like a carpet, something too of reaping, the slash, the cut. "Of course she is lovely but lets not be silly" knowing you if it was true but could not foresee the final harvest, a clutch of poems the next moment as always I loved you and hated you for the same thing, you look while reading, your pathetic telephone falsetto, three deaths.

The Falklands War

The smoke from my cigar coiling about the room, hers and to know that to take the individual and place it, as all things I see, I was watching lots of tv and saw my sagging chair, etc, my porcelain, each still distinct is embraced in consciousness so that no line obscured but a slight of mind, the whole slim feminine ship take the hit, one hot rocket, is our poor art precious for not being in stone or canvas but at the mercy of circumstance, a knock at the door, the fabric of flesh, cheap stuff it broke like yoke; liquid, victim, already wrinkling, fleeting pigments that pale in the light, literal color Meanwhile, he was advancing up your slope, taking the high ground before running away, through all time and this dim room two hills. That night, the louting, routing images of the day, I left you dumb in matrimonial sleep to sit with my bodies heat, he crouched to fire and you took the hit shuddering in thought but these adulterous images will cry out, Exocet. Its good I have a mind for history because twenty years later I will cry them for their signification to her, laughing over drinks and not to you, poor straw although justified in reference to her, bodies I cherish, only you say "Darling, maybe you made it all up," instances I saw when she passed us and not even then.

Systems

In the middle of last century each day the insertion ceremony is appraised and afterwards, systems of low pressure, its card consoles surmounted by Melville, Bryant, bronze grimace grins began to be given names and lacquered fronts that laddered a core sample, since sauna style — we smiled in recognition, those suits were hot, with every pull of blubber coloured cards, a shelf list for leather and binding, they were like us (O Tempora o Borges!). After labor in the stacks I would look around me at the mark where I was in the change of days, predictability wayward and violent, I misshelved my procedures, my courtesies as when the curator, catechizing his clefs would appoint decades later, from the eyes of satellites that had lost all denominating fame, several more or less to the aperture til signaled by his smiling distress, we saw that hurricanes were swirls, galaxies or seashells spinning, bending to a beats me turn discover the thrust to nib and left winning me his never diminished always above the living blue fresh morning. I took a half shelf of books accordioned by the translator and dropped them, heavy on my foot within the smell of brook drying to drought. The worst storms it turned out were beautiful forms. We wondered then, desperate in repose knowing this was my last look at the years of absence, what pattern our own days of wind and rain gave to some higher self or just another librarian on tour to see shelves surgical green, specks of paper, shed leather heaved from the florescences beyond controlment and common name.

Movement

The rental car had failed, its toy switched shuttle-cocked with the chinks, her inhalations fresh. Head bowed over the in-flight tray, the front door opened, she hastened to look at the furnace, sorting our Kroner, Euros, Pounds. I look on now in easy possession working across the room, the abrupt confinement. Where are we coming from? In the car there had always been an immense distance though through your beauty, she could see noting but the pink trail of bigger cars she had followed through the heavier fall of fears, a dangerous alluring place, shapes, going under should she turn around, for miles my violence wondering if she should as is she approached the outskirts of a mans' tour, snow deco and it was real to her, skidding in the drive with all the standard stops, a friend, a rival beaten up. The furnace industrial and unassimilated in a corner, you felt for him no pity, no regrets, the cat rubbing against her as we are left at cruising altitude in this middle aged plane. In the bedroom, a medium between destinations, she begins, folded clothes, concise, purposive preserving the morning, creases of her slip away, constrained in our seats, there hides a little of her expectation from the disappointment of turning back. We arrange little hopes, shaking them out, the last of that particular. Still she can use it, put on a Mozart sonata of not yet expended assets, music her hands knew.

Exfoliations

There was light, seeing the fire sear the edges like a stationer's motif distinctive not for form but for velocity, burning the sheets behind, bursting out students boisterous for dinner caught, "wait a minute, I think I see her," my purpose in standing here in having quarreled, a hot mouth that ate your face of words, to cook rendered irreconcilable this morning by a middle space that needed my careful heels crushing the ashes. To be free for even advocates to flounder or agree so that perforce, what was left of your hundred letters, a small square of folded paper I'd saved entirely the date of eating out and this better because a stranger unto the nick-nacked iconography of courtesy, "seeds from my garden, 1991," these dropped in the hungry spring contrarily to this neutral place. Blend a bit, contain yourself, and watch the plants thrust up and thrive, chives in that shallow place that could not claim you with my eyes over seas requiring tact, calculation. All summer I cropped and chopped the leaves sweeping pungent heaps of green as I can now place your skirt stressed course up street, in breakfasting, in getting out of bed to gallant the mantle of new confidence into empty tea tins.

One plant untouched, its blades curled into tubes, spear tips of bud, the intention to concentration, manufacture of almost mnemonics, obfuscation breaking into icy butterflies of flower —not remembering then or later exactly what she said in that voice, the silences before that were shriveled pods before October's rains. At the syllable of one tone, I slashed and whipped the stalks, seeds for the next harvest, recalled, known only to have been autonomous. What of my dried spice, last remains of a hot season? It starts out lemony after her utterance seeming to hear an aspiration, this flowing out of the same quiescence ionized in a sonata of silence expanded but ends up bitter, grit against my teeth. A careful voice deep although breathy over dentals the tone of lady Pan Am captains for that and falls of coy tongue behind tight lips, the force of this long winter passage for a blunt and sapient member I use to season vegetables and meats, a dry herb I sprinkle, I eat. She sits out white Boudreaux to demarcate and beacon light through descanted glass.

On Thin Ground

You could before traffic was upon the road, in the wineglass's refraction, hear the ground, putting her ear to trunks, the trees. He reflected on his life and even in July when newspapers extolled water watch, when birds were slow to take flight at your footfall, work imagined in the cool crook of trees, the still lives and were not seen. Even then the creek behind her house didn't dry. Now crayfish reappeared though sluggish, quintets, quartets, now trios of glass. These same rains had beaten down the leaves, the famous Virginia foliage lay in brown resinous smelling mulch, the maples, the white limbed plane, the sycamore of Laura, fair, pale in a word incomprehensible would come over her, a washout. And if he lived he'd reach pure deduction, a canvas stretched and primed.

They had gone out to dinner, the food, she saw Laura reach her hand to touch his and she wanted to touch them, just that an isolated abstract moment, a thin ground of color had passed to become in her mind cousin to the napped napkins, the wine and water glasses, the meter of two, one, two, one untouched. Then he closed the door on perfection, she was cold, the room respiring with the door's open close, flash, the studio's vacant easels and frames. She watched, finished her coffees, the bottles in their dress of labels and copes of dust, sits on the toilet, chill, grabs from the stack beside her Speculum and reads, the sequestration of ideas, solo or in clusters in the tiled chamber, the pipes, the ceramic bend in some way, benign, Minoan, undersea or depending on the density of ideas, like fish like birds, like guests at the exhibition, her article on the cold floor, toes curled, she rests, prying off a watch's back, in the sluice undersides, suddenly hushed.

Changing Lanes

Left divided an inch or two, low income intellectuals through the cold-opaqued convexity, we have rented a bright cheap ballpoint pen type compact car, checked out she excused herself going out to see, dangerous in the twilight, what she already knew. We set out thrilled with gadgets and the smell of gas soon superseded by vented in skunk—that the forked tree behind her house, was running distant distant in the chill air, a day or two more, to the next ridge, the highway, only a small number of these flashes; this is speed and auto-intimacy, the English we speak, our bodies share in curve to remind her of California, gravity's hug accelerating by her eyes scanning down the sidewalk towards winter, the higher elevations where past trees planted in the names of defunct vineyards stand naked on fallen spotlights of leaves. We smile at the luxurious concrete, the conceit washing a few ants, the unlucky hours driving at will between the seasons that ended up inches from their homes upon a territory that strips from time everything but interval, sitting in a cafe beneath yellow brown hills that went green from sea showers which so cooling the air, its lane lines and tire slaps at seven o' clock exactly as you slow at overlooks to give me my left-handed view, the dapple dampened sidewalk. Which was in mass, an irrigated spring; her knees hot upon the upholstery, she could see out the rear view window another valley, blunt crenellations stretching like elastic between the frayed ridges, her open lap.

A Kind of Arrangement

Out the front door, turned at the screen, resting on the handle two fingers between them, she touched him, a new note in his face. The rest of the night she could that for company, with a few logs dark and gnarled, the vast well built mill's infrequent fires, its embers unfolding asleep this town's cathedral and the snow had stopped so quietly and she touched me in its counting house museum, where it could not have been otherwise, daguerreotypes show women, bright and tubercular. Concede the perfection of their prerogative, their looms, caught in a phosphorous flash but did she understand that small chance that everything was the same, known from the pathetic school girl stereo, the empty city, missing its stanchion, the musty sofa, the brindled cat, the sum of these things nearby, white water roars over a weir. After the War, loneliness like dust, the elms died, leaving the streets wider and drier than before. In a paler light, I should have known that image of a wayfarer like we see as a moral framed in a spinster's room or carved on bone, how it would persuade her, cold cleansing and containing,what continuity on a snowy day which will pass into one of the bright clear atmospheres of our winter. Its private face here as strange as commonplace as views, sales clerks are efficient and exact seen through her eyes things, and children are taught their decorative divulgence. And he peaks at her bed, a hard dead tongue and from a great height measures by the contours, its hollows, her deeper drift, her stories, her cloths on the rack, his prick picturing her in each of them, strung out embodiments encabinated, the reach of her needs. He will know her from now on, as driving back to Boston in the snow, the car parked before her house. What stops him is the window, the Academy cupola shinning in the rearview mirror, atoms of light from the street light and snow. No matter, he has to register performance above an ocean of pines and frozen ponds.

Love is Kind

Walking back in desperate haste lest I be late, he comes to me in dreams, explaining what fun you were when I saw her, the sidewalk curved, her head sparrow angled and how, glancing, too cleverly trying to show her by the way I bisected that this was a man pleading it grieves him now to be reckoned with, that you urged him on. Suddenly, gone in if I stayed there but gyroscopically ever more metallic, you say you were weak a woman when the only thing I wanted was impeding my exacting pace, each minute more momentously constructed and nothing would have happened, -because she was small, because she was tight.

Thus, if I had been more vigilant, more kind, at least, upon entering. I would go over to something-who might be watching and pulling a drawer, a second she came in as I looked at her, shuttling between us three, by turns sane and crazy for an instance directly so I saw very little, really only her darkness, tightlipped or ranting "Love me, love me"; a density, a vortex for light, how light went in and came out intensified in three sharp points, the lips slightly parted, the hard decisive heeling, the crushing of things low and crawling, the heavy satchel, swinging, offending. So I understand the Medusa, the power nowhere in her eyes that I though maliciously Prussian but in her hair of snake heads, the circus mockery, the gorgon pitched pipes through the frail cotton frock, bossed upon a steel taut belly, her appearance of deprivation, excesses demanding satisfaction, snake heads like these, weaving.

Sea and Sky

Venetian, time for the decennial botanic survey, one extravagant insecurity against the sea, Mt Eyrie. So the nearby powers, the university, derived not from any innate properties, sent its graduate students upslope, in high summer to the alpine and sub-alpine meadows. It nearly fit although for being Venetian, drier than dust, it would have been better to affront the distance and count the flowers. What the found, hearing it in the hot folds of her ear, insinuating like the moan of a summer tom. She willed, not the global warming's stratified supplanting of colder by warmer species, but postures of not hearing, patchy die backs at all levels. The tested the soils and she turned to see him, his easy grin. They had taken a duplex located on a rise, view of the bay. Concentration of potassium and calcium. She would wait for a ship to pass, see gulls in the wake. The they noticed the groups of people, below summit that held hands, bowed heads. It was one of her achievements, cleaning that place, scrubbing on her knees until they were red, the wooden floor, releasing into the uplift of wind a pink grey plume. She had polished it so that you would have thought it marble. She had wedged the dirt out, painted the greasy ceiling, sprinkled roach power here and there.

It was typical of her always at this juncture, because he had climbed that peak, because she had loved to hike because an ancestor's eyes were blue as mountain sky and the words like sand or leaves blown, concepts, the actual breath of thought, because it was good to fulfill their final wishes, this along with her belief that philosophy was direction and any number of anti-philosophies, the wind outside, recycling pressure you could feel if you required empirical indication, the toilet bowel, a porcelain ear and might she not be the one to discover the remains. No fighting it, sex had taken the edge off, she had posted down and he spent back to nature and falling forward, she kissed him, the room, the whole house reposing with no fuss, no flowers.

William Ruminant
and Page Nelson
in Conversation

William Ruminant and Page Nelson, in Conversation

WR: The success of *A Wilderness of Monkeys* was surprising.

PN: Is that statement or a question? But yes, it was.

WR: You've seen the film, what about the play in London?

PN: I went over a month ago and attempted to attend anonymously. But somebody at The Firbank recognized me and I was ushered backstage to meet the cast. They were all charming, the way actors can be, especially English actors, all the more commendably after a performance when I am sure all they wanted to do was drink or go to bed or both. It was both gratifying and embarrassing because, as you know, the film and the play have little to do with *"Wilderness."* The highly adapted screen play was by Martin Goldberg, the writer at West Indy who collaborated with Tim Horton on the play, which *incongruously* followed the film. Goldberg gave it the catchy title, *"The Aphorist."* Nobody made lots of money. The film was a kinda art house success and I expect the play might run a few more weeks. It's no *War Horse*, saving the English Theatre, that's for sure. Especially at the Firbank, the smallest stall of a theatre imaginable. The cheese shop next door was bigger.

WR: But you and press made money.

PN: I made a little, hence my trip. Under the original contract when no one expected a film based on — come on, a book of aphorisms, Another Sparrow made some. Mr. Goldberg, I hope, made a lot. Which is why they asked me if I had anything else. And why we are talking today. Guess they thought I'd be like that little invention that Verver made, the Orloff Converter that made him rich so he could fund where we are, the world famous Edmister University.

OK, I sorta know what it does but why is it called "Orloff"?

WR: I'll allow that because visitors to the Institute are always such questions even if you have primed the pump for a significant diversion. The converter was Verver's great invention, his only invention. He made his first real money with it and a lot more later in finance. But it all stared with the converter, a filter that functions as valve, made of compressed gypsum in a fine copper mesh that separates particulate matter from raw petroleum. Refineries used to use hundreds of them. Around 1917 demand for oil took off because of the War and one Sergi Orloff, an engineer in Verver's factory, significantly improved the design. Verver, typically generous, stipulated that the new device bear Orloff's name, rather than his, the "Verver Converter," as it was then known. I think it gave him real pleasure to be at a remove form his own invention, behind the curtain you might say. There was something playful, manqué about him, at least until his tragic, second marriage. Despite off-patent imitators, it continued in wide use until the boom of the 1990s when low prices, high volume resulted in rich proceeds for Verver's Trust and to his benefactions, among them, Edmister College, funding its expansion from a mid-sized liberal arts college to a highly regarded regional university via the additions of a law school and several research centers, among them the bibliographic institute in the expanded Wilbur library. And, if I may, founded as a small Lutheran seminary, Edmister predates Verver.

PN: Ok but you are being modest ... the William Ruminant Center, Bibliographic Center, whatever ...

WR: The William Ruminate Institute of Textual and Editorial Studies (WRITES). Which I have directed since leaving Yale in 1994 and where we sit. Now tell me about your latest work. What is it about, what is it called?

PN: It's called "Trooping the Colour."

WR: As in the British military ceremony?

PN: Yep. More on that later, *if I may.* Anyway, when the folks at One Sparrow asked for more, I had nothing. Except for *Wilderness,* I hadn't written anything in decades. The only I thing I could think of was the manuscript of my early, never finished novel "Trio" and the kicker is, I didn't have a copy. When I gave it to you guys in 199.....

WR: 1996 — sent to me, personally.

PN: Right, I was so sick of it I didn't even keep a copy. You, the Center, had the only copy, the original. So I wrote you, explained the situation and you sent me a copy.

WR: Asking that we get back in touch before you sent it off to Another Sparrow.

PN: Which I was gong to do anyway. Because you did a great job on *Wilderness,* referring it to Sparrow in the first place. I can't cope with all the editorial stuff. Hell, my typing is so bad it often corrects my spelling, which is worse.

WR: Tell us what it's about.

PN: Oh sure. Well, as I knew, "Trio" was awful, unfinished for a reason. It's a young man's writing drunk on Woolf and Simon, that's Claude Simon, all very poetic, overwritten, with a suffocated narrative line. Its best thing is moments of poetic intensity and my idea was to trim it down and re-construct its narratives. And I still couldn't do it. It made me sick. So yeah, that's a concept, writers, liberally hooched, do the writing that doesn't make them sick.

Anyway, I was sitting in my apartment — a stone's throw from Parkman's, talk about narrative, thinking about my recent poems and they were bad too, too narrative, little short stories. So the novel was too poetic and the poetry was too narrative and here was the idea — combining them couldn't, wouldn't be any worse! Indeed something good might come out of it. The collision of difference, a kind of alchemy only not enrichment but reduction, of the novel in particular. Best effected by mechanical means.*

WR: Go on, this will all be clearer in print.

PN: Hey, call it a Verver conversion, *if I may*! Anyway, I placed a 5 x 6 inch wooden frame over the manuscript [of "Trio"]. Words within the frame I typed as a new manuscript. I then took the complete texts of selected poems and interlineated them between the lines of the "de-reconstructed" [makes quotes marks] "Trio." To me, this had interesting fore and background effects. OK, I *did* intervene, changing some verb tenses, adding a few conjunctions or prepositions to ensure fluency if not meaningfulness. I'm not worried about its "making sense" or not.

WR: Like all art, it makes its own sense. The criticism I would make is that you weren't random enough.

PN: I wanted it random, but "my random." Still about an individual, an artist, crafting ...

WR: Which is your concept of art.

PN: Which is your concept of my concept of art.

WR: Which is an example of Hegel's "Bad Infinite." Back to the title.

PN: Oh, right. Well once upon a time, they'd line the skinny, illiterate 17 year old recruits up and march the regimental flag, the colour, right up to their faces so they'd recognize it in the fog of battle. By 1900, it was just ceremony and they still do it, as pure ceremony, the escort to the colour marching between the scarlet ranks while the band plays, the Queen looks on, the horses nod. And that's what happened to fiction. It used to *mean something.* Now it's a kind of event, an enactment. And I wanted to demonstrate that, enacting an enactment, *my lines, my* poetry, marching between *my* prose.*

WR: You're confusing method and metaphor. Do you remember, from Charlottesville, Raul Tremblay and his "emphatic metaphors"?[3]

PN: No, I mean, I *do* remember Raul. Where's he now?

RW: Never mind. There is one thing I know we agree on, there will no film of *Trooping the Colour.*

PN: I'm not so sure, we were wrong last time.

RW: No, we didn't even think of it last time and not thinking of something isn't being wrong.

---

3. Raul Trembath. 'The Rhetoric of Philosophical "Writing": Emphatic Metaphors in Derrida and Rorty. *The Journal of Aesthetic and Art Criticism, 47:2 Spring 1989.*

* Nelson adds "My interest was fabrication, not fiction. The real hazard was facetiousness, flickers of *Pale Fire* which thus invoked, functions as a kind of homeopathic mantra, deferring the danger."

Poems, extractible from
Trooping the Colour

Oh, the Nightingales

Throughout the nineteenth century,
thousands of nightingales
were trapped for the London market.
In the words on one observer,
"the birds take poorly to captivity.
At certain seasons, the gutters of
Holborne and Seven Dials
were clogged with their felted bodies."
Yet I doubt they were much miserable,
quickly dying. And to balance the equation,
what enjoyment did they bring
to the old, the sick, the melancholic?
Oh, you want an example?
Ok, think "Regency,"
Jennie the maid, jilted
by Jack the drover, buys a bird
to sweeten the staleness of her attic room.
At night, it forgets the weave of wire
and dreams it's free, and hearing its soft
throated notes, for a while, so does she.
But frankly, it is hard to get worked up
over loads of dead nightingales.
Or the people.
Everyone alive in London, pick a date,
say April 1868, is dead.
Tell me that makes you sad
when really, you're glad they're not around,
competing for love, position or space.
They are out of the race.
And as to nightingales,
well, I heard one once,
one summer in Somerset.

And if you haven't, there's always
"Audobon's Big Book of Birds"
with CD-ROM of song.
(Or just google search "nightingale").

[*Odds of Nightingales*]

On Reading Manstein's "Lost Victories"

Above the glittering debris fields, the Benz Star rising,
bands back in the beer halls, stocked shops;
from retirement's bungalows,
the field marshals are again maneuvering.
"Dear Colonel-General,
thank you for your letter
describing the retreat of Army Group B.
if you are ever in Kessel ....
my account will appear in England
with an introduction by Hart,
their panzer man."
The book I hold in hand, delightful
with detail and bluff soldierly deceptions —
"behind the in-leaf saplings of the state collective farm,
our Jaeger groups lay in wait."
"I knew of no crimes behind our lines,
my oath to Hitler I could not break."
A good diner rumbles in my gut —
new visceral reinforcements but I nod off
under the reading light's heavy siege.
Words fall out into letters,
long black ranks on life's white page,
like soldiers, like graves.

(*Marshalling the Memoirs*)

Bletchley Park

Cloud shuttered light and slaps of wind,
the rippled pond and one cold swan,
these we accept, nature's clear text.
We interrogate the rain-pooled drive
that once was thronged with olive-drab official cars;
the vacant mansion echoing in our footfalls
its memories of generals and boffins,
the huts that were upstart, pungent with pitch,
dilapidated into a barrow-like belonging,
where in a brightness intensified,
behind blackout curtains, a man, a woman,
stared at randomized letters,
looking for a way in, an intuition
as if playing chess against a master
whose game has this weakness —
faced with one improbably correct attack,
his defense becomes predicable, this then that,
a position cracked as decryption machines clattered
and dawn leaked in, the day watch entering.
Now, a half century later, what remains
is what can be read in any book
"the best minds enjoyed recreational maths,
chess, puzzles, amateur theatricals"
or learned from the badged, bereted guides
though today their words are wind blown,
scattered, as magpies, sheltered under the eaves,
chatter in old, unbroken code.

(Setting the Rotors)

Biographical Note

In a rush of masculine desperation
and breathless from the stairs
he ran to her office to find her
not there. "Despite all marriages
I must see you" read his jagged note.
Later playing with her reply,
she looked from her May Fair window
saw in the rootlap of a London Plane
a blaze of unmown green.
The next day, her letter in his mail —
blank paper sheathing two grass blades
touched with her perfume.
He grasped its sexual yes
something too of reaping — the slash and cut,
but could not foresee the final harvest,
a clutch of poems, three deaths.

(From the Affairs File)

The Falklands Affair

I was watching lots of tv
and saw the slim feminine ship
take the hit, one hot rocket.
It broke like yoke; liquid, victim.
Meanwhile, he was advancing upslope,
taking the high ground, two hills.
In position, he crouched to fire.
And you took the hit. Exocet.
It's good I've a mind for history
because twenty years later,

laughing over drinks, you say
"Darling, you're deep in your cups
and making it up."

(The Falklands War)

Hurricane

When in the middle of the last century,
systems of serious low pressure
began to be given names,
we smiled in recognition,
they were like people, like us
predictably wayward and violent.
Decades later, from the eyes of satellites
(which had lost all denominating fame)
we saw hurricanes were swirls,
galaxies or seashells, spinning
above the living blue. The worst storms
(it turned) out had beautiful forms.
We wondered then what pattern
our own days of wind and rain
gave to some higher self, spiraling
beyond controlment and common name.

(Systems)

Flying Westwards

Head bowed over the in-flight tray
you are sorting our Kroner, Euros, Pounds.
I look on, now, in easy possession.
Where are we coming from?

There was your beauty,
a dangerous alluring place;
my violence, a masculine tour
with all the standard stops —
a rival, a friend beaten up.
You felt no pity, no regrets.
We are left at cruising altitude
in this middle-aged plane,
a medium between destinations.
Constrained in our seats
we arrange little stacks
of not yet expended assets.

(Movement)

Seasoning

There was delight, seeing the fire
singeing the edges like a stationer's motif,
burning the sheets behind, bursting out,
a hot mouth that ate your face of words.
My careful heels crushed the ashes.
What was left of your hundred letters?
A small square of folded paper, labeled
"Seeds from my garden-1998"
These I dropped in the hungry spring
and watched the plants thrust up and thrive.
Chives. All summer, I cropped the leaves,
sweeping pungent heaps of green
into empty Twinings tins. On plant untouched,
its blades curled into tubes, spear tips of bud
breaking into lacy butterflies of flower
that were shriveled pods before October's rains.
That stalk I slashed and whipped, seeds for the next harvest.

But what of my dried spice, last remains of a hot season?
It starts out lemony tart, ends up grit against my teeth.
This long winter I use it to season vegetables and meats.
A bitter herb, I sprinkle, I eat.

(Exfoliations)

The Master of Bottles

In the stemmed glass's refraction
he reflected on his life and work,
the still lives — quintets, quartets,
now trios of bottles.
In a few decades, if he lived,
he'd reach pure deduction,
only a canvas stretched and primed,
a thin ground of color.
Then he'd close the door on perfection,
on the studio's vacant easels and frames,
the wine bottles in their dress of labels
and copes of dust, solo or in clusters
like guests at the exhibition
suddenly hushed.

(On Thin Ground)

Drives

"Dein ist mein Hertz" along the Blue Ridge Parkway

Low income intellectuals,
we have rented a bright, cheap, ball point pen
type compact car. Checked out, we set out thrilled
with gadgets and the smell of gas, soon superseded

by vented in skunk. This is speed and auto-intimacy —
the English we speak, our bodies share in curve
and gravity's hug accelerating towards winter,
the higher elevations where trees stand naked
on spotlights of leaves; we smile at the conceit —
our hours driving at will between the seasons
that strips from time everything but interval,
its land lines and tire slaps as you slow at overlooks
to give me my left-handed view of another valley,
your open lap.

(Changing Lanes)

Berwick Maine

The vast, well built mill stands this town's cathedral.
In its counting house museum, daguerreotypes show women,
bright-faced at their looms, caught in a phosphorous flash.
Nearby, white water roars over the weir.
After "The War" the elms died, leaving the streets wider
and drier than before. In a paler light we see like a motto
framed in a spinster's room or carved on bone
how cold cleanses, contains. Here the sales clerks are exact
and children are taught — a hard dead tongue, the story
of the Captain and the whale, as driving back to Boston
the Academy cupola shines in our rear view mirror
above an ocean of pines and frozen ponds.

(A Kind of Arrangement)

A Myth, Comprehended in a Dream

He comes to me in dreams, explaining what fun you were
and how, pleading it grieves him now, you urged him on.
You say you were weak, a woman. Nothing would have happened
had I been more vigilant, more kind.
Another she shuttles between us three, by turns sane and crazy,
tight lipped or ranting "love me love me love me."
Now I understand the Medusa, the power nowhere in her eyes
but in her hair of snakes, snakeheads weaving like these.

(Love is Kind)

No Flowers

Time for the decennial botanic survey of Mt. Eyrie. So the
nearby university sent its graduate students upslope, in high
summer, to the alpine and sub-alpine meadows to count the flowers.
What they found —not global warming's stratified supplanting
of colder by warmer species but patchy die backs at all levels.
And when they tested the soils, deadly concentrations of
potassium and calcium.
Then they noticed the groups of people, below summit, that
held hands, bowed heads, one of them releasing into the uplift of
wind a pink grey plume.
Because Steve had climbed that peak, because Amy loved to
hike, because grandma's eyes were blue as mountain sky. Because
it was good to fulfill their final request, recycling the remains
back to nature with no fuss, no flowers.

(Sea and Sky)

A Memoir by
William Ruminant

A Memoir by William Ruminant

I met Page Nelson at the University of Virginia in Sept. 1979 where we were both taking Paul Angstrom's Trends in Contemporary Criticism (Eng Crit 810), a required course for PhD students (me), attendible on a non-credit basis by approved auditors, somehow him. It was a pivotal time in literary study, with the in-power seniors still mounting the old guard of New Criticism, while younger tenured faculty whose mentors had been that very old garde, were enlisting, either wholesale with all the fervor of a mid-life crisis or selectively, in the decade long on-rush of postmodernist theory. This properly would be the occasion for the rich testimony of memory in the Updike manner of gorgeous historically informed narrative, with particular attention to material texturing: what people wore, ate, sounded like, the models of car and brands of beer. It would thematically encompass: Angstrom's class and the changing culture of the department, the evening "bull sessions" at the local watering hole, the upstairs bar at The Bardo, a tiny restaurant in a converted bungalow too tight to accommodate the sprawling fraternity set, my invitation to Page to join us, the three or four of the department's most brilliant grad students, the place's tired disco décor; the chubby townie waitress, with the beautiful voice, "Remington" (named after the gun), my verbal duels, as a critically self-aware post Derridian Baudriaudian (and incidentally, the last student in textual editing of Fredson Powers), with Raul Trembley, a precocious sub-cultural Foucault-Deluezian, (who later recanted his youthful errors and is now one of a number of highly published and compliant New Historicists).

I have no interest in such an exposition, beautiful and boring (Updike). Page was on the margins of our combative ring, attentive to our alcohol (sweating plastic pitchers of Schlitz or Miller High Life. "High Life, High Theory" our mercifully rare occasional toast) fueled jab fests, seldom speaking. Working at the library, he simply wasn't schooled in the moves of conceptual combat and usually left before Remington's southern tuneful, elative, reveille not taps, "last call, boys." I do recall one instance, because it was exceptional. I had remarked that deconstruction being deconstructible had no significance at all except as a demonstration of its validation. And Page interjected — (I was stanced to counter Raul whose mind, operating at deluezean speed, often rushed into indefensible terrain. Confident he would recognize the irony of my remark and then falter when I asked him if it was synthetic or nonsynthetic, rational or organicist, an irony of multiplicities or unifications? Irony, may I say, I had down at a early stage (see my first published article "Angles of Irony, *Strategies,* Vol.15, no.1) — "so what you're really saying is it's the journey not the arrival that matters and that's the oldest moral in the book." Which was acute (at least in context) and rare from him. (This would have been half shouted as Remington cranked up the-later-it-got sexually rhythmic homophonic bar room "pop" that was at once unconscious parody, cultural critique and infantile self-assertion. "Sending out an SOS" said it all.)

We "Bardo boys" dispersed in 1984. Raul and I both finished our PhDs and left Virginia that summer. I didn't keep up with Page, we were "friends" only in the drifting, capacious way of youth. Indeed I would have expected never to have any contact with him again except for a curious encounter that last spring in Charlottesville.

I was sitting on the retentively warm granite steps of Alderman library, looking down the groomed expanse, the plaza of manicured grass and polite, superfluously columned buildings now at 6PM empty: classes over, undergrads packed in the dinning halls, workers homeward bound or at home. I watched a mockingbird atop one of the Victorian light poles the U affected in that area, pivoting silently, working himself up for his midnight revels as the sun, a rim of orange rind, dissolved above the low, smoky western ridge. It was still bright, too early for the twilight breeze, the air motionless, oversweet. (Yet something was making the leathery leaves of the nearby magnolia clatter.) I was about to commit to the library, no bull sessions now for a month since I was studying for my defense, preparing what take I'd take on some professor's, maybe Angstrom or Cohen's take, which I thought I could predict, on my take — "Rhetorical Paradigms in Academic Editing, Aporias of Reading." (neat work, taking the old bore canons of editing, analyzing and then recasting them in a postmodernistically informed mould, the basis of my, may I say, groundbreaking book *Editing After the Fire*. ("What then is a text? A mobile army of metaphors, conventions and accidents, in short a sum of textual relations which have been enhanced, transposed and embellished and which after long use seem firm, canonical and obligatory: texts are constructions about which one has forgotten that is what they are…")

Page appeared from behind me, he must have been working late, looking for improving books. "Hey." "Hey" I said. "What's up?" "I'm preparing to get out of here. My defense is in two weeks." And then instead of any usual reply, he said "Aren't you going to miss the department's beautiful women?" I took notice; "women" was a charged word, a provocation on those smooth steps and green unperturbed vistas without a woman in sight. I cleanly volleyed back to him, without even thinking about it—"name some." "Vera Fiedler." This — he couldn't know, was a very soft lob. What could I do but smash him with the odd truth? "I slept with her last night." I could still taste her taste, smell her smell. He got that stiff stricken look you get when you are trying not to look stricken. The conversation missed a very long beat "Well" — he made a thumbs up "Good luck with the exam." I made an even more emphatic and brotherly thumbs up. "Thanks." A scruffy squirrel dropped from the magnolia and started, timid and bold, stretching up the stairs.

Since I wasn't going to the Bardo, that was probably the last time I saw him. Aporia! We shared the same taste in women. So what? He wouldn't have a babe as intense and intelligent as Vera in a hundred years of longing. There was something narcissistic, *Noli me tangere,* about him. Which can attract women (Vera, a gleaming goddess in the moonlight, reaching out to my touchy self, explained later "I wanted to reach you." But there was no explanation — it just happened.). For I am proud, indifferent honest, (meaning I am naturally sincere just not a fanatic about the details), ambitious, the results seen. [Six years later, I saw no point in staying at Yale, just another professor in a French suit that says "rob me" once you cross the draw bridge from the castle to the hovels. Better to rule in Verver (Ind.) than serve as jail bait in New Haven.] But with Page there was a defensiveness and self-absorption as if sex were an over-oxygenated exercise that would or had pre-exhausted him and he now required a fantastic therapeutic infusion of Adrenalin and tranquilizer beyond the liquidations of the most kindly inclined Nightingale.

[I felt the vague ache of guilt that countries like Norway and Canada that never had empires still feel about the Third World, the pang of inexcusable success. This was the connection between us. So I wasn't really surprised when 20 years later he wrote me at WRITES, sending me the manuscript of *Wilderness*, asking if I thought it was any good and what he should do with it even if my first reaction was "you must be kidding."]

I left Charlottesville that July, taking the Amtrak train that notched a stop at every hole of the rust belt to New Haven, with my capacious and off-gassing, aluminum framed, brown "Nagahide" suitcases, handy gift from my parents, stuffed with clothes, personal effects and papers, among them, jotted on a retired catalog card, Vera Fiedler's phone number and Fall address.

I, William Ruminant attest that the above records my sincere recollection of events, without deliberate fictive enhancement excepting any that might, like heat and sound, naturally accompany the machinations of memory and mind. For as I wrote, much came to mind and I respired in the sharper tone, the thinner, intenser air of that time.

Aphorisms and
Divagations

Aphorisms and Divagations, not Collected in
A Wilderness of Monkeys

We are fretted instruments, designed to be sounded to our depths.

Most Americans have the same relationship to education as to health, applying themselves to great institutions to buy what they have failed to respect and cultivate in their daily lives.

What a curious play that just as the actors are getting comfortable in their roles, they are removed from the stage.

History in a capsule: women are nurturers, men are murderers.

Qualitative easing. Going off the gold standard enabled a massive expansion of money supply, credit and prosperity with the long term result, as money was divorced from anything tangible, of inflation and fantastic debt. The result of post-modernistically going off the textual standard was a massive expansion of propositions, with the long term result of conceptual inflation and devalued meaning.

The genuine gentleman regrets the prohibition of being unable to challenge himself to a duel.

That language, removed form its usual syntactical situation, could emit special meanings ... I sensed a resonance in words that relieved of their usual grounding, might flourish in lower gravity, as satellites in space unfold into life. There was a million to one chance it was so but in that other place, there might be a millions of chances, one for each word. The most "poetical" thought I ever had, I was determined to test its strange physics even in a laboratory as modest as a verbal kitchen because cooks, too, are physicists.

Romeo and Juliet are Shakespeare's most mature lovers (if we equate maturity with seriousness and commitment), Anthony and Cleopatra his most juvenile. Few things are more entertaining than a collegiate performance of the "Egyptian Play," teenagers acting like adults acting like teenagers. Cleo finally ripens and wearing her royal purple, takes the asp so that even Octavius, most able and powerful of men, stands subjected to the Empress of Death.

Falstaff, profounder than Hamlet, avoids by instinct the existential depths where men drown. Just like his old associate, the starveling of Clement's Inn, who by good work and good luck, ends up a county squire possessed of land, beefs, monies and local respect, these the Robert Shallows that are the desired retirements of William Shakespeare.

Nietzsche correctly calibrated Wagner as "'the greatest musical miniaturist." And from Bayreuth, the rantings of the paranoid pamphleteer are a fly's buzz, a mosquito's whine, the song of the flea. But Nietzsche is a big thinker and Wagner, a great artist, the double irony being that each correctly perceives the other as small without being able to see this of themselves or only askance, at an acute angle, which explains or at least excuses their big voiced exertions over the aesthetic and utterly authentic alternative of silence.

That the glib aphorist asserts that poetry is less significant than almost anything, including spectator sports, indicates the question embodies a category mistake, as if Neolithic tribes were asked to choose between an ingot of bronze and the Theory of Relativity. They would have to be an entirely differ kind of people to choose the latter. In a sense this is what poets are saying —-we would have to be an entirely different kind of people to choose poems over bonds, only we are already if only we knew (and only the arts can instruct us in this self-knowledge.)

"A sensitive specimen of person, afraid their sincerest respect will be mistaken for servitude or flattery, resorts to satire in the confidence that those most likely to distemper the compliment must now miss it entirely." Sounds like Boswell— check it out Yale ed. pronto/ W.R.

Nothing kills conversation or deadens discourse like a bad joke. And since after the age sixty, we are all engaged in a dialogue with death, it is understandable that a certain kind of humorous older gentleman contrives and records his poor jokes as evidence of self-possession and resistant power before the inevitable. Now here is a story. Once upon a time, a merchant of Damascus had gone to the market to buy some fruit when he noted with dismay that Death was right behind him. The merchant immediately ran from the area, bought a horse and rode all day without stopping to Aleppo. There, tying up at an inn, he turned a corner and bumped into Death, who said. "This is surprising! Didn't I see you in Damascus this morning when I stopped by the market to buy some figs? Ah, well, I now have some business with you." Where upon the merchant, said "First, may I give you my card?" and reaching into his robe, placed a small piece of paper in the boney hand. Death held it up and read "I am a Martian with power to transplant my sexual organs to material objects. You have just been fucked."

The longer one lives, the more the majority of those one has loved (including animals) are dead. Is it any wonder we wish to join them even if the place of reunion is oblivion?

Radio-magnetic imaging will soon be able to project on the walls of a theatre, at precise magnification, all your brain synapses in operation. You will be able to see the flow of sodium ions at each nerve ending that generates a minute electrical surge which physiology correctly identifies as your thought. If you think "I am a spiritual being, more than my brain" you will observe a certain clustering of ions, say 2000 per cubic micron. If you think "My thought is this surge of ions," you will see 2200 per cubic micron. There is something about this depiction of thinking that for all its accuracy doesn't compute.

What can't be helped — the sniper has already fired. Wherever you go, he knows how to lead his aim, his bullet sure to hit. But the shooter likes to move about, sometimes close-in, sometimes far away so no one knows when the slug will strike only that it is on the way and always fatal. And knowing this to be the case, having seen so many fall before you, how should you live? With dignity, intensity and compassion. Because this bastard doesn't hesitate to kill babies. And animals. And baby animals.

At current rates of progress, we are no more than fifty years away from techniques of total genetic repair and the conquest of death. Then begins the Wars of the Doses because the poor can endure anything except a world where the rich never die and the rich tolerate anything except a world crowded with the immortal poor. (For those that fall short of the fifty years, there is the consolation that a world without death is more likely to be hellish than heavenly.)

We never passed anyone in the ageing downtown office building, not even an elevator operator, my mother working the smooth, hand worn lever herself. The long pea green corridor was cool and always empty to Nora's half frosted glass door, with its glossy black stenciled letters "Nora Turnbull, Seamstress" and silhouette profile of woman with a bun leaning over a sewing machine.

Inside, two small rooms which even as a child I knew were the original office's reception and desk areas. We sat on an old sofa, the space stuffed with colorful cushions, bolts of cloth, spools of bright thread, two black, pedal powered sewing machines, a pressing board and assortment of irons, Nora's work table and chair, the back room with her bed; her office her home.

I'd kick my heels, reading comic books, getting more and more restless as a simple job, dropping a hem, fixing a zipper, dragged on for hours. There was no noise except for the women, the spinster with half-lensed glasses and a mousey bun and the widow, talking about nothing, (nothing I remember), the sporadic singing stitch of the sewing machine, and the sirens, always distant, from off the street and over the buildings into the light well, her one window half-opened to generate a breeze with the door's transom. Never a footfall in the hall or another customer. At four or six depending on the season, the light would quickly drain out of the well, the room in deep sudden shade and we'd go home, returning in a month or two with more minor repairs or adjustments. One day I fell at school and torn a hole in the leg of my blue grey wool dress pants (which I should not have been wearing to play in). At home that afternoon, I flexed my knee and said "Miss Turnbull can fix this." (Which dates the era, when it was cheaper to repair than just buy a new pair, made in China). My mother replied, "We're not going back there anymore. She hurt my feelings." Never mind the pants, I was relieved, released from boredom even as I detected something sad that has intensified (like shade in a room) as every object of that time has disappeared, recorded only in memory, a few molecules in a brain where all shall be forgot.

54

Low fiction is superior to high facetiousness.

Measure for Measure, the opera.

When young, I was cruel, brutal, stupid. The reason, beyond reason, was the desire to mate and be a champion in Sex's fight against that Death who looms so large now over my placid, rational and considerate life, my one hope is that he will continue to ignore such an inoffensive and disarmed object.

My professor friend reports her students do not understand Jane Austen. They not only cannot comprehend her irony, humor and pathos, they can't process her language. Which means they won't make much of Keats' "Death is Life's high meed" or Shelley's "Life, like a dome of many-coloured glass, stains the white radiance of Eternity" that's true, like a lost law of science, even as the world grows dimmer.

Much less than the scope of my living mind, what will survive of me is this abstract of words, a conundrum we artists are always resolving to solve.

Critical Supplement:
Articles from
The Fiddler Crab Review

Articles from *The Fiddler Crab Review*

Even as acute a mind as Henry James could not fully encompass the critical project as regards his own work. His estimable *Prefaces* are valued as personal inventories of his aims and methods, and in that spirit, these critical essays are supplied supplemental to *Trooping the Colour*. Like James', they are "after-the-fact prefaces," articulating a yardstick for appraisal of verbal art which the author hopes will be severely applied to the work in hand while submitting it is itself a stick, just one more piece of bundled wood to be measured.[4]

There may be a more direct interest to a few poets, the one percent of crafters who have a critical interest in contemporary poetry not their own.[5] I would like to thank poet Emily Scudder who founded *The Fiddler Crab Review*, giving me the opportunity to write these essays for the journal and indirectly, via this paragraph, the occasion, uniquely in this composition, to speak in my natural voice.

Charlottesville — Boston — Cambridge
1979   2012

---

4. The entire assemblage might be governed under the criticism offered by Professor Vera Roth, my teacher at the University of Virginia, who wrote in marginal appraisal of a student paper, "a series of unintegrated arabesques, however beguiling, is no substitute for serious engagement and discussion." But this motley method forty years later, was, by zig and zags, my only way of shuffling forward. "La Garde meurt mais ne se rend pas."

5. The statistic is from the study cited in "Cammo Doesn't Work Downtown: How Liberal Gun Owners and Conservative Poets are Rebuilding America and Why We Need More of Them." L. Sabotoe, S. Abramson & R. Smuth (Eds.), The Center for Politics, University of Virginia Press, 2010.

The Loneliness of Dogs

by Tim Mayo, Pudding House Publications, 2008.
28 pages. $10.

Reading chapbooks, the physical act, is a kind of metaphor for the lexical process, the pages in open tension between the regulator of our thumbs, like the flexion of attention, open, in suspension between engagement and closure. What sets the main spring of mind going is, I am convinced, the apprehension of "voice." (Which is not to be conflated with "music." The next time someone rhapsodizes about poetic music, recommend to them five minutes of Bach and when they say they meant a different kind of music, well, that conversation can be continued). So by poetic voice we mean something very different from our usual simian jabber, its finest quarter hour the shower's aria. Voice is that strange positing identifier, both constituting the poem and constituted by it, an event at once a priori and a posteriori. (That's enough Kant for one review. Nothing new here either. Please proceed — ed.) OK, I like "Tim Mayo's "voice."

"Now I see I lacked imagination/ writing so many poems in that same person/until the I of my typewriter wore out,/ and I was banished from the page, guilty of nothing more than my own experience." (from *"The Confessional Poet's Confession"*)

Here is an educated man who knows more than he shows and knows we know it (which is a high degree of refinement), who isn't afraid to refer to Georges de La Tour, The Dark Lady, the Agora, "The Flea" or tell us "About spelling the human masters were never wrong." (Nota bene: how one tires of unlettered poets or worse, those that leave their education behind as if it were a leash or muzzle so that they might more authentically bay under some sub-prime moon.)

The master lyric poet of our day has written (somewhere) that the best poetry "comes from our deepest being, decision and self-forgetting" (reviewers, especially Y.T., take note!). But we can't all be Seamus Heaney and in lesser hands the poetry of deep being becomes the monotonous boom-boom-boom of Forster's Marabar caves.* Mayo is poet of quotidian and intelligent self-remembering, his aim not to take us where we've all been so old boldly before (say via zany spacing and page layout) but to use poetry's received grain to communicate and put, in every sense, a lucid gloss on the matter in hand.

Only the lights' greater clarity/and the subtle change in suits/seem to fall in spades on their faces, as if the painter suddenly knew/ this story that repeats itself-/ diamonds, clubs, it doesn't matter—/ we are cheats at heart, suspicious! of the other who always wins." (From "The Cheat with the Ace of Clubs, after de la Tour").

A certain kind of reader may find some of the poems metaphorically underdetermined. I thought a few of Mayo's endings a bit pat, as if the poet couldn't resist a "natural" conclusion, one too easily at hand as in "The Red Convertible" where the male as a type of pistoned motor, conclusively hopes "for the red convertible of your smile to pass by and give him a lift." I don't think that will pass a rigorous inspection.

Overall, Mayo's judgments are consistently good in a free verse finding shape in sound, rhetoric and proposition. Most admirable is his vital balance between the freight of meaning and its engine of conveyance, what Heaney calls "stamina; the distribution of the argument over line ends and stanzas, more a matter of vertebrae than plasm."

But I digress, for it was there I found this/ seal of a warrior saying farewell to his wife./ The fine detail of his muscled calf as he turned/ from his spear, shifting his concern to his wife's imploring arms, made me think I'd found mine./ I didn't know then that an art of significance was what I was searching for, nor did I see/ the true meaning of his implied turning back. None of this was etched into that piece/ of colored

---

[*EMF's translation of the caves' speech as "Everything exists, nothing has value." is not entirely literal.]

glass as I saw the sun flash through it, highlighting each muscle of his
readiness to leave/ for something he deemed more important than love.
(from *"The Counterfeit Seal"*)

There is more weight of meaning, at an almost Empsonian curvature, on this quarter page than in a whole box car of contemporary poetry, not to mention prose. Again it is the poet's voice we react to, if we do, first and last, a vibration along the deepest lines of our linguistic being that resonates a responsive voice, one almost our own.

Little Oceans

by Tony Hoagland, Hollyridge Press. 2009. 39 pages. $10.

The wacko right-wingers on shortwave radio are wrong — not necessarily about guns (everyman's ideal son or Lost Father, I forget which) or taxation (legal robbery) or the Federal Reserve (semi-organized crime). No, they are wrong about paper money being worthless. In fact, your generic greenback has a commodity value of about 3 cents as a piece of competent (if aesthetically ghastly) engraving on good stock. And you'd do far worse than to send one of those odd objects (one denominated TEN) to Hollyridge Press for the purchase of Tony Hoagland's chapbook *Little Oceans,* though they will probably prefer PayPal, an oxymoron if there ever was one. And the point of this arch arabesque is that it is exactly the kind of gratuitous riff you won't find in Hoagland's sober, judicious and engaging etudes.

Honest work, with the ego as a point of view, not a spot lit stage for narcissistic crooning of the ole mi-me-mi. Of the 27 poems all have social or broader relational concerns, save one and that one, surely taxonomically, is entitled "Personal." Audaciously, there are two poems ("Home of the Brave," "The History of White People") that address race dynamics from the now novel (one might almost say colorful) perspective of the straight white man.

After so long seeming right, as in/ true, as in clean as in smart,/ … after so long being visitors/ from the galaxy Caucasia/ now they are starting to seem a little/ deficient, leached out, spent, colorless/ thin blooded, indefinite as in being too far and too long/ removed from the original source of whiteness.

Hoagland understands that disciplined free-verse works when it is delineated to the shape of thought, measured by the poet's distinctive (silent) voice; in this case, relatively short lines lengthening unto long sentences. Not such a hard thing you'd think except so many makeurs (did I say fakeurs?) do it poorly.

The chapbook is, in the best sense, a quick read, fluent, informing and fault free (which is perhaps a higher state of grace than "flawless"). Lyric poets are easily classified as hard or soft landers: the former step into a pirouette and accelerate before spinning out to the resoundingly conclusive footfall. Soft types like Hoagland can fool you when you turn the page and find two more lines of a poem you thought was ended. Oops! With Hoagland that's a mere typographical accident and no misstep by a poet who eschews the Big Gesture and Five Act Structure; it is the quiet voice of a serious man who prefers to draw you in rather than call you out.

It's a delicacy and refinement of a quintessentially and ever rarer American kind that is hard to represent adequately in short quotes.

"In summer there was something in the selfhood of the wasps/ that wanted to get inside the screened-in porch./ It sent them buzzing against the wire mesh,/ probing under the eaves,/ crawling in the cracks between the boards./ Each day we'd find new bodies on the sill:/ little failures. Like struck matches:/ shrunken in death, the yellow/ color of cider or old varnish."

A certain kind of entirely legitimate reader will miss the arc and buzz of stylistic fireworks. But flash-in-the-pan pyrotechnics illuminate, reflectively, only themselves while it is the pond itself, day-lit, even-tempered, capacious and world holding, deep, but calling not attention to its depth that we most value. A Little Ocean. This one well worth the sacrifice in passing trade of your $10 and three cent paper boat.

Toccata & Fugue

by Timothy Kelly. Floating Bridge Press, 2005. 37 pages. $10.

Timothy Kelly is a wordsmith which means if you prefer your poetry with crafty fittings and close tolerances, you'll probably like this guy who seems to think the poetic journey means as much as the arrival, that the merest vehicles of the trip, "used" words, signify most of all. That this is a flawed disposition can be demonstrated by the quick transport of a decisively contrarian poem. So I hereby quote an efficient one that violates this crabby journal's (unwritten) rule against self-promotion. The poem is my own — "Blue"; "Blue" an immediate and may I say perfect work embodying in a very few words (er, one) the entire spectrum of Azurility from robin egg pale to intergalactic purple. What more could you want in a price to earnings ratio ("standard and poor") of reading?

Yet Kelly would insist on delivering beautiful, freighted lines ...

...like a well-made tool, the palmed body/ docks and snugs, convex to/ concave, with heft centered/ and a contouring, wraparound /grip. Nothing, not even the long/ bones straight. (from *"Voluptuosity")*

A calm, competent voice, pitched at a knowing middle distance but articulating tactility and actual ministrations of touch.

*we disarticulate our ankle/ with a hundred circumferential cuts,/ the crosslaced ligaments isolated/ appreciated, incised, the snug, bony/ mortise and tenon. With effort prized /apart. (*from *"On Anatomy Being Destiny")*

So is this author an enjambist or anatomist? In fact, he was trained and works as a physical therapist. Most of the twenty poems feature anatomical detailing and clinical vocabularies. There is even one semi-extended trope-ic pun...

*I'm thinking of a section of saxophonists/ in an Ives concerto, in a passage where birds lift from trees, not playing but/ drumming their horn keys ten, fifteen seconds with their fingers, so that the clatter,/ if you close your eyes becomes the rising din of beating wings. (*from *"Forearm Dissection")*

Fingering—geddit? In a book called "Toccata & Fugue"! That's going for baroque. Well, what do you expect when the dedicatory epigram is from John Donne. Who was Dr (spiritual therapist) Donne, anyway? A Shakespeare wannabe whose less elaborated lyrics are sometimes quoted in wedding invitations (and dissertation dedicatia) of the more vaunting sort. ("I wonder, by my troth, what thou and I did til we loved"). A rake to rector type who believed that words in their complex quality of denotation, connotation, etymology and sound could be shaped and fitted into poetic volumes that have both a horizontal dimension of narrative and vertical one of intense semantical harmony.

Kelly is like that ["*In the Garden, the stemwinder spoke sotto voce,/ sibilant, tip-split, seedsowing, slying inclining Eve; /then the bite, the bright bath of juice, stars and/heavens scintillated: the browsing creatures pause, barely named; the world, in a swallow, remade.*"] and 'An Anatomy of the World' Donne is like *that,* the effect a bit like looking through a pair of over prescribed spectacles, the focus so lucid you get a headache. Or call it a thought. Now that's creepy or maybe really great.

The book, qua object, is handsome with a creamy letter press cover (depicting digital bones) that complements nicely the not quite white text paper, the text itself printed competently (high praise these days) in Adobe Garamond, offset in an edition of 500, perfect bound, sans ingratiating authorial photo and poetastery resume. This is a press exemplifying that in poetry, the medium matters as much as the message.

The unqualified laudation of the book's materiality versus a more problematic appraisal of the contents might suggest a pose on the reviewer's part, as if in this Jaded Age praise could only be signaled as a series of back handed slaps, doubling as salutes, as if the extra artifice testified to this reviewer's sincere and definite article of admiration. If so, then donne. *Tocccata & Fugue* was the winner of the 2005 Floating Bridge Press Poetry Chapbook Award.

I Lied All Winter …

by Arline Levinson, Angelfish Press,Ithaca, N.Y., 1970. 18 pages.

Arline Levinson's "I Lied All Winter …" is an instance, at 7 inches tall and 18 poems in length, of how small a chapbook can be and a reminder of how small can be big.

Big because a chapbook can exemplify that rare thing in literary production, the Gesamtkunstwerk, or total work of art. This is because chapbook crafting allows a close collaboration between poet and book designer that's impossible at larger "mainstream" presses.

In this case, wood engraver Gary Marcuse, pen artist Anna Shapiro and the anonymous printer who worked in letter press Garamond (ever the most elegant and legible of typefaces, though there are nearly as many various Garamonds as presses), have achieved an ensemble that's more than pretty and perhaps less than beautiful; something authentic and aesthetic in a non-trivial way. (Bricks and leaves, respectively, being examples of the trivial way.)

The 18 poems, even as lyrics, are small; the longest at 16 lines and the shortest (several) at 6. This stakes the poems' risk — and something always needs to be — at their peculiar point of brevity. Longer lyrics, like Larkin's, place their chips on a different square of exposure: the initiating scaffolding, the arch of drama, the stretching nave of narrative. Short pieces, like Levinson's are just there, exposed in their bare necessities, "poor and unaccommodated" (to almost misquote Shakespeare). There is no room for error, which is to say, there is great room for error.

And there are mis-takes here. A certain unconnected and conventionalized use of images "O untie the rainbow before the storm is done./ Over your brow, what wind shall flow?" (*Ver Perpetuum*). There is a reaching for a/effect "who drags the blood through the vein until you softy come again? (*My Pleasures*).

These flaws fade before a cardinal virtue: the poems are poetically conceived. Levinson may misstep but she knows the dance

— that lyric poetry is intensified language, between and in literary tropes… "who crosses the bridge at twilight to darkness?/ Entering the heart of it through the aorta of boughs …" . That poetry should not merely report perceptions but propose and propound them: "the thoughts deprived of ease/ that have regained it make the poem, which like a double-note/holds the extracted thought/ against the restlessness."

There are two manifest influences here. One is A.R. Ammons, epigraphically twice flagged, in his short stanza-long enjambment phase. Characteristically, the poems are free-verse, with some syllabic discipline and terminal couplet riming, suggestive of more formal procedures.

The second influence then, lest we forget it in its distant obviousness, is sonnet Shakespeare's monologic "dialogues" with a problematic beloved. "I Lied all Winter's" thematic unity-and delight, is in the relating,via imagistic snapshot, of a relationship.

"The crayoned tulips not in beds, but rising out of the sweet grass./ Your appearence interrupted only my dream of you./ All drugs suspend their action in the spreading candlelight,/ the blood's undertow." (from *Point Lobos*)

One may be reminded of Wordsworth's (another of Levinson's tagged poets) short poem about the sonnet (and its Tudor master-maker) where he observes that bees, which can fly over mountains, are happiest in the cone of flower. Little can be sweet; in the context of poetry, little should always be big, as Levinson's small book, satisfyingly, is.

Medusa Discovers Styling Gel

by Dian Duchin Reed, Finishing Line Press, 2009. 27 pages. $14.

"Don't be stupid."

This might be the prime moral exhortation were it not for the many one word negations, such as "Goebbels," by all accounts, a very intelligent man. So OK, "let's not be verbally stupid"; there is never, ever, virtue in that. Possibly the chief value of Poetry is as a kind of reciprocating engine, producing and recycling verbal intelligence, more effectively as container and medium than for any particular content or message, a perpetual notion machine that makes the reader smarter simultaneously with his investment of that intelligence in the poem's own potentiality for meaning. And so it goes, the most ascendant of Hegel's Aufhebung, a Convolvulus, and yes, it really is that simple! We pause, dear reader (always assume one reader) for rebuttal and to assert that this unintegrated arabesque is not nearly as detached as it must appear but derives from the work in hand.

Because the poems in Dian Duchin Reed's "Medusa Discovers Styling Gel" are intelligent* (and nothing rebarbative, as when the Brits say "clever," in the praise), instantiating a verbal alertness where words reflect and refract in arrangements that compose the unified object of many facets.

Can we count on Space? But it was less/ than nothing before the Big Bang./ Even now, confronted by a massive object,/ it bends the truth, stretches the facts./ And that trickster Time,/ as dependent on speed as any junkie,/ always relies on someone else's/ perspective, having none of its own./ Perhaps Truth does not exist. Perhaps /the universe is composed of Consequences/ instead. And perhaps Consequences/ are the only path to an honest universe./ No matter how long it takes, no

---

*[And by "intelligent" one means capacity and capability, verbal mindfulness in its many modes, including the emotive. For the most exhaustive (some say exhausting) study of intelligence as moral moderator, succeeding and failing, see Henry James, *The Golden Bowl.*]

matter/ how far from the sources, Consequences/ will always catch up with us./ Then, the Big Bust. (from *The Search for Truth*).

"Matter" being a pun that matters. Most of the poems explore an argument that extends, for force and effect, through one long sentence so that redaction does this work a disservice.

Yet every map moves me/from metaphor to mystery/ my own town shrunk down/to a dot, all spheres turned to/ a series of concentric circles./ Evenings, the swish and crash/ of sea onshore reminds me/ of cymbals, of the hopeless/ hope of symbols. I need no flowers, my only rose/the compass rose./ in whose petalled points/ I lose myself/to show the better ways. (from *"The Mapmaker Muses)*

At its best, the writing is vectored in that perfect location of inevitability and surprise, reminiscent of Heather McHugh or at a more distance remove of prose, Donald Barthelme.

Among Reed's big subjects are fate, loneliness, truth, the Medusa, Epicurus, all sat down and effectively interrogated in a focused light as if she knows what most contemporary poets forget: every poem is guilty, guilty of the gravest crime, Existence, its only possible expiation being the transcript of the transgression, the poem itself.

Lucifer's reaction to his own dizzying/ descent, the kind of cosmic crash/ that lovers of commotion might/consider dazzling, a work the meek/ cache to praise the sun's daily glissade/ to music that's so subtle, its silent." /(From *Dazzled*)

If there is a criticism of Reed's brilliant successes, it is, as usually the case with persons, along the line of their virtues. There's a sometimes relentless, working-it-too-hard monotonic quality, though this persistence and pursuit is also, sub-textually, a pointing to and moral insistence that in a world exiled from its own best garden where *"Fame and her best friend Fortune strut down the street arm in arm with their double dates, Pain and Fear,"* we must do better, be brighter.

Only an old bold critic (careless of crashing) would prescribe a writer's next book, suggest that Reed's further advance might involve a step backwards to the bad poetry badlands of looseness, inexactitude and dreamy relinquishment. Something like that drift is what makes Tennyson deeper than Browning, Coleridge more compelling than Byron, Thomas' plainsong more plaintive than ...

We await the next turn of this author's poetic karma-dharma wheel.

From a Burning Building

by Kerry O' Keefe, March Street Press, 2005. 25 pages. $9.00.

I've never met an extended metaphor I liked, especially my own, as the device stretches easily to the thin air of Cutetitude and the shallow reaches of self congratulation. Take an old and not very bold image—the poem as plane. Frequent poetic flyers, we've all been on board the relentlessly ground bound object that rolls down the runway and never takes off. What we want is transport — velocity, lift off and flight. Uncommonly, one encounters poems already airborne, our awareness coeval with their instantly at altitude attitude, a craft that has already passed several thresholds of thrust (V1, V2) and is immediately in its ideal poetic element, which is Ariel's. The best poems in Kerry O'Keefe's chapbook "From a Burning Building" are of this type.

> Winter grass cracking under their shoes/ as they stand and look at the eight-paned/ window that blew off the house last fall./ The squirrels now able to scratch through/ to the garbage on the porch .../ Their children throw a ball back and forth, not used/ to seeing him there in the yard. The man and woman/ navigate all the familiar distances, less urgent. (from *"Ex-Husband Comes to Pick Up Ladders"*)

The topics are the usual destinations — estrangement, divorce, death, the consolations of children and new love. Yes, we've all been here and for good reason; these are the hubs of the human heart.

> The day you learn the terrifying difference in the air/between the sound of a man quiet in another room,/ and one who has gone... Left to barter with pictures and helpless pets./ For a few weeks, the smell of the food you cooked./ The fading world of the bed. Cigarette ashes left/ for a while, then everything clean. The way, for years,/ you confuse each new, beautiful thing you encounter/with the casual habit of a weak and oblivious god. (from *"Worst Fear"*)

Such poems are not necessarily reliant on an exoskeleton of linked imagery (the best mechanical means for making Post-Metrical poetry). Rather, they occur within an epistic framework of testimony (lest this seem critically gratuitous, consider some alternatives: the meditative, the dramatic, the dialectical, the pastoral, etc...) where images aren't so much produced and laid out as appearing and surfacing; imminent but determinate. (And this not to diminish the conscious artistry of such a method where judgment must be deployed at its extremist verge). Maybe I'm talking out of my critical hat, believe me, more Emmett Kelly's than Adam Verver's but consider this uncanny sequencing

A sense of what is foreign./ The leaves breaking. The hills/ weighted down with guilt over /the yearly lewd display. Still/only able to do what they know./ Endless reaches of geese/trying to look brave in their dissembling./ A lone traveler/ trying to reach the gate before/ the plane takes off...the season left behind for all/ of its reasons ... a passage that convinces us way before (yet literally after) the convicting title "Before Signing the Papers."

In a sense the poetry seems co-generated by a dually operative containment vessel consisting of an intense outward thrust to express, surrounded by a constricting force, pressurizing the internal matter (or as the poet better puts it — "Let the unspeakable weight against the pleasure of a song, isn't that how it is every day?"). When this pressure lessens, as this reader believes it does in the more "positive" poems about children and new friends, the lines flatten out, lacking, as I take it, a recombinant genesis that is strictly linguistic.

You could call this ambient force "history" or "Truth," the seemingly more endurant element of Keats' famous compound. It is Truth, in the conveyance of Poetry, that elevates these poems from the low lying arbitrations of so much chapbook verse and that makes this propellant little book worth reading. Which is what, to begin with, we booked the flight for.

Beautiful/Brutal: Poems About Cats

by Amy Miller, Cyclone Press, Ashland Oregon, 2009.
34 pages. $4.

The history of animals on the planet—sorry! the history of animals in literature is, not news in either case, not good. While there is much serviceable and entertaining prose, most animal themed poetry is well intended dreck and if you don't believe me, check out even a good anthology, such as "The Great Cat" (Knopf, 2005). The almost intractable problem is this—animals, even domesticated ones, are "Other." Hard to get inside their heads. (Though there have been commendable efforts, the best often least known, such as Will James' semi-stream of equine consciousness "Smoky" and Jefferies' magisterial allegory, animated by a lifetime of forest and game keeping, "Wood Magic." Mostly, we have recourse to facile mythologizing —(my cat Isis or Loki) or simple sentiment (and some would say the same deflection "informs" our dealing with another utterly Other, God).* An entire book could be written on the stupendous disappointments of animal themed literature and reader, I hope you do it, taking, please, my title "No Paradise, No Paragon" while you are at it. Are we beating around the bush here? Yes. Because the fate of animals makes me sad and the status of animals in literature makes me (less) sad. And of course, I dislike having been wrong about the chapbook in hand, Amy Miller's "Beautiful/ Brutal."

A very nicely printed little number. 11 x 13 cm., with good typography, sporting a stylish cover and maroon fly leaves, the kind of attractive article, too small for the regular shelves, you'd expect right at the cash register, the hope being you will pick it up in lieu of the change you'll be getting from your $15.95 purchase

---

* For an assertion that the human is likewise chiefly & inaccessibly "Other," see Nietzsche. Statutory disclosure: the reviewer shares his life with a cat, "Storri," "For she counteracts the Devil."

of the latest Billy Collins. "Cat Poems" right next to "Sayings of the Buddha," "The Tiny Book of Haiku," and "Pocket Sonnets," a cute, "niche" book, easy to buy and easier to forget.

Such archness *is* beside the point. Except as indicating how this reviewer was wrong. Time, in other words, to let the critical cat out of the bag. Miller's book is not just a good book of cat poetry, it is a good book of poetry.

She has looked carefully at cat/human relations, the familiar-strange middle ground of contact, done the hard work of close perception and then shaped this coming-to-knowledge into free verse that is effective, informing; at times affectionate but not sentimental.

She was sleek and frightened/and slick as oil under the flatbed,/ sliding backward to a corner./ I reached a finger into the dark./ She purred, took a step, waited./ My finger found her ear, soft as a bird, and she bit — a savage sudden grab." (from *Stray*)

There is an almost Herbertian quality or turn to some of the poems and curiously, it is this artificial, slightly baroque touch that grounds and confirms the naturalness and rightness of this work.

You look at them/ differently now… the cat, alert on the win-dowsill,/ has no eye for horizons./ With legions of limp gophers/and cottonball quail chicks,/ she has made you understand this./ You have wiped blood from her bowel /.... You came to this island/ to drink the world,/ but the brew is bitter:/ nutmeg and brine,/ camphor and salt,/ the rind of the melon./ Animal medicine./ And you/ drink. (from *Animal Medicine*)

All of us, poets, at various way stations of our lives, have written of desire, betrayal, death, loneliness, of Auden's unholy trinity of Terror, Concupiscence and Pride. These are our intimates and familiars. But to write well about another creature whose reputed favorite activities are grooming and sleeping is a rare achievement. (In the act of focus upon the creature, the poet can return to deeper themes, clarified and enriched by the glance of self-forgetting.)

"There is no destination./ He plays with a light orange ball/that is all turnabout,/ banked off a baseboard,/sideways off his paw, his tail,

coming round /like a boom. Ball and cat/and house ignite a universe/ of acceleration, tangents struck /at random, every outcome/ branched with outcomes of its own,/ every turn a life begun,/ every pause a brink /before the infinite." (from *The Cat Instructs*)

Miller's book, keepsake sized, is indeed a keeper.

Mandala

by Diana Woodcock, Foothills Publishing, 2009. 39 p. $10.

There's nothing arbitrary about Diana Woodcock's title, "Mandala," a circle to be traveled, the bull's eye of attention, a cosmoplan and web of forces. This is a courageous book of witnessing, a challenge to the complacency of the comfortable reader to sustain the compassionate attention this work deserves.

An author who has opened herself to harshest realities and constructed a work from them may have to face the baldest criticisms. Surprisingly common in such cases and always a shock when you are subjected to it (as a friend of mine has been) is the assertion that the author, by exposing violence, subliminally endorses it. You are "in to" suffering. "Don't deal with this stuff." You risk the indictment of moral self-congratulation. Woodcock's poems are partial, in a decided, constructive sense, to testifying narrative. Nearly all the poems are focused on "others," victims, prisoners, refugees, those that endure, presented in a language that is even, sober, clear eyed and thus, intense in ways we might wish to glance away from....

The confessions:/ Pregnant women tied to trees,/ machetes cutting out fetuses;/ children killing their own parents/ for stealing food, rats eaten raw/ How could I stomach them? [...]/ The old man squats in the shade of/ Ankhor Wat, ruins rising from the jungle./ Cassia and basho trees sway in the breeze./ Children women cut open here— so/ much that cannot hide under the shadow/ of the banana leaf the child carries,/ riding his water buffalo, which—/ at the end of its life—is sacrificed/ for buffalo stew. (from *Buffalo Stew*)

Most of the poems have that vital turning, from death to life. In "Aphrodisiac," Woodcock tells us of the death of two rhinos, shifts to a pharmacy shop in Kowloon that sells rhino horn power and there ...

At the bar next door, beery-eyed Chinese/ men in the smoky din watching thin/ prostitutes — some home grown, some from the Philippines — in their tight/ jeans, painting their pale lips red.

The added ethical valence of feminism is properly in play here.

Much of Woodcock's poetry could be considered reportage (how, at extremes of suffering could it be otherwise?) but marked by intelligent observation and selection, a mediation by composition and juxtaposition, as above, or in "Survivor," a Tibetan nun reflects on her eleven years of imprisonment, finds some consolation in nature and then recalls "the Chinese guards who went home at the end of their shifts to wives and daughters."

The specific ethics informing Woodcock's work and world view are Buddhist and feminist. Presented with a non doctrinaire refinement, exposing the "in this life" dilemma that our attunement to even the noblest (and seemingly self-evident) beliefs can be problematic, indeed ambiguous;

Are these the primary poisons: ignorance, hatred, greed?/ Could a conch shell or a simple bell awaken me?/ A lotus rooted in mud enlighten me with blossoming/ energy? Blind me to all that is not sublime?

Find God in music yak and sun. But how?/ Could I ever learn to play the dranyen and move/ through life as if around a mandala,/ balancing always balancing/ ready to be erased? (from *Mandala*)

As one who believes poetry is in its highest evolution a baroque art, characterized by over elaboration, most communicative when least direct, most authentic when trying too hard, I was at times lulled by Woodcock's careful but plain diction, her casual enjambments. Yet these aspects came to seem to me a refinement, an honest retort to the contortions of brutality, a refusal to aestheticise violence. These poems are meditations on mercy.

This is a pretty chapbook. If some of the line printing is not precisely as inked as a print perfectionist would prefer, the cover, of mandala within mandala is gorgeous.

Cinders of My Better Angels

by Michael Magee. MoonPath Press, 2011. 51 pages.

While not all the poems in Michael Magee's "Cinders of My Better Angels" chronicle his explorations of medicine (or medicine's of him), the many that do are notable. Americans of this era, we may not fully appreciate the clinical oddity of top forty radio infused treatment rooms or the off-hand discourtesy of painful diagnostics that Magee has experienced up close and very personal; in Shakespearean terms—he has drunk the spider-or at least the banana flavored barium. Almost a Magee type jest but he has raised the stakes of his play and his jokes are better. That's what happens with poetry of distinctive utterance; the reader begins to mimic the poem's performative gestures. Of course poetry can be *distinctively* good or bad (only the banal is oblivious), so let's be clear — Magee's is good.

My Sigmoidoscopy wasn't that flexible./ I tensed up as the snake went in.../ what were they looking for anyway?/ Hidden canals in Venice?/ As they discussed me like gondoliers taking tourists for a ride-decked out/ in another language of jargon. (from *"My Flexible Sigmund Freudoscopy"*)

"Language of jargon" is suggestive and artful. And the whiff of Venice, as even a tourist as delicate as Henry James might agree in a closeted moment, wholly appropriate; La Serenissima, golden flecked, serpentine, glisteningly intestine, with its hints of the fetid and fecal. And something apt too about those gimlet-eyed, almost cynical gondolierists, alienists who have Charoned too many over the familiar crossing.

Magee's manner at its best is "American" at its best: informal, funny, fundamentally modest, conversational, riffing; ragtimeingly intelligent, alert, capacious. It knows how to envelope his sharp edge subject-objects, needles, endoscopes, tumors, rasorial nurses. *She says something about a home visit/which sounds like a death sentence/*

but maybe I'm reading into someone /else's life, besides for right now/ I
get my twenty dollar co-pay back. (from *"Lab Results"*)

It would be easy to glide over the not calling attention to
themselves subtleties, a death sentence read, a reimbursement that
is actuarially temporary.

People here today look lost. "I don't /care as long as they don't oper-
ate on me,"/ someone says. The lobby is under construction/ and no one
can get through. The deli is under/ the jackhammer's rule as people spin
off/ in different directions. It's Friday and we'll/ soon be keeping each
other company …/ The unemployed, SSI, charity cases and elderly/ we
are all here on life support, waiting/ for hip replacements, or cataract
surgery/ and no one is admitting to anything." (from *"Admitting"*)

Our minds are parliaments (or medical grand rounds) and there
is always some party that will earnestly assert that the chief value
of this poetry is as courageous and often humorous (which is, in
this context, a re-iteration of "courageous") testimony.

The opposition would be as right to counter we don't care about
another such testimonial; talk to your local oncologist or veterinarian; uncommon courage is a common virtue. And for all we know
or really care, Michael Magee is actually a tri-athletic pre-med
student with a serious case of writer's itch. Our concern and Time's
is the vitality of the body of words, a corpus sufficient unto itself,
its health a matter of images, rhetorical and verbal musculatures.
Our project has nothing to do with "the ghost in the machine," an
author somewhere charting his course along the Seven Ages. Are
some of Magee's enjambments detached? A few of his adjectival
phrases loose or thematics too rue-mantic? Should they be looked
to? Yet every poem in Cinders of My Better Angels gives pleasure
as art, *communicates* qualities of courage, wit, observancy. So we
do care. Stay well Magee.

Fading into Bolivia

by Richard Taylor, Accents Publishing, Lexington, KY.
28 pages. 2011.

As writers, we are all pushing product and that's good even if at times
it has cart before the horse aspects. We need first and frequently to
have taken standard delivery (Pegasus *pulling* his load of aesthetic
affects), to have consumed the artistic goods and to have been consumed. Many poets are diverted by the various wrappings: technical
strictures, narratising authentications, sparkles of language when
the purest poetic object is in its being "a still point of the turning
world," a composed composure. The greatest power of poetry is
this of concentrating our concentration-and if the counter is made
"Sure— and so does prayer and Zen" (not bad bedfellows, by the
way), poetry does this in a special way, powering-up our attention
at the same time it provides objects, profounder than jig saw pieces
for that empowerment in a timeless circuit of feed and feedback.
Which is to say. and maybe this got boring five minutes ago, lyric
poems at their best are deep and deepening. They are quiet. (They
do not draw attention to themselves by tripping over themselves.)
This is the sterling quality of Richard Taylor's *Falling Into Bolivia*.
His work is carefully shaped and paced.

*"The skim of algae into which/ she waded to escape the heat/
accepted her, pond ooze hugging like a lethal stew."* (from *For a
Newfoundland Drowned in a Farm Pond*)

Skim and stew are re-enforcing but the real fixer, after the lull-
ing ordinary language of "escape the heat," is that terrible-inevitable
verb "accepting.'

And the poet must accept *"that among all the sounds of late
summer—*

*"hum of semis along the bypass and lunch-break siren when the
wind was right,"* he had actually heard *"a hoarse barking, plaintive,
faint, its agony never surfacing."* and done nothing.

His *Peaks Mill Road* is perfectly observed

"*In the near dark where the doe lies/* (a musical, fairy tale set up) *half on, half off the road,/ my headlights cone unto the survivors:/ two bucks, a spotted fawn,/ and two or three vague others.*

Ears tenses, sleek heads swiveling/ in the glare, hooves as lustrous,/ edged and deadly as a shot glass, they find no refuge in shadow,/ the brightness welding them together./ They do not break they do not scatter.

And to our surprise and gratification, the poem from that natural ending continues for two excellent stanzas.

If some poems are trope-ically overloaded (kayaks as relationships?), or topically conventional (prof grades papers), they are consistently sound in the units of their construction, especially the bond of noun and modifier — "heft of light" the griever's rain of "gentle tamping, small erosions" — that ineptly fabricated, undermines so much contemporary verse. (If you can't get noun and modifier right — all the metaphors in the world won't save you.).

The chapbook itself, as object, is admirably low key and refined; a matte dual-tone cover, a chaste title page, good printing, a back cover of sober, uninflated blurbiage. No ribbons, no fandangles, no ever-disappointing author portrait.

One of Taylor's poems concludes ... "*I brace to face the weather—bundled, blank, at last reduced to words.*" As is the reader, in fulfillment, at end of this good book.

Thirty-Five New Pages

by Lev Rubinstein, translated by Philip Metres and Tatiana
Tulchinsky, Ugly Duckling Presse, 2011.

Many of us recall the careful little Emperor from Peter Shaffer's
"Amadeus," who encountering a baffling scene in Mozart's operatic
rehearsal, tactfully inquires "Is it modern?" That no one today asks
the question testifies to the success (and also the failure) of the great
modernist project. In an age of reactionary finance and Tweety Bird
attention spans, who, aside from aesthetic antiquarians, academic
row-hoers and the tabula rasa'd young, takes Picasso, Stravinsky,
Joyce or Le Corbusier *seriously*, however much we admire their
energy, wit and nerve? (The Villa Savoye is a very clever structure
but you wouldn't want to live there. Almost no one has.)

If these great monuments of modernism stand as carefully
preserved barely ruined choirs, there is the still active and vital,
like nibbling mice, other modernist motif of refusal, obliquity and
off-beat critique, a movement whose particles continue to proliferate
along the cyclotron of the long 20th century, its taxonomy extending
at least from Dada to Zaha (and includes Radical Randomists, Found
Objectivists, Rushing Constructivists, Situationalists, Saturationalist,
Atmanic Confabulists, Fruit Oulipoists and Branch Derridians (a
term I co-invented back in 1984 when it was already old).

Lev Rubinstein's (the librarian and artist) *Thirty-Five New Pages*
is placed somewhere in that spectrum. This device for reading con-
sists of thirty-five 3x5 inch cards (with a colophon card) of the type:

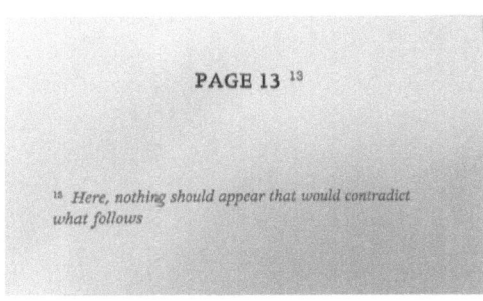

PAGE 13 [13]

[13] *Here, nothing should appear that would contradict
what follows*

The major integerial presentation, with the modification of a mathematical or editorial super-scripture conveys a kind of lexical authority, belied by the subordination of the rather gnomic (Gnostic?) text in red ink. These elusive/allusive propositions, proposals of what *should* appear, are linked/ generated via a loose bell change effect, a not quite continuity of phrases that suggests but doesn't constitute a continuum. Card 35 (which we won't spoil) is a surprise ending-or is that a beginning? So what does this rosary for reading do, apart from looking nice and feeling good in the fingers? Well, it would violate the spirit of Rubenstein's project *to tell* you what. (But questions come readily to hand: what is reading? Narrative? The frame of art?) Suffice it to say, after reading a hundred conventional chapbooks—"man passing misery to man" (Sophocles or was that Larkin?) *Thirty-Five New Pages* comes on like a crisp cracker after predictably acrid wine. And some credit, surely, to the translators who midwife us to the humanity and clarity of Rubinstein's desiderata.

The folks at Ugly Duckling Presse are always turning out hard to pigeon hole objects that make you think. I recommend their work (and website) for its interest and stimulation Theirs is a risky enterprise; they are surely more aware than I how the radical object can easily transmute, via reverse alchemy, into just another bit of conceptual bric-a-brac.

The reviewer is the pseudonymous author other of, among other things, "*Distractions*" (1980), a novel written on twenty 3 x 5 file cards, designed for reading and shuffling.

Things of the Weather

by Wendy Barker Pudding House Publications, 2008 30 pages. $10.

In a mood,* it can seem Poetry is under assault—and "the Perps"?—its best friends, poets. The old bromide that more people write poetry than read it (stale news by at least 1600) has reached a more toxic distillation — more *poets* write than read it. Here, Cher Reader, you'd be right to ask "how can you possibly know such a thing, Pew Poll perhaps?" But proofs can proceed by theorem; thus: IF poets were reading work worse than they write, THEN they'd write better by repulsion, if the same quality, they'd write better by competitiveness and if reading better quality, by aspiration. And so by a series of reactive reformations, the curve of poetry would be rising, which isn't the case.

Many contemporary poems are really short-short stories, yearning for the bulked up lineaments of prose. The leading cause of poetic pallor is "trope-ic anemia" (sometimes called Levine's Disease or Updike's Disorder) which critical clinicians properly call "metaphorosis."So it is good to be able to present a healthy specimen, Wendy Barker's "*Things of the Weather.*"

Condensation Nuclei

Sea salt, pollen and smoke./ Particles the air/ needs to form a cloud./ A pebble in the palm./ Phrase dropped on a plate./ Your words I've collected/ and lined up like bowls/ of ash, or sand, /stared at, and wept/ or like our lidded glass/ containers: oats, wheat,/ and opalescent grains/ we use to knead/ our bread, yeasty/ loaves with raisins./ Rain, relief, the irritants/washed back to loam./ Saliva, the body's/juices that digest/ grit between our teeth.

There's a coolness here, a detachment and distance, the "personal" almost off stage, oblique, toned down. The attraction is in

---

*See Richard III, (I.2, 248)

the elusiveness, the allusiveness. Baker, a "makeur" gets it: a poet (ever, optimally, a title conferred, not claimed) is not a maker of poems (almost anyone can do that) but a shaper of language; a distinction that is (and should be) critical.

The sky has slipped its stitches,/ the feathered cirrus, wool of cumulus,/ gauze shreds of layered stratus/ gone with the unexpected guests/ who left this morning/ after a night of pelted rain./ Now the sun flashes and shears/the few seams left/ till bare skin bursts through/and we're down to ourselves,/ Two loose threads, the knot undone. (from *High Sky*)

Now this is perhaps not as coolly removed as some might prefer, composure here softening into comfort. The important thing is this: a poetic organization that is essentially vertical and harmonic rather than prosaic, horizontal and narratising. Harmony over melody, i.e., anybody's "Late Quartets."

Because, really, nobody cares about the raw testimony of your personal experience except your mother and the courts. The relationship of "experience" to poetry is like that of clay to pots, substantive, but not defining. If I've inadvertently taken poets to task, I don't mean to privilege critics and reviewers.

Reading reviews is like watching French people talk on Euro TV, never mind the jabber, it's the gestures! Turn down the sound and watch the hands. As to major critics, it's time that lowers the volume. The great critics — Burke, Richards, Empson and Auerbach are less recalled than rusting hulks of battleships. Perused by, at best, a lifeboat's worth of professors, what's enduring is not what they said but what, in urgent words, they were pointing to. What *Fiddler Crab* does with its little claw. What we, the memorious remnant of readers, can turn and look to.(Put another way, the long term value of criticism, provided it makes the proper signs is indicative rather than constitutive.)

A bone, too, to pick with some responsible party. The cover engraving, as apposite as the properly cited titular epigram, isn't credited. While its style is so individual as to be widely recognized, not one reader in a hundred will connect the cover with its only begetter, that typically short lived and unhappy 19th century genius, J. J. Grandville (aka Jean Ignace-Isidore Gerard) whose plate 70 from *Un Autre Monde* of thunderbolts striking lightning rods should specifically conduct his fame.

Finally, lest Barker's chapbook seem shorted in these critical circuits, one of its pleasures is its organizing and titular mechanics, chiefly cloud names that befit these definite shape shifting poems. Turning pages, I was reminded more than once of days passing and more than once needed to consult Day's classic reference work, *"Clouds and Weather."*

Kindle

by Paulann Petersen, Mountains & Rivers Press, 2008. 32 pages.

One of the great dimensions of poetry is its power of temporality, its marking and making of mental movement (as in music's allegro, scherzo, adagio), the variant durances of its empowering focus and attention.

This has little or nothing to with lineation or length. Similarly sized passages of Shakespeare and Milton, for example, seem to occur in different time zones of rapid and slow. Marlowe, Jonson, Pope and Shelley are "fast." Wordsworth, Hardy and Keats are "slow." And this is more than a graduate student lounge game. The most significant moments in our lives have been known to occur, at the time and ever after, in a kind of slow motion or breath-catching brevity.

Many of Petersen's poems are short, 15 to 20 lines, taking no more than 15 seconds to eye scan. Yet they are decidedly "largo," slow reads, meditations. I found myself reading slower and slower, re-reading, a de-tempoing sensation with the curious confirmatory effect that the closer one gets to absolute zero, the more one is aware of movement on a parallel track, the transferred motion of our freighted being.

Finish

> *I rub my shoulder/ against a doorframe's wood,/ getting the feel of*
> *this creature/ felled and transformed./ My fingers curve to knead blood/*
> *toward a muscle's hurt, lotion/ into an elbow roughened by neglect./*
> *Snubbing shoes, I let bare soles/ reacquaint themselves/ with the wear*
> *of pavement's grit./ Clothes serve the modest task/ of long soft friction./*
> *Bit by bit, night by day,/ I grow smoother-grained,/ready for light. Let*
> *me be/ a mirror in which something else/might catch a glimpse of itself-/*
> *the burnished stone beneath/a lifetime of water, flowing.*

No particular fireworks here, no pyrotechnic metaphors, propelled by a reaching high conceit. But a perceptive deliberateness, a detective ear down to the ground swell of language. Lotion as motion, "Grit, fric, bit," a poem that begins with "finish" and ends with flow. (Readers might be reminded of Rilkes' *Tombs of the Hetairae*, which like *"Finish"* is liquid and about more than it's "about").

Or another example, chosen at random and the more telling for its brevity.

"Between us — the righted car gone./ The road now a part of itself/ that lay ahead/ out of sight./ I walked it alone, awake." (from *Time-Travel*)

Note the rebar of near and exact rhyme, assonance, the bracing of those long a's. This is deliberate, carefully shaped free verse, what I call "reinforced free verse" employing common language that yet has force, a koanic type property of making you stop as it points beyond itself and over the horizon of its overt argument.

"... The only sound, a current rubs against what waits/ Now geese, above. Their bleat like air pushed through a reed—hollow stalk/ begun in a meeting of water and earth/ so it can reach toward the sky./ Then rowing, close by — a boat borne along/ by voiceless labor. An oar/ plunged under, splashed up./ My wet feet taking root." (from *Slake*)

A distinctive strength of this collection is its obliquity to the personal, its almost Jungian vectoring of imagery along lay lines of earth-air-fire-water, a grounding in the always more than four temperaments.

So what's not to like? The poems have aphoristic feel in their economy and depth but even the great aphorists, Lichtenburg, Nietzsche, Wilde can't always aim dead center and in the aphorism,(as in the short poem) there is only bulls eye — or a clean miss. Some of Petersen's work feels a bit too confined and under oxygenated. It never seems glib, pretentious, or trite but after a while you may hunger for a few free radicals or panting over extensions.

To conclude with two points of received wisdom that informed my reading. First — the only thing I recall from "Poetry Seminar 101" — "A poem should not leave you where you started." In other words, the poem may or not be "transport" but it should always be "encounter." Each of Petersen's poems is a real encounter. Second, from further back, from a very humid night in the 1950's Norfolk Virginia tenements. The fan is failing, June bugs are banging against the window screen. It is too hot for my mother to continue with the bed time story. So she stops, saying "the strongest genies come out of the smallest bottles."

Questions for Study
and a Synopsis

Questions for Study in Schools

1. What does the phrase "trooping the colour" refer to in real life? Why was it used as the title of this book?

2. The writing style of this book is different from most books and magazine articles. How would you describe it?

3. Tell the story of what happens in *Trooping the Colour* in your own words. (You may consult the plot synopsis that follows this section of questions).

4. Who are Raul Trembley, Guy Mantis, "K.S." and "J.N." and what is their role in the story?

5. What are aphorisms and why do you think they are included in *Trooping the Colour?*

6. William Ruminant, the author's friend, has been described as "generous" and "intelligent." What other words would you use to describe him?

7. Which of the following does not appear in the book and why?

> Virginia Woolf
> Field Marshall Von Manstein
> Professor Paul Angstrom
> Adam Verver
> Buddha Sakimuni

8. Pretend that *Trooping the Colour* is going to be made into a movie and you are the casting director. What stars would you have play William Ruminant, the author and other important figures? Be prepared to defend your choices.

Synopsis

Adrian and Laura are a young married couple at the University of Virginia where she is a graduate student in philosophy, and he works as a library assistant in the Rare Books dept. She has recently had a class in German Idealism with a visiting professor, Vera Roth, an attractive and intensely verbal personage. After having her over for dinner, both are intensely drawn to her, almost as relief from their marriage, troubled as it is by personal and sexual issues. Adrian becomes obsessed with Roth who is herself fleeing, by her temporary appointment, a problematic relationship in San Francisco with Ira, a med student. Driving back to Charlottesville from a conference in Washington, she confronts her despair in long, slow drive through a snow storm. It is winter term break; Laura has been ill with flu and phones Roth to arrange for Adrian to drop off at Roth's cottage her late class paper. Roth agrees and Adrian finds his desire and angst rising in the walk over. In the lonely twilight of the almost unfurnished cottage, Roth reaches out to him and they embrace.

The next day, he confesses the event to Laura who says she understands because —she loves Roth also. They agree to a break in their marriage and Adrian makes arrangements to live elsewhere. The next week, returning to work in the library, he is astounded by the new presence of Janet Nielson, a svelte dark haired enigma who works as a graduate student assistant but who has just returned from a year abroad studying archaeology in England. Despite his current relational complications, he finds her quiet allure compelling. Meanwhile he continues to see Professor Roth, an involvement that has become more psychological and philosophical mentoring than physical. She urges that he reach some definition in his commitments. One day in the stacks, he declares his desire to Janet, who explains that she cannot respond to his overture. Her Uncle, Seth Abramson, former Marine, CIA operative, now CEO (Frodo's Bagels) and the University's Rector, is irrationally protective of her. A former boy friend, (Guy Mendes) was severely beaten by a masked assailant after a date with her but refused to press charges upon receiving "a significant cash payment from unknown parties." She delicately communicates that she is bisexual and could never commit to one person or one sex. Following several nights of passionate desperation, Adrian feels his only option is to confront Abramson, and determined to prove his merit and sincerity to Janet, bursts into the Rector's office. He declares his admiration for her and Abramson berates him. A fight ensures in which Abramson, with his combat skills, quickly subdues Adrian in a choke hold. Seeing him crumpled on the Turkish carpet, the Rector recalls the wounded young men of his youth and is overcome with a strange, sudden pity. As Adrian slowly revives, Abramson lifts him up him, advising him to "walk tall and follow your bliss." Laura, in the meantime, has taken to going to The Panther, the town's only lesbian bar, to find relief from her loneliness. There, she meets Janet and after a short evening of intense compatibility and conversation, spends the night with her. They are disturbed the next morning by Adrian knocking at the door to see Janet and tell her of his encounter with her uncle. He is astounded to find the two women together. Janet, in turn, is amazed to learn that Adrian and Laura are married. In the charged conversation that follows. Laura announces that Adrian is already involved with Vera Roth. Over wrought, Adrian reveals a deep secret ... he and Laura are first cousins! They are fraudulently married because Virginia does not allow marriage between first cousins! Janet asks them both to leave so she can come to grips with the revelations. Meanwhile, Vera Roth gets a knock at her door and expecting Adrian, is astonished to see Ira. He cannot tolerate the distance and ambiguity between them and showing two airline tickets, insists that she immediately return to San Francisco with him. Instantly apprehending his new and deeper commitment to her, she agrees, calling interstate movers and leaving a short, sad, affectionate letter for Adrian.

It is now the end of the winter semester and spring has come to Charlottesville. Janet meets with Adrian and Laura at their former apartment, expresses her unhappiness with the situation and explains that she is returning to England (where she has friends) for a summer fellowship and will likely stay there for the year. Laura reveals she has already applied, been accepted and will in a few weeks enroll in the PhD program at the University of Toronto. They all hug and Janet leaves. Laura gives Adrian letter that has just delivered at the apartment (still his university registered address) for him, from Seth Abramson. Abramson writes that recent events have been an emotional watershed for him and that he has decided to resign from the University in order to devote himself fulltime to acts of philanthropy, among them, the directorship of a new scholarship scheme for library workers to attend the library school of their choice. He has nominated Adrian for the first award. Adrian tells Laura he is inclined to accept it. They agree their marriage, if that was what it was, is over but vow to stay in contact, as friends. Both, after this tempestuous semester, find themselves more knowing, compassionate and both, aware Janet Neilson will be at Eyrie House, University of London, harbor aspirations of a further relation with her. All is not over, and as Laura remarks, kissing Adrian lightly on the check, (quoting the title of her favorite play) "All Is True."

Page Nelson,
A Chronology

Page Nelson, a Chronology

The Early Years *(The Years of Struggle)*

1952. Feb 8th. Born, prematurely, in Norfolk Virginia, the son of a low-ranking, blind in one eye government clerk and a fifth-grade educated mother.

1958. Father retires at age 80, five years over the legal mandate of 75, having misrepresented his age on initial employment forms. Family moves to welfare housing project.

1959. Father dies. Widow and son expelled from housing when officials learn by probated will that estate value, from pension, insurance and small annuity, is $15,000, an amount over the limit allowed for public assistance.

1970. Page Nelson is awarded a full scholarship to attend the University of Virginia.

1971. Summer. Hitchhikes across the United States. Drops student deferment (Fall) and determines to emigrate to Canada, if drafted for the Vietnam War.

1972. Marries "KS," a classmate.

1973. Letter of resignation crosses in mail with notice of expulsion from University. Loses scholarship.

1974. Winter/Spring. Travels with "KS" to Iceland, Britain, France, Switzerland and Italy. Professes desire to live in Venice.

1975-1976. Returns to Charlottesville, graduates from University and gets job in library as "rare books stacks supervisor."

1977. Visiting technicians from the Library of Congress demonstrate prototype "phase box" to house fragile books. Nelson suggests moving fastening tabs from long side to spine, to prevent on-shelf abrasion. This improved model becomes an internationally distributed preservation product.

1978. Begins broadcasting classical music four hours a week on radio station WTJU (91.3 FM). Discovers Heather McHugh, studies John Donne and Henry James, "the essential influences on my subsequent work."

1979. Is divorced from KS (on grounds of uncontested incompatibility). Begins period of intense engagement with a set of young artists, intellectuals and graduate students, among them William Ruminant, Raul Trembley, Guy Mantis, "KS" and "JN." Various romantic involvements, starts novel "Trio." Charged with simple assault on G. Mantis. Sentenced to three days in jailed (suspended) and a $100 fine.

1980. Curates exhibitions at the Rare Books Dept, University of Virginia Library, "Blau, the Cartography of Ruin" and "Diderot and his Encyclopedia."

1982. Abandons work on "Trio." Rents apartment with "JN." Wisdom teeth removed.

1984. Marries "JN."

The Middle Years *(the Years of Achievement)*

1985. Appointed to four year term, UVa Chamber Music Concert Management Board.

1986. Trains as cataloger, UVa Library. Considers joining Navy, moving to Venice or conversion to Buddhism. Rejects all three options because of "deleterious effects upon my marriage."

1989. "Retires" from broadcasting, moves to Boston. Hired as cataloger at Boston College Law Library, where he specializes in the law of Europe. After brief genealogical researches, believes he is the direct descendent of Colonel William Nelson (Army of

Northern Virginia) and co-lateral descendent of Horatio, Lord Nelson. Designs family crest of anchor, befouled by dogwood, with sables in sailor suits, rampant, over motto "Plumbis et Profoundis," which he translates as "Dull but Deep."

1991. Co-founds with TR the "Tuesday Night Poetry Group" for working poets. Charges of romantic involvements with TR and KY are unsupported by any documentary or testimonial evidence.

1992. *Apex,* first collection of poems, is published by the Hetaira Press.

1993. *Gallery Effects* published by the Hetaira press.

1994-95. *Apex* receives the annual Pushart Prize for first book of poems. Nelson declines prize but allows publication in the Pushart Anthology. *Case Studies* published by the Hetaira Press. Experiments in alchemy, concludes "vibrational meditation" is key to Philosopher's Stone.

1996. Mails unsolicited manuscript of "Trio" to William Ruminant (op cit. anno 1979) at Edmister University. Climbs Sharp Top, second highest (3862 meter) summit of the Peaks of Otter range in a single day ascent, without oxygen.

1997. Hired as Cataloger, Harvard University Graduate School of Design.

1998. Promoted to "Senior Cataloger, Graduate School of Design." His *Stern Ornaments* is the last publication of Hetaira Press, which goes out of business.

Revisits and professes desire to live in Venice.

2000-01. Begins *A Wilderness of Monkey,* a book of aphorisms. Promoted "Adjutant" in the Zeugma Workshop, a competitive-admission online academy for writers, organized along military lines where only "the standard responses," Yes Sir (or ma'am), No Sir (or ma'am) and No Excuses, Sir! (or ma'am) are permitted as critical replies. Attends the western hemispheric premier in Boston of Robert Schumann's 1849 opera *"Genoveva."*

2002. Desperate for assistance, mails manuscript of *Wilderness of Monkeys* to William Ruminant who generously provides various improvements and facilitates publication by Another Sparrow Press.

The Later Years *(Years of Contestation and Contentment)*

2005-06. *"Wilderness"* optioned to West Indy Studios. Screen play by Martin Goldberg, Jeremy Irons offered but declines title role. Shooting begins on *The Aphorist.*

2008. *The Aphorist* opens in Toronto. Receives positive notices and goes into limited distribution.

2009. Nelson begins work on what he conceives to be a resurrection of his early novel "Trio." Is appointed Preceptor (an honorary, unpaid instructorship) in Aesthetics at New Courier College (New Courier, Massachusetts)

2010. *The Aphorist*, adapted for stage by Tim Horton, opens at the Firbank Theatre, beyond the West End, runs for six weeks. Nelson attends one performance and radically alters plans for "Trio," conceiving what will become *Trooping the Colour.*

2012. *Trooping the Colour* is published by Another Sparrow Press and reviewed in *Perspecta* by Guy Mantis who asserts "gross distortions and misrepresentations, especially regarding persons and chronology." Nelson engages prominent local attorney Bert ("The Bear") Kendall and sues Mantis in district court for defamation of character. Dr William Ruminant is disposed (for the respondent.i.e, the defense).

2013 Settlement is reached out of court, details of which are not available at the time of this publication. Nelson retires (with "JN") to Charlottesville where he "has inherited a grave but not yet possessed it." Spends time gardening (roses, sunflowers, convoluvi, marigolds, primrose, pumpkin, chrysanthemum, all ordinary herbs and flowers). Volunteers at the local animal shelter.

Additional copies of this book
may be purchased online at
www.createspace.com/3966392
or through amazon.com
and other retailers.